THE MOORLAND COTTAGE
AND OTHER STORIES

MRS GASKELL was born Elizabeth Cleghorn Stevenson in 1810. The daughter of a Unitarian, who was a civil servant and journalist, she was brought up after her mother's death by her aunt in Knutsford, Cheshire, which became the model not only for Cranford but also for Hollingford (in *Wives and Daughters*). In 1832 she married William Gaskell, a Unitarian minister in Manchester, with whom she lived very happily. Her first novel, *Mary Barton*, published in 1848, was immensely popular and brought her to the attention of Charles Dickens, who was looking for contributors to his new periodical, *Household Words*, for which she wrote the famous series of papers subsequently reprinted as *Cranford*. Her later novels include *Ruth* (1853), *North and South* (1854–5), *Sylvia's Lovers* (1863), and *Wives and Daughters* (1864–6). She also wrote many stories and her remarkable *Life of Charlotte Brontë*. She died in 1865.

SUZANNE LEWIS is a graduate of the University of Sydney. She is the editor of Gaskell's *A Dark Night's Work and Other Stories* in the World's Classics series.

THE WORLD'S CLASSICS

ELIZABETH GASKELL

The Moorland Cottage

and Other Stories

Edited with an Introduction by
SUZANNE LEWIS

Oxford   New York
OXFORD UNIVERSITY PRESS
1995

Oxford University Press, Walton Street, Oxford OX2 6DP

Oxford New York
Athens Auckland Bangkok Bombay
Calcutta Cape Town Dar es Salaam Delhi
Florence Hong Kong Istanbul Karachi
Kuala Lumpur Madras Madrid Melbourne
Mexico City Nairobi Paris Singapore
Taipei Tokyo Toronto

and associated companies in
Berlin Ibadan

Oxford is a trade mark of Oxford University Press

Editorial material © Suzanne Lewis 1995
First published as a World's Classics paperback 1995

British Library Cataloguing in Publication Data
Data available

Library of Congress Cataloging in Publication Data
Gaskell, Elizabeth Cleghorn, 1810–1865.
The Moorland cottage, and other stories / Elizabeth Gaskell;
edited with an introduction by Suzanne Lewis.
p.   cm.—(The World's classics)
Includes bibliographical references—.
1. England—Social life and customs—19th century—Fiction.
I. Lewis, Suzanne.   II. Title.   III. Series.
PR4710.M66 1995   823'.8—dc20   94–33159
ISBN 0–19–282321–3

1 3 5 7 9 10 8 6 4 2

Typeset by Pure Tech Corporation, Pondicherry, India
Printed in Great Britain
BPC Paperbacks Ltd.
Aylesbury, Bucks

CONTENTS

CONTENTS

INTRODUCTION

'I BELIEVE the art of telling a story is born with some people, and these have it to perfection,' wrote Elizabeth Gaskell in her essay 'Company Manners'.[1] Gaskell herself was a born storyteller and in her letters, novels, short tales, and essays her talent is displayed to perfection. This selection of one short novel and eight stories shows Gaskell the storyteller working in different genres and with a wide range of material. Four of the stories were published as Christmas tales, one commissioned specifically for the lucrative seasonal trade and two forming part of the chain stories which Charles Dickens put together for the extra Christmas numbers of his journals *Household Words* and *All the Year Round*; two use familiar historical backgrounds—the English Civil War and the French Revolution; four are written as first-person narratives, moving the storyteller's role into greater prominence, and in two of these Gaskell is innovative in successfully adopting a male, working-class persona. All demonstrate that Elizabeth Gaskell deserves recognition as a short fiction writer of great skill, quite apart from her fine reputation as a novelist and biographer.

Gaskell's mastery of her art derives from her talent, not only as a storyteller but also as a social observer. Of *Ruth* (1853), her controversial novel about seduction, betrayal, and illegitimacy, she confessed, 'I did feel as if I had something to say about it that I *must* say, and you know I can tell stories better than any other way of expressing myself'.[2] Such a statement reveals the dual motivation behind much of her writing. She is rarely didactic but her stories provoke a moral response, sometimes spelt out for the reader, but usually arising out of an emotional response to a particular character or to the quiet understatement of the writing itself.

In 1854 the feminist and journalist Frances Power Cobbe, who considered herself a pragmatist and a gatherer of knowledge

---

[1] Elizabeth Gaskell, 'Company Manners', *Household Words*, 9 (20 May 1854), 329.

[2] Letter to Mary Green, January 1853, in the collection of letters in the possession of Dr R. R. Jamison. Quoted in Jenny Uglow, *Elizabeth Gaskell: A Habit of Stories* (London, 1993), 236.

through facts, read 'a pretty little story by Mrs Gaskell'. Her reaction was so intense that she recorded the event in her autobiography, published some forty years later. Through Gaskell's writing, she confessed, 'it came to me to see that Love is greater than Knowledge; that it is more beautiful to serve our brothers freely and tenderly, than to "hive up learning with each studious year" '.[3] Although it is not certain to which story Cobbe was referring, her remarks could apply to most of Elizabeth Gaskell's short fiction, and certainly to all the tales in this selection. Indeed, the common thread which runs through all the stories collected here is love.

Gaskell explores different kinds of love—true and false, selfish and self-sacrificing, within families, between lovers, friends, or even strangers—and she examines ways in which love is manifested in actions, words, or even silence. She claimed, when she was working on *The Moorland Cottage*, that she 'could not write about virtues to order',[4] but the tales in this volume show that she was an acute observer of human behaviour, who recognized virtues and failings in the lives of the great and the humble, and recorded them with irony and sympathy. For Gaskell, love could be both a virtue and a failing and she explores this paradox in *The Moorland Cottage* and in the stories that follow, through humour and pathos, and through the tragic, the extraordinary, and the everyday.

In 1850 Elizabeth Gaskell was, somewhat against her will, writing a Christmas book for Edward Chapman who had published her immensely successful *Mary Barton* two years earlier. In September 1850 she wrote to Lady Kay-Shuttleworth, 'I am almost sorry you know I am going to publish another because I don't think you will like it. Mr Chapman asked me to write a Xmas story, "recommending benevolence, charity, etc", to which I agreed, why I cannot think now, for it was very foolish indeed. However I could not write about virtues to order, so it is simply a little country love-story called Rosemary' (*Letters*, 132). The story became *The*

---

[3] *Life of Frances Power Cobbe, by Herself*, 2 vols. (3rd edn.; London, 1894), i. 96. Also quoted in the *Gaskell Society Christmas Newsletter*, 1991, by Brenda Colloms who suggests that the story was 'Libbie Marsh's Three Eras' (available in *A Dark Night's Work and Other Stories*, ed. Suzanne Lewis (World's Classics edn.; Oxford, 1992)).

[4] *The Letters of Mrs Gaskell*, ed. J. A. V. Chapple and Arthur Pollard (Manchester, 1966), 132. All subsequent references are to this edition.

Moorland Cottage but not before the alternative titles of 'The Fagot' (Chapman's dreadful suggestion) and 'December Days' (Gaskell's own choice) had been considered (see *Letters*, 141). Writing to Chapman in 1856 to remind him of payments due to her, she referred to *The Moorland Cottage* as 'that unfortunate tale' (*Letters*, 407) but to George Smith the following year she commented that while the title was poor, she thought it a pretty tale.[5] Her irritation about the book may have been due less to her opinion of its literary merit than to her troubled relationship with her first publisher. Although she received fifty pounds for the manuscript of *The Moorland Cottage* (as opposed to one hundred pounds for the copyright of *Mary Barton*), she always felt she had made a poor bargain.

However, her readers and reviewers were more kindly disposed towards the story. Elizabeth Gaskell sent a copy of *The Moorland Cottage* to Charlotte Brontë, to which Brontë responded with a copy of *Wuthering Heights* and with high praise of Gaskell's tale. She wrote, 'I told you that book opened like a daisy; I now tell you it finished like a herb—a balsamic herb with healing in its leaves. That small volume has beauty for commencement, gathers power in progress, and closes in pathos. . . . The little story is fresh, natural, religious; no more need be said.'[6] And Mary Forster described her brother, Matthew Arnold, during Christmas 1850— 'Matt is stretched out full length on the sofa, reading a Christmas tale of Mrs Gaskell's which moves him to tears, and the tears to complacent admiration of his own sensibility.'[7]

As Matthew Arnold's reaction suggests, the story is sentimental at times, particularly in its treatment of the invalid Mrs Buxton. It is also melodramatic in its final chapters which include forgery, flight from the law, a fire, and a shipwreck. Henry Fothergill

[5] The *Letters* give this line as 'a poor little, pretty—I thought' (484) but in a footnote to p. 140 Chapple and Pollard suggest the alternative reading, 'A poor title'.

[6] Transcribed from MSS f EL B 91 in the John Rylands University Library of Manchester. Quoted in Angus Easson (ed.), *Elizabeth Gaskell: The Critical Heritage* (London, 1991), 193.

[7] Transcript of a letter from Mrs W. E. Forster to Mr Thomas Arnold, 30 Dec. 1850, in The Brotherton Special Collection, Brotherton Library, University of Leeds. Quoted in Uglow, *Gaskell: A Habit of Stories*, 252.

Chorley, who reviewed the story for the *Athenaeum*, wrote that 'there is a touch of the *Deus ex machinâ* in the catastrophe' but that 'it would be hypercriticism to reckon severely with the authoress for introducing what belongs to the class of *coups de théâtre* at the close of a story so unforced yet so forcible, so natural yet so new, as "The Moorland Cottage" '.[8] For the most part, as Chorley infers, this tale of a young girl's growth to maturity and her negotiation of relationships within the limited circle of her family and friends is quiet and restrained in tone.

In fact, most of the stories in this selection focus, like *The Moorland Cottage,* on tracing fluctuations of feeling and development of character. Character and incident are integrated by a common thread of memory, association, experience, love, and loyalty that runs through an individual life, and the communality of this experience is reinforced in the writing as Gaskell draws on a shared heritage of folklore, parable, fairy tale, biblical lore, and history. Gaskell also uses landscape very effectively to elucidate character. *The Moorland Cottage*, in particular, features an interplay between the outer physical world and the inner emotional world which is seen in some of her finest writing.

These aspects of the stories show that Gaskell owes much to the subtle but profound influence of Wordsworth and the early Romantic movement generally. Poetry was the common literary ground on which William and Elizabeth Gaskell met and, in the early years of their married life at least, they were immersed in Wordsworth and in 'The Poets and Poetry of Humble Life' (*Letters*, 33). However, Gaskell's use of Romantic conventions is not entirely straightforward. For instance, in the opening lines of *The Moorland Cottage*, which recall the beginning of Wordsworth's 'Michael', the narrator addresses the reader as 'you' and sets the scene by giving directions to a traveller, directions which draw the reader into the imagined world of the story and, by implication, into the heroine's emotional world. Gaskell suggests the way in which Maggie Browne's moral horizons will expand beyond the limits of her home, in part through the agency of her finely tuned response to nature. For example, when Maggie is troubled she

---

[8] [Henry Fothergill Chorley], 'The Moorland Cottage. By the Author of "Mary Barton." Chapman & Hall', *Athenaeum*, 1208 (21 Dec. 1850), 1337–8.

climbs the moors to a thorn tree where she 'forgot her little home griefs to . . . imagine what lay beyond those old grey holy hills, which seemed to bear up the white clouds of Heaven. . . . She always came down from the thorn, comforted, and meekly gentle.' The thorn tree becomes the focus of Maggie's emotional existence in much the same way that Wordsworth uses another 'thorn' to concentrate the intense emotions described in his ballad of the same name.[9] But the influence of the thorn tree is harmful as well as beneficial; it reconciles her to her moorland home which, while it acts as a balm to her spirit, is also a prison which binds her to duty and obedience.

At one point in the story Maggie is described using lines from Wordsworth's 'Three Years She Grew in Sun and Shower' (*Lyrical Ballads*, 1800). This is an example of one of Gaskell's favourite methods of characterization in which she places certain of her heroines in a particular relationship to nature indicated by Wordsworth's 'Lucy' poems. She uses the device in connection with Phillis Holman in 'Cousin Phillis' (1863–4), Ruth Benson in *Ruth* and Molly Gibson in *Wives and Daughters* (1864–6). Gaskell draws on the Romantic tradition which associated solitary female figures with nature to suggest the sensitivity, intuitive knowledge, and instinctive goodness of her heroines. However, her use of the 'Lucy' poems is ambiguous because these poems imply that the price of such closeness to nature is a loss of identity and individuality which reaches its most extreme form in the death of the subject.

Maggie does, ultimately, risk death in her attempt to satisfy the onerous and often opposing demands made on her by her mother, brother, lover, and her lover's ambitious father. As Chorley puts it, 'The poor girl, as too often happens, had to stand between these conflicting impersonations of selfishness, under deadly peril of the happiness and joy of her life being trampled out in the struggle'. He calls *The Moorland Cottage* a 'study of self-sacrifice', yet Gaskell holds back from allowing her heroine to give up everything for others. Maggie demands and retains a portion of happiness for

<hr>

[9] Alan Shelston notes these Wordsworthian connections in his study of Myles Birket Foster's illustrations for the first edition of *The Moorland Cottage* in the *Gaskell Society Journal*, 2 (1988), 41–58.

herself. She recognizes not only a personal motive but also a moral imperative to refrain from a course of total self-abnegation. In such imperatives Gaskell always resists the easy commonplace fate of the traditional Victorian heroine, for a stronger, more powerful recognition of the value of womens' lives.

In this way Maggie Browne differs from the character with whom she is often compared, George Eliot's Maggie Tulliver. Swinburne noted that the author of *The Mill on the Floss* (1860) owed a 'palpable and weighty and direct obligation—to Mrs Gaskell's beautiful story of "The Moorland Cottage" '.[10] Certainly there are similarities of name, characterization, and plot between the two works. But perhaps the strongest argument for regarding *The Mill on the Floss* as, in part, a reply to issues raised by Elizabeth Gaskell some ten years earlier, is the common theme of female heroism. For Maggie Tulliver is, as Maggie Browne is described, 'in danger of becoming too little a dweller in the present, from the habit of anticipating the occasion for some great heroic action'. Mrs Buxton corrects this tendency in Maggie Browne by speaking of characters who might have stepped out of one of Wordsworth's poems (or one of Gaskell's own stories), 'those whose names will never be blazoned on earth—some poor maid-servant, or hard-worked artisan, or weary governess—who have gone on through life quietly . . . in a soft, still, succession of resolute days', and such words could also apply to the life Maggie Tulliver faces after her renunciation of Stephen Guest.

Regardless of whether George Eliot was indebted to Gaskell's story, certainly Gaskell herself reworked certain elements from *The Moorland Cottage* very successfully in her last novel *Wives and Daughters*, particularly the device of contrasting 'sister' figures, the step-sisters Molly and Cynthia in *Wives and Daughters*, and Maggie and her wealthy friend Erminia, Mrs Buxton's niece, in *The Moorland Cottage*. Erminia is described as 'gay, volatile, wilful, warm-hearted', but 'the distractions of wealth' have meant that her life is 'a shattered mirror; every part dazzling and brilliant, but wanting the coherency and perfection of a whole'. Similarly, Cynthia Kirkpatrick's 'constant brilliancy' is wearying for 'it was not the sunshiny rest of a placid lake, it was rather the glitter of the

[10] Algernon Charles Swinburne, *A Note on Charlotte Brontë* (London, 1877), 31.

pieces of a broken mirror, which confuses and bewilders'.[11] In contrast, Maggie Browne and Molly Gibson, with their homely names, are quiet, thoughtful, sympathetic, and unselfishly generous, conforming closely to Victorian models of ideal female adolescent behaviour. Yet for both girls the 'reward' for such goodness is domestic oppression and social rejection (Molly is considered by Squire Hamley as unsuitable to marry his son just as the wealthy Mr Buxton tries to break the engagement between Maggie and his son Frank).

Elizabeth Gaskell's exploration of the negative aspects of goodness is, in fact, one of the most interesting themes of both *The Moorland Cottage* and *Wives and Daughters*. Like Molly Gibson, Maggie Browne's happiness and, indeed, her life are placed at risk by her own, and other people's, expectations of her unselfishness and her capacity for heroism and sacrifice in the name of love. But all the characters interpret and define love differently, usually according to their own needs and in ways that are revealing of their own personality.

These issues resonate in the second story in this volume, 'The Sexton's Hero'. The tale is predicated on the question asked by one of the passing travellers who listens to the sexton's story, ' "How would you then define a hero?" ' Standing in intimate relation to Gaskell's text, although never named, are two other texts, Thomas Carlyle's *On Heroes, Hero Worship and the Heroic in History* (1841), and, from the Gospel of St John, 'Greater love hath no man than this, that a man lay down his life for his friends' (15: 13). The sexton's hero, Gilbert Dawson, is a quiet rebuttal of Carlyle's rhetoric of heroism for he is, to borrow the words of Mrs Buxton in *The Moorland Cottage*, one 'of those whose names will never be blazoned on earth'. Gilbert is a Christ-like figure, as shown by his pacifism, his ability to attract small children around him, and the Gospel texts 'marked broad with his carpenter's pencil' in his Bible; and while the story itself is full of action, it begins and ends with the quietness and simplicity of a parable, echoing the rhythms of biblical language.

If the theme of the tale was close to Gaskell's heart, then so too was

[11] Elizabeth Gaskell, *Wives and Daughters* (1864–6), ed. Angus Easson (World's Classics edn.; Oxford, 1987), 362.

the setting, Morecambe Bay. In July 1843, Elizabeth Gaskell and her children stayed at Silverdale, a farming and fishing village on the eastern side of the Bay to which they returned for many holidays, joyous accounts of which are to be found in Gaskell's letters. On a more sombre note, however, she wrote to Charles Eliot Norton that from their holiday accommodation they looked 'down on the Bay with it's [sic] slow moving train of crossers led over the treacherous sands by the Guide, a square man sitting stern on his *white* horse, (the better to be seen when daylight ebbs). . . . On foggy nights the guide, (who has let people drown before now, who could not pay him his fee . . .) may be heard blowing an old ram's horn trumpet, to guide by the sound' (*Letters*, 505). For Silverdale overlooks the sands which lie at the junction of the Bay and the mouth of the River Kent. Gaskell was aware of the dangers in crossing the sands using the routes which appeared at low tide, and she used these dangers to heighten the tension and tragedy of her story.

'The Sexton's Hero' was published in William and Mary Howitt's rather didactic, stodgy, and short-lived *Journal*, as was the story which follows it in this volume, 'Christmas Storms and Sunshine'. Gaskell had confessed, 'I cannot write a Xmas book',[12] but *The Moorland Cottage* and 'Christmas Storms and Sunshine' disprove her opinion. Henry Chorley's review in the *Athenaeum* summed up *The Moorland Cottage* as 'a story intended to soften the heart and sweeten the charities at Christmas time by the agency of pity and sympathy'. Add the ingredient of humour and this description could apply equally well to Gaskell's story of feuding neighbours in 'Christmas Storms and Sunshine'. Jenkins and Hodgson are compositors on rival provincial newspapers—'the *Flying Post* . . . long established and respectable—alias bigoted and Tory; the *Examiner* . . . spirited and intelligent—alias new-fangled and democratic'. Their wives enter into the quarrel with as much vigour as themselves, and the two sides are well-matched by the addition of the Hodgsons' baby '("such a baby!—a poor, puny little thing")' and the Jenkinses' cat '("such a cat! a great, nasty miowling

---

[12] Letter, possibly to Edward Chapman, tentatively dated early 1850, in *Letters*, 104.

tom-cat, that was always stealing the milk put by for little Angel's supper")'.

The playful, satirical opening paragraphs establish the dominant tone of the tale which has been compared to Charles Dickens's Christmas stories. In 'Christmas Storms and Sunshine' Gaskell's characterization approaches Dickensian caricature but, although the plot turns on the threat to a child's life, she avoids Dickensian sentimentality. Instead, she draws again on that line of feeling and memory which links her characters' present to their past and operates as a benign influence in their lives. Thus, after the superbly comic episode in which Mary Hodgson beats the Jenkinses' cat for stealing, Mary's thoughts turn to the past, to 'her dear, dear mother', and she reflects, 'What would her mother say if she knew how cross and cruel her little Mary was getting? If she should live to beat her child in one of her angry fits?' The darkening tone of Mary's thoughts foreshadows the crisis which is about to threaten her child. Their unlikely rescuer, Mrs Jenkins, equally comic in her sour self-righteousness, mellows too as she listens to children singing a Christmas carol in the street below and begins 'to think over long-past days, on softening remembrances of the dead and gone, on words long forgotten, on holy stories heard at her mother's knee'.

The story ends happily, with Christmas feasting and songs and, in a sense, would have been better suited to the purposes of Charles Dickens's *Household Words* and *All the Year Round*, the magazines for which Gaskell wrote the majority of her short fiction including the remaining stories in this volume, than to the Howitts' more serious *Journal*. Both Dickens and the Howitts had a political manifesto for their journals, which sought a general improvement of social conditions, especially for the poor. However, Dickens, the consummate business impresario, sought financial success too with his 'solemn and continual Conductorial Injunction' to 'KEEP "HOUSEHOLD WORDS" IMAGINATIVE!'[13] and his instruction to W. H. Wills, his editor: ' "Brighten it, brighten it,

[13] 'To W.H. Wills, 17 November 1853', in *The Letters of Charles Dickens*, vii, ed. Graham Storey, Kathleen Tillotson, and Angus Easson (Pilgrim edn.; Oxford, 1993), 200.

brighten it!" [14] His remarks reveal a crucial difference between the two publications which ensured the great success of the one and the rapid failure of the other.

While Dickens always welcomed Gaskell's contributions to *Household Words* and *All the Year Round*, his opinions of her work varied from extravagant praise to criticism which was sometimes ill-natured but often very perceptive. For instance, he remarked that Gaskell had 'a way of rather abusing her strength by making her victims unjustly unhappy sometimes'.[15] This is certainly true of Nest Gwynn, heroine of the next story in this volume, 'The Well of Pen-Morfa'. Nest's prospects for happiness, which are dependent on the conventional channels for women—beauty, marriage, children—are blighted by a sudden accident, and her fate does seem unjust. However, as in so many of Gaskell's stories, Nest finds a certain measure of happiness and fulfilment in a course of action that seems outwardly difficult and unpromising, but requires and nurtures an enlargement of spirit inspired by humble duties faithfully carried out.

'The Well of Pen-Morfa' is set in north-west Wales, 'Welsh Wales' as Gaskell describes it, and is informed by her personal response to the country. She had family connections in the area and holidayed there before and after her marriage, and on her honeymoon. She delighted in the local people, their legends and customs, and her response to the landscape is reflected in that of her heroine Ruth, in the novel of the same name, for whom Snowdonia 'was opening a new sense; vast ideas of beauty and grandeur filled her mind at the sight of the mountains now first beheld in full majesty. She was almost overpowered by the vague and solemn delight; but by and by her love for them equalled her awe'.[16]

But the beauty is tinged with great tragedy for it was at Ffestiniog, in Snowdonia, that Gaskell's daughter Marianne contracted scarlet fever during a holiday in July 1845. Marianne recovered but the infection spread to Gaskell's infant son Willie who died at

[14] Quoted in Uglow, *Gaskell: A Habit of Stories*, 254.

[15] Written in relation to Gaskell's 'Crowley Castle' in a letter to Lady Cowley, 13 Dec. 1863. Quoted in Angus Easson, *Elizabeth Gaskell* (London, 1979), 220.

[16] Elizabeth Gaskell, *Ruth* (1853), ed. Alan Shelston (World's Classics edn.; Oxford, 1985), 65.

Porthmadog, the town at the entrance to the Lleyn Peninsula where the village of Pen-Morfa is situated. Thus these wild and beautiful places feature in Elizabeth Gaskell's stories as the backdrop to tales of great unhappiness, loss of love, betrayal, and abandonment.

Upon receiving the manuscript of 'The Well of Pen-Morfa' Dickens wrote to Gaskell saying that he had 'read it with avidity' and was 'delighted to have it'.[17] The publication of the short story 'Lizzie Leigh'[18] in March–April of 1850, on the first page of the first number of *Household Words*, had been a bright and promising start to a professional relationship which brought rewards and frustrations to both editor and author. If Dickens had been hoping for regular contributions from Gaskell he was already disappointed for, after a silence of some months, he wrote to her in July, 'This is a brief letter, but—if you only knew it!—a very touching one in its earnestness. Can't you—won't you—don't you ever mean to—write me another story?'[19] But it was October before she responded with 'The Well of Pen-Morfa', and December when 'The Heart of John Middleton' appeared on Dickens's desk.

Dickens's letter to Wills about 'The Heart of John Middleton' identifies, albeit jokingly and unconsciously, his predilection for editorial tinkering with the work of his contributors, which was one of the rocks on which he and Gaskell were later to split. 'The story is very clever—I think the best thing of hers I have seen, not excepting Mary Barton—and if it had ended happily (which is the whole meaning of it) would have been a great success. As it is, it . . . will not do much, and will link itself painfully, with the girl who fell down at the well ['The Well of Pen-Morfa'], and the child who tumbled down stairs ['Lizzie Leigh']. I wish to Heaven, her people would keep a little firmer on their legs!'[20] The heroine of this story also suffers an accident, the consequences of which seem unnecessarily harsh. Dickens's correspondence with Gaskell shows

[17] 'To Mrs Gaskell, 6 October 1850', in *The Letters of Charles Dickens*, vi, ed. Graham Storey, Kathleen Tillotson, and Nina Burgis (Pilgrim edn.; Oxford, 1988), 188.

[18] In *Cousin Phillis and Other Tales*, ed. Angus Easson (World's Classics edn.; Oxford, 1981).

[19] 'To Mrs Gaskell, 3 July 1850', *Letters of Charles Dickens*, vi. 121.

[20] 'To W.H. Wills, 12 December 1850', ibid. 231.

that he did formally propose to her that the story have a happy ending and that Gaskell would have agreed to the alteration had the proposal reached her in time. However, as the story stands, Nelly's fate is in keeping with Gaskell's underlying theme, the exploration of opposing ethics, New Testament love and forgiveness versus Old Testament revenge.

Dickens was acute in describing 'The Heart of John Middleton' as 'a story of extraordinary power, worked out with a vigor [*sic*] and truthfulness that very very few people could reach'.[21] In fact, here Gaskell achieves a marvellous integration of plot, characterization, setting, and language in a story which could be described as her most overt examination of Christian philosophy, but which is notable for its understatement and absence of didacticism. The story is set on the bleak moors between Yorkshire and Lancashire and, as in 'The Sexton's Hero', the working-class narrator uses language which is a blend of regional dialect and biblical rhythms. However, unlike the sexton, whose story is imbued with the New Testament message of love, sacrifice, and forgiveness, John Middleton draws on the language and stories of the Old Testament, and on the rantings of a fanatical itinerant preacher, to express his interpretation of Christianity that shapes and focuses his own personal motive for revenge. He reads 'the mighty act of God's vengeance, in the Old Testament, with a kind of triumphant faith that, sooner or later, He would take my cause in hand, and revenge me on mine enemy'. The language is powerful, even shocking, for, as John Middleton admits, 'I liked strong things; and I liked the bare, full truth'. Of course this is implicitly challenged in a story which presents various versions of the truth, but it gives a clue to the success of the tale, which lies in Gaskell's daring adoption of a male, working-class persona.

One of the features of this selection of stories is the diversity of narratorial voices used. Elizabeth Gaskell, a consummate storyteller, experiments with first- and third-person narratives and male and female personae, drawn from a range of social backgrounds and regional settings. In stories such as 'The Sexton's Hero' and 'The Heart of John Middleton' Gaskell is more adventurous in her use of

[21] 'To Mrs Gaskell, 17 December 1850', ibid. 238.

personae but in the next tale in this volume, 'Morton Hall', Gaskell is on familiar territory with Bridget Sidebotham, a narrator who might have stepped out of the pages of *Cranford* (1851–3).

In a notice in the *Athenaeum* on the occasion of Elizabeth Gaskell's death, Henry Fothergill Chorley, who had reviewed most of her work for the magazine, selected 'Morton Hall' as 'expressly to be commemorated as powerful, pathetic and individual'.[22] Certainly some of the historical episodes described in this story of several generations of the aristocratic Morton family are very powerful, dealing as they do with exile, imprisonment, madness, penury, starvation, and self-sacrificing love. But the subject-matter sits oddly with the style of the narrator, whose forte is not the broad sweep of history, the decline and restoration of aristocratic fortunes, but observation of the small details of human behaviour, of the kind which has made *Cranford* such an enduring success. Thus, her description of a gay party of seventeeth-century Cavaliers is universally applicable, as Bridget herself recognizes: 'If you'll notice, when many people are talking merrily out of doors in sunlight, they will stop talking for an instant, when they come into the cool green shade, and either be silent for some little time, or else speak graver, and slower, and softer.'

'My French Master', the next story in this selection, also contains pertinent observations of human foibles. The narrator recalls that when she was a child, 'A sort of hieroglyphic or cypher talk was used in order to conceal the meaning of much that was said if children were present. My mother was a proficient in this way of talking, and took, we fancied, a certain pleasure in perplexing my father by inventing a new cypher, as it were, every day. For instance, for some time, I was called Martia, because I was very tall of my age; and, just as my father began to understand the name—and, it must be owned, a good while after I had learnt to prick up my ears whenever Martia was named—my mother suddenly changed me into the "buttress," from the habit I had acquired of leaning my languid length against a wall. I saw my father's perplexity about this "buttress" for some days, and could have helped him out of it, but I durst not.'

Like 'Morton Hall', 'My French Master' is also set against

[22] 'Henry Fothergill Chorley, from an unsigned notice, the *Athenaeum*, 18 November 1865, 689–90', quoted in Easson (ed.), *Gaskell: The Critical Heritage*, 508.

momentous historical events, in this case the French Revolution and its aftermath. But because these events take place at a distance, the unnamed narrator does not have to deal directly with history; instead she is free to observe the reshaping of Monsieur de Chalabre's character and the inevitable approach of his own personal tragedy which take place precisely *because* he is removed from the historical events which affect him, and from the country he loves so passionately.

'My French Master', like Gaskell's other 'historical' story, 'Morton Hall', ends with a marriage, a double, 'Shakespearian' marriage in fact, which ameliorates previous tragedies, turns alienation into reconciliation, and re-establishes the continuum from past to present. The story that follows it, 'The Manchester Marriage', is a study of marriage in which the ghost of the past actually materializes in human form and threatens to tear husband and wife apart. Gaskell contrasts the past and present marriages of Alice Openshaw in an extremely shrewd look at the institution of matrimony. 'The perpetual requirement of loving words, looks, and caresses, and misconstruing their absence into absence of love, had been the great trial of her former married life', whereas her second husband, while he learns to love her deeply, is primarily motivated by mutual advantage when he proposes to her with the words ' "Mrs Frank, is there any reason why we two should not put up our horses together?" ' Alice's second wooing is comic but the profit motive which underlies both the proposal and the acceptance is disturbing in that it allows Alice little real choice in answer to Mr Openshaw's question.

One of the most interesting aspects of the story is the way in which Gaskell shifts the focus from Alice's thoughts and feelings in order to explore her husband's emotional life. Mr Openshaw changes from an utterly prosaic businessman—'I do not think he ever saw a group of flowers in the fields without thinking whether their colours would, or would not, form harmonious contrasts in the coming spring muslins and prints'—to a vulnerable human being who acts out of pity, sympathy, and love.

If 'The Manchester Marriage' is a study of rational affection deepened into undemonstrative but enduring love, then 'Crowley Castle', the last story in this volume, is a tale of wild, irrational, jealous love and its terrible consequences. Here Gaskell pursues a theme already explored in 'Morton Hall', and in other tales such as 'The Grey Woman'[23] and her first published work, 'Clopton Hall'.[24] In these pieces, ancestral homes and an aristocratic lineage are prison vaults for the women of these families who are hemmed in by forces of history and tradition, and by imposed, unreasonable, misinterpreted expectations of love and loyalty. Victorine, the villainess in 'Crowley Castle', offers a powerful symbol of the oppression of the past and the oppression of love when she says to her mistress Theresa Crowley, ' "In my country they reckon a building secure against wind and storm and all the ravages of time, if the first mortar used has been tempered with human blood. But not even our joint secret, though it was tempered well with blood, can hold our lives together! How much less all the care, all the love, that I lavished upon you in the days of my youth and strength!" ' As a storyteller, Gaskell would have relished this piece of folklore as a device for heightening the pleasurable terror of telling wild tales around the fire.

Victorine interprets love as a bond, a contract, solid as a building of stone and mortar, whereas John Middleton describes love as 'a little golden, filmy thread' woven into the black, coarse web of his life. These contrasting images illustrate the way in which Elizabeth Gaskell plays the variations on the theme of love in all the stories selected here. Bound up with her exploration of love is her analysis of heroism. The sexton's hero, and Gaskell's heroes, are no Carlylean giants, no Dantes or Shakespeares, Cromwells or Napoleons, but rather, 'Some mute inglorious Milton . . . | Some Cromwell guiltless of his country's blood'.[25]

Furthermore, unlike Carlyle or Gray, Elizabeth Gaskell's heroes are usually women and her male characters often manifest their heroism in ways that Gaskell construes as particularly characteristic of women—suffering, endurance, silence. Of course such a gender-based interpretation of heroism is itself problematic, particularly for those who would claim Gaskell as a feminist. What is

---

[23] In Gaskell, *A Dark Night's Work*.

[24] In 1838 Elizabeth Gaskell sent William and Mary Howitt a four-page account of a visit to Clopton House which William used verbatim in his *Visits to Remarkable Places* (1840; Philadelphia, 1842), 117–20, acknowledging his source only as 'a fair lady'.

[25] Thomas Gray, 'Elegy Written in a Country Churchyard' (1751). Elizabeth Gaskell's father William Stevenson gave her Gray's *Poems* in 1825 (see Uglow, *Gaskell: A Habit of Stories*, 41).

significant, however, is that such characters appear in her fiction at all. Crippled women, unmarried women (above a certain age), poor women, childless women, just did not feature in the fiction of most of her contemporaries, unless treated sentimentally or comically.

It is relatively easy to see the romance in the life of a dispossessed French aristocrat such as Monsieur de Chalabre, or a beautiful, wayward baronet's daughter such as Theresa Crowley. Gaskell does not deny that characters such as these, despite all their apparent advantages of birth and position, will be called upon to display great heroism and endure great suffering. But she also recognizes and acknowledges the quiet heroism of everyday life, and 'the romance in the lives of some of those who elbowed me daily in the busy streets'.[26] The stories in this selection are all in some way a response to Elizabeth Gaskell's belief that 'the beauty and poetry of many of the common things and daily events of life in its humblest aspect does not seem to me sufficiently appreciated' (*Letters*, 33).

[26] Elizabeth Gaskell, Preface to *Mary Barton* (1848), ed. Edgar Wright (World's Classics edn.; Oxford, 1987), xxxv.

NOTE ON THE TEXT

THE text of each story is that of the last publication during Elizabeth Gaskell's lifetime, over which it may be assumed she had some editorial control. In general, however, it was not Gaskell's practice to revise her work to any great extent.

The Moorland Cottage was first published as a Christmas book by Chapman and Hall (London, 1850; present text). It was not reprinted in Elizabeth Gaskell's lifetime.

'The Sexton's Hero' appeared in *Howitt's Journal of Literature and Popular Progress*, vol. 2, in September 1847, and was reprinted several times during the author's lifetime. For example, in 1850 the story was published together with 'Christmas Storms and Sunshine' as a sixpenny pamphlet sold at Capesthorne Fête for the benefit of the Macclesfield Public Baths and Wash-houses. These two stories were also reprinted by F. D. Maurice and Charles Kingsley in *The Christian Socialist*, vol. 1, March–April 1851. Chapman and Hall included 'The Sexton's Hero' in the collection *Lizzie Leigh; and Other Tales* (Cheap Edition, London, 1855), and Smith, Elder reprinted it in *Cousin Phillis, and Other Tales* (London, 1865; present text).

'Christmas Storms and Sunshine' was first published in *Howitt's Journal*, vol. 3, in the New Year's Day number, 1848. Apart from the reprintings mentioned above, the story also appeared in Chapman and Hall's 1855 edition of *Lizzie Leigh; and Other Tales*, and in Smith, Elder's collection *The Grey Woman and Other Tales* (London, 1865; present text).

The next four stories in this volume all appeared first in *Household Words*—'The Well of Pen-Morfa' in vol. 2, 16 and 23 November 1850; 'The Heart of John Middleton' in vol. 2, 28 December 1850; 'Morton Hall' in vol. 8, 19 and 26 November 1853; and 'My French Master' also in vol. 8, 17 and 24 December 1853. All four were reprinted by Chapman and Hall in *Lizzie Leigh; and Other Tales*, and by Smith, Elder in a collection of the same name (London, 1865; present text).

'The Manchester Marriage' first appeared as part of the chain story *A House to Let*, the Extra Christmas Number of *Household*

Words for 1858. It was reprinted in *Right at Last and Other Tales*, a selection of Gaskell's stories put out by Sampson Low (London, 1860; present text), with a few emendations to the text to allow the story to stand independently of the chain story context.

'Crowley Castle' was first published as 'How the First Floor Went to Crowley Castle', part of the chain story *Mrs Lirriper's Lodgings*, the Extra Christmas Number of *All the Year Round* for 1863. Approximately the first three-quarters of this story exists in manuscript form (MS. F. 823.894 Z1, Manchester Central Reference Library). Collation of the two versions reveals compression of the *All the Year Round* text, probably the result of editing by Charles Dickens rather than by Elizabeth Gaskell. The present text follows the version printed in *All the Year Round*, except for the first paragraph where the manuscript version has been used in order to allow the story to stand independently of the chain story context.

A few obvious errors have been corrected and in some instances Gaskell's spelling and punctuation have been modernized or otherwise emended. All except the most minor changes are referred to in the explanatory notes.

SELECT BIBLIOGRAPHY

ELIZABETH GASKELL is an important nineteenth-century English writer whose work is currently experiencing a great revival of interest and critical scrutiny. The present flourishing state of Gaskell scholarship is attested to by the recent publication of four major works. Angus Easson has edited a volume on Elizabeth Gaskell for the Critical Heritage series (London, 1991), thus making available in easily accessible form a wide range of responses to Gaskell's work from her contemporaries. Two full-length critical studies of Gaskell's fiction have also been published recently, Hilary Schor's *Scheherezade in the Marketplace: Elizabeth Gaskell and the Victorian Novel* (New York, 1992), and Felicia Bonaparte's *The Gypsy-Bachelor of Manchester: The Life of Mrs Gaskell's Demon* (Charlottesville, 1992). Finally, Jenny Uglow has written an outstanding new biography, *Elizabeth Gaskell: A Habit of Stories* (London, 1993). As Uglow herself acknowledges, Gaskell scholars and enthusiasts continue to be indebted to J. A. V. Chapple and Arthur Pollard for *The Letters of Mrs Gaskell* (Manchester, 1966).

Uglow's biography goes far towards redressing the imbalance which has, to date, seen Elizabeth Gaskell's considerable output of short fiction receive scant critical attention. Nevertheless, there are a number of studies of Gaskell's writing which devote a chapter, or a significant section, to the short fiction. These include Aina Rubenius, *The Woman Question in Mrs Gaskell's Life and Works* (Upsala and Cambridge, Mass., 1950); Arthur Pollard, *Mrs Gaskell: Novelist and Biographer* (Manchester, 1965); Edgar Wright, *Mrs Gaskell: The Basis for Reassessment* (London, 1965); Margaret Ganz, *Elizabeth Gaskell: The Artist in Conflict* (New York, 1969); Angus Easson, *Elizabeth Gaskell* (London, 1979); Enid Duthie, *The Themes of Elizabeth Gaskell* (London, 1980); Coral Lansbury, *Elizabeth Gaskell* (Boston, 1984); and Patsy Stoneman, *Elizabeth Gaskell* (Brighton, 1987). J. G. Sharps makes use of detailed background material and biographical information in his study of the novels and the short fiction, *Mrs Gaskell's Observation and Invention* (Fontwell, Sussex, 1970).

There are three comprehensive editions of Elizabeth Gaskell's works. The eight-volume Knutsford edition, *The Works of Mrs Gaskell* (London, 1906) edited by A. W. Ward, and the eleven-volume World's Classics edition, *The Novels and Tales of Mrs Gaskell* (London, 1906–19) edited by Clement Shorter, are out of print. Both Ward and Shorter provide useful introductions which include consideration of the short stories. The World's Classics series published by Oxford University Press has the most extensive collection of Elizabeth Gaskell's work currently in print. The introductions to the three volumes of short stories, *Cousin Phillis and Other Tales* (ed. Angus Easson, Oxford, 1981), *My Lady Ludlow and Other Stories* (ed. Edgar Wright, Oxford, 1989), and *A Dark Night's Work and Other Stories* (ed. Suzanne Lewis, Oxford, 1992) contain both biographical material and critical comment on Gaskell as a writer of short fiction. Anna Walters's introduction to *Elizabeth Gaskell: Four Short Stories* (London, 1983), provides detailed critical comment on 'The Well of Pen-Morfa' and 'The Manchester Marriage' (together with 'Libbie Marsh's Three Eras' and 'Lizzie Leigh').

However, the individual stories in this selection have, in general, received little critical attention. In '(Re) Visions of Virtue: Elizabeth Gaskell's *Moorland Cottage* and George Eliot's *The Mill on the Floss*' (*Studies in the Novel*, 23/4 (Winter 1991), 432–42), Ramona Lumpkin offers a detailed consideration of the interchange between these two texts; and Alan Shelston has examined *The Moorland Cottage* in relation to Myles Birket Foster's illustrations for the first edition of the story in '*The Moorland Cottage*: Elizabeth Gaskell and Myles Birket Foster', *Gaskell Society Journal*, 2 (1988), 41–58. Peter Skrine mentions the story in the context of Elizabeth Gaskell's personal and literary connections with Germany, and considers several other short stories in some detail in 'Mrs Gaskell and Germany', *Gaskell Society Journal*, 7 (1993), 37–49. Elizabeth Gaskell's personal and literary connections with France have been examined by Philip Yarrow in 'Mrs Gaskell and France', *Gaskell Society Journal*, 7 (1993), 16–36, in which he mentions 'My French Master' and 'The Manchester Marriage'. 'My French Master' is also discussed by Enid Duthie in 'Echoes of the French Revolution in the Work of Elizabeth Gaskell', *Gaskell Society Journal*, 2 (1988), 34–40.

A CHRONOLOGY OF
ELIZABETH GASKELL

1810   Elizabeth Cleghorn Stevenson, second surviving child of William Stevenson and Elizabeth Holland, born in Chelsea 29 September.

1811   (November) After her mother's death, Elizabeth is taken to Knutsford to live with her Aunt Hannah Lumb.

1822–7 Attends school at Misses Byerley's in Warwick and Stratford-upon-Avon.

1828–9 Her elder brother, John Stevenson (b. 1799), disappears while on a voyage to India. Elizabeth goes to Chelsea to live with her father and stepmother.

1829   (22 March) Elizabeth's father dies; she goes to Newcastle upon Tyne, to the home of the Revd William Turner.

1831   Spends much of this year in Edinburgh with Mr Turner's daughter. Visits Manchester.

1832   (30 August) Marries the Revd William Gaskell, assistant Minister at Cross Street Chapel, Manchester, at St John's Parish Church, Knutsford. They live at 14 Dover Street, Manchester.

1833   Her first child, a daughter, born dead.

1834   Her second daughter, Marianne, born.

1837   A poem, 'Sketches among the Poor', by Mr and Mrs Gaskell, appears in *Blackwood's Magazine* (January). Her third daughter, Margaret Emily (Meta), born. Mrs Hannah Lumb dies.

1840   Her description of Clopton Hall included by William Howitt in *Visits to Remarkable Places*.

1841   Mr and Mrs Gaskell visit the Continent, touring the Rhine country.

1842   Her fourth daughter, Florence Elizabeth, born. The family move to 121 Upper Rumford Street, Manchester.

1844   Her only son, William, born; dies of scarlet fever at Porthmadog, 1845.

1846   Her fifth daughter, Julia Bradford, born.

1847   'Libbie Marsh's Three Eras' published in *Howitt's Journal*.

1848   'Christmas Storms and Sunshine' in *Howitt's Journal*. Her first novel, *Mary Barton*, published.

1849   Visits London, where she meets Dickens and other literary figures. Meets Wordsworth while on holiday in Ambleside. 'Hand and Heart' published in the *Sunday School Penny Magazine*, 'The Last Generation in England' in *Sartain's Union Magazine*, America.

1850   The family move to 84 Plymouth Grove, Manchester. Dickens invites Mrs Gaskell to contribute to *Household Words*: 'Lizzie Leigh' begins in first number, followed by 'The Well of Pen-Morfa' and 'The Heart of John Middleton'. *The Moorland Cottage* published. First meets Charlotte Brontë in August.

1851   'Mr Harrison's Confessions' appears in the *Ladies' Companion*. Continues to write for *Household Words*, the first episode of *Cranford* appearing in December. Visited by Charlotte Brontë in June. Her portrait, now in the National Portrait Gallery, painted by Richmond.

1852   'The Schah's English Gardener' and 'The Old Nurse's Story' in *Household Words*. 'Bessy's Troubles at Home' in the *Sunday School Penny Magazine*. Gives Charlotte Brontë the outline of *Ruth* (April). Visited by Dickens (September).

1853   *Ruth* (January) and *Cranford* (June) published. 'Cumberland Sheep-Shearers', 'Traits and Stories of the Huguenots', 'Morton Hall', 'My French Master', 'The Squire's Story' all in *Household Words*. Begins *North and South*. Visits exchanged with Charlotte Brontë.

1854   'Modern Greek Songs', 'Company Manners' in *Household Words*; *North and South* begins to appear in September. Her husband succeeds as Minister of Cross Street Chapel, Manchester. Visits France with Marianne: meets Mme Mohl and William W. Story. Meets Florence Nightingale in London. Last meeting with Charlotte Brontë.

1855   'An Accursed Race', 'Half a Lifetime Ago' in *Household Words*. *North and South* and *Lizzie Leigh; and Other Tales* published. In June, Charlotte Brontë's father asks her to write his daughter's *Life*. She and Meta spend a month in Paris with Mme Mohl.

1856   'The Poor Clare' in *Household Words*.

1857   *Life of Charlotte Brontë* published. Visits Paris and Rome with her two eldest daughters and Catherine Winkworth.

1858   'My Lady Ludlow', 'Right at Last', and 'The Manchester Marriage' in *Household Words*. 'The Doom of the Griffiths' in *Harper's Magazine*.

1859   *Round the Sofa and Other Tales* published. 'Lois the Witch' and 'The Crooked Branch' in *All the Year Round*. Visits Whitby where she collects material for *Sylvia's Lovers*. Takes her daughters Meta and Florence to Germany, returning via Paris.

1860   *Right at Last and Other Tales* published. 'Curious, if True' in *The Cornhill*. Visits to France.

1861   'The Grey Woman' in *All the Year Round*.

1862   Visits Paris, Normandy, and Brittany with Meta and a friend, returning to London for the Exhibition. Back in Manchester she over-exerts herself in relief work among the workmen, and has to recuperate. Writes a Preface to Vecchi's *Garibaldi*.

1863   'A Dark Night's Work', 'An Italian Institution', 'The Cage at Cranford', and 'Crowley Castle' in *All the Year Round*. 'Cousin Phillis' in *The Cornhill*. *Sylvia's Lovers* published by Smith, Elder. Visits Mme Mohl in Paris, going on to Rome with three of her daughters. Her daughter Florence marries.

1864   'French Life' in *Fraser's Magazine*. *Wives and Daughters* begins to appear in *The Cornhill*.

1865   *Cousin Phillis, and Other Tales* and *The Grey Woman and Other Tales* published. Visits Dieppe, and Mme Mohl in Paris. Buys a house, The Lawns, nr. Holybourne in Hampshire, and dies there suddenly on 12 November.

1866   *Wives and Daughters* published posthumously.

The Moorland Cottage
and Other Stories

THE MOORLAND COTTAGE

CHAPTER 1

IF you take the turn to the left, after you pass the lyke-gate* at Combehurst Church, you will come to the wooden bridge over the brook; keep along the field-path which mounts higher and higher, and, in half a mile or so, you will be in a breezy upland field, almost large enough to be called a down, where sheep pasture on the short, fine, elastic turf. You look down on Combehurst and its beautiful church-spire. After the field is crossed, you come to a common, richly coloured with the golden gorse and the purple heather, which in summer-time send out their warm scents into the quiet air. The swelling waves of the upland make a near horizon against the sky; the line is only broken in one place by a small grove of Scotch firs, which always look black and shadowed even at mid-day, when all the rest of the landscape seems bathed in sunlight. The lark quivers and sings high up in the air; too high—in too dazzling a region, for you to see her. Look! she drops into sight;—but, as if loth to leave the heavenly radiance, she balances herself and floats in the ether. Now she falls suddenly right into her nest, hidden among the ling,* unseen except by the eyes of Heaven, and the small bright insects that run hither and thither on the elastic flower-stalks. With something like the sudden drop of the lark, the path goes down a green abrupt descent; and in a basin, surrounded by the grassy hills, there stands a dwelling, which is neither cottage nor house, but something between the two in size. Nor yet is it a farm, though surrounded by living things. It is, or rather it was, at the time of which I speak, the dwelling of Mrs Browne, the widow of the late curate of Combehurst. There she lived with her faithful old servant and her only children, a boy and girl. They were as secluded in their green hollow as the households in the German forest-tales.* Once a week they emerged and crossed the common, catching on its summit the first sounds of the sweet-toned bells, calling them to church. Mrs Browne walked first, holding Edward's hand. Old Nancy followed with Maggie;

but they were all one party, and all talked together in a subdued and quiet tone, as beseemed the day. They had not much to say, their lives were too unbroken; for, excepting on Sundays, the widow and her children never went to Combehurst. Most people would have thought the little town a quiet, dreamy place; but to those two children it seemed the world; and after they had crossed the bridge, they each clasped more tightly the hands which they held, and looked shyly up from beneath their drooped eyelids when spoken to by any of their mother's friends. Mrs Browne was regularly asked by some one to stay to dinner after morning church, and as regularly declined, rather to the timid children's relief; although in the week-days they sometimes spoke together in a low voice of the pleasure it would be to them if mama would go and dine at Mr Buxton's, where the little girl in white and that great tall boy lived. Instead of staying there, or anywhere else, on Sundays, Mrs Browne thought it her duty to go and cry over her husband's grave. The custom had arisen out of true sorrow for his loss, for a kinder husband, and more worthy man, had never lived; but the simplicity of her sorrow had been destroyed by the observation of others on the mode of its manifestation. They made way for her to cross the grass towards his grave; and she, fancying that it was expected of her, fell into the habit I have mentioned. Her children, holding each a hand, felt awed and uncomfortable, and were sensitively conscious how often they were pointed out, as a mourning group, to observation.

'I wish it would always rain on Sundays,' said Edward one day to Maggie, in a garden-conference.

'Why?' asked she.

'Because then we bustle out of church, and get home as fast as we can, to save mama's crape;* and we have not to go and cry over papa.'

'I don't cry,' said Maggie. 'Do you?'

Edward looked round before he answered, to see if they were quite alone, and then said:

'No; I was sorry a long time about papa, but one can't go on being sorry for ever. Perhaps grown-up people can.'

'Mama can,' said little Maggie. 'Sometimes I am very sorry too; when I am by myself, or playing with you, or when I am wakened up by the moonlight in our room. Do you ever waken and fancy you heard papa calling you? I do sometimes; and then I am very sorry to think we shall never hear him calling us again.'

'Ah, it's different with me, you know. He used to call me to lessons.'

'Sometimes he called me when he was displeased with me. But I always dream that he was calling us in his own kind voice, as he used to do when he wanted us to walk with him, or to show us something pretty.'

Edward was silent, playing with something on the ground. At last he looked round again, and, having convinced himself that they could not be overheard, he whispered—

'Maggie,—sometimes I don't think I'm sorry that papa is dead—when I'm naughty, you know; he would have been so angry with me if he had been here; and I think,—only sometimes, you know,—I'm rather glad he is not.'

'Oh, Edward! you don't mean to say so, I know. Don't let us talk about him. We can't talk rightly, we're such little children. Don't, Edward, please.'

Poor little Maggie's eyes filled with tears; and she never spoke again to Edward, or indeed to any one, about her dead father. As she grew older, her life became more actively busy. The cottage and small outbuildings, and the garden and field, were their own; and on the produce they depended for much of their support. The cow, the pig, and the poultry took up much of Nancy's time. Mrs Browne and Maggie had to do a great deal of the house-work; and when the beds were made, and the rooms swept and dusted, and the preparations for dinner ready, then, if there was any time, Maggie sat down to her lessons. Ned, who prided himself considerably on his sex, had been sitting all the morning, in his father's arm-chair, in the little book-room, 'studying,' as he chose to call it. Sometimes Maggie would pop her head in, with a request that he would help her to carry the great pitcher of water upstairs, or do some other little household service; with which request he occasionally complied, but with so many complaints about the interruption, that at last she told him she would never ask him again. Gently as this was said, he yet felt it as a reproach, and tried to excuse himself.

'You see, Maggie, a man must be educated to be a gentleman. Now, if a woman knows how to keep a house, that's all that is wanted from her. So my time is of more consequence than yours. Mama says I'm to go to college, and be a clergyman; so I must get on with my Latin.'

Maggie submitted in silence; and almost felt it as an act of gracious condescension when, a morning or two afterwards, he came to meet her as she was toiling in from the well, carrying the great brown jug full of spring-water ready for dinner. 'Here,' said he, 'let us put it in the shade behind the horse-mount. Oh, Maggie! look what you've done! Spilt it all, with not turning quickly enough when I told you. Now you may fetch it again for yourself, for I'll have nothing to do with it.'

'I did not understand you in time,' said she, softly. But he had turned away, and gone back in offended dignity to the house. Maggie had nothing to do but return to the well, and fill it again. The spring was some distance off, in a little rocky dell. It was so cool after her hot walk, that she sat down in the shadow of the grey lime-stone rock, and looked at the ferns, wet with the dripping water. She felt sad, she knew not why. 'I think Ned is sometimes very cross,' thought she. 'I did not understand he was carrying it there. Perhaps I am clumsy. Mama says I am; and Ned says I am. Nancy never says so, and papa never said so. I wish I could help being clumsy and stupid. Ned says all women are so. I wish I was not a woman. It must be a fine thing to be a man. Oh dear! I must go up the field again with this heavy pitcher, and my arms do so ache!' She rose and climbed the steep brae.* As she went she heard her mother's voice.

'Maggie! Maggie! there's no water for dinner, and the potatoes are quite boiled. Where *is* that child?'

They had begun dinner, before she came down from brushing her hair and washing her hands. She was hurried and tired.

'Mother,' said Ned, 'mayn't I have some butter to these potatoes, as there is cold meat? They are so dry.'

'Certainly, my dear. Maggie, go and fetch a pat of butter out of the dairy.'

Maggie went from her untouched dinner without speaking.

'Here, stop, you child!' said Nancy, turning her back in the passage. 'You go to your dinner,—I'll fetch the butter. You've been running about enough to-day.'

Maggie durst not go back without it, but she stood in the passage till Nancy returned; and then she put up her mouth to be kissed by the kind rough old servant.

'Thou'rt a sweet one,' said Nancy to herself, as she turned into the kitchen; and Maggie went back to her dinner with a soothed and lightened heart.

When the meal was ended, she helped her mother to wash up the old-fashioned glasses and spoons, which were treated with tender care and exquisite cleanliness in that house of decent frugality; and then, exchanging her pinafore for a black silk apron, the little maiden was wont to sit down to some useful piece of needlework, in doing which her mother enforced the most dainty neatness of stitches. Thus every hour in its circle brought a duty to be fulfilled; but duties fulfilled are as pleasures to the memory, and little Maggie always thought those early childish days most happy, and remembered them only as filled with careless contentment.

Yet, at the time, they had their cares.

In fine summer days Maggie sat out of doors at her work. Just beyond the court lay the rocky moorland, almost as gay as that with its profusion of flowers. If the court had its clustering noisettes, and fraxinellas, and sweetbriar, and great tall white lilies, the moorland had its little creeping scented rose, its straggling honeysuckle, and an abundance of yellow cistus; and here and there a grey rock cropped out of the ground, and over it the yellow stone-crop and scarlet-leaved crane's-bill grew luxuriantly. Such a rock was Maggie's seat. I believe she considered it her own, and loved it accordingly; although its real owner was a great lord, who lived far away, and had never seen the moor, much less the piece of grey rock, in his life.

The afternoon of the day which I have begun to tell you about, she was sitting there, and singing to herself as she worked: she was within call of home, and could hear all home sounds, with their shrillness softened down. Between her and it, Edward was amusing himself; he often called upon her for sympathy, which she as readily gave.

'I wonder how men make their boats steady; I have taken mine to the pond, and she has toppled over every time I sent her in.'

'Has it?—that's very tiresome! Would it do to put a little weight in it, to keep it down?'

'How often must I tell you to call a ship "her;" and there you will go on saying—it,—it!'

After this correction of his sister, Master Edward did not like the condescension of acknowledging her suggestion to be a good one; so he went silently to the house in search of the requisite ballast; but not being able to find anything suitable, he came back to his turfy hillock, littered round with chips of wood, and tried to insert some pebbles into his vessel; but they stuck fast, and he was obliged to ask again.

'Supposing it was a good thing to weight her, what could I put in?'

Maggie thought a moment.

'Would shot* do?' asked she.

'It would be the very thing; but where can I get any?'

'There is some that was left of papa's. It is in the right-hand corner of the second drawer of the bureau, wrapped up in a news-paper.'

'What a plague! I can't remember your "seconds," and "right-hands," and fiddle-faddles.' He worked on at his pebbles. They would not do.

'I think if you were good-natured, Maggie, you might go for me.'

'Oh, Ned! I've all this long seam to do. Mama said I must finish it before tea; and that I might play a little if I had done it first,' said Maggie, rather plaintively; for it was a real pain to her to refuse a request.

'It would not take you five minutes.'

Maggie thought a little. The time would only be taken out of her playing, which, after all, did not signify; while Edward was really busy about his ship. She rose, and clambered up the steep grassy slope, slippery with the heat.

Before she had found the paper of shot, she heard her mother's voice calling, in a sort of hushed hurried loudness, as if anxious to be heard by one person, yet not by another—'Edward, Edward, come home quickly. Here's Mr Buxton coming along the Fell-Lane;—he's coming here, as sure as sixpence; come, Edward,—come.'

Maggie saw Edward put down his ship and come. At his mother's bidding it certainly was; but he strove to make this as little appar-ent as he could, by sauntering up the slope, with his hands in his pockets, in a very independent and *négligé* * style. Maggie had no time to watch longer; for now she was called too, and down stairs she ran.

'Here, Maggie,' said her mother, in a nervous hurry; 'help Nancy to get a tray ready all in a minute. I do believe here's Mr Buxton coming to call. Oh, Edward! go and brush your hair, and put on your Sunday jacket; here's Mr Buxton just coming round. I'll only run up and change my cap; and you say you'll come up and tell me, Nancy; all proper, you know.'

'To be sure, ma'am. I've lived in families afore now,' said Nancy, gruffly.

'Oh, yes, I know you have. Be sure you bring in the cowslip wine. I wish I could have stayed to decant some port.'

Nancy and Maggie bustled about, in and out of the kitchen and dairy; and were so deep in their preparations for Mr Buxton's reception that they were not aware of the very presence of that gentleman himself on the scene. He had found the front door open, as is the wont in country places, and had walked in; first stopping at the empty parlour, and then finding his way to the place where voices and sounds proclaimed that there were inhabitants. So he stood there, stooping a little under the low-browed lintels of the kitchen door, and looking large, and red, and warm, but with a pleased and almost amused expression of face.

'Lord bless me, sir! what a start you gave me!' said Nancy, as she suddenly caught sight of him. 'I'll go and tell my missus in a minute that you're come.'

Off she went, leaving Maggie alone with the great, tall, broad gentleman, smiling at her from his frame in the door-way, but never speaking. She went on dusting a wine-glass most assiduously.

'Well done, little girl,' came out a fine strong voice at last. 'Now I think that will do. Come and show me the parlour where I may sit down, for I've had a long walk, and am very tired.'

Maggie took him into the parlour, which was always cool and fresh in the hottest weather. It was scented by a great beau-pot* filled with roses; and, besides, the casement was open to the fragrant court. Mr Buxton was so large, and the parlour so small, that when he was once in, Maggie thought, when he went away, he would carry the room on his back, as a snail does its house.

'And so, you are a notable little woman, are you?' said he, after he had stretched himself (a very unnecessary proceeding), and unbuttoned his waistcoat. Maggie stood near the door, uncertain whether to go or to stay. 'How bright and clean you were making that glass! Do you think you could get me some water to fill it? Mind, it must be that very glass I saw you polishing. I shall know it again.'

Maggie was thankful to escape out of the room; and in the passage she met her mother, who had made time to change her gown as well as her cap. Before Nancy would allow the little girl to return with the glass of water, she smoothed her short-cut glossy hair; it was all that was needed to make her look delicately neat. Maggie was conscientious in trying to find out the identical glass; but I am afraid Nancy was not quite so truthful in avouching that one of the six, exactly similar, which were now placed on the tray, was the same she had found on the dresser, when she came back from telling her mistress of Mr Buxton's arrival.

Maggie carried in the water, with a shy pride in the clearness of the glass. Her mother was sitting on the edge of her chair, speaking in unusually fine language, and with a higher pitched voice than common. Edward, in all his Sunday glory, was standing by Mr Buxton, looking happy and conscious. But when Maggie came in, Mr Buxton made room for her between Edward and himself, and, while he went on talking, lifted her on to his knee. She sat there as on a pinnacle of honour; but as she durst not nestle up to him, a chair would have been the more comfortable seat.

'As founder's line, I have a right of presentation;* and for my dear old friend's sake' (here Mrs Browne wiped her eyes), 'I am truly glad of it; my young friend will have a little form of examination to go through; and then we shall see him carrying every prize before him, I have no doubt. Thank you,—just a little of your sparkling cowslip wine. Ah! this gingerbread is like the gingerbread I had when I was a boy. My little lady here must learn the receipt, and make me some. Will she?'

'Speak to Mr Buxton, child, who is kind to your brother. You will make him some gingerbread, I am sure.'

'If I may,' said Maggie, hanging down her head.

'Or, I'll tell you what. Suppose you come to my house, and teach us how to make it there; and then, you know, we could always be making gingerbread when we were not eating it. That would be best, I think. Must I ask mama to bring you down to Combehurst, and let us all get acquainted together? I have a great boy and a little girl at home, who will like to see you, I'm sure. And we have got a pony for you to ride on, and a peacock and guinea fowls, and I don't know what all. Come, madam, let me persuade you. School begins in three weeks. Let us fix a day before then.'

'Do, mama,' said Edward.

'I am not in spirits for visiting,' Mrs Browne answered. But the quick children detected a hesitation in her manner of saying the oft spoken words, and had hopes, if only Mr Buxton would persevere in his invitation.

'Your not visiting is the very reason why you are not in spirits. A little change, and a few neighbourly faces, would do you good, I'll be bound. Besides, for the children's sake you should not live too secluded a life. Young people should see a little of the world.'

Mrs Browne was much obliged to Mr Buxton for giving her so decent an excuse for following her inclination, which, it must be owned, tended to the acceptance of the invitation. So, 'for the children's sake,' she consented. But she sighed, as if making a sacrifice.

'That's right,' said Mr Buxton. 'Now for the day.'

It was fixed that they should go on that day week; and after some further conversation about the school at which Edward was to be placed, and some more jokes about Maggie's notability, and an inquiry if she would come and live with him the next time he wanted a housemaid, Mr Buxton took his leave.

His visit had been an event; and they made no great attempt at settling again that day to any of their usual employments. In the first place, Nancy came in to hear and discuss all the proposed plans. Ned, who was uncertain whether to like or dislike the prospect of school, was very much offended by the old servant's remark, on first hearing of the project.

'It's time for him. He'll learn his place there, which, it strikes me, he and others too are apt to forget at home.'

Then followed discussions and arrangements respecting his clothes. And then they came to the plan of spending a day at Mr Buxton's, which Mrs Browne was rather shy of mentioning, having a sort of an idea of inconstancy and guilt connected with the thought of mingling with the world again. However, Nancy approved: 'It was quite right,' and 'just as it should be,' and 'good for the children.'

'Yes; it was on their account I did it, Nancy,' said Mrs Browne.

'How many children has Mr Buxton?' asked Edward.

'Only one. Frank, I think, they call him. But you must say Master Buxton; be sure.'

'Who is the little girl, then,' asked Maggie, 'who sits with them in church?'

'Oh! that's little Miss Harvey, his niece, and a great fortune.'

'They do say he never forgave her mother till the day of her death,' remarked Nancy.

'Then they tell stories, Nancy!' replied Mrs Browne (it was she herself who had said it; but that was before Mr Buxton's call). 'For d'ye think his sister would have left him guardian to her child, if they were not on good terms?'

'Well! I only know what folks say. And, for sure, he took a spite at Mr Harvey for no reason on earth; and every one knows he never spoke to him.'

'He speaks very kindly and pleasantly,' put in Maggie.

'Ay; and I'm not saying but what he is a very good, kind man in the main. But he has his whims, and keeps hold on 'em when he's got 'em. There's them pies burning, and I'm talking here!'

When Nancy had returned to her kitchen, Mrs Browne called Maggie up stairs, to examine what clothes would be needed for Edward. And when they were up, she tried on the black satin gown, which had been her visiting dress ever since she was married, and which she intended should replace the old, worn-out bombazine* on the day of the visit to Combehurst.

'For Mrs Buxton is a real born lady,' said she; 'and I should like to be well dressed, to do her honour.'

'I did not know there was a Mrs Buxton,' said Maggie. 'She is never at church.'

'No; she is but delicate and weakly, and never leaves the house. I think her maid told me she never left her room now.'

The Buxton family, root and branch, formed the *pièce de résistance* * in the conversation between Mrs Browne and her children for the next week. As the day drew near, Maggie almost wished to stay at home, so impressed was she with the awfulness of the visit. Edward felt bold in the idea of a new suit of clothes, which had been ordered for the occasion, and for school afterwards. Mrs Browne remembered having heard the rector say, 'A woman never looked so lady-like as when she wore black satin,' and kept her spirits up with that observation; but when she saw how worn it was at the elbows, she felt rather depressed, and unequal to visiting. Still, for her children's sake, she would do much.

After her long day's work was ended, Nancy sat up at her sewing. She had found out that among all the preparations, none were going on for Margaret;* and she had used her influence over her mistress (who half-liked and half-feared, and entirely depended upon her) to obtain from her an old gown, which she had taken to pieces, and washed and scoured, and was now making up, in a way a little old-fashioned to be sure; but, on the whole, it looked so nice when completed and put on, that Mrs Browne gave Maggie a strict lecture about taking great care of such a handsome frock, and forgot that she had considered the gown from which it had been made as worn out and done for.

CHAPTER II

AT length they were dressed, and Nancy stood on the court-steps, shading her eyes, and looking after them, as they climbed the heathery slope leading to Combehurst.

'I wish she'd take her hand sometimes, just to let her know the feel of her mother's hand. Perhaps she will, at least after Master Edward goes to school.'

As they went along, Mrs Browne gave the children a few rules respecting manners and etiquette.

'Maggie! you must sit as upright as ever you can; make your back flat, child, and don't poke. If I cough, you must draw up. I shall cough whenever I see you do anything wrong, and I shall be looking at you all day; so remember. You hold yourself very well, Edward. If Mr Buxton asks you, you may have a glass of wine, because you're a boy. But mind and say, "Your good health, sir," before you drink it.'

'I'd rather not have the wine if I'm to say that,' said Edward, bluntly.

'Oh, nonsense! my dear. You'd wish to be like a gentleman, I'm sure.'

Edward muttered something which was inaudible. His mother went on—

'Of course you'll never think of being helped more than twice. Twice of meat, twice of pudding, is the genteel thing. You may take less, but never more.'

'Oh, mama! how beautiful Combehurst spire is, with that dark cloud behind it!' exclaimed Maggie, as they came in sight of the town.

'You've no business with Combehurst spire when I'm speaking to you. I'm talking myself out of breath to teach you how to behave, and there you go looking after clouds, and such like rubbish. I'm ashamed of you.'

Although Maggie walked quietly by her mother's side all the rest of the way, Mrs Browne was too much offended to resume her instructions on good-breeding. Maggie might be helped three times if she liked: she had done with her.

They were very early. When they drew near the bridge, they were met by a tall, fine-looking boy, leading a beautiful little Shetland pony, with a side-saddle on it. He came up to Mrs Browne, and addressed her.

'My father thought your little girl would be tired, and he told me to bring my cousin Erminia's pony for her. It's as quiet as can be.'

Now this was rather provoking to Mrs Browne, as she chose to consider Maggie in disgrace. However, there was no help for it: all she could do was to spoil the enjoyment as far as possible, by looking and speaking in a cold manner, which often chilled Maggie's little heart, and took all the zest out of the pleasure now. It was in vain that Frank Buxton made the pony trot and canter; she still looked sad and grave.

'Little dull thing!' he thought; but he was as kind and considerate as a gentlemanly boy could be.

At last they reached Mr Buxton's house. It was in the main street, and the front door opened upon it by a flight of steps. Wide on each side extended the stone-coped* windows. It was in reality a mansion, and needed not the neighbouring contrast of the cottages on either side to make it look imposing. When they went in, they entered a large hall, cool even on that burning July day, with a black and white flag floor, and old settees round the walls, and great jars of curious china, which were filled with pot-pourrie. The dusky gloom was pleasant, after the glare of the street outside; and the requisite light and cheerfulness were given by the peep into the garden, framed, as it were, by the large doorway that opened into it. There were roses, and sweet-peas, and poppies,—a rich mass of colour, which looked well, set in the somewhat sombre coolness of the hall. All the house told of wealth—wealth which had accumulated for generations, and which was shown in a sort of comfortable, grand, unostentatious way. Mr Buxton's ancestors had been yeomen;* but, two or three generations back, they might, if ambitious, have taken their place as county gentry, so much had the value of their property increased, and so great had been the amount of their savings. They, however, continued to live in the old farm till Mr Buxton's grandfather built the house in Combehurst of which I am speaking, and then he felt rather ashamed of what he had done; it seemed like stepping out of his position. He and his wife always sat in the best kitchen; and it was only after his son's marriage that the entertaining rooms were furnished. Even then they were kept with closed shutters and bagged-up furniture during the lifetime of the old couple, who, nevertheless, took a pride in adding to the rich-fashioned ornaments and grand old china of the apartments. But they died, and were gathered to their fathers, and young Mr and Mrs Buxton (aged respectively fifty-one and forty-five) reigned in their stead. They had the good taste to make no sudden change; but gradually the rooms assumed an inhabited appearance, and their son and daughter grew up in the enjoyment of great wealth, and no small degree of refinement. But as yet they held back modestly from putting themselves in any way on a level with the county people. Lawrence Buxton was sent to the same school as his father had been before him; and the notion of his going to college to complete his education was, after some deliberation, negatived. In process of time he succeeded his father, and married a sweet gentle lady, of a decayed and very poor county family, by whom he had one boy before she fell into delicate health. His sister had married a man whose character was worse than his fortune, and had been left a widow. Everybody thought her husband's death a blessing; but she loved him, in spite of negligence and many grosser faults; and so, not many years after, she died, leaving her little daughter to her brother's care, with many a broken-voiced entreaty that he would never speak a word against the dead father of her child. So the little Erminia was taken home by her self-reproaching uncle, who felt now how hardly he had acted towards his sister in breaking off all communication with her on her ill-starred marriage.

'Where is Erminia, Frank?' asked his father, speaking over Maggie's shoulder, while he still held her hand. 'I want to take Mrs Browne to your mother. I told Erminia to be here to welcome this little girl.'

'I'll take her to Minnie; I think she's in the garden. I'll come back to you,' nodding to Edward, 'directly, and then we will go to the rabbits.'

So Frank and Maggie left the great lofty room, full of strange rare things, and rich with books, and went into the sunny scented garden, which stretched far and wide behind the house. Down one of the walks, with a hedge of roses on either side, came a little tripping fairy, with long golden ringlets, and a complexion like a china rose. With the deep blue of the summer sky behind her, Maggie thought she looked like an angel. She neither hastened nor slackened her pace when she saw them, but came on with the same dainty light prancing step.

'Make haste, Minnie,' cried Frank.

But Minnie stopped to gather a rose.

'Don't stay with me,' said Maggie, softly, although she had held his hand like that of a friend, and did not feel that the little fairy's manner was particularly cordial or gracious. Frank took her at her word, and ran off to Edward.

Erminia came a little quicker when she saw that Maggie was left alone; but for some time after they were together, they had nothing to say to each other. Erminia was easily impressed by the pomps and vanities of the world; and Maggie's new handsome frock seemed to her made of old ironed brown silk. And though Maggie's voice was soft, with a silver ringing sound in it, she pronounced her words in Nancy's broad country way. Her hair was cut short all round; her shoes were thick, and clumped as she walked. Erminia patronized her, and thought herself very kind and condescending; but they were not particularly friendly. The visit promised to be more honourable than agreeable, and Maggie almost wished herself at home again. Dinner-time came. Mrs Buxton dined in her own room. Mr Buxton was hearty, and jovial, and pressing; he almost scolded Maggie because she would not take more than twice of his favourite pudding: but she remembered what her mother had said, and that she would be watched all day; and this gave her a little prim, quaint manner, very different from her usual soft charming unconsciousness. She fancied that Edward and Master Buxton were just as little at their case with each other as she and Miss Harvey. Perhaps this feeling on the part of the boys made all four children unite after dinner.

'Let us go to the swing in the shrubbery,' said Frank, after a little consideration; and off they ran. Frank proposed that he and Edward should swing the two little girls; and for a time all went on very well. But by-and-by Edward thought that Maggie had had enough, and that he should like a turn; and Maggie, at his first word, got out.

'Don't you like swinging?' asked Erminia.

'Yes! but Edward would like it now.' And Edward accordingly took her place. Frank turned away, and would not swing him. Maggie strove hard to do it, but he was heavy, and the swing bent unevenly. He scolded her for what she could not help, and at last jumped out so roughly, that the seat hit Maggie's face, and knocked her down. When she got up, her lips quivered with pain, but she did not cry; she only looked anxiously at her frock. There was a great rent across the front breadth. Then she did shed tears,—tears of fright. What would her mother say?

Erminia saw her crying.

'Are you hurt?' said she, kindly. 'Oh, how your cheek is swelled! What a rude, cross boy your brother is!'

'I did not know he was going to jump out. I am not crying because I am hurt, but because of this great rent in my nice new frock. Mama will be so displeased.'

'Is it a new frock?' asked Erminia.

'It is a new one for me. Nancy has sat up several nights to make it. Oh! what shall I do?'

Erminia's little heart was softened by such excessive poverty. A best frock made of shabby old silk! She put her arms round Maggie's neck, and said—

'Come with me; we will go to my aunt's dressing-room, and Dawson will give me some silk, and I'll help you to mend it.'

'That's a kind little Minnie,' said Frank. Ned had turned sulkily away. I do not think the boys were ever cordial again that day; for, as Frank said to his mother, 'Ned might have said he was sorry; but he is a regular tyrant to that little brown mouse of a sister of his.'

Erminia and Maggie went, with their arms round each other's necks, to Mrs Buxton's dressing-room. The misfortune had made them friends. Mrs Buxton lay on the sofa; so fair and white and colourless, in her muslin dressing-gown, that when Maggie first saw the lady lying with her eyes shut, her heart gave a start, for she thought she was dead. But she opened her large languid eyes, and called them to her, and listened to their story with interest.

'Dawson is at tea. Look, Minnie, in my work-box; there is some silk there. Take off your frock, my dear, and bring it here, and let me see how it can be mended.'

'Aunt Buxton,' whispered Erminia, 'do let me give her one of my frocks. This is such an old thing.'

'No, love. I'll tell you why afterwards,' answered Mrs Buxton.

She looked at the rent, and arranged it nicely for the little girls to mend. Erminia helped Maggie with right good will. As they sat on the floor, Mrs Buxton thought what a pretty contrast they made; Erminia, dazzlingly fair, with her golden ringlets, and her pale-blue frock: Maggie's little round white shoulders peeping out of her petticoat; her brown hair as glossy and smooth as the nuts that it resembled in colour; her long black eye-lashes drooping over her clear smooth cheek, which would have given the idea of delicacy, but for the coral lips that spoke of perfect health: and when she glanced up, she showed long, liquid, dark-grey eyes. The deep red of the curtain behind, threw out these two little figures well.

Dawson came up. She was a grave elderly person, of whom Erminia was far more afraid than she was of her aunt; but at Mrs Buxton's desire she finished mending the frock for Maggie.

'Mr Buxton has asked some of your mama's old friends to tea, as I am not able to go down. But I think, Dawson, I must have these two little girls to tea with me. Can you be very quiet, my dears; or shall you think it dull?'

They gladly accepted the invitation; and Erminia promised all sorts of fanciful promises as to quietness; and went about on her tiptoes in such a laboured manner, that Mrs Buxton begged her at last not to try and be quiet, as she made much less noise when she did not. It was the happiest part of the day to Maggie. Something in herself was so much in harmony with Mrs Buxton's sweet resigned gentleness, that it answered like an echo, and the two understood each other strangely well. They seemed like old friends. Maggie, who was reserved at home because no one cared to hear what she had to say, opened out, and told Erminia and Mrs Buxton all about her way of spending her day, and described her home.

'How odd!' said Erminia. 'I have ridden that way on Abdel-Kadr, and never seen your house.'

'It is like the place the Sleeping Beauty* lived in; people sometimes seem to go round it and round it, and never find it. But unless you follow a little sheep-track, which seems to end at a grey piece of rock, you may come within a stone's throw of the chimneys and never see them. I think you would think it so pretty. Do you ever come that way, ma'am?'

'No, love,' answered Mrs Buxton.

'But will you some time?'

'I am afraid I shall never be able to go out again,' said Mrs Buxton, in a voice which, though low, was very cheerful. Maggie thought how sad a lot was here before her; and by-and-by she took a little stool, and sat by Mrs Buxton's sofa, and stole her hand into hers.

Mrs Browne was in full tide of pride and happiness down stairs. Mr Buxton had a number of jokes, which would have become dull from repetition (for he worked a merry idea threadbare before he would let it go), had it not been for his jovial blandness and good-nature. He liked to make people happy, and, as far as bodily wants went, he had a quick perception of what was required. He sat like a king (for, excepting the rector, there was not another gentleman of his standing at Combehurst), among six or seven ladies, who laughed merrily at all his sayings, and evidently thought Mrs Browne had been highly honoured in having been asked to dinner as well as to tea. In the evening, the carriage was ordered to take her as far as a carriage could go; and there was a little mysterious hand-shaking between her host and herself on taking leave, which made her very curious for the lights of home by which to examine a bit of rustling paper that had been put in her hand with some stammered-out words about Edward.

When every one had gone, there was a little gathering in Mrs Buxton's dressing-room. Husband, son, and niece, all came to give her their opinions on the day and the visitors.

'Good Mrs Browne is a little tiresome,' said Mr Buxton, yawning. 'Living in that moorland hole, I suppose. However, I think she has enjoyed her day; and we'll ask her down now and then, for Browne's sake. Poor Browne! what a good man he was!'

'I don't like that boy at all,' said Frank. 'I beg you'll not ask him again while I'm at home: he is so selfish and self-important; and yet he's a bit snobbish now and then. Mother! I know what you mean by that look. Well! if I am self-important sometimes, I'm not a snob.'

'Little Maggie is very nice,' said Erminia. 'What a pity she has not a new frock! Was not she good about it, Frank, when she tore it?'

'Yes, she's a nice little thing enough, if she does not get all spirit cowed out of her by that brother. I'm thankful that he is going to school.'

When Mrs Browne heard where Maggie had drank tea, she was offended. She had only sat with Mrs Buxton for an hour before dinner. If Mrs Buxton could bear the noise of children, she could not think why she shut herself up in that room, and gave herself such airs. She supposed it was because she was the grand-daughter of Sir Henry Biddulph that she took upon herself to have such whims, and not sit at the head of her table, or make tea for her company in a civil decent way. Poor Mr Buxton! What a sad life for a merry light-hearted man to have such a wife! It was a good thing for him to have agreeable society sometimes. She thought he looked a deal better for seeing his friends. He must be sadly moped with that sickly wife.

(If she had been clairvoyante at that moment, she might have seen Mr Buxton tenderly chafing his wife's hands, and feeling in his innermost soul a wonder how one so saint-like could ever have learnt to love such a boor as he was; it was the wonderful mysterious blessing of his life. So little do we know of the inner truths of the households, where we come and go like intimate guests!)

Maggie could not bear to hear Mrs Buxton spoken of as a fine lady assuming illness. Her heart beat hard as she spoke. 'Mama! I am sure she is really ill. Her lips kept going so white; and her hand was so burning hot all the time that I held it.'

'Have you been holding Mrs Buxton's hand? Where were your manners? You are a little forward creature, and ever were. But don't pretend to know better than your elders. It is no use telling me Mrs Buxton is ill, and she able to bear the noise of children.'

'I think they are all a pack of set-up people, and that Frank Buxton is the worst of all,' said Edward.

Maggie's heart sank within her to hear this cold unkind way of talking over the friends who had done so much to make their day happy. She had never before ventured into the world, and did not know how common and universal is the custom of picking to pieces those with whom we have just been associating; and so it pained her. She was a little depressed too with the idea that she should never see Mrs Buxton and the lovely Erminia again. Because no future visit or intercourse had been spoken about, she fancied it would never take place; and she felt like the man in the Arabian Nights, who caught a glimpse of the precious stones and dazzling glories of the cavern, which was immediately after closed, and shut up into the semblance of hard, barren rock.* She tried to recall the house. Deep blue, crimson red, warm brown draperies, were so striking after the light chintzes of her own house; and the effect of a suite of rooms opening out of each other was something quite new to the little girl; the apartments seemed to melt away into vague distance, like the dim endings of the arched aisles in church. But most of all she tried to recall Mrs Buxton's face; and Nancy had at last to put away her work, and come to bed, in order to soothe the poor child, who was crying at the thought that Mrs Buxton would soon die, and that she should never see her again. Nancy loved Maggie dearly, and felt no jealousy of this warm admiration of the unknown lady. She listened to her story and her fears till the sobs were hushed; and the moon fell through the casement on the white closed eyelids of one, who still sighed in her sleep.

CHAPTER III

IN three weeks, the day came for Edward's departure. A great cake and a parcel of gingerbread soothed his sorrows on leaving home.

'Don't cry, Maggie!' said he to her on the last morning; 'you see I don't. Christmas will soon be here, and I dare say I shall find time to write to you now and then. Did Nancy put any citron in the cake?'

Maggie wished she might accompany her mother to Combehurst to see Edward off by the coach; but it was not to be. She went with them, without her bonnet, as far as her mother would allow her; and then she sat down, and watched their progress for a long, long way. She was startled by the sound of a horse's feet, softly trampling through the long heather. It was Frank Buxton's.

'My father thought Mrs Browne would like to see the Woodchester Herald. Is Edward gone?' said he, noticing her sad face.

'Yes! he is just gone down the hill to the coach. I dare say you can see him crossing the bridge, soon. I did so want to have gone with him,' answered she, looking wistfully towards the town.

Frank felt sorry for her, left alone to gaze after her brother, whom, strange as it was, she evidently regretted. After a minute's silence, he said—

'You liked riding the other day. Would you like a ride now? Rhoda is very gentle, if you can sit on my saddle. Look! I'll shorten the stirrup. There now; there's a brave little girl! I'll lead her very carefully. Why, Erminia durst not ride without a side-saddle! I'll tell you what; I'll bring the newspaper every Wednesday till I go to school, and you shall have a ride. Only I wish we had a side-saddle for Rhoda. Or, if Erminia will let me, I'll bring Abdel-Kadr, the little Shetland you rode the other day.'

'But will Mr Buxton let you?' asked Maggie, half delighted—half afraid.

'Oh, my father! to be sure he will. I have him in very good order.'

Maggie was rather puzzled by this way of speaking.

'When do you go to school?' asked she.

'Towards the end of August; I don't know the day.'

'Does Erminia go to school?'

'No. I believe she will soon though, if mama does not get better.' Maggie liked the change of voice, as he spoke of his mother.

'There, little lady! now jump down. Famous! you've a deal of spirit, you little brown mouse.'

Nancy came out, with a wondering look, to receive Maggie.

'It is Mr Frank Buxton,' said she, by way of an introduction. 'He has brought mama the newspaper.'

'Will you walk in, sir, and rest? I can tie up your horse.'

'No, thank you,' said he. 'I must be off. Don't forget, little Mousey, that you are to be ready for another ride next Wednesday.' And away he went.

It needed a good deal of Nancy's diplomacy to procure Maggie this pleasure; although I don't know why Mrs Browne should have denied it, for the circle they went was always within sight of the knoll in front of the house, if any one cared enough about the matter to mount it, and look after them. Frank and Maggie got great friends in these rides. Her fearlessness delighted and surprised him, she had seemed so cowed and timid at first. But she was only so with people, as he found out before his holidays ended. He saw her shrink from particular looks and inflexions of voice of her mother's; and learnt to read them, and dislike Mrs Browne accordingly, notwithstanding all her sugary manner towards himself. The result of his observations he communicated to his mother, and in consequence, he was the bearer of a most civil and ceremonious message from Mrs Buxton to Mrs Browne, to the effect that the former would be much obliged to the latter if she would allow Maggie to ride down occasionally with the groom, who would bring the newspapers on the Wednesdays (now Frank was going to school), and to spend the afternoon with Erminia. Mrs Browne consented, proud of the honour, and yet a little annoyed that no mention was made of herself. When Frank had bid good-bye, and fairly disappeared, she turned to Maggie.

'You must not set yourself up if you go amongst these fine folks. It is their way of showing attention to your father and myself. And you must mind and work doubly hard on Thursdays to make up for playing on Wednesdays.'

Maggie was in a flush of sudden colour, and a happy palpitation of her fluttering little heart. She could hardly feel any sorrow that the kind Frank was going away, so brimful was she of the thoughts of seeing his mother; who had grown strangely associated in her dreams, both sleeping and waking, with the still calm marble effigies that lay for ever clasping their hands in prayer on the altar-tombs in Combehurst church. All the week was one happy season of anticipation. She was afraid her mother was secretly irritated at her natural rejoicing; and so she did not speak to her about it, but she kept awake till Nancy came to bed, and poured into her sympathizing ears every detail, real or imaginary, of her past or future intercourse with Mrs Buxton. And the old servant listened with interest, and fell into the custom of picturing the future with the ease and simplicity of a child.

'Suppose, Nancy! only suppose, you know, that she did die. I don't mean really die, but go into a trance like death; she looked as if she was in one when I first saw her; I would not leave her, but I would sit by her, and watch her, and watch her.'

'Her lips would be always fresh and red,' interrupted Nancy.

'Yes, I know; you've told me before how they keep red,—I should look at them quite steadily; I would try never to go to sleep.'

'The great thing would be to have air-holes left in the coffin.' But Nancy felt the little girl creep close to her at the grim suggestion, and, with the tact of love, she changed the subject.

'Or supposing we could hear of a doctor who could charm away illness. There were such in my young days; but I don't think people are so knowledgeable now. Peggy Jackson, that lived near us when I was a girl, was cured of a waste by a charm.'

'What is a waste, Nancy?'

'It is just a pining away. Food does not nourish, nor drink strengthen them, but they just fade off, and grow thinner and thinner, till their shadow looks grey instead of black at noon day; but he cured her in no time by a charm.'

'Oh, if we could find him.'

'Lass, he's dead, and she's dead, too, long ago!'

While Maggie was in imagination going over moor and fell, into the hollows of the distant mysterious hills, where she imagined all strange beasts and weird people to haunt, she fell asleep.

Such were the fanciful thoughts which were engendered in the little girl's mind by her secluded and solitary life. It was more solitary than ever, now that Edward was gone to school. The house missed his loud cheerful voice, and bursting presence. There seemed much less to be done, now that his numerous wants no longer called for ministration and attendance. Maggie did her task of work on her own grey rock; but as it was sooner finished, now that he was not there to interrupt and call her off, she used to stray up the Fell Lane at the back of the house; a little steep stony lane, more like stairs cut in the rock than what we, in the level land, call a lane: it reached on to the wide and open moor, and near its termination there was a knotted thorn-tree; the only tree for apparent miles. Here the sheep crouched under the storms, or stood and shaded themselves in the noontide heat. The ground was brown with their cleft round foot-marks; and tufts of wool were hung on the lower part of the stem, like votive offerings on some shrine.

Here Maggie used to come and sit and dream in any scarce half-hour of leisure. Here she came to cry, when her little heart was overfull at her mother's sharp fault-finding, or when bidden to keep out of the way, and not be troublesome. She used to look over the swelling expanse of moor, and the tears were dried up by the soft low-blowing wind which came sighing along it. She forgot her little home griefs to wonder why a brown-purple shadow always streaked one particular part in the fullest sunlight; why the cloud-shadows always seemed to be wafted with a sidelong motion; or she would imagine what lay beyond those old grey holy hills, which seemed to bear up the white clouds of Heaven on which the angels flew abroad. Or she would look straight up through the quivering air, as long as she could bear its white dazzling, to try and see God's throne in that unfathomable and infinite depth of blue. She thought she should see it blaze forth sudden and glorious, if she were but full of faith. She always came down from the thorn, comforted, and meekly gentle.

But there was danger of the child becoming dreamy, and finding her pleasure in life in reverie, not in action, or endurance, or the holy rest which comes after both, and prepares for further striving or bearing. Mrs Buxton's kindness prevented this danger just in time. It was partly out of interest in Maggie, but also partly to give Erminia a companion, that she wished the former to come down to Combehurst.

When she was on these visits, she received no regular instruction; and yet all the knowledge, and most of the strength of her character, was derived from these occasional hours. It is true her mother had given her daily lessons in reading, writing, and arithmetic; but both teacher and taught felt these more as painful duties to be gone through, than understood them as means to an end. The 'There! child; now that's done with,' of relief, from Mrs Browne, was heartily echoed in Maggie's breast, as the dull routine was concluded.

Mrs Buxton did not make a set labour of teaching; I suppose she felt that much was learned from her superintendence, but she never thought of doing or saying anything with a latent idea of its indirect effect upon the little girls, her companions. She was simply, herself; she even confessed (where the confession was called for) to short-comings, to faults, and never denied the force of temptations, either of those which beset little children, or of those which occasionally assailed herself. Pure, simple, and truthful to the heart's core, her life, in its uneventful hours and days, spoke many homilies. Maggie, who was grave, imaginative, and somewhat quaint, took pains in finding words to express the thoughts to which her solitary life had given rise, secure of Mrs Buxton's ready understanding and sympathy.

'You are so like a cloud,' said she to Mrs Buxton, 'Up at the thorn-tree, it was quite curious how the clouds used to shape themselves, just according as I was glad or sorry. I have seen the same clouds, that, when I came up first, looked like a heap of little snow-hillocks over babies' graves, turn, as soon as I grew happier, to a sort of long bright row of angels. And you seem always to have had some sorrow when I am sad, and to turn bright and hopeful as soon as I grow glad. Dear Mrs Buxton! I wish Nancy knew you.'

The gay, volatile, wilful, warm-hearted Erminia was less earnest in all things. Her childhood had been passed amid the distractions of wealth; and passionately bent upon the attainment of some object at one moment, the next found her angry at being reminded of the vanished anxiety she had shown but a moment before. Her life was a shattered mirror; every part dazzling and brilliant, but wanting the coherency and perfection of a whole. Mrs Buxton strove to bring her to a sense of the beauty of completeness, and the relation which qualities and objects bear to each other; but in all her striving she retained hold of the golden clue of sympathy. She would enter into Erminia's eagerness, if the object of it varied twenty times a day; but by-and-by, in her own mild, sweet, suggestive way, she would place all these objects in their right and fitting places, as they were worthy of desire. I do not know how it was, but all discords, and disordered fragments, seemed to fall into harmony and order before her presence.

She had no wish to make the two little girls into the same kind of pattern character. They were diverse as the lily and the rose. But she tried to give stability and earnestness to Erminia; while she aimed to direct Maggie's imagination, so as to make it a great minister to high ends, instead of simply contributing to the vividness and duration of a reverie.

She told her tales of saints and martyrs, and all holy heroines, who forgot themselves, and strove only to be 'ministers of Him, to do His pleasure.'* The tears glistened in the eyes of hearer and speaker, while she spoke in her low, faint voice, which was almost choked at times when she came to the noblest part of all.

But when she found that Maggie was in danger of becoming too little a dweller in the present, from the habit of anticipating the occasion for some great heroic action, she spoke of other heroines. She told her how, though the lives of these women of old were only known to us through some striking glorious deed, they yet must have built up the temple of their perfection by many noiseless stories; how, by small daily offerings laid on the altar, they must have obtained their beautiful strength for the crowning sacrifice. And then she would turn and speak of those whose names will never be blazoned on earth—some poor maid-servant, or hard-worked artisan, or weary governess—who have gone on through life quietly, with holy purposes in their hearts, to which they gave up pleasure and ease, in a soft, still, succession of resolute days. She quoted those lines of George Herbert's,

> All may have,
> If they dare choose, a glorious life, or grave.*

And Maggie's mother was disappointed because Mrs Buxton had never offered to teach her 'to play on the piano,' which was to her the very head and front of a genteel education. Maggie, in all her time of yearning to become Joan of Arc,* or some great heroine, was unconscious that she herself showed no little heroism, in bearing meekly what she did every day from her mother. It was hard to be questioned about Mrs Buxton, and then to have her answers turned into subjects for contempt, and fault-finding with that sweet lady's ways.

When Ned came home for the holidays, he had much to tell. His mother listened for hours to his tales; and proudly marked all that she could note of his progress in learning. His copy-books and writing-flourishes were a sight to behold; and his account-books contained towers and pyramids of figures.

'Ay, ay!' said Mr Buxton, when they were shown to him; 'this is grand! when I was a boy I could make a flying eagle with one stroke of my pen, but I never could do all this. And yet I thought myself a fine fellow, I warrant you. And these sums! why man! I must make you my agent. I need one, I'm sure; for though I get an accountant every two or three years to do up my books, they somehow have the knack of getting wrong again. Those quarries, Mrs Browne, which every one says are so valuable, and for the stone out of which I receive orders amounting to hundreds of pounds, what d'ye think was the profit I made last year, according to my books?'

'I'm sure I don't know, sir; something very great, I've no doubt.'

'Just seven-pence three farthings,' said he, bursting into a fit of merry laughter, such as another man would have kept for the announcement of enormous profits. 'But I must manage things differently soon. Frank will want money when he goes to Oxford, and he shall have it. I'm but a rough sort of fellow, but Frank shall take his place as a gentleman. Aha, Miss Maggie! and where's my gingerbread? There you go, creeping up to Mrs Buxton on a Wednesday, and have never taught Cook how to make gingerbread yet. Well, Ned! and how are the classics going on? Fine fellow, that Virgil!* Let me see, how does it begin?

> Arma, virumque cano, Troiae qui primus ab oris*

'That's pretty well, I think, considering I've never opened him since I left school, thirty years ago. To be sure, I spent six hours a day at it when I was there. Come now, I'll puzzle you. Can you construe this?

> Infir dealis, inoak noneis; inmud eelis, inclay noneis.'*

'To be sure I can,' said Edward, with a little contempt in his tone. 'Can you do this, sir?

> 'Apud in is almi des ire,
> Mimis tres i neve require,
> Alo veri findit a gestis,
> His miseri ne ver at restis.'*

But though Edward had made much progress, and gained three prizes, his moral training had been little attended to. He was more tyrannical than ever, both to his mother and Maggie. It was a drawn battle between him and Nancy, and they kept aloof from each other as much as possible. Maggie fell into her old humble way of submitting to his will, as long as it did not go against her conscience; but that, being daily enlightened by her habits of pious aspiring thought, would not allow her to be so utterly obedient as formerly. In addition to his imperiousness, he had learned to affix the idea of cleverness to various artifices and subterfuges, which utterly revolted her by their meanness.

'You are so set up, by being intimate with Erminia, that you won't do a thing I tell you; you're as selfish and self-willed as—' he made a pause. Maggie was ready to cry.

'I will do anything, Ned, that is right.'

'Well! and I tell you this is right.'

'How can it be?' said she, sadly, almost wishing to be convinced.

'How—why it is, and that's enough for you. You must always have a reason for everything now. You're not half so nice as you were. Unless one chops logic with you, and convinces you by a long argument, you'll do nothing. Be obedient, I tell you. That is what a woman has to be.'

'I could be obedient to some people, without knowing their reasons, even though they told me to do silly things,' said Maggie, half to herself.

'I should like to know to whom,' said Edward, scornfully.

'To Don Quixote,' answered she, seriously; for, indeed, he was present in her mind just then, and his noble, tender, melancholy character had made a strong impression there.

Edward stared at her for a moment, and then burst into a loud fit of laughter. It had the good effect of restoring him to a better frame of mind. He had such an excellent joke against his sister, that he could not be angry with her. He called her Sancho Panza* all the rest of the holidays, though she protested against it, saying she could not bear the Squire, and disliked being called by his name.

Frank and Edward seemed to have a mutual antipathy to each other, and the coldness between them was rather increased than diminished by all Mr Buxton's efforts to bring them together. 'Come, Frank, my lad!' said he, 'don't be so stiff with Ned. His father was a dear friend of mine, and I've set my heart on seeing you friends. You'll have it in your power to help him on in the world.'

But Frank answered, 'He is not quite honourable, sir. I can't bear a boy who is not quite honourable. Boys brought up at those private schools* are so full of tricks!'

'Nay, my lad, there thou'rt wrong. I was brought up at a private school, and no one can say I ever dirtied my hands with a trick in my life. Good old Mr Thomson would have flogged the life out of a boy who did anything mean or underhand.'

CHAPTER IV

SUMMERS and winters came and went, with little to mark them, except the growth of the trees, and the quiet progress of young creatures. Erminia was sent to school somewhere in France, to receive more regular instruction than she could have in the house with her invalid aunt. But she came home once a year, more lovely and elegant and dainty than ever; and Maggie thought, with truth, that ripening years were softening down her volatility, and that her aunt's dewlike sayings had quietly sunk deep, and fertilized the soil. That aunt was fading away. Maggie's devotion added materially to her happiness; and both she and Maggie never forgot that this devotion was to be in all things subservient to the duty which she owed to her mother.

'My love,' Mrs Buxton had more than once said, 'you must always recollect that your first duty is towards your mother. You know how glad I am to see you; but I shall always understand how it is, if you do not come. She may often want you when neither you nor I can anticipate it.'

Mrs Browne had no great wish to keep Maggie at home, though she liked to grumble at her going. Still she felt that it was best, in every way, to keep on good terms with such valuable friends; and she appreciated, in some small degree, the advantage which her intimacy at the house was to Maggie. But yet she could not restrain a few complaints, nor withhold from her, on her return, a recapitulation of all the things which might have been done if she had only been at home, and the number of times that she had been wanted; but when she found that Maggie quietly gave up her next Wednesday's visit as soon as she was made aware of any necessity for her presence at home, her mother left off grumbling, and took little or no notice of her absence.

When the time came for Edward to leave school, he announced

that he had no intention of taking orders, but meant to become an attorney.*

'It's such slow work,' said he to his mother. 'One toils away for four or five years, and then one gets a curacy of seventy pounds a-year, and no end of work to do for the money. Now the work is not much harder in a lawyer's office, and if one has one's wits about one, there are hundreds and thousands a-year to be picked up with mighty little trouble.'

Mrs Browne was very sorry for this determination. She had a great desire to see her son a clergyman, like his father. She did not consider whether his character was fitted for so sacred an office; she rather thought that the profession itself, when once assumed, would purify the character; but, in fact, his fitness or unfitness for holy orders entered little into her mind. She had a respect for the profession, and his father had belonged to it.

'I had rather see you a curate at seventy pounds a-year, than an attorney with seven hundred,' replied she. 'And you know your father was always asked to dine everywhere,—to places where I know they would not have asked Mr Bish, of Woodchester, and he makes his thousand a-year. Besides, Mr Buxton has the next presentation to Combehurst, and you would stand a good chance for your father's sake. And in the meantime you should live here, if your curacy was any way near.'

'I dare say! Catch me burying myself here again. My dear mother, it's a very respectable place for you and Maggie to live in, and I dare say you don't find it dull; but the idea of my quietly sitting down here, is something too absurd!'

'Papa did, and was very happy,' said Maggie.

'Yes! after he had been at Oxford,' replied Edward, a little nonplussed by this reference to one whose memory even the most selfish and thoughtless must have held in respect.

'Well! and you know you would have to go to Oxford first.'

'Maggie! I wish you would not interfere between my mother and me. I want to have it settled and done with, and that it will never be if you keep meddling. Now, mother, don't you see how much better it will be for me to go into Mr Bish's office? Harry Bish has spoken to his father about it.'

Mrs Browne sighed.

'What will Mr Buxton say?' asked she, dolefully.

'Say! Why don't you see it was he who first put it into my head, by telling me, that first Christmas holidays, that I should be his agent. That would be something, would it not? Harry Bish says he thinks a thousand a-year might be made of it.'

His loud, decided, rapid talking overpowered Mrs Browne; but she resigned herself to his wishes with more regret than she had ever done before. It was not the first case in which fluent declamation has taken the place of argument.

Edward was articled to Mr Bish, and thus gained his point. There was no one with power to resist his wishes, except his mother and Mr Buxton. The former had long acknowledged her son's will as her law; and the latter, though surprised and almost disappointed at a change of purpose which he had never anticipated in his plans for Edward's benefit, gave his consent, and even advanced some of the money requisite for the premium.

Maggie looked upon this change with mingled feelings. She had always from a child pictured Edward to herself as taking her father's place. When she had thought of him as a man, it was as contemplative, grave, and gentle, as she remembered her father. With all a child's deficiency of reasoning power, she had never considered how impossible it was that a selfish, vain, and impatient boy could become a meek, humble, and pious man, merely by adopting a profession in which such qualities are required. But now, at sixteen, she was beginning to understand all this. Not by any process of thought, but by something more like a correct feeling, she perceived that Edward would never be the true minister of Christ. So, more glad and thankful than sorry, though sorrow mingled with her sentiments, she learned the decision that he was to be an attorney.

Frank Buxton all this time was growing up into a young man. The hopes both of father and mother were bound up in him; and, according to the difference in their characters was the difference in their hopes. It seemed, indeed, probable that Mr Buxton, who was singularly void of worldliness or ambition for himself, would become worldly and ambitious for his son. His hopes for Frank were all for honour and distinction here. Mrs Buxton's hopes were prayers. She was fading away, as light fades into darkness on a summer evening. No one seemed to remark the gradual progress; but she was fully conscious of it herself. The last time that Frank was at home from college before her death, she knew that she should never see him again; and when he gaily left the house, with a cheerfulness, which was partly assumed, she dragged herself with languid steps into a room at the front of the house, from which she could watch him down the long, straggling little street, that led to the inn from which the coach started. As he went along, he turned to look back at his home; and there he saw his mother's white figure gazing after him. He could not see her wistful eyes, but he made her poor heart give a leap of joy by turning round and running back for one more kiss and one more blessing.

When he next came home, it was at the sudden summons of her death.

His father was as one distracted. He could not speak of the lost angel without sudden bursts of tears, and oftentimes of self-up-braiding, which disturbed the calm, still, holy ideas, which Frank liked to associate with her. He ceased speaking to him, therefore, about their mutual loss; and it was a certain kind of relief to both when he did so; but he longed for some one to whom he might talk of his mother, with the quiet reverence of intense and trustful affection. He thought of Maggie, of whom he had seen but little of late; for when he had been at Combehurst, she had felt that Mrs Buxton required her presence less, and had remained more at home. Possibly Mrs Buxton regretted this; but she never said anything. She, far-looking, as one who was near death, foresaw that, probably, if Maggie and her son met often in her sick-room, feelings might arise which would militate against her husband's hopes and plans, and which, therefore, she ought not to allow to spring up. But she had been unable to refrain from expressing her gratitude to Maggie for many hours of tranquil happiness, and had unconsciously dropped many sentences which made Frank feel, that, in the little brown mouse of former years, he was likely to meet with one who could tell him much of the inner history of his mother in her last days, and to whom he could speak of her without calling out the passionate sorrow which was so little in unison with her memory.

Accordingly, one afternoon, late in the autumn, he rode up to Mrs Browne's. The air on the heights was so still, that nothing seemed to stir. Now and then a yellow leaf came floating down from the trees, detached from no outward violence, but only be-cause its life had reached its full limit, and then ceased. Looking down on the distant sheltered woods, they were gorgeous in orange and crimson, but their splendour was felt to be the sign of the decaying and dying year. Even without an inward sorrow, there was a grand solemnity in the season which impressed the mind, and hushed it into tranquil thought. Frank rode slowly along, and quietly dismounted at the old horse-mount, beside which there was an iron bridle-ring fixed in the grey stone wall. He saw the casement of the parlour-window open, and Maggie's head bent down over her work. She looked up as he entered the court, and his footsteps sounded on the flag-walk. She came round and opened the door. As she stood in the door-way, speaking, he was struck by her resemblance to some old painting. He had seen her young, calm face, shining out with great peacefulness, and the large, grave, thoughtful eyes, giving the character to the features which other-wise they might, from their very regularity, have wanted. Her brown dress had the exact tint which a painter would have admired. The slanting mellow sunlight fell upon her as she stood; and the vine-leaves, already frost-tinted, made a rich, warm border, as they hung over the old house-door.

'Mama is not well; she is gone to lie down. How are you? How is Mr Buxton?'

'We are both pretty well; quite well, in fact, as far as regards health. May I come in? I want to talk to you, Maggie!'

She opened the little parlour-door, and they went in; but for a time they were both silent. They could not speak of her who was with them, present in their thoughts. Maggie shut the casement, and put a log of wood on the fire. She sat down with her back to the window; but as the flame sprang up, and blazed at the touch of the dry wood, Frank saw that her face was wet with quiet tears. Still her voice was even and gentle, as she answered his questions. She seemed to understand what were the very things he would care most to hear. She spoke of his mother's last days; and without any word of praise (which, indeed, would have been impertinence), she showed such a just and true appreciation of her who was dead and gone, that he felt as if he could listen for ever to the sweet-dropping words. They were balm to his sore heart. He had thought it possible that the suddenness of her death might have made her life in-complete, in that she might have departed without being able to express wishes and projects, which would now have the sacred force of commands. But he found that Maggie, though she had never intruded herself as such, had been the depositary of many little thoughts and plans; or, if they were not expressed to her, she knew that Mr Buxton or Dawson was aware of what they were, though, in their violence of early grief, they had forgotten to name them. The flickering brightness of the flame had died away; the gloom of evening had gathered into the room, through the open door of which the kitchen fire sent a ruddy glow, distinctly marked against carpet and wall. Frank still sat, with his head buried in his hands against the table, listening.

'Tell me more,' he said, at every pause.

'I think I have told you all now,' said Maggie, at last. 'At least, it is all I recollect at present; but if I think of anything more, I will be sure and tell you.'

'Thank you; do.' He was silent for some time.

'Erminia is coming home at Christmas. She is not to go back to Paris again. She will live with us. I hope you and she will be great friends, Maggie.'

'Oh yes,' replied she. 'I think we are already. At least we were last Christmas. You know it is a year since I have seen her.'

'Yes; she went to Switzerland with Mademoiselle Michel, instead of coming home the last time. Maggie, I must go, now. My father will be waiting dinner for me.'

'Dinner! I was going to ask if you would not stay to tea. I hear mama stirring about in her room. And Nancy is getting things ready, I see. Let me go and tell mama. She will not be pleased unless she sees you. She has been very sorry for you all,' added she, dropping her voice.

Before he could answer, she ran up stairs.

Mrs Browne came down.

'Oh, Mr Frank! Have you been sitting in the dark? Maggie, you ought to have rung for candles! Ah! Mr Frank, you've had a sad loss since I saw you here—let me see—in the last week of September. But she was always a sad invalid; and no doubt your loss is her gain. Poor Mr Buxton, too! How is he? When one thinks of him, and of her years of illness, it seems like a happy release.'

She could have gone on for any length of time, but Frank could not bear this ruffling up of his soothed grief, and told her that his father was expecting him home to dinner.

'Ah! I am sure you must not disappoint him. He'll want a little cheerful company more than ever now. You must not let him dwell on it, Mr Frank, but turn his thoughts another way by always talking of other things. I am sure if I had some one to speak to me in a cheerful, pleasant way, when poor dear Mr Browne died, I should never have fretted after him as I did; but the children were too young, and there was no one to come and divert me with any news. If I'd been living in Combehurst, I am sure I should not have let my grief get the better of me as I did. Could you get up a quiet rubber* in the evenings, do you think?'

But Frank had shaken hands and was gone. As he rode home he thought much of sorrow, and the different ways of bearing it. He decided that it was sent by God for some holy purpose, and to call out into existence some higher good; and he thought that if it were faithfully taken as His decree, there would be no passionate, despairing resistance to it; nor yet, if it were trustfully acknowledged to have some wise end, should we dare to baulk it, and defraud it by putting it on one side, and, by seeking the distractions of worldly things, not let it do its full work. And then he returned to his conversation with Maggie. That had been real comfort to him. What an advantage it would be to Erminia to have such a girl for a friend and companion!

It was rather strange that, having this thought, and having been struck, as I said, with Maggie's appearance while she stood in the doorway (and I may add that this impression of her unobtrusive beauty had been deepened by several succeeding interviews), he should reply as he did to Erminia's remark, on first seeing Maggie after her return from France.

'How lovely Maggie is growing! Why, I had no idea she would ever turn out pretty. Sweet-looking she always was; but now her style of beauty makes her positively distinguished. Frank! speak! is not she beautiful?'

'Do you think so?' answered he, with a kind of lazy indifference, exceedingly gratifying to his father, who was listening with some eagerness to his answer. That day, after dinner, Mr Buxton began to ask his opinion of Erminia's appearance.

Frank answered at once—

'She is a dazzling little creature. Her complexion looks as if it were made of cherries and milk; and, it must be owned, the little lady has studied the art of dress to some purpose in Paris.'

Mr Buxton was nearer happiness at this reply than he had ever been since his wife's death; for the only way he could devise to satisfy his reproachful conscience towards his neglected and unhappy sister, was to plan a marriage between his son and her child. He rubbed his hands, and drank two extra glasses of wine.

'We'll have the Brownes to dinner, as usual, next Thursday,' said he. 'I am sure your mother would have been hurt if we had omitted it; it is now nine years since they began to come, and they have never missed one Christmas since. Do you see any objection, Frank?'

'None at all, sir,' answered he. 'I intend to go up to town soon after Christmas, for a week or ten days, on my way to Cambridge. Can I do anything for you?'

'Well, I don't know. I think I shall go up myself some day soon. I can't understand all these lawyer's letters, about the purchase of the Newbridge estate; and I fancy I could make more sense out of it all, if I saw Mr Hodgson.'

'I wish you would adopt my plan, of having an agent, sir. Your affairs are really so complicated now, that they would take up the time of an expert man of business. I am sure all those tenants at Dumford ought to be seen after.'

'I do see after them. There's never a one that dares cheat me, or that would cheat me if they could. Most of them have lived under the Buxtons for generations. They know that if they dared to take advantage of me, I should come down upon them pretty smartly.'

'Do you rely upon their attachment to your family,—or on their idea of your severity?'

'On both. They stand me instead of much trouble in account-keeping, and those eternal lawyers' letters some people are always despatching to their tenants. When I'm cheated, Frank, I give you leave to make me have an agent, but not till then. There's my little Erminia singing away, and nobody to hear her.'

CHAPTER V

CHRISTMAS-DAY was strange and sad. Mrs Buxton had always contrived to be in the drawing-room, ready to receive them all after dinner. Mr Buxton tried to do away with his thoughts of her by much talking; but every now and then he looked wistfully towards the door. Erminia exerted herself to be as lively as she could, in order, if possible, to fill up the vacuum. Edward, who had come over from Woodchester for a walk, had a good deal to say; and was, unconsciously, a great assistance with his never-ending flow of rather clever small-talk. His mother felt proud of her son, and his new waistcoat, which was far more conspicuously of the latest fashion than Frank's could be said to be. After dinner, when Mr Buxton and the two young men were left alone, Edward launched out still more. He thought he was impressing Frank with his knowledge of the world, and the world's ways. But he was doing all in his power to repel one who had never been much attracted towards him. Worldly success was his standard of merit. The end seemed with him to justify the means; if a man prospered, it was not necessary to scrutinize his conduct too closely. The law was viewed in its lowest aspect; and yet with a certain cleverness, which preserved Edward from being intellectually contemptible. Frank had entertained some idea of studying for a barrister himself; not so much as a means of livelihood as to gain some idea of the code which makes and shows a nation's conscience: but Edward's details of the ways in which the letter so often baffles the spirit, made him recoil. With some anger against himself, for viewing the profession with disgust, because it was degraded by those who embraced it, instead of looking upon it as what might be ennobled and purified into a vast intelligence by high and pureminded men, he got up abruptly and left the room.

The girls were sitting over the drawing-room fire, with unlighted candles on the table, talking, he felt, about his mother; but when he came in they rose, and changed their tone. Erminia went to the piano, and sang her newest and choicest French airs. Frank was gloomy and silent; but when she changed into more solemn music his mood was softened. Maggie's simple and hearty admiration, untinged by the slightest shade of envy for Erminia's accomplishments, charmed him. The one appeared to him the perfection of elegant art, the other of graceful nature. When he looked at Maggie, and thought of the moorland home from which she had never wandered, the mysteriously beautiful lines of Wordsworth seemed to become sun-clear to him.

> And she shall lean her ear
> In many a secret place
> Where rivulets dance their wayward round,
> And beauty born of murmuring sound
> Shall pass into her face.*

Mr Buxton, in the dining-room, was really getting to take an interest in Edward's puzzling cases. They were like tricks at cards. A quick motion, and out of the unpromising heap, all confused together, presto! the right card turned up. Edward stated his case, so that there did not seem a loophole for the desired verdict; but, through some conjuration, it always came uppermost at last. He had a graphic way of relating things; and, as he did not spare epithets in his designation of the opposing party, Mr Buxton took it upon trust that the defendant or the prosecutor (as it might happen) was a 'pettifogging knave,' or a 'miserly curmudgeon,' and rejoiced accordingly in the triumph over him gained by the ready wit of 'our governor,' Mr Bish. At last he became so deeply impressed with Edward's knowledge of law, as to consult him about some cottage property he had in Woodchester.

'I rather think there are twenty-one cottages, and they don't bring me in four pounds a-year; and out of that I have to pay for collecting. Would there be any chance of selling them? They are in Doughty-street; a bad neighbourhood, I fear.'

'Very bad,' was Edward's prompt reply. 'But if you are really anxious to effect a sale, I have no doubt I could find a purchaser in a short time.'

'I should be very much obliged to you,' said Mr Buxton. 'You would be doing me a kindness. If you meet with a purchaser, and can manage the affair, I would rather that you drew out the deeds for the transfer of the property. It would be the beginning of business for you; and I only hope I should bring you good luck.'

Of course Edward could do this; and when they left the table, it was with a feeling on his side that he was a step nearer to the agency which he coveted; and with a happy consciousness on Mr Buxton's of having put a few pounds in the way of a deserving and remarkably clever young man.

Since Edward had left home, Maggie had gradually, but surely, been gaining in importance. Her judgement and her untiring unselfishness could not fail to make way. Her mother had some respect for, and great dependence on her; but still it was hardly affection that she felt for her; or if it was, it was a dull and torpid kind of feeling, compared with the fond love and exulting pride which she took in Edward. When he came back for occasional holidays, his mother's face was radiant with happiness, and her manner towards him was even more caressing than he approved of. When Maggie saw him repel the hand that fain would have stroked his hair as in childish days, a longing came into her heart for some of these uncared-for tokens of her mother's love. Otherwise she meekly sank back into her old secondary place, content to have her judgement slighted and her wishes unasked as long as he stayed. At times she was now beginning to disapprove and regret some things in him; his flashiness of manner jarred against her taste; and a deeper, graver feeling was called out by his evident want of quick moral perception. 'Smart and clever,' or 'slow and dull,' took with him the place of 'right and wrong.' Little as he thought it, he was himself narrow-minded and dull; slow and blind to perceive the beauty and eternal wisdom of simple goodness.

Erminia and Maggie became great friends. Erminia used to beg for Maggie, until she herself put a stop to the practice; as she saw her mother yielded more frequently than was convenient, for the honour of having her daughter a visitor at Mr Buxton's, about which she could talk to her few acquaintances who persevered in calling at the cottage. Then Erminia volunteered a visit of some days to Maggie, and Mrs Browne's pride was redoubled; but she made so many preparations, and so much fuss, and gave herself so much trouble, that she was positively ill during Erminia's stay; and Maggie felt that she must henceforward deny herself the pleasure of having her friend for a guest, as her mother could not be persuaded from attempting to provide things in the same abundance and style as that to which Erminia was accustomed at home; whereas, as Nancy shrewdly observed, the young lady did not know if she was eating jelly, or porridge, or whether the plates were common delf or the best China,* so long as she was with her dear Miss Maggie. Spring went, and summer came. Frank had gone to and fro between Cambridge and Combehurst, drawn by motives of which he felt the force, but into which he did not care to examine. Edward had sold the property of Mr Buxton; and he, pleased with the possession of half the purchase money (the remainder of which was to be paid by instalments), and happy in the idea that his son came over so frequently to see Erminia, had amply rewarded the young attorney for his services.

One summer's day, as hot as day could be, Maggie had been busy all morning; for the weather was so sultry that she would not allow either Nancy or her mother to exert themselves much. She had gone down with the old brown pitcher, coeval with herself, to the spring for water; and while it was trickling, and making a tinkling music, she sat down on the ground. The air was so still that she heard the distant wood-pigeons cooing; and round about her the bees were murmuring busily among the clustering heath. From some little touch of sympathy with these low sounds of pleasant harmony, she began to try and hum some of Erminia's airs. She never sang out loud, or put words to her songs; but her voice was very sweet, and it was a great pleasure to herself to let it go into music. Just as her jug was filled, she was startled by Frank's sudden appearance. She had thought he was at Cambridge, and, from some cause or other, her face, usually so faint in colour, became the most vivid scarlet. They were both too conscious to speak. Maggie stooped (murmuring some words of surprise) to take up her pitcher.

'Don't go yet, Maggie,' said he, putting his hand on hers to stop her; but, somehow, when that purpose was effected, he forgot to take it off again. 'I have come all the way from Cambridge to see you. I could not bear suspense any longer. I grew so impatient for certainty of some kind, that I went up to town last night, in order to feel myself on my way to you, even though I knew I could not be here a bit earlier to-day for doing so. Maggie,—dear Maggie! how you are trembling! Have I frightened you? Nancy told me you were here; but it was very thoughtless to come so suddenly upon you.'

It was not the suddenness of his coming; it was the suddenness of her own heart, which leaped up with the feelings called out by his words. She went very white, and sat down on the ground as before. But she rose again immediately, and stood, with drooping, averted head. He had dropped her hand, but now sought to take it again.

'Maggie, darling, may I speak?' Her lips moved, he saw, but he could not hear. A pang of affright ran through him that, perhaps, she did not wish to listen. 'May I speak to you?' he asked again, quite timidly. She tried to make her voice sound, but it would not; so she looked round. Her soft grey eyes were eloquent in that one glance. And, happier than his words, passionate and tender as they were, could tell, he spoke till her trembling was changed into bright flashing blushes, and even a shy smile hovered about her lips, and dimpled her cheeks.

The water bubbled over the pitcher unheeded. At last she remembered all the work-a-day world. She lifted up the jug, and would have hurried home, but Frank decidedly took it from her.

'Henceforward,' said he, 'I have a right to carry your burdens.' So with one arm round her waist, and with the other carrying the water, they climbed the steep turfy slope. Near the top she wanted to take it again.

'Mama will not like it. Mama will think it so strange.'

'Why, dearest, if I saw Nancy carrying it up this slope I would take it from her. It would be strange if a man did not carry it for any woman. But you must let me tell your mother of my right to help you. It is your dinner-time, is it not? I may come in to dinner as one of the family, may not I, Maggie?'

'No,' she said softly. For she longed to be alone; and she dreaded being overwhelmed by the expression of her mother's feelings, weak and agitated as she felt herself. 'Not to-day.'

'Not to-day!' said he, reproachfully. 'You are very hard upon me. Let me come to tea. If you will, I will leave you now. Let me come to early tea. I must speak to my father. He does not know I am here. I may come to tea. At what time is it? Three o'clock. Oh, I know you drink tea at some strange early hour; perhaps it is at two. I will take care to be in time.'

'Don't come till five, please. I must tell mama; and I want some time to think. It does seem so like a dream. Do go, please.'

'Well! if I must, I must. But I don't feel as if I were in a dream, but in some real blessed heaven, so long as I see you.'

At last he went. Nancy was awaiting Maggie, at the side-gate.

'Bless us and save us, bairn! what a time it has taken thee to get the water. Is the spring dry with the hot weather?'

Maggie ran past her. All dinner-time she heard her mother's voice in long-continued lamentation about something. She answered at random, and startled her mother by asserting that she thought 'it' was very good; the said 'it' being milk turned sour by thunder. Mrs Browne spoke quite sharply, 'No one is so particular as you, Maggie. I have known you drink water, day after day, for breakfast, when you were a little girl, because your cup of milk had a drowned fly in it; and now you tell me you don't care for this, and don't mind that, just as if you could eat up all the things which are spoiled by the heat. I declare my head aches so, I shall go and lie down as soon as ever dinner is over.'

If this was her plan, Maggie thought she had no time to lose in making her confession. Frank would be here before her mother got up again to tea. But she dreaded speaking about her happiness; it seemed as yet so cobweb-like, as if a touch would spoil its beauty.

'Mama, just wait one minute. Just sit down in your chair while I tell you something. Please, dear mama.' She took a stool, and sat at her mother's feet; and then she began to turn the wedding-ring on Mrs Browne's hand, looking down and never speaking, till the latter became impatient.

'What is it you have got to say, child? Do make haste, for I want to go up-stairs.'

With a great jerk of resolution, Maggie said—

'Mama, Frank Buxton has asked me to marry him.'

She hid her face in her mother's lap for an instant; and then she lifted it up, as brimful of the light of happiness as is the cup of a water-lily of the sun's radiance.

'Maggie—you don't say so,' said her mother, half incredulously. 'It can't be, for he's at Cambridge, and it's not post-day. What do you mean?'

'He came this morning, mother, when I was down at the well; and we fixed that I was to speak to you; and he asked if he might come again for tea.'

'Dear! dear! and the milk all gone sour! We should have had milk of our own, if Edward had not persuaded me against buying another cow.'

'I don't think Mr Buxton will mind it much,' said Maggie, dimpling up, as she remembered, half-unconsciously, how little he had seemed to care for anything but herself.

'Why, what a thing it is for you!' said Mrs Browne, quite roused up from her languor and her head-ache. 'Everybody said he was engaged to Miss Erminia. Are you quite sure you made no mistake, child? What did he say? Young men are so fond of making fine speeches; and young women are so silly in fancying they mean something. I once knew a girl who thought that a gentleman who sent her mother a present of a sucking-pig, did it as a delicate way of making her an offer. Tell me his exact words.'

But Maggie blushed, and either would not or could not. So Mrs Browne began again,

'Well, if you're sure, you're sure. I wonder how he brought his father round. So long as he and Erminia have been planned for each other! That very first day we ever dined there after your father's death, Mr Buxton as good as told me all about it. I fancied they were only waiting till they were out of mourning.'

All this was news to Maggie. She had never thought that either Erminia or Frank was particularly fond of the other; still less had she had any idea of Mr Buxton's plans for them. Her mother's surprise at her engagement jarred a little upon her too: it had become so natural, even in these last two hours, to feel that she belonged to *him*. But there were more discords to come, Mrs Browne began again, half in soliloquy:

'I should think he would have four thousand a-year. He did not tell you, love, did he, if they had still that bad property in the canal, that his father complained about? But he will have four thousand. Why you'll have your carriage, Maggie. Well! I hope Mr Buxton has taken it kindly, because he'll have a deal to do with the settlements. I'm sure I thought he was engaged to Erminia.'

Ringing changes on these subjects all the afternoon, Mrs Browne sat with Maggie. She occasionally wandered off to speak about Edward, and how favourably his future prospects would be advanced by the engagement.

'Let me see—there's the house in Combehurst; the rent of that would be a hundred and fifty a year, but we'll not reckon that. But there's the quarries' (she was reckoning upon her fingers in default of a slate, for which she had vainly searched), 'we'll call them two hundred a-year, for I don't believe Mr Buxton's stories about their only bringing him in sevenpence; and there's Newbridge, that's certainly thirteen hundred,—where had I got to, Maggie?'

'Dear mama, do go and lie down for a little; you look quite flushed,' said Maggie, softly.

Was this the manner to view her betrothal with such a man as Frank? Her mother's remarks depressed her more than she could have thought it possible; the excitement of the morning was having its reaction, and she longed to go up to the solitude under the thorn-tree, where she had hoped to spend a quiet, thoughtful afternoon.

Nancy came in to replace glasses and spoons in the cupboard. By some accident, the careful old servant broke one of the former. She looked up quickly at her mistress, who usually visited all such offences with no small portion of rebuke.

'Never mind, Nancy,' said Mrs Browne. 'It's only an old tumbler; and Maggie's going to be married, and we must buy a new set for the wedding-dinner.'

Nancy looked at both, bewildered; at last a light dawned into her mind, and her face looked shrewdly and knowingly back at Mrs Browne. Then she said, very quietly,

'I think I'll take the next pitcher to the well myself, and try my luck. To think how sorry I was for Miss Maggie this morning! "Poor thing," says I to myself, "to be kept all this time at that confounded well" (for I'll not deny that I swear a bit to myself at times—it sweetens the blood), "and she so tired." I e'en thought I'd go help her; but I reckon she'd some other help. May I take a guess at the young man?'

'Four thousand a-year! Nancy;' said Mrs Browne exultingly.

'And a blithe look, and a warm, kind heart,—and a free step,—and a noble way with him to rich and poor,—aye, aye, I know the name. No need to after all my neat MBs, done in turkey-red cotton. Well, well! every one's turn comes sometime, but mine's rather long a-coming.'

The faithful old servant came up to Maggie, and put her hand caressingly on her shoulder. Maggie threw her arms round her neck, and kissed the brown, withered face.

'God bless thee, bairn,' said Nancy, solemnly. It brought the low music of peace back into the still recesses of Maggie's heart. She began to look out for her lover; half-hidden behind the muslin window curtain, which waved gently to and fro in the afternoon breezes. She heard a firm, buoyant step, and had only time to catch one glimpse of his face, before moving away. But that one glance made her think that the hours which had elapsed since she saw him had not been serene to him any more than to her.

When he entered the parlour, his face was glad and bright. He went up in a frank, rejoicing way to Mrs Browne; who was evidently rather puzzled how to receive him—whether as Maggie's betrothed, or as the son of the greatest man of her acquaintance.

'I am sure, sir,' said she, 'we are all very much obliged to you for the honour you have done our family!'

He looked rather perplexed as to the nature of the honour which he had conferred without knowing it; but as the light dawned upon him, he made answer in a frank, merry way, which was yet full of respect for his future mother-in-law—

'And I am sure I am truly grateful for the honour one of your family has done me.'

When Nancy brought in tea she was dressed in her fine-weather Sunday gown; the first time it had ever been worn out of church, and the walk to and fro.

After tea, Frank asked Maggie if she would walk out with him; and accordingly they climbed the Fell-Lane and went out upon the moors, which seemed vast and boundless as their love.

'Have you told your father?' asked Maggie; a dim anxiety lurking in her heart.

'Yes,' said Frank. He did not go on; and she feared to ask, although she longed to know, how Mr. Buxton had received the intelligence.

'What did he say?' at length she inquired.

'Oh! it was evidently a new idea to him that I was attached to you; and he does not take up a new idea speedily. He has had some notion, it seems, that Erminia and I were to make a match of it; but she and I agreed, when we talked it over, that we should never have fallen in love with each other if there had not been another human being in the world. Erminia is a little sensible creature, and says she does not wonder at any man falling in love with you. Nay, Maggie, don't hang your head so down; let me have a glimpse of your face.'

'I am sorry your father does not like it,' said Maggie, sorrowfully.

'So am I. But we must give him time to get reconciled. Never fear but he will like it in the long run; he has too much good taste and good feeling. He must like you.'

Frank did not choose to tell even Maggie how violently his father had set himself against their engagement. He was surprised and annoyed at first to find how decidedly his father was possessed with the idea that he was to marry his cousin, and that she, at any rate, was attached to him, whatever his feelings might be towards her;

but after he had gone frankly to Erminia and told her all, he found that she was as ignorant of her uncle's plans for her as he had been; and almost as glad at any event which should frustrate them.

Indeed she came to the moorland cottage on the following day, after Frank had returned to Cambridge. She had left her horse in charge of the groom, near the fir-trees on the heights, and came running down the slope in her habit. Maggie went out to meet her, with just a little wonder at her heart if what Frank had said could possibly be true; and that Erminia, living in the house with him, could have remained indifferent to him. Erminia threw her arms round her neck, and they sat down together on the court-steps.

'I durst not ride down that hill; and Jem is holding my horse, so I may not stay very long; now begin, Maggie, at once, and go into a rhapsody about Frank. Is not he a charming fellow? Oh! I am so glad. Now don't sit smiling and blushing there to yourself; but tell me a great deal about it. I have so wanted to know somebody that was in love, that I might hear what it was like; and the minute I could, I came off here. Frank is only just gone. He has had another long talk with my uncle, since he came back from you this morning; but I am afraid he has not made much way yet.'

Maggie sighed. 'I don't wonder at his not thinking me good enough for Frank.'

'No! the difficulty would be to find any one he did think fit for his paragon of a son.'

'He thought you were, dearest Erminia.'

'So Frank has told you that, has he? I suppose we shall have no more family secrets now,' said Erminia, laughing. 'But I can assure you I had a strong rival in Lady Adela Castlemayne, the Duke of Wight's daughter; she was the most beautiful lady my uncle had ever seen (he only saw her in the Grand Stand at Woodchester races, and never spoke a word to her in his life). And if she would have had Frank, my uncle would still have been dissatisfied as long as the Princess Victoria* was unmarried; none would have been good enough while a better remained. But Maggie,' said she, smiling up into her friend's face, 'I think it would have made you laugh, for all you look as if a kiss would shake the tears out of your eyes, if you could have seen my uncle's manner to me all day. He will have it that I am suffering from an unrequited attachment; so he watched me and watched me over breakfast; and at last, when I had eaten a whole nest-full of eggs, and I don't know how many pieces of toast, he rang the bell and asked for some potted charr.* I was quite unconscious that it was for me, and I did not want it when it came; so he sighed in a most melancholy manner, and said, "My poor Erminia!" If Frank had not been there, and looking dreadfully miserable, I am sure I should have laughed out.'

'Did Frank look miserable?' said Maggie, anxiously.

'There now! you don't care for anything but the mention of his name.'

'But did he look unhappy?' persisted Maggie.

'I can't say he looked happy, dear Mousey; but it was quite different when he came back from seeing you. You know you always had the art of stilling any person's trouble. You and my aunt Buxton are the only two I ever knew with that gift.'

'I am so sorry he has any trouble to be stilled,' said Maggie.

'And I think it will do him a world of good. Think how success-ful his life has been! the honours he got at Eton! his picture taken, and I don't know what! and at Cambridge just the same way of going on. He would be insufferably imperious in a few years, if he did not meet with a few crosses.'

'Imperious!—oh, Erminia, how can you say so?'

'Because it's the truth. He happens to have very good disposi-tions; and therefore his strong will is not either disagreeable, or offensive; but once let him become possessed by a wrong wish, and you would then see how vehement and imperious he would be. Depend upon it, my uncle's resistance is a capital thing for him. As dear sweet Aunt Buxton would have said, "There is a holy purpose in it;" and as Aunt Buxton would not have said, but as I, a "fool, rush in where angels fear to tread,"* I decide that the purpose is to teach Master Frank patience and submission.'

'Erminia—how could you help—' and there Maggie stopped.

'I know what you mean; how could I help falling in love with him? I think he has not mystery and reserve enough for me. I should like a man with some deep, impenetrable darkness round him; something one could always keep wondering about. Besides, think what clashing of wills there would have been! My uncle was very short-sighted in his plan; but I don't think he thought so much about the fitness of our characters and ways, as the fitness of our fortunes!'

'For shame, Erminia! No one cares less for money than Mr Buxton!'

'There's a good little daughter-in-law elect! But seriously, I do think he is beginning to care for money; not in the least for himself, but as a means of aggrandizement for Frank. I have observed, since I came home at Christmas, a growing anxiety to make the most of his property; a thing he never cared about before. I don't think he is aware of it himself; but from one or two little things I have noticed, I should not wonder if he ends in being avaricious in his old age.' Erminia sighed.

Maggie had almost a sympathy with the father, who sought what he imagined to be for the good of his son, and that son, Frank. Although she was as convinced as Erminia, that money could not really help any one to happiness, she could not at the instant resist saying—

'Oh! how I wish I had a fortune! I should so like to give it all to him.'

'Now Maggie! don't be silly! I never heard you wish for anything different from what *was*, before, so I shall take this opportunity of lecturing you on your folly. No! I won't either, for you look sadly tired with all your agitation; and besides I must go, or Jem will be wondering what has become of me. Dearest cousin-in-law, I shall come very often to see you; and perhaps I shall give you my lecture yet.'

CHAPTER VI

IT was true of Mr Buxton, as well as of his son, that he had the seeds
of imperiousness in him. His life had not been such as to call them
out into view. With more wealth than he required; with a gentle
wife, who if she ruled him never showed it, or was conscious of the
fact herself; looked up to by his neighbours, a simple affectionate
set of people, whose fathers had lived near his father and grandfather in the same kindly relation, receiving benefits cordially
given, and requiting them with good will and respectful attention:
such had been the circumstances surrounding him; and until his
son grew out of childhood, there had not seemed a wish which he
had it not in his power to gratify as soon as formed. Again, when
Frank was at school and at college, all went on prosperously; he
gained honours enough to satisfy a far more ambitious father.
Indeed, it was the honours he gained that stimulated his father's
ambition. He received letters from tutors, and headmasters, prophesying that, if Frank chose, he might rise to the 'highest honours in
church or state;' and the idea thus suggested, vague as it was,
remained, and filled Mr Buxton's mind; and, for the first time in
his life, made him wish that his own career had been such as would
have led him to form connexions among the great and powerful.
But, as it was, his shyness and *gêne**, from being unaccustomed to
society, had made him averse to Frank's occasional requests that he
might bring such and such a schoolfellow, or college-chum, home
on a visit. Now he regretted this, on account of the want of those
connexions which might thus have been formed; and, in his visions,
he turned to marriage as the best way of remedying this. Erminia
was right in saying that her uncle had thought of Lady Adela
Castlemayne for an instant; though how the little witch had found
it out I cannot say, as the idea had been dismissed immediately
from his mind. He was wise enough to see its utter vanity, as long
as his son remained undistinguished. But his hope was this. If
Frank married Erminia, their united property (she being her
father's heiress) would justify him in standing for the shire; or if he
could marry the daughter of some leading personage in the county,
it might lead to the same step; and thus at once he would obtain a
position in parliament, where his great talents would have scope

and verge enough. Of these two visions, the favourite one (for his sister's sake) was that of marriage with Erminia.

And, in the midst of all this, fell, like a bomb-shell, the intelligence of his engagement with Maggie Browne; a good sweet little girl enough, but without fortune or connexion,—without, as far as Mr Buxton knew, the least power, or capability, or spirit, with which to help Frank on in his career to eminence in the land! He resolved to consider it as a boyish fancy, easily to be suppressed; and pooh-poohed it down, to Frank, accordingly. He remarked his son's set lips, and quiet determined brow, although he never spoke in a more respectful tone, than while thus steadily opposing his father. If he had shown more violence of manner, he would have irritated him less; but, as it was, it was the most miserable interview that had ever taken place between the father and son.

Mr Buxton tried to calm himself down with believing that Frank would change his mind, if he saw more of the world; but, somehow, he had a prophesying distrust of this idea internally. The worst was, there was no fault to be found with Maggie herself, although she might want the accomplishments he desired to see in his son's wife. Her connexions, too, were so perfectly respectable (though humble enough in comparison with Mr Buxton's soaring wishes), that there was nothing to be objected to on that score; her position was the great offence. In proportion to his want of any reason but this one, for disapproving of the engagement, was his annoyance under it. He assumed a reserve towards Frank; which was so unusual a restraint upon his open genial disposition, that it seemed to make him irritable towards all others in contact with him, excepting Erminia. He found it difficult to behave rightly to Maggie. Like all habitually cordial persons, he went into the opposite extreme, when he wanted to show a little coolness. However angry he might be with the events of which she was the cause, she was too innocent and meek to justify him in being more than cool; but his awkwardness was so great, that many a man of the world has met his greatest enemy, each knowing the other's hatred, with less freezing distance of manner than Mr Buxton's to Maggie. While she went simply on in her own path, loving him the more through all, for old kindness' sake, and because he was Frank's father, he shunned meeting her with such evident and painful anxiety, that at last she tried to spare him the encounter, and hurried out of church, or lingered behind all, in order to avoid the only chance they now had of being forced to speak; for she no longer went to the dear house in Combehurst, though Erminia came to see her more than ever.

Mrs Browne was perplexed and annoyed beyond measure. She upbraided Mr Buxton to every one but Maggie. To her she said,—'Any one in their senses might have foreseen what had happened, and would have thought well about it, before they went and fell in love with a young man of such expectations as Mr Frank Buxton.'

In the middle of all this dismay, Edward came over from Woodchester for a day or two. He had been told of the engagement, in a letter from Maggie herself; but it was too sacred a subject for her to enlarge upon to him; and Mrs Browne was no letter-writer. So this was his first greeting to Maggie, after kissing her—

'Well, Sancho, you've done famously for yourself. As soon as I got your letter I said to Harry Bish,—"Still waters run deep; here's my little sister Maggie, as quiet a creature as ever lived, has managed to catch young Buxton, who has five thousand a-year if he's a penny." Don't go so red, Maggie. Harry was sure to hear of it soon from some one, and I see no use in keeping it secret, for it gives consequence to us all.'

'Mr Buxton is quite put out about it,' said Mrs Browne, querulously; 'and I'm sure he need not be, for he's enough of money, if that's what he wants; and Maggie's father was a clergyman, and I've seen "yeoman," with my own eyes, on old Mr Buxton's (Mr Lawrence's father's) carts; and a clergyman is above a yeoman any day. But if Maggie had had any thought for other people, she'd never have gone and engaged herself, when she might have been sure it would give offence. We are never asked down to dinner now. I've never broken bread there since last Christmas.'

'Whew'—said Edward to this. It was a disappointed whistle; but he soon cheered up. 'I thought I could have lent a hand in screwing old Buxton up about the settlements; but I see it's not come to that yet. Still I'll go and see the old gentleman. I'm a bit of a favourite of his, and I've no doubt I can turn him round.'

'Pray, Edward, don't go,' said Maggie. 'Frank and I are content to wait; and I'm sure we would rather not have any one speak to Mr Buxton, upon a subject which evidently gives him so much pain; please, Edward, don't!'

'Well, well. Only I must go about this property of his. Besides, I don't mean to get into disgrace; so I shan't seem to know anything about it, if it would make him angry. I want to keep on good terms, because of the agency. So, perhaps, I shall shake my head, and think it great presumption in you, Maggie, to have thought of becoming his daughter-in-law. If I can do you no good, I may as well do myself some.'

'I hope you won't mention me at all,' she replied.

One comfort (and almost the only one arising from Edward's visit) was, that she could now often be spared to go up to the thorn-tree, and calm down her anxiety, and bring all discords into peace, under the sweet influences of nature. Mrs Buxton had tried to teach her the force of the lovely truth, that the 'melodies of the everlasting chime'* may abide in the hearts of those who ply their daily task in towns, and crowded populous places; and that solitude is not needed by the faithful for them to feel the immediate presence of God; nor utter stillness of human sound necessary, before they can hear the music of His angels' footsteps: but, as yet, her soul was a young disciple; and she felt it easier to speak to Him, and come to Him for help, sitting lonely, with wild moors swelling and darkening around her, and not a creature in sight but the white specks of distant sheep, and the birds that shun the haunts of men, floating in the still mid-air.

She sometimes longed to go to Mr Buxton and tell him how much she could sympathize with him, if his dislike to her engagement arose from his thinking her unworthy of his son. Frank's character seemed to her grand in its promise. With vehement impulses, and natural gifts, craving worthy employment, his will sat supreme over all, like a young emperor calmly seated on his throne, whose fiery generals and wise counsellors stand alike ready to obey him. But if marriage were to be made by due measurement and balance of character, and if others, with their scales, were to be the judges, what would become of all the beautiful services rendered by the loyalty of true love? Where would be the raising up of the weak by the strong? or the patient endurance? or the gracious trust of her——

> Whose faith is fixt and cannot move;
> She darkly feels him great and wise,
> She dwells on him with faithful eyes,
> 'I cannot understand: I love.'*

Edward's manners and conduct caused her more real anxiety than anything else. Indeed, no other thoughtfulness could be called anxiety compared to this. His faults, she could not but perceive, were strengthening with his strength, and growing with his growth. She could not help wondering whence he obtained the money to pay for his dress, which she thought was of a very expensive kind. She heard him also incidentally allude to 'runs up to town,' of which, at the time, neither she nor her mother had been made aware. He seemed confused when she questioned him about these, although he tried to laugh it off; and asked her how she, a country girl, cooped up among one set of people, could have any idea of the life it was necessary for a man to lead who 'had any hope of getting on in the world.' He must have acquaintances and connexions, and see something of life, and make an appearance. She was silenced, but not satisfied. Nor was she at ease with regard to his health. He looked ill, and worn; and, when he was not rattling and laughing, his face fell into a shape of anxiety and uneasiness, which was new to her in it. He reminded her painfully of an old German engraving she had seen in Mrs Buxton's portfolio, called, 'Pleasure digging a Grave;'* Pleasure being represented by a ghastly figure of a young man, eagerly industrious over his dismal work.

A few days after he went away, Nancy came to her in her bed-room.

'Miss Maggie,' said she, 'may I just speak a word?' But when the permission was given, she hesitated.

'It's none of my business, to be sure,' said she at last: 'only, you see, I've lived with your mother ever since she was married; and I care a deal for both you and Master Edward. And I think he drains Missus of her money; and it makes me not easy in my mind. You did not know of it, but he had his father's old watch when he was over last time but one; I thought he was of an age to have a watch, and that it was all natural. But, I reckon, he's sold it, and got that gimcrack one instead. That's perhaps natural too. Young folks like young fashions. But, this time, I think he has taken away your mother's watch; at least, I've never seen it since he went. And this morning she spoke to me about my wages. I'm sure I've never asked for them, nor troubled her; but I'll own it's now near on to twelve months since she paid me; and she was as regular as clock-work till then. Now, Miss Maggie, don't look so sorry, or I shall wish I had never spoken. Poor Missus seemed sadly put about, and said something as I did not try to hear; for I was so vexed she should think I needed apologies, and them sort of things. I'd rather live with you without wage than have her look so shame-faced as she did this morning. I don't want a bit for money, my dear; I've a deal in the bank. But I'm afeard Master Edward is spending too much, and pinching Missus.'

Maggie was very sorry indeed. Her mother had never told her anything of all this, so it was evidently a painful subject to her; and Maggie determined (after lying awake half the night) that she would write to Edward, and remonstrate with him; and that in every personal and household expense, she would be, more than ever, rigidly economical.

The full, free, natural intercourse between her lover and herself, could not fail to be checked by Mr Buxton's aversion to the engagement. Frank came over for some time in the early autumn. He had left Cambridge, and intended to enter himself at the Temple* as soon as the vacation was ended. He had not been very long at home before Maggie was made aware, partly through Erminia, who had no notion of discreet silence on any point, and partly by her own observation, of the increasing estrangement between father and son. Mr Buxton was reserved with Frank for the first time in his life; and Frank was depressed and annoyed at his father's obstinate repetition of the same sentence, in answer to all his arguments in favour of his engagement——arguments which were overwhelming to himself, and which it required an effort of patience on his part to go over and recapitulate, so obvious was the conclusion: and then to have the same answer for ever, the same words even,——

'Frank! it's no use talking. I don't approve of the engagement; and never shall.'

He would snatch up his hat, and hurry off to Maggie to be soothed. His father knew where he was gone without being told; and was jealous of her influence over the son who had long been his first and paramount object in life.

He needed not have been jealous. However angry and indignant Frank was when he went up to the moorland cottage, Maggie almost persuaded him, before half an hour had elapsed, that his father was but unreasonable from his extreme affection. Still she saw that such frequent differences would weaken the bond between father and son; and, accordingly, she urged Frank to accept an invitation into Scotland.

'You told me,' said she, 'that Mr Buxton will have it, it is but a boy's attachment; and that when you have seen other people, you will change your mind; now do try how far you can stand the effects of absence.' She said it playfully, but he was in a humour to be vexed.

'What nonsense, Maggie! You don't care for all this delay yourself; and you take up my father's bad reasons as if you believed them.'

'I don't believe them; but still they may be true.'

'How should you like it, Maggie, if I urged you to go about and see something of society, and try if you could not find some one you liked better? It is more probable in your case than in mine; for you have never been from home, and I have been half over Europe.'

'You are very much afraid, are not you, Frank?' said she, her face bright with blushes, and her grey eyes smiling up at him. 'I have a great idea that if I could see that Harry Bish that Edward is always talking about, I should be charmed. He must wear such beautiful waistcoats! Don't you think I had better see him before our engagement is quite, quite final?'

But Frank would not smile. In fact, like all angry persons, he found fresh matter for offence in every sentence. She did not consider the engagement as quite final: thus he chose to understand her playful speech. He would not answer. She spoke again:

'Dear Frank, you are not angry with me, are you? It is nonsense to think that we are to go about the world, picking and choosing men and women, as if they were fruit, and we were to gather the best; as if there was not something in our own hearts which, if we listen to it conscientiously, will tell us at once when we have met the one of all others. There now, am I sensible? I suppose I am, for your grim features are relaxing into a smile. That's right. But now listen to this. I think your father would come round sooner, if he were not irritated every day by the knowledge of your visits to me. If you went away, he would know that we should write to each other, yet he would forget the exact time when; but now he knows as well as I do where you are when you are up here; and I fancy, from what Erminia says, it makes him angry the whole time you are away.'

Frank was silent. At last he said: 'It is rather provoking to be obliged to acknowledge that there is some truth in what you say. But even if I would, I am not sure that I could go. My father does not speak to me about his affairs, as he used to do; so I was rather surprised yesterday to hear him say to Erminia (though I'm sure he meant the information for me), that he had engaged an agent.'

'Then there will be the less occasion for you to be at home. He won't want your help in his accounts.'

'I've given him little enough of that. I have long wanted him to have somebody to look after his affairs. They are very complicated, and he is very careless. But I believe my signature will be wanted for some new leases; at least he told me so.'

'That need not take you long,' said Maggie.

'Not the mere signing. But I want to know something more about the property, and the proposed tenants. I believe this Mr Henry that my father has engaged, is a very hard sort of man. He is what is called scrupulously honest and honourable; but I fear a little too much inclined to drive hard bargains for his client. Now I want to be convinced to the contrary, if I can, before I leave my father in his hands. So, you cruel judge, you won't transport me yet, will you?'

'No,' said Maggie, over-joyed at her own decision, and blushing her delight that her reason was convinced it was right for Frank to stay a little longer.

The next day's post brought her a letter from Edward. There was not a word in it about her enquiry or remonstrance; it might never have been written, or never received; but a few hurried anxious lines, asking her to write by return of post, and say if it was really true that Mr Buxton had engaged an agent. 'It's a confounded shabby trick if he has, after what he said to me long ago. I cannot tell you how much I depend on your complying with my request. Once more, *write directly*. If Nancy cannot take the letter to the post, run down to Combehurst with it yourself. I must have an answer to-morrow, and every particular as to who,—when to be appointed, &c. But I can't believe the report to be true.'

Maggie asked Frank if she might name what he had told her the day before to her brother. He said:—

'Oh, yes, certainly, if he cares to know. Of course, you will not say anything about my own opinion of Mr Henry. He is coming to-morrow, and I shall be able to judge how far I am right.'

CHAPTER VII

THE next day Mr Henry came. He was a quiet, stern-looking man, of considerable intelligence and refinement, and so much taste for music as to charm Erminia, who had rather dreaded his visit. But all the amenities of life were put aside when he entered Mr Buxton's sanctum—his 'office,' as he called the room where he received his tenants and business-people. Frank thought Mr Henry was scarce commonly civil in the open evidence of his surprise and contempt for the habits, of which the disorderly books and ledgers were but too visible signs. Mr Buxton himself felt more like a school-boy, bringing up an imperfect lesson, than he had ever done since he was thirteen.

'The only wonder, my good sir, is that you have any property left; that you have not been cheated out of every farthing.'

'I'll answer for it,' said Mr Buxton, in reply, 'that you'll not find any cheating has been going on. They dared not, sir; they know I should make an example of the first rogue I found out.'

Mr Henry lifted up his eyebrows, but did not speak.

'Besides, sir, most of these men have lived for generations under the Buxtons. I'd give you my life, they would not cheat me.'

Mr Henry coldly said:

'I imagine a close examination of these books by some accountant will be the best proof of the honesty of these said tenants. If you will allow me, I will write to a clever fellow I know, and desire him to come down and try and regulate this mass of papers.'

'Anything—anything you like,' said Mr Buxton, only too glad to escape from the lawyer's cold, contemptuous way of treating the subject.

The accountant came; and he and Mr Henry were deeply engaged in the office for several days. Mr Buxton was bewildered by the questions they asked him. Mr Henry examined him in the worrying way in which an unwilling witness is made to give evidence. Many a time and oft did he heartily wish he had gone on in the old course to the end of his life, instead of putting himself into an agent's hands; but he comforted himself by thinking that, at any rate, they would be convinced he had never allowed himself to be cheated or imposed upon, although he did not make any parade of exactitude.

What was his dismay when, one morning, Mr Henry sent to request his presence, and, with a cold, clear voice, read aloud an admirably drawn up statement, informing the poor landlord of the defalcations, nay more, the impositions of those whom he had trusted. If he had been alone, he would have burst into tears, to find how his confidence had been abused. But as it was, he became passionately angry.

'I'll prosecute them, sir. Not a man shall escape. I'll make them pay back every farthing, I will. And damages, too. Crayston, did you say, sir? Was that one of the names? Why, that is the very Crayston who was bailiff under my father for years. The scoundrel! And I set him up in my best farm when he married. And he's been swindling me, has he?'

Mr Henry ran over the items of the account,—'421*l*. 13*s*. 4 $\frac{3}{4}$ *d*. Part of this I fear we cannot recover—'

He was going on, but Mr Buxton broke in: 'But I will recover it. I'll have every farthing of it. I'll go to law with the viper. I don't care for money, but I hate ingratitude.'

'If you like, I will take counsel's opinion on the case,' said Mr Henry, coolly.

'Take anything you please, sir. Why, this Crayston was the first man that set me on a horse,—and to think of his cheating me!'

A few days after this conversation, Frank came on his usual visit to Maggie.

'Can you come up to the thorn-tree, dearest?' said he. 'It is a lovely day, and I want the solace of a quiet hour's talk with you.'

So they went, and sat in silence some time, looking at the calm and still blue air about the summits of the hills, where never tumult of the world came to disturb the peace, and the quiet of whose heights was never broken by the loud passionate cries of men.

'I am glad you like my thorn-tree,' said Maggie.

'I like the view from it. The thought of the solitude which must be among the hollows of those hills pleases me particularly to-day. Oh, Maggie! it is one of the times when I get depressed about men and the world. We have had such sorrow, and such revelations, and remorse, and passion at home to-day. Crayston (my father's old tenant) has come over. It seems,—I am afraid there is no doubt, of it,—he has been peculating to a large amount. My father has been too careless, and has placed his dependants in great temptation; and Crayston—he is an old man, with a large extravagant family—has yielded. He has been served with notice of my father's intention to prosecute him; and came over to confess all, and ask for forgiveness, and time to pay back what he could. A month ago, my father would have listened to him, I think; but now, he is stung by Mr Henry's sayings, and gave way to a furious passion. It has been a most distressing morning. The worst side of everybody seems to have come out. Even Crayston, with all his penitence and appearance of candour, had to be questioned closely by Mr Henry before he would tell the whole truth. Good God! that money should have such power to corrupt men. It was all for money, and money's worth, that this degradation has taken place. As for Mr Henry, to save his client money, and to protect money, he does not care,—he does not even perceive,—how he induces deterioration of character. He has been encouraging my father in measures which I cannot call anything but vindictive. Crayston is to be made an example of, they say. As if my father had not half the sin on his own head! As if he had rightly discharged his duties as a rich man! Money was as dross to him; but he ought to have remembered how it might be as life itself to many, and be craved after, and coveted, till the black longing got the better of principle, as it has done with this poor Crayston. They say the man was once so truthful, and now his self-respect is gone; and he has evidently lost the very nature of truth. I dread riches. I dread the responsibility of them. At any rate, I wish I had begun life as a poor boy, and worked my way up to competence. Then I could understand and remember the temptations of poverty. I am afraid of my own heart becoming hardened as my father's is. You have no notion of his passionate severity to-day, Maggie! It was quite a new thing even to me!'

'It will only be for a short time,' said she. 'He must be much grieved about this man.'

'If I thought I could ever grow as hard and indifferent to the abject entreaties of a criminal as my father has been this morning,—one whom he has helped to make, too,—I would go off to Australia at once. Indeed, Maggie, I think it would be the best thing we could do. My heart aches about the mysterious corruptions and evils of an old state of society such as we have in England.——What do you say, Maggie? Would you go?'

She was silent,——thinking.

'I would go with you directly, if it were right,' said she, at last. 'But would it be? I think it would be rather cowardly. I feel what you say; but don't you think it would be braver to stay, and endure much depression and anxiety of mind, for the sake of the good those always can do who see evils clearly. I am speaking all this time as if neither you nor I had any home duties, but were free to do as we liked.'

'What can you or I do? We are less than drops in the ocean, as far as our influence can go to re-model a nation?'

'As for that,' said Maggie, laughing, 'I can't remodel Nancy's old-fashioned ways; so I've never yet planned how to remodel a nation.'

'Then what did you mean by the good those always can do who see evils clearly? The evils I see are those of a nation whose god is money.'

'That is just because you have come away from a distressing scene. To-morrow you will hear or read of some heroic action meeting with a nation's sympathy, and you will rejoice and be proud of your country.'

'Still I shall feel the evils of her complex state of society keenly; and where is the good I can do?'

'Oh! I can't tell in a minute. But cannot you bravely face these evils, and learn their nature and causes; and then has God given you no powers to apply to the discovery of their remedy? Dear Frank, think! It may be very little you can do,——and you may never see the effect of it, any more than the widow saw the world-wide effect of her mite.* Then, if all the good and thoughtful men run away from us to some new country, what are we to do with our poor, dear Old England?'

'Oh, you must run away with the good thoughtful men——(I mean to consider that as a compliment to myself, Maggie!) Will you let me wish I had been born poor, if I am to stay in England? I should not then be liable to this fault into which I see the rich men fall, of forgetting the trials of the poor.'

'I am not sure whether, if you had been poor, you might not have fallen into an exactly parallel fault, and forgotten the trials of the rich. It is so difficult to understand the errors into which their position makes all men liable to fall. Do you remember a story in *Evenings at Home*, called the 'Transmigrations of Indra'?* Well! when I was a child, I used to wish I might be transmigrated (is that the right word?) into an American slave-owner for a little while, just that I might understand how he must suffer, and be sorely puzzled, and pray and long to be freed from his odious wealth, till at last he grew hardened to its nature;—and since then, I have wished to be the Emperor of Russia, for the same reason, Ah! you may laugh; but that is only because I have not explained myself properly.'

'I was only smiling to think how ambitious any one might suppose you were who did not know you.'

'I don't see any ambition in it—I don't think of the station—I only want sorely to see the "What's resisted" of Burns, in order that I may have more charity for those who seem to me to have been the cause of such infinite woe and misery.'

> 'What's done we partly may compute;
> But know not what's resisted,'*

repeated Frank, musingly. After some time he began again:

'But, Maggie, I don't give up this wish of mine to go to Australia,—Canada, if you like it better,—anywhere where there is a newer and purer state of society.'

'The great objection seems to be your duty, as an only child, to your father. It is different to the case of one out of a large family.'

'I wish I were one in twenty, then I might marry where I liked to-morrow.'

'It would take two people's consent to such a rapid measure,' said Maggie, laughing. 'But now I am going to wish a wish, which it won't require a fairy godmother to gratify. Look, Frank, do you see in the middle of that dark brown purple streak of moor a yellow gleam of light? It is a pond, I think, that at this time of the year catches a slanting beam of the sun. It can't be very far off. I have wished to go to it every autumn. Will you go with me now? We shall have time before tea.'

Frank's dissatisfaction with the stern measures that, urged on by Mr Henry, his father took against all who had imposed upon his carelessness as a landlord, increased rather than diminished. He spoke warmly to him on the subject, but without avail. He remonstrated with Mr Henry, and told him how he felt that, had his father controlled his careless nature, and been an exact, vigilant landlord, these tenantry would never have had the great temptation to do him wrong; and that therefore he considered some allowance should be made for them, and some opportunity given them to redeem their characters, which would be blasted and hardened for ever by the publicity of a law-suit. But Mr Henry only raised his eyebrows and made answer:

'I like to see these notions in a young man, sir. I had them myself at your age. I believe I had great ideas then, on the subject of temptation and the force of circumstances; and was as Quixotic* as any one about reforming rogues. But my experience has convinced me that roguery is innate. Nothing but outward force can control it, and keep it within bounds. The terrors of the law must be that outward force. I admire your kindness of heart; and in three-and-twenty we do not look for the wisdom and experience of forty or fifty.'

Frank was indignant at being set aside as an unripe youth. He disapproved so strongly of all these measures, and of so much that was now going on at home under Mr Henry's influence, that he determined to pay his long promised visit to Scotland; and Maggie, sad at heart to see how he was suffering, encouraged him in his determination.

CHAPTER VIII

AFTER he was gone, there came a November of the most dreary and characteristic kind. There was incessant rain, and closing-in mists, without a gleam of sunshine to light up the drops of water, and make the wet stems and branches of the trees glisten. Every colour seemed dimmed and darkened; and the crisp autumnal glory of leaves fell soddened to the ground. The latest flowers rotted away without ever coming to their bloom; and it looked as if the heavy monotonous sky had drawn closer and closer, and shut in the little moorland cottage as with a shroud. In doors, things were no more cheerful. Maggie saw that her mother was depressed, and she thought that Edward's extravagance must be the occasion. Oftentimes she wondered how far she might speak on the subject; and once or twice she drew near it in conversation; but her mother winced away, and Maggie could not as yet see any decided good to be gained from encountering such pain. To herself it would have been a relief to have known the truth,—the worst, as far as her mother knew it; but she was not in the habit of thinking of herself. She only tried, by long tender attention, to cheer and comfort her mother; and she and Nancy strove in every way to reduce the household expenditure, for there was little ready money to meet it. Maggie wrote regularly to Edward; but since the note inquiring about the agency, she had never heard from him. Whether her mother received letters she did not know; but at any rate she did not express anxiety, though her looks and manner betrayed that she was ill at ease. It was almost a relief to Maggie when some change was given to her thoughts by Nancy's becoming ill. The damp gloomy weather brought on some kind of rheumatic attack, which obliged the old servant to keep her bed. Formerly, in such an emergency, they would have engaged some cottager's wife to come and do the house-work; but now it seemed tacitly understood that they could not afford it. Even when Nancy grew worse, and required attendance in the night, Maggie still persisted in her daily occupations. She was wise enough to rest when and how she could; and, with a little forethought, she hoped to be able to go through this weary time without any bad effect. One morning (it was on the second of December; and even the change of name in the month, although it brought no change of circumstances or weather, was a relief,—December brought glad tidings even in its very name), one morning, dim and dreary, Maggie had looked at the clock on leaving Nancy's room, and finding it was not yet half-past five, and knowing that her mother and Nancy were both asleep, she determined to lie down and rest for an hour before getting up to light the fires. She did not mean to go to sleep; but she was tired out, and fell into a sound slumber. When she awoke it was with a start. It was still dark; but she had a clear idea of being wakened by some distinct, rattling noise. There it was once more—against the window, like a shower of shot. She went to the lattice, and opened it to look out. She had that strange consciousness, not to be described, of the near neighbourhood of some human creature, although she neither saw nor heard any one for the first instant. Then Edward spoke in a hoarse whisper, right below the window, standing on the flower-beds.

'Maggie! Maggie! Come down and let me in. For your life, don't make any noise. No one must know.'

Maggie turned sick. Something was wrong, evidently; and she was weak and weary. However, she stole down the old creaking stairs, and undid the heavy bolt, and let her brother in. She felt that his dress was quite wet, and she led him, with cautious steps, into the kitchen, and shut the door, and stirred the fire, before she spoke. He sank into a chair, as if worn out with fatigue. She stood, expecting some explanation. But when she saw he could not speak, she hastened to make him a cup of tea; and, stooping down, took off his wet boots, and helped him off with his coat, and brought her own plaid to wrap round him. All this time her heart sunk lower and lower. He allowed her to do what she liked, as if he were an automaton; his head and his arms hung loosely down, and his eyes were fixed, in a glaring way, on the fire. When she brought him some tea, he spoke for the first time; she could not hear what he said till he repeated it, so husky was his voice.

'Have you no brandy?'

She had the key of the little wine-cellar, and fetched up some. But as she took a tea-spoon to measure it out, he tremblingly clutched at the bottle, and shook down a quantity into the empty tea-cup, and drank it off at one gulp. He fell back again in his chair; but in a few minutes he roused himself, and seemed stronger.

'Edward, dear Edward, what is the matter?' said Maggie, at last; for he got up, and was staggering towards the outer door, as if he were going once more into the rain, and dismal morning-twilight.

He looked at her fiercely, as she laid her hand on his arm.

'Confound you! Don't touch me. I'll not be kept here, to be caught and hung!'

For an instant she thought he was mad.

'Caught and hung!' she echoed. 'My poor Edward! what do you mean?'

He sat down suddenly on a chair, close by him, and covered his face with his hands. When he spoke, his voice was feeble and imploring.

'The police are after me, Maggie! What must I do? Oh! can you hide me? Can you save me?'

He looked wild, like a hunted creature. Maggie stood aghast. He went on:

'My mother!—Nancy! Where are they? I was wet through and starving, and I came here. Don't let them take me, Maggie, 'till I'm stronger, and can give battle.'

'Oh! Edward! Edward! What are you saying?' said Maggie, sitting down on the dresser, in absolute, bewildered despair. 'What have you done?'

'I hardly know. I'm in a horrid dream. I see you think I'm mad; I wish I were. Won't Nancy come down soon? You must hide me.'

'Poor Nancy is ill in bed!' said Maggie.

'Thank God,' said he. 'There's one less. But my mother will be up soon, will she not?'

'Not yet,' replied Maggie. 'Edward, dear, do try and tell me what you have done. Why should the police be after you?'

'Why, Maggie,' said he with a kind of forced, unnatural laugh, 'they say I've forged.'

'And have you?' asked Maggie, in a still, low tone of quiet agony.

He did not answer for some time, but sat, looking on the floor with unwinking eyes. At last he said, as if speaking to himself:—

'If I have, it's no more than others have done before, and never been found out. I was but borrowing money. I meant to repay it. If I had asked Mr Buxton, he would have lent it me.'

'Mr Buxton!' said Maggie.

'Yes!' answered he, looking sharply and suddenly up at her. 'Your future father-in-law. My father's old friend. It is he that is hunting me to death! No need to look so white and horror-struck, Maggie! It's the way of the world, as I might have known, if I had not been a blind fool.'

'Mr Buxton!' she whispered, faintly.

'Oh, Maggie!' said he, suddenly throwing himself at her feet, 'save me! You can do it. Write to Frank, and make him induce his father to let me off. I came to see you, my sweet, merciful sister! I knew you would save me. Good God! What noise is that? There are steps in the yard!'

And before she could speak, he had rushed into the little china closet, which opened out of the parlour, and crouched down in the darkness. It was only the man who brought their morning's supply of milk from a neighbouring farm. But when Maggie opened the kitchen door, she saw how the cold, pale light of a winter's day had filled the air.

'You're late with your shutters to-day, miss,' said the man. 'I hope Nancy has not been giving you all a bad night. Says I to Thomas, who came with me to the gate, "It's many a year since I saw them parlour shutters barred up at half-past eight." '

Maggie went, as soon as he was gone, and opened all the low windows, in order that they might look as usual. She wondered at her own outward composure, while she felt so dead and sick at heart. Her mother would soon get up; must she be told? Edward spoke to her now and then from his hiding-place. He dared not go back into the kitchen, into which the few neighbours they had were apt to come, on their morning's way to Combehurst, to ask if they could do any errands there for Mrs Browne or Nancy. Perhaps a quarter of an hour or so had elapsed since the first alarm, when, as Maggie was trying to light the parlour fire, in order that the doctor, when he came, might find all as usual, she heard the click of the garden gate, and a man's step coming along the walk. She ran up stairs to wash away the traces of the tears which had been streaming down her face as she went about her work, before she opened the door. There, against the watery light of the rainy day without, stood Mr Buxton. He hardly spoke to her, but pushed past her, and entered the parlour. He sat down, looking as if he did not know what he was doing. Maggie tried to keep down her shivering alarm. It was long since she had seen him; and the old idea of his kind, genial disposition, had been sadly disturbed by what she had heard from Frank, of his severe proceedings against his unworthy tenantry; and now, if he was setting the police in search of Edward, he was indeed to be dreaded; and with Edward so close at hand, within earshot! If the china fell! He would suspect nothing from that; it would only be her own terror. If her mother came down! But, with all these thoughts, she was very still, outwardly, as she sat waiting for him to speak.

'Have you heard from your brother lately?' asked he, looking up in an angry and disturbed manner. 'But I'll answer for it he has not been writing home for some time. He could not, with the guilt he has had on his mind. I'll not believe in gratitude again. There perhaps was such a thing once; but now-a-days the more you do for a person, the surer they are to turn against you, and cheat you. Now, don't go white and pale. I know you're a good girl in the main; and I've been lying awake all night, and I've a deal to say to you. That scoundrel of a brother of yours!'

Maggie could not ask (as would have been natural, if she had been ignorant) what Edward had done. She knew too well. But Mr Buxton was too full of his own thoughts and feelings to notice her much.

'Do you know he has been like the rest? Do you know he has been cheating me—forging my name? I don't know what besides. It's well for him that they've altered the laws, and he can't be hung for it' (a dead heavy weight was removed from Maggie's mind), 'but Mr Henry is going to transport him. It's worse than Crayston. Crayston only ploughed up the turf, and did not pay rent, and sold the timber, thinking I should never miss it. But your brother has gone and forged my name. He had received all the purchase-money, while he only gave me half, and said the rest was to come after-wards. And the ungrateful scoundrel has gone and given a forged receipt! You might have knocked me down with a straw when Mr Henry told me about it all last night. "Never talk to me of virtue and such humbug again," I said, "I'll never believe in them. Every one is for what he can get." However, Mr Henry wrote to the superintendent of police at Woodchester; and has gone over him-self this morning to see after it. But to think of your father having such a son!'

'Oh, my poor father!' sobbed out Maggie. 'How glad I am you are dead before this disgrace came upon us!'

'You may well say disgrace. You're a good girl yourself, Maggie. I have always said that. How Edward has turned out as he has done, I cannot conceive. But now, Maggie, I've something to say to you.' He moved uneasily about, as if he did not know how to begin. Maggie was standing leaning her head against the chimney-piece, longing for her visitor to go, dreading the next minute, and wishing to shrink into some dark corner of oblivion where she might forget all for a time, till she regained a small portion of the bodily strength that had been sorely tried of late. Mr Buxton saw her white look of anguish, and read it in part, but not wholly. He was too intent on what he was going to say.

'I've been lying awake all night, thinking. You see the disgrace it is to you, though you are innocent; and I'm sure you can't think of involving Frank in it.'

Maggie went to the little sofa, and, kneeling down by it, hid her face in the cushions. He did not go on, for he thought she was not listening to him. At last he said,

'Come now, be a sensible girl, and face it out, I've a plan to propose.'

'I hear,' said she, in a dull veiled voice.

'Why, you know how against this engagement I have always been. Frank is but three-and-twenty, and does not know his own mind, as I tell him. Besides, he might marry any one he chose.'

'He has chosen me,' murmured Maggie.

'Of course, of course. But you'll not think of keeping him to it, after what has passed. You would not have such a fine fellow as Frank pointed at as the brother-in-law of a forger, would you? It was far from what I wished for him before; but now! Why you're glad your father is dead, rather than he should have lived to see this day; and rightly too, I think. And you'll not go and disgrace Frank.—From what Mr Henry hears, Edward has been a discredit to you in many ways. Mr Henry was at Woodchester yesterday, and he says if Edward has been fairly entered as an attorney, his name may be struck off the Rolls* for many a thing he has done. Think of my Frank having his bright name tarnished by any connexion with such a man! Mr Henry says, even in a court of law what has come out about Edward would be excuse enough for a breach of promise of marriage.'

Maggie lifted up her wan face; the pupils of her eyes were dilated, her lips were dead white. She looked straight at Mr Buxton with indignant impatience—

'Mr Henry! Mr Henry! What has Mr Henry to do with me?'

Mr Buxton was staggered by the wild, imperious look, so new upon her mild, sweet face. But he was resolute for Frank's sake, and returned to the charge after a moment's pause.

'Mr Henry is a good friend of mine, who has my interest at heart. He has known what a subject of regret your engagement has been to me; though really my repugnance to it was without cause formerly, compared to what it is now. Now be reasonable, my dear. I'm willing to do something for you if you will do something for me. You must see what a stop this sad affair has put to any thoughts between you and Frank. And you must see what cause I have to wish to punish Edward for his ungrateful behaviour, to say nothing of the forgery. Well now! I don't know what Mr Henry will say to me, but I have thought of this. If you'll write a letter to Frank, just saying distinctly that, for reasons which must for ever remain a secret—'

'Remain a secret from Frank?' said Maggie, again lifting up her head. 'Why?'

'Why? my dear! You startle me with that manner of yours—just let me finish out my sentence. If you'll say that, for reasons which must for ever remain a secret, you decidedly and unchangeably give up all connexion, all engagement with him (which, in fact, Edward's conduct has as good as put an end to), I'll go over to Woodchester and tell Mr Henry and the police that they need not make further search after Edward, for that I won't appear against him. You can save your brother; and you'll do yourself no harm by writing this letter, for of course you see your engagement is broken off. For you never would wish to disgrace Frank.'

He paused, anxiously awaiting her reply. She did not speak.

'I'm sure, if I appear against him, he is as good as transported,' he put in, after a while.

Just at this time there was a little sound of displaced china in the closet. Mr Buxton did not attend to it, but Maggie heard it. She got up, and stood quite calm before Mr Buxton.

'You must go,' said she. 'I know you; and I know you are not aware of the cruel way in which you have spoken to me, while asking me to give up the very hope and marrow of my life,—' she could not go on for a moment; she was choked up with anguish.

'It was the truth, Maggie,' said he, somewhat abashed.

'It was the truth that made the cruelty of it. But you did not mean to speak cruelly to me, I know. Only it is hard all at once to be called upon to face the shame and blasted character of one who was once an innocent child at the same father's knee.'

'I may have spoken too plainly,' said Mr Buxton, 'but it was necessary to set the plain truth before you, for my son's sake. You will write the letter I ask?'

Her look was wandering and uncertain. Her attention was distracted by sounds which to him had no meaning; and her judgement she felt was wavering and disturbed.

'I cannot tell. Give me time to think; you will do that, I'm sure. Go now, and leave me alone. If it is right, God will give me strength to do it, and perhaps He will comfort me in my desolation. But I do not know—I cannot tell. I must have time to think. Go now, if you please, sir,' said she, imploringly.

'I am sure you will see it is a right thing I ask of you,' he persisted.

'Go now,' she repeated.

'Very well. In two hours, I will come back again; for your sake, time is precious. Even while we speak he may be arrested. At eleven, I will come back.'

He went away, leaving her sick and dizzy with the effort to be calm and collected enough to think. She had forgotten for the moment how near Edward was; and started when she saw the closet-door open, and his face put out.

'Is he gone? I thought he never would go. What a time you kept him, Maggie! I was so afraid, once, you might sit down to write the letter in this room; and then I knew he would stop and worry you with interruptions and advice, so that it would never be ended; and my back was almost broken. But you sent him off famously. Why, Maggie! Maggie!—you're not going to faint, surely!'

His sudden burst out of a whisper into a loud exclamation of surprise, made her rally; but she could not stand. She tried to smile, for he really looked frightened.

'I have been sitting up for many nights,—and now this sorrow!' Her smile died away into a wailing, feeble cry.

'Well, well! it's over now, you see. I was frightened enough myself this morning, I own; and then you were brave and kind. But I knew you could save me, all along.'

At this moment the door opened, and Mrs Browne came in.

'Why, Edward, dear! who would have thought of seeing you! This is good of you; what a pleasant surprise! I often said, you might come over for a day from Woodchester. What's the matter, Maggie, you look so fagged? She's losing all her beauty, is not she, Edward? Where's breakfast? I thought I should find all ready. What's the matter? Why don't you speak?' said she, growing anxious at their silence. Maggie left the explanation to Edward.

'Mother,' said he, 'I've been rather a naughty boy, and got into some trouble; but Maggie is going to help me out of it, like a good sister.'

'What is it?' said Mrs Browne, looking bewildered and uneasy.

'Oh—I took a little liberty with our friend Mr Buxton's name; and wrote it down to a receipt—that was all.'

Mrs Browne's face showed that the light came but slowly into her mind.

'But that's forgery—is not it?' asked she at length, in terror.

'People call it so,' said Edward; 'I call it borrowing from an old friend, who was always willing to lend.'

'Does he know?—is he angry?' asked Mrs Browne.

'Yes, he knows; and he blusters a deal. He was working himself up grandly at first. Maggie! I was getting rarely frightened, I can tell you.'

'Has he been here?' said Mrs Browne, in bewildered fright.

'Oh, yes! he and Maggie have been having a long talk, while I was hid in the china-closet. I would not go over that half-hour again for any money. However, he and Maggie came to terms, at last.'

'No, Edward, we did not!' said Maggie, in a low quivering voice.

'Very nearly. She's to give up her engagement, and then he will let me off.'

'Do you mean that Maggie is to give up her engagement to Mr Frank Buxton?' asked his mother.

'Yes. It would never have come to anything, one might see that. Old Buxton would have held out against it till dooms-day. And sooner or later, Frank would have grown weary. If Maggie had had any spirit, she might have worked him up to marry her before now; and then I should have been spared even this fright, for they would never have set the police after Mrs Frank Buxton's brother.'

'Why, dearest Edward, the police are not after you, are they?' said Mrs Browne, for the first time alive to the urgency of the case.

'I believe they are, though,' said Edward. 'But after what Mr Buxton promised this morning, it does not signify.'

'He did not promise anything,' said Maggie.

Edward turned sharply to her, and looked at her. Then he went and took hold of her wrists with no gentle grasp, and spoke to her through his set teeth.

'What do you mean, Maggie—what do you mean?' (giving her a

little shake). 'Do you mean that you'll stick to your lover, through thick and thin, and leave your brother to be transported? Speak, can't you?'

She looked up at him, and tried to speak, but no words came out of her dry throat. At last she made a strong effort.

'You must give me time to think. I will do what is right, by God's help.'

'As if it was not right,—and such cant,—to save your brother,' said he, throwing her hands away in a passionate manner.

'I must be alone,' said Maggie, rising, and trying to stand steadily in the reeling room. She heard her mother and Edward speaking, but their words gave her no meaning, and she went out. She was leaving the house by the kitchen door, when she remembered Nancy, left alone and helpless all through this long morning; and, ill as she could endure detention from the solitude she longed to seek, she patiently fulfilled her small duties, and sought out some breakfast for the poor old woman.

When she carried it upstairs, Nancy said:

'There's something up. You've trouble in your sweet face, my darling. Never mind telling me,—only don't sob so. I'll pray for you, bairn, and God will help you.'

'Thank you, Nancy. Do!' and she left the room.

CHAPTER IX

WHEN she opened the kitchen-door, there was the same small, mizzling rain that had obscured the light for weeks, and now it seemed to obscure hope. She clambered slowly (for indeed she was very feeble) up the Fell Lane, and threw herself under the leafless thorn, every small branch and twig of which was loaded with rain-drops. She did not see the well-beloved and familiar landscape, for her tears; and did not miss the hills in the distance that were hidden behind the rain-clouds, and sweeping showers.

Mrs Browne and Edward sat over the fire. He told her his own story: making the temptation, strong; the crime a mere trifling, venial error, which he had been led into, through his idea that he was to become Mr Buxton's agent.

'But if it is only that,' said Mrs Browne, 'surely Mr Buxton will not think of going to law with you?'

'It's not merely going to law that he will think of, but trying and transporting me. That Henry he has got for his agent is as sharp as a needle, and as hard as a nether mill-stone.* And the fellow has obtained such a hold over Mr Buxton, that he dare but do what he tells him. I can't imagine how he had so much free-will left as to come with his proposal to Maggie; unless, indeed, Henry knows of it,—or, what is most likely of all, has put him up to it. Between them, they have given that poor fool Crayston a pretty dose of it; and I should have come yet worse off, if it had not been for Maggie. Let me get clear this time, and I will keep to windward of the law* for the future.'

'If we sold the cottage we could repay it,' said Mrs Browne, meditating. 'Maggie and I could live on very little. But you see this property is held in trust for you two.'

'Nay mother! you must not talk of repaying it. Depend upon it he will be so glad to have Frank free from his engagement, that he won't think of asking for the money. And if Mr Henry says anything about it, we can tell him it's not half the damages they would have had to have given Maggie, if Frank had been extricated in any other way. I wish she would come back; I would prime her a little as to what to say. Keep a look out, mother, lest Mr Buxton return and find me here.'

'I wish Maggie would come in too,' said Mrs Browne. 'I'm afraid she'll catch cold this damp day, and then I shall have two to nurse. You think she'll give it up, don't you, Edward? If she does not, I'm afraid of harm coming to you. Had you not better keep out of the way?'

'It's fine talking. Where am I to go out of sight of the police, this wet day; without a shilling in the world, too? If you'll give me some money I'll be off fast enough, and make assurance doubly sure.* I'm not much afraid of Maggie. She's a little yea-nay thing, and I can always bend her round to what we want. She had better take care, too,' said he, with a desperate look on his face, 'for by G— I'll make her give up all thoughts of Frank, rather than be taken and tried. Why! it's my chance for all my life; and do you think I'll have it frustrated for a girl's whim!'

'I think it's rather hard upon her too,' pleaded his mother. 'She's very fond of him; and it would have been such a good match for her.'

'Pooh! she's not nineteen yet, and has plenty of time before her to pick up somebody else; while, don't you see, if I'm caught and transported, I'm done for for life. Besides, I've a notion Frank had already begun to be tired of the affair; it would have been broken off in a month or two, without her gaining anything by it.'

'Well, if you think so,' replied Mrs Browne. 'But I'm sorry for her. I always told her she was foolish to think so much about him; but I know she'll fret a deal if it's given up.'

'Oh! she'll soon comfort herself with thinking that she has saved me. I wish she'd come. It must be near eleven. I do wish she would come. Hark! is not that the kitchen-door?' said he, turning white, and betaking himself once more to the china-closet. He held it ajar, till he heard Maggie stepping softly and slowly across the floor. She opened the parlour-door; and stood looking in, with the strange imperceptive gaze of a sleep-walker. Then she roused herself, and saw that he was not there; so she came in a step or two, and sat down in her dripping cloak on a chair near the door.

Edward returned, bold, now there was no danger.

'Maggie!' said he, 'what have you fixed to say to Mr Buxton?'

She sighed deeply; and then lifted up her large innocent eyes to his face.

'I cannot give up Frank,' said she, in a low, quiet voice.

Mrs Browne threw up her hands and exclaimed in terror:

'Oh Edward, Edward! go away—I will give you all the plate I have; you can sell it—my darling, go!'

'Not till I have brought Maggie to reason,' said he, in a manner as quiet as her own; but with a subdued ferocity in it, which she saw, but which did not intimidate her.

He went up to her, and spoke below his breath.

'Maggie, we were children together,—we two,—brother and sister of one blood! Do you give me up to be put in prison,—in the hulks,*—among the basest of criminals,—I don't know where,—all for the sake of your own selfish happiness?'

She trembled very much; but did not speak, or cry, or make any noise.

'You were always selfish. You always thought of yourself. But this time I did think you would have shown how different you could be. But it's self—self—paramount above all.'

'Oh, Maggie! how can you be so hard-hearted and selfish?' echoed Mrs Browne, crying and sobbing.

'Mother!' said Maggie, 'I know that I think too often and too much of myself. But this time I thought only of Frank. He loves me; it would break his heart if I wrote as Mr Buxton wishes, cutting our lives asunder, and giving no reason for it.'

'He loves you so!' said Edward, tauntingly, 'A man's love break his heart! You've got some pretty notions! Who told you that he loved you so desperately? How do you know it?'

'Because I love him so,' said she, in a quiet earnest voice. 'I do not know of any other reason; but that is quite sufficient to me. I believe him when he says he loves me; and I have no right to cause him the infinite—the terrible pain, which my own heart tells me he would feel, if I did what Mr Buxton wishes me.'

Her manner was so simple and utterly truthful, that it was as quiet and fearless as a child's; her brother's fierce looks of anger had no power over her; and his blustering died away before her, into something of the frightened cowardliness he had shown in the morning. But Mrs Browne came up to Maggie; and took her hand between both of hers, which were trembling. 'Maggie, you can save Edward. I know I have not loved you as I should have done; but I will love and comfort you for ever, if you will but write as Mr Buxton says. Think! Perhaps Mr Frank may not take you at your word, but may come over and see you, and all may be right, and yet Edward may be saved. It is only writing this letter; you need not stick to it.'

'No!' said Edward. 'A signature, if you can prove compulsion, is not valid. We will all prove that you write this letter under compulsion; and if Frank loves you so desperately, he won't give you up without a trial to make you change your mind.'

'No!' said Maggie, firmly. 'If I write the letter I abide by it. I will not quibble with my conscience. Edward! I will not marry,—I will go, and live near you, and come to you whenever I may,—and give up my life to you if you are sent to prison;—my mother and I will go, if need be;—I do not know yet what I can do, or cannot do, for you, but all I can, I will;—but this one thing I cannot.'

'Then I'm off!' said Edward. 'On your death-bed may you remember this hour, and how you denied your only brother's request. May you ask my forgiveness with your dying breath, and may I be there to deny it you.'

'Wait a minute!' said Maggie, springing up, rapidly. 'Edward, don't curse me with such terrible words till all is done. Mother, I implore you to keep him here. Hide him,—do what you can to conceal him. I will have one more trial.' She snatched up her bonnet, and was gone, before they had time to think or speak to arrest her.

On she flew along the Combehurst road. As she went, the tears fell like rain down her face, and she talked to herself.

'He should not have said so. No! he should not have said so. We were the only two.' But still she pressed on, over the thick, wet, brown heather. She saw Mr Buxton coming; and she went still quicker. The rain had cleared off, and a yellow watery gleam of sunshine was struggling out. She stopped him, or he would have passed her unheeded; little expecting to meet her there.

'I wanted to see you,' said she, all at once resuming her composure, and almost assuming a dignified manner. 'You must not go down to our house; we have sorrow enough there. Come under these fir-trees, and let me speak to you.'

'I hope you have thought of what I said, and are willing to do what I asked you.'

'No!' said she. 'I have thought and thought. I did not think in a selfish spirit, though they say I did. I prayed first. I could not do that earnestly, and be selfish, I think. I cannot give up Frank. I know the disgrace; and if he, knowing all, thinks fit to give me up, I shall never say a word, but bow my head, and try and live out my appointed days quietly and cheerfully. But he is the judge, not you; nor have I any right to do what you ask me.' She stopped, because the agitation took away her breath.

He began in a cold manner: 'I am very sorry. The law must take its course. I would have saved my son from the pain of all this knowledge, and that which he will of course feel in the necessity of giving up his engagement. I would have refused to appear against your brother, shamefully ungrateful as he has been. Now, you cannot wonder that I act according to my agent's advice; and prosecute your brother as if he were a stranger.'

He turned to go away. He was so cold and determined that for a moment Maggie was timid. But she then laid her hand on his arm.

'Mr Buxton,' said she, 'you will not do what you threaten. I know you better. Think! My father was your old friend. That claim is, perhaps, done away with by Edward's conduct. But I do not believe you can forget it always. If you did fulfil the menace you uttered just now, there would come times as you grew older, and life grew fainter and fainter before you,—quiet times of thought, when you remembered the days of your youth, and the friends you then had and knew;—you would recollect that one of them had left an only son, who had done wrong; who had sinned; sinned against you in his weakness;—and you would think them—you could not help it—how you had forgotten mercy in justice; and, as justice required he should be treated as a felon, you threw him among felons; where every glimmering of goodness was darkened for ever. Edward is, after all, more weak than wicked;—but he will become wicked if you put him in prison, and have him transported. God is merciful,—we cannot tell or think how merciful. Oh, sir, I am so sure you will be merciful, and give my brother—my poor sinning brother—a chance, that I will tell you all. I will throw myself upon your pity. Edward is even now at home,—miserable and desperate;—my mother is too much stunned to understand all our wretchedness,—for very wretched we are in our shame.'

As she spoke, the wind arose and shivered in the wiry leaves of the fir-trees, and there was a moaning sound as of some Ariel imprisoned in the thick branches* that, tangled over-head, made a shelter for them. Either the noise, or Mr Buxton's fancy called up an echo to Maggie's voice—a pleading with her pleading—a sad tone of regret, distinct yet blending with her speech, and a falling, dying sound, as her voice died away in miserable suspense.

It might be that, formed as she was by Mrs Buxton's care and love, her accents and words were such as that lady, now at rest from all sorrow, would have used;—somehow, at any rate, the thought flashed into Mr Buxton's mind, that as Maggie spoke, his dead wife's voice was heard, imploring mercy in a clear distinct tone, though faint, as if separated from him by an infinite distance of space. At least, this is the account Mr. Buxton would have given of the manner in which the idea of his wife became present to him, and what she would have wished him to do a powerful motive in his conduct. Words of hers, long ago spoken, and merciful forgiving expressions, made use of in former days to soften him in some angry mood, were clearly remembered while Maggie spoke; and their influence was perceptible in the change of his tone, and the wavering of his manner henceforward.

'And yet you will not save Frank from being involved in your disgrace,' said he; but more as if weighing and deliberating on the case than he had ever spoken before.

'If Frank wishes it, I will quietly withdraw myself out of his sight for ever;—I give you my promise, before God, to do so. I shall not utter one word of entreaty or complaint. I will try not to wonder or feel surprise;—I will bless him in every action of his future life;— but think how different would be the disgrace he would voluntarily incur, to my poor mother's shame, when she wakens up to know what her child has done! Her very torpor about it now is more painful than words can tell.'

'What could Edward do?' asked Mr Buxton. 'Mr Henry won't hear of my passing over any frauds.'

'Oh, you relent!' said Maggie, taking his hand, and pressing it. 'What could he do? He could do the same, whatever it was, as you thought of his doing, if I had written that terrible letter.'

'And you'll be willing to give it up, if Frank wishes, when he knows all?' asked Mr Buxton.

She crossed her hands and drooped her head, but answered steadily:

'Whatever Frank wishes, when he knows all, I will gladly do. I will speak the truth. I do not believe that any shame surrounding me, and not in me, will alter Frank's love one tittle.'

'We shall see,' said Mr Buxton. 'But what I thought of Edward's doing, in case—Well, never mind!' (seeing how she shrunk back from all mention of the letter he had asked her to write)—'was to go to America, out of the way. Then Mr Henry would think he had escaped, and need never be told of my connivance. I think he would throw up the agency, if he were; and he's a very clever man. If Ned is in England, Mr Henry will ferret him out. And, besides, this affair is so blown, I don't think he could return to his profession. What do you say to this, Maggie?'

'I will tell my mother. I must ask her. To me it seems most desirable. Only, I fear he is very ill; and it seems lonely; but never mind! We ought to be thankful to you for ever. I cannot tell you how I hope and trust he will live to show you what your goodness has made him.'

'But you must lose no time. If Mr Henry traces him, I can't answer for myself. I shall have no good reason to give, as I should have had, if I could have told him that Frank and you were to be as strangers to each other. And even then I should have been afraid, he is such a determined fellow; but uncommonly clever. Stay!' said he, yielding to a sudden and inexplicable desire to see Edward, and discover if his criminality had in any way changed his outward appearance. 'I'll go with you. I can hasten things. If Edward goes, he must be off, as soon as possible, to Liverpool, and leave no trace. The next packet* sails the day after to-morrow. I noted it down from the *Times*.'

Maggie and he sped along the road. He spoke his thoughts aloud:

'I wonder if he will be grateful to me for this. Not that I ever mean to look for gratitude again. I mean to try, not to care for anybody but Frank. "Govern men by outward force," says Mr Henry. He is an uncommonly clever man, and he says, the longer he lives, the more he is convinced of the badness of men. He always looks for it now, even in those who are the best, apparently.'

Maggie was too anxious to answer, or even to attend to him. At the top of the slope she asked him to wait while she ran down, and told the result of her conversation with him. Her mother was alone, looking white and sick. She told her that Edward had gone into the hay-loft, above the old, disused shippen.*

Maggie related the substance of her interview with Mr Buxton, and his wish that Edward should go to America.

'To America!' said Mrs Browne. 'Why that's as far as Botany Bay.* It's just like transporting him. I thought you'd done something for us, you looked so glad.'

'Dearest mother, it *is* something. He is not to be subjected to imprisonment nor trial. I must go and tell him, only I must beckon to Mr Buxton first. But when he comes, do show him how thankful we are for his mercy to Edward.'

Mrs Browne's murmurings, whatever was their meaning, were lost upon Maggie. She ran through the court, and up the slope, with the lightness of a fawn; for though she was tired in body to an excess she had never been before in her life, the opening beam of hope in the dark sky made her spirit conquer her flesh for the time.

She did not stop to speak, but turned again as soon as she had signed to Mr Buxton to follow her. She left the house-door open for his entrance, and passed out again through the kitchen into the space behind, which was partly an unenclosed yard, and partly rocky common. She ran across the little green to the shippen, and mounted the ladder into the dimly-lighted loft. Up in a dark corner Edward stood, with an old rake in his hand.

'I thought it was you, Maggie!' said he, heaving a deep breath of relief. 'What have you done? Have you agreed to write the letter? You've done something for me, I see by your looks.'

'Yes! I have told Mr Buxton all. He is waiting for you in the parlour. Oh! I know he could not be so hard!' She was out of breath.

'I don't understand you!' said he. 'You've never been such a fool as to go and tell him where I am?'

'Yes, I have. I felt I might trust him. He has promised not to prosecute you. The worst is, he says you must go to America. But come down, Ned, and speak to him. You owe him thanks, and he wants to see you.'

'I can't go through a scene. I'm not up to it. Besides, are you sure he is not entrapping me to the police? If I had a farthing of money I would not trust him, but be off to the moors.'

'Oh, Edward! How do you think he would do anything so treacherous and mean! I beg you not to lose time in distrust. He says himself, if Mr Henry comes before you are off, he does not know what will be the consequence. The packet sails for America in two days. It is sad for you to have to go. Perhaps even yet he may think of something better, though I don't know how we can ask or expect it.'

'I don't want anything better,' replied he, 'than that I should have money enough to carry me to America. I'm in more scrapes than this (though none so bad) in England; and in America there's many an opening to fortune.'

He followed her down the steps while he spoke. Once in the yellow light of the watery day, she was struck by his ghastly look. Sharp lines of suspicion and cunning seemed to have been stamped upon his face, making it look older by many years than his age warranted. His jaunty evening dress, all weather-stained and dirty, added to his forlorn and disreputable appearance; but most of all—deepest of all—was the impression she received that he was not long for this world; and Oh! how unfit for the next! Still if time was given—if he were placed far away from temptation—she thought that her father's son might yet repent, and be saved. She took his hand, for he was hanging back as they came near the parlour-door, and led him in. She looked like some guardian angel, with her face that beamed out trust, and hope, and thankfulness. He, on the contrary, hung his head in angry, awkward shame; and half wished he had trusted to his own wits, and tried to evade the police, rather than have been forced into this interview.

His mother came to him; for she loved him all the more fondly, now he seemed degraded and friendless. She could not, or would not, comprehend the extent of his guilt; and had upbraided Mr Buxton to the top of her bent for thinking of sending him away to America. There was a silence when he came in which was insupportable to him. He looked up with clouded eyes, that dared not meet Mr Buxton's.

'I am here, sir, to learn what you wish me to do. Maggie says I am to go to America: if that is where you want to send me, I'm ready.'

Mr Buxton wished himself away as heartily as Edward. Mrs Browne's upbraidings, just when he felt that he had done a kind action, and yielded, against his judgement, to Maggie's entreaties, had made him think himself very ill used. And now here was Edward speaking in a sullen, savage kind of way, instead of showing any gratitude. The idea of Mr Henry's stern displeasure loomed in the background.

'Yes!' said he, 'I'm glad to find you come into the idea of going to America. It's the only place for you. The sooner you can go, and the better.'

'I can't go without money,' said Edward, doggedly. 'If I had had money, I need not have come here.'

'Oh, Ned! would you have gone without seeing me?' said Mrs Browne, bursting into tears. 'Mr Buxton, I cannot let him go to America. Look how ill he is. He'll die if you send him there.'

'Mother, don't give way so,' said Edward, kindly, taking her hand. 'I'm not ill, at least not to signify. Mr Buxton is right:

America is the only place for me. To tell the truth, even if Mr Buxton is good enough' (he said this as if unwilling to express any word of thankfulness) 'not to prosecute me, there are others who may—and will. I'm safer out of the country. Give me money enough to get to Liverpool and pay my passage, and I'll be off this minute.'

'You shall not,' said Mrs Browne, holding him tightly. 'You told me this morning you were led into temptation, and went wrong because you had no comfortable home, nor any one to care for you, and make you happy. It will be worse in America. You'll get wrong again, and be away from all who can help you. Or you'll die all by yourself, in some back-wood or other. Maggie! you might speak and help me—how can you stand so still, and let him go to America without a word!'

Maggie looked up bright and steadfast, as if she saw something beyond the material present. Here was the opportunity for self-sacrifice of which Mrs Buxton had spoken to her in her childish days—the time which comes to all, but comes unheeded and unseen to those whose eyes are not trained to watching.

'Mother! could you do without me for a time? If you could, and it would make you easier, and help Edward to ——' The word on her lips died away; for it seemed to imply a reproach on one who stood in his shame among them all.

'You would go!' said Mrs Browne, catching at the unfinished sentence. 'Oh! Maggie, that's the best thing you've ever said or done since you were born. Edward, would not you like to have Maggie with you?'

'Yes,' said he, 'well enough. It would be far better for me than going all alone; though I dare say I could make my way pretty well after a time. If she went, she might stay till I felt settled, and had made some friends, and then she could come back.'

Mr Buxton was astonished at first by this proposal of Maggie's. He could not all at once understand the difference between what she now offered to do, and what he had urged upon her only this very morning. But as he thought about it, he perceived that what was her own she was willing to sacrifice; but that Frank's heart once given into her faithful keeping, she was answerable for it to him and to God. This light came down upon him slowly; but when he understood, he admired with almost a wondering admiration. That little timid girl brave enough to cross the ocean and go to a foreign land, if she could only help to save her brother!

'I'm sure, Maggie,' said he, turning towards her, 'you are a good, thoughtful little creature. It may be the saving of Edward—I believe it will. I think God will bless you for being so devoted.'

'The expense will be doubled,' said Edward.

'My dear boy! never mind the money. I can get it advanced upon this cottage.'

'As for that, I'll advance it,' said Mr Buxton.

'Could we not,' said Maggie, hesitating from her want of knowledge, 'make over the furniture, papa's books, and what little plate we have, to Mr Buxton—something like pawning them—if he would advance the requisite money? He, strange as it may seem, is the only person you can ask in this great strait.'

And so it was arranged, after some demur on Mr Buxton's part. But Maggie kept steadily to her point as soon as she found that it was attainable; and Mrs Browne was equally inflexible, though from a different feeling. She regarded Mr Buxton as the cause of her son's banishment, and refused to accept of any favour from him. If there had been time, indeed, she would have preferred obtaining the money in the same manner from any one else. Edward brightened up a little when he heard the sum could be procured; he was almost indifferent how; and, strangely callous, as Maggie thought, he even proposed to draw up a legal form of assignment. Mr Buxton only thought of hurrying on the departure; but he could not refrain from expressing his approval and admiration of Maggie whenever he came near her. Before he went, he called her aside.

'My dear, I'm not sure if Frank can do better than marry you, after all. Mind! I've not given it as much thought as I should like. But if you come back as we plan, next autumn, and he is steady to you till then,—and Edward is going on well (if he can but keep good, he'll do, for he is very sharp—yon is a knowing paper he drew up),—why, I'll think about it. Only let Frank see a bit of the world first. I'd rather you did not tell him I've any thoughts of coming round, that he may have a fair trial; and I'll keep it from Erminia if I can, or she will let it all out to him. I shall see you to-morrow at the coach. God bless you, my girl, and keep you on the great wide sea.' He was absolutely in tears when he went away—tears of admiring regret over Maggie.

CHAPTER X

THE more Maggie thought, the more she felt sure that the impulse on which she had acted in proposing to go with her brother was right. She feared there was little hope for his character, whatever there might be for his worldly fortune, if he were thrown, in the condition of mind in which he was now, among the set of adventurous men who are continually going over to America in search of an El Dorado* to be discovered by their wits. She knew she had but little influence over him at present; but she would not doubt or waver in her hope that patience and love might work him right at last. She meant to get some employment—in teaching—in needlework—in a shop—no matter how humble—and be no burden to him, and make him a happy home, from which he should feel no wish to wander. Her chief anxiety was about her mother. She did not dwell more than she could help on her long absence from Frank; it was too sad, and yet too necessary. She meant to write and tell him all about herself and Edward. The only thing which she would keep for some happy future, should be the possible revelation of the proposal which Mr Buxton had made, that she should give up her engagement as a condition of his not prosecuting Edward.

There was much sorrowful bustle in the moorland cottage that day. Erminia brought up a portion of the money Mr Buxton was to advance, with an entreaty that Edward would not show himself out of his home; and an account of a letter from Mr Henry, stating that the Woodchester police believed him to be in London, and that search was being made for him there.

Erminia looked very grave and pale. She gave her message to Mrs Browne, speaking little beyond what was absolutely necessary. Then she took Maggie aside, and suddenly burst into tears.

'Maggie, darling—what is this going to America? You've always and always been sacrificing yourself to your family, and now you're setting off, nobody knows where, in some vain hope of reforming Edward. I wish he was not your brother, that I might speak of him as I should like.'

'He has been doing what is very wrong,' said Maggie. 'But you—none of you—know his good points,—nor how he has been exposed to all sorts of bad influences, I am sure; and never had the advantage of a father's training and friendship, which are so inestimable to a son. Oh! Minnie, when I remember how we two used to kneel down in the evenings at my father's knee, and say our prayers; and then listen in awe-struck silence to his earnest blessing, which grew more like a prayer for us as his life waned away; I would do anything for Edward rather than that wrestling agony of supplication should have been in vain. I think of him as the little innocent boy, whose arm was round me as if to support me in the Awful Presence, whose true name of Love we had not learned. Minnie! he has had no proper training—no training, I mean, to enable him to resist temptation; and he has been thrown into it without warning or advice. Now he knows what it is; and I must try, though I am but an unknowing girl, to warn and to strengthen him. Don't weaken my faith. Who can do right if we lose faith in them?'

'And Frank!' said Erminia, after a pause. 'Poor Frank!'

'Dear Frank!' replied Maggie, looking up, and trying to smile; but, in spite of herself, her eyes filled with tears. 'If I could have asked him, I know he would approve of what I am going to do. He would feel it to be right that I should make every effort—I don't mean,' said she, as the tears would fall down her cheeks in spite of her quivering effort at a smile, 'that I should not have liked to have seen him. But it is no use talking of what one would have liked. I am writing a long letter to him at every pause of leisure.'

'And I'm keeping you all this time,' said Erminia, getting up, yet loth to go. 'When do you intend to come back? Let us feel there is a fixed time. America! Why, it's thousands of miles away. Oh, Maggie! Maggie!'

'I shall come back the next autumn, I trust,' said Maggie, comforting her friend with many a soft caress. 'Edward will be settled then, I hope. You were longer in France, Minnie. Frank was longer away, that time he wintered in Italy with Mr Monro.'

Erminia went slowly to the door. Then she turned, right facing Maggie.

'Maggie! tell the truth. Has my uncle been urging you to go? Because if he has, don't trust him; it is only to break off your engagement.'

'No, he has not, indeed. It was my own thought at first. Then in a moment I saw the relief it was to my mother—my poor mother!

Erminia, the thought of her grief at Edward's absence is the trial; for my sake, you will come often and often, and comfort her in every way you can.'

'Yes! that I will; tell me everything I can do for you.' Kissing each other, with long lingering delay they parted.

Nancy would be informed of the cause of the commotion in the house; and when she had in some degree ascertained its nature, she wasted no time in asking further questions, but quietly got up and dressed herself; and appeared among them, weak and trembling indeed, but so calm and thoughtful, that her presence was an infinite help to Maggie.

When day closed in, Edward stole down to the house once more. He was haggard enough to have been in anxiety and concealment for a month. But when his body was refreshed, his spirits rose in a way inconceivable to Maggie. The Spaniards who went out with Pizarro* were not lured on by more fantastic notions of the wealth to be acquired in the New World than he was. He dwelt on these visions in so brisk and vivid a manner, that he even made his mother cease her weary weeping (which had lasted the livelong day, despite all Maggie's efforts), to look up and listen to him.

'I'll answer for it,' said he: 'before long I'll be an American judge, with miles of cotton plantations.'

'But in America,' sighed out his mother.

'Never mind, mother!' said he, with a tenderness which made Maggie's heart glad. 'If you won't come over to America to me, why I'll sell them all, and come back to live in England. People will forget the scrapes that the rich American got into in his youth.'

'You can pay back Mr Buxton then,' said his mother.

'Oh, yes—of course,' replied he, as if falling into a new and trivial idea.

Thus the evening whiled away. The mother and son sat, hand in hand, before the little glinting blazing parlour fire, with the unlighted candles on the table behind. Maggie, busy in preparations, passed softly in and out. And when all was done that could be done before going to Liverpool, where she hoped to have two days to prepare their outfit more completely, she stole back to her mother's side. But her thoughts would wander off to Frank, 'working his way south through all the hunting-counties,' as he had written her word. If she had not urged his absence, he would have been here for her to see his noble face once more; but then, perhaps, she might never have had the strength to go.

Late, late in the night, they separated. Maggie could not rest, and stole into her mother's room. Mrs Browne had cried herself to sleep, like a child. Maggie stood and looked at her face, and then knelt down by the bed and prayed. When she arose, she saw that her mother was awake, and had been looking at her.

'Maggie dear! you're a good girl, and I think God will hear your prayer whatever it was for. I cannot tell you what a relief it is to me to think you're going with him. It would have broken my heart else. If I've sometimes not been as kind as I might have been, I ask your forgiveness, now, my dear; and I bless you and thank you for going out with him; for I'm sure he's not well and strong, and will need somebody to take care of him. And you shan't lose with Mr Frank, for as sure as I see him I'll tell him what a good daughter and sister you've been; and I shall say, for all he is so rich, I think he may look long before he finds a wife for him like our Maggie. I do wish Ned had got that new great coat he says he left behind him at Woodchester.'

Her mind reverted to her darling son; but Maggie took her short slumber by her mother's side, with her mother's arms around her; and awoke and felt that her sleep had been blessed. At the coach-office the next morning they met Mr Buxton, all ready as if for a journey, but glancing about him as if in fear of some coming enemy.

'I'm going with you to Liverpool,' said he. 'Don't make any ado about it, please. I shall like to see you off; and I may be of some use to you, and Erminia begged it of me; and, besides, it will keep me out of Mr Henry's way for a little time, and I'm afraid he will find it all out, and think me very weak; but you see he made me too hard upon Crayston, so I may take it out in a little soft-heartedness towards the son of an old friend.'

Just at this moment Erminia came running through the white morning mist all glowing with haste.

'Maggie,' said she, 'I'm come to take care of your mother. My uncle says she and Nancy must come to us for a long, long visit. Or if she would rather go home, I'll go with her till she feels able to come to us, and do anything I can think of for her. I will try to be a daughter till you come back, Maggie; only don't be long, or Frank and I shall break our hearts.'

Maggie waited till her mother had ended her long clasping embrace of Edward, who was subdued enough this morning; and then, with something like Esau's craving for a blessing,* she came to bid her mother good-bye, and received the warm caress she had longed for for years. In another moment the coach was away; and before half an hour had elapsed, Combehurst church-spire had been lost in a turn of the road.

Edward and Mr Buxton did not speak to each other, and Maggie was nearly silent. They reached Liverpool in the afternoon; and Mr Buxton, who had been there once or twice before, took them directly to some quiet hotel. He was far more anxious that Edward should not expose himself to any chance of recognition, than Edward himself. He went down to the Docks to secure berths in the vessel about to sail the next day, and on his return he took Maggie out to make the requisite purchases.

'Did you pay for us, sir?' said Maggie, anxious to ascertain the amount of money she had left, after defraying the passage.

'Yes,' replied he, rather confused. 'Erminia begged me not to tell you about it, but I can't manage a secret well. You see she did not like the idea of your going as steerage-passengers as you meant to do; and she desired me to take you cabin places* for her. It is no doing of mine, my dear. I did not think of it; but now I have seen how crowded the steerage is, I am very glad Erminia had so much thought. Edward might have roughed it well enough there, but it would never have done for you.'

'It was very kind of Erminia,' said Maggie, touched at this consideration of her friend; 'but—'

'Now don't "but" about it,' interrupted he. 'Erminia is very rich, and has more money than she knows what to do with. I'm only vexed I did not think of it myself. For, Maggie, though I may have my own ways of thinking on some points, I can't be blind to your goodness.'

All evening Mr Buxton was busy, and busy on their behalf. Even Edward, when he saw the attention that was being paid to his physical comfort, felt a kind of penitence; and, after choking once or twice in the attempt, conquered his pride (such I call it for want of a better word) so far as to express some regret for his past conduct, and some gratitude for Mr Buxton's present kindness. He did it awkwardly enough, but it pleased Mr Buxton.

'Well—well—that's all very right,' said he, reddening from his own uncomfortableness of feeling. 'Now don't say any more about it, but do your best in America; don't let me feel I've been a fool in letting you off. I know Mr Henry will think me so. And, above all, take care of Maggie. Mind what she says, and you're sure to go right.'

He asked them to go on board early the next day, as he had promised Erminia to see them there, and yet wished to return as soon as he could. It was evident that he hoped, by making his absence as short as possible, to prevent Mr Henry's ever knowing that he had left home, or in any way connived at Edward's escape.

So, although the vessel was not to sail till the afternoon's tide, they left the hotel soon after breakfast, and went to the *Anna-Maria*. They were among the first passengers on board. Mr Buxton took Maggie down to her cabin. She then saw the reason of his business the evening before. Every store that could be provided was there. A number of books lay on the little table—books just suited to Maggie's taste. 'There!' said he, rubbing his hands. 'Don't thank me. It's all Erminia's doing. She gave me the list of books. I've not got all; but I think they'll be enough. Just write me one line, Maggie, to say I've done my best.'

Maggie wrote with tears in her eyes—tears of love towards the generous Erminia. A few minutes more and Mr Buxton was gone. Maggie watched him as long as she could see him; and as his portly figure disappeared among the crowd on the pier, her heart sank within her.

Edward's, on the contrary, rose at his absence. The only one, cognisant of his shame and ill-doing, was gone. A new life lay before him, the opening of which was made agreeable to him, by the position in which he found himself placed, as a cabin-passenger; with many comforts provided for him; for although Maggie's wants had been the principal object of Mr Buxton's attention, Edward was not forgotten.

He was soon among the sailors, talking away in a rather consequential manner. He grew acquainted with the remainder of the cabin-passengers, at least those who arrived before the final bustle began; and kept bringing his sister such little pieces of news as he could collect.

'Maggie, they say we are likely to have a good start, and a fine moon-light night.' Away again he went.

'I say, Maggie, there's an uncommonly pretty girl come on board, with those old people in black. Gone down into the cabin, now; I wish you would scrape up an acquaintance with her, and give me a chance.'

CHAPTER XI

MAGGIE sat on deck, wrapped in her duffel-cloak; the old familiar cloak, which had been her wrap in many a happy walk in the haunts near her moorland home. The weather was not cold for the time of year, but still it was chilly to any one that was stationary. But she wanted to look her last on the shoals of English people, who crowded backwards and forwards, like ants, on the pier. Happy people! who might stay among their loved ones. The mocking daemons gathered round her, as they gather round all who sacrifice self, tempting. A crowd of suggestive doubts pressed upon her. 'Was it really necessary that she should go with Edward? Could she do him any real good? Would he be in any way influenced by her?' Then the daemon tried another description of doubt. 'Had it ever been her duty to go? She was leaving her mother alone. She was giving Frank much present sorrow. It was not even yet too late!' She could not endure longer; and replied to her own tempting heart.

'I was right to hope for Edward; I am right to give him the chance of steadiness which my presence will give. I am doing what my mother earnestly wished me to do; and what to the last she felt relieved by my doing. I know Frank will feel sorrow, because I myself have such an aching heart; but if I had asked him whether I was not right in going, he would have been too truthful not to have said yes. I have tried to do right, and though I may fail, and evil may seem to arise rather than good out of my endeavour, yet still I will submit to my failure, and try and say "God's will be done!"* If only I might have seen Frank once more, and told him all face to face!'

To do away with such thoughts, she determined no longer to sit gazing, and tempted by the shore; and, giving one look to the land which contained her lover, she went down below, and busied herself, even through her blinding tears, in trying to arrange her own cabin, and Edward's. She heard boat after boat arrive, loaded with passengers. She learnt from Edward, who came down to tell her the fact, that there were upwards of two hundred steerage passengers. She felt the tremulous shake which announced that the ship was loosed from her moorings, and being tugged down the river. She wrapped herself up once more, and came on deck, and sat down among the many who were looking their last look at England. The early winter evening was darkening in, and shutting out the Welsh coast, the hills of which were like the hills of home. She was thankful when she became too ill to think and remember.

Exhausted and still, she did not know whether she was sleeping or waking; or whether she had slept, since she had thrown herself down on her cot; when suddenly, there was a great rush, and then Edward stood like lightning by her, pulling her up by the arm.

'The ship is on fire,—to the deck, Maggie! Fire! Fire!' he shouted, like a maniac, while he dragged her up the stairs—as if the cry of Fire could summon human aid on the great deep. And the cry was echoed up to heaven by all that crowd, in an accent of despair.

They stood huddled together, dressed and undressed; now in red lurid light, showing ghastly faces of terror,—now in white wreaths of smoke,—as far away from the steerage as they could press; for there, up from the hold, rose columns of smoke, and now and then a fierce blaze leaped out, exulting—higher and higher every time; while from each crevice on that part of the deck, issued harbingers of the terrible destruction that awaited them.

The sailors were lowering the boats; and above them stood the captain, as calm as if he were on his own hearth at home—his home where he never more should be. His voice was low—was lower; but as clear as a bell in its distinctness; as wise in its directions as collected thought could make it. Some of the steerage passengers were helping; but more were dumb and motionless with affright. In that dead silence was heard a low wail of sorrow, as of numbers whose power was crushed out of them by that awful terror. Edward still held his clutch of Margaret's arm.

'Be ready!' said he, in a fierce whisper.

The fire sprung up along the main-mast, and did not sink or disappear again. They knew, then, that all the mad efforts made by some few below to extinguish it were in vain; and then went up the prayers of hundreds, in mortal agony of fear:

'Lord! have mercy upon us!'

Not in quiet calm of village church did ever such a pitiful cry go up to heaven; it was like one voice—like the day of judgement in the presence of the Lord.

And after that there was no more silence; but a confusion of terrible farewells, and wild cries of affright, and purposeless rushes hither and thither.

The boats were down, rocking on the sea. The captain spoke:

'Put the children in first; they are the most helpless.'

One or two stout sailors stood in the boats to receive them. Edward drew nearer and nearer to the gangway, pulling Maggie with him. She was almost pressed to death, and stifled. Close in her ear, she heard a woman praying to herself. She, poor creature, knew of no presence but God's in that awful hour, and spoke in a low voice to Him.

'My heart's darlings are taken away from me. Faith! faith! Oh, my great God! I will die in peace, if Thou wilt but grant me faith in this terrible hour, to feel that Thou wilt take care of my poor orphans. Hush! dearest Billy,' she cried out shrill to a little fellow in the boat, waiting for his mother; and the change in her voice, from despair to a kind of cheerfulness, showed what a mother's love can do. 'Mother will come soon. Hide his face, Anne, and wrap your shawl tight round him.' And then her voice sank down again, in the same low, wild prayer for faith. Maggie could not turn to see her face, but took the hand which hung near her. The woman clutched at it with the grasp of a vice; but went on praying, as if unconscious. Just then the crowd gave way a little. The captain had said, that the women were to go next; but they were too frenzied to obey his directions, and now pressed backward and forward. The sailors, with mute, stern obedience, strove to follow out the captain's directions. Edward pulled Maggie, and she kept her hold on the mother. The mate, at the head of the gangway, pushed him back.

'Only women are to go!'

'There are men there.'

'Three, to manage the boat.'

'Come on, Maggie! while there's room for us,' said he, unheeding. But Maggie drew back, and put the mother's hand into the mate's. 'Save her first!' said she. The woman did not know of anything, but that her children were there; it was only in after days, and quiet hours, that she remembered the young creature who pushed her forwards to join her fatherless children, and, by losing her place in the crowd, was jostled—where, she did not know; but dreamed until her dying day. Edward pressed on, unaware that Maggie was not close behind him. He was deaf to reproaches; and, heedless of the hand stretched out to hold him back, sprang towards the boat. The men there pushed her off—full, and more than full, as she was; and overboard he fell into the sullen heaving waters.

His last shout had been on Maggie's name—a name she never thought to hear again on earth, as she was pressed back, sick and suffocating. But suddenly a voice rang out above all confused voices and moaning hungry waves, and above the roaring fire.

'Maggie, Maggie! My Maggie!'

Out of the steerage side of the crowd a tall figure issued forth, begrimed with smoke. She could not see, but she knew. As a tame bird flutters to the human breast of its protector when affrighted by some mortal foe, so Maggie fluttered and cowered into his arms. And, for a moment, there was no more terror or thought of danger in the hearts of those twain, but only infinite and absolute peace. She had no wonder how he came there: it was enough that he was there. He first thought of the destruction that was present with them. He was as calm and composed as if they sat beneath the thorn-tree on the still moorlands, far away. He took her, without a word, to the end of the quarter-deck. He lashed her to a piece of spar. She never spoke.

'Maggie,' he said, 'my only chance is to throw you overboard. This spar will keep you floating. At first, you will go down—deep, deep down. Keep your mouth and eyes shut. I shall be there when you come up. By God's help, I will struggle bravely for you.'

She looked up; and by the flashing light he could see a trusting, loving smile upon her face. And he smiled back at her; a grave, beautiful look, fit to wear on his face in heaven. He helped her to the side of the vessel, away from the falling burning pieces of mast. Then for a moment he paused.

'If—Maggie, I may be throwing you in to death.' He put his hand before his eyes. The strong man lost courage. Then she spoke.

'I am not afraid; God is with us, whether we live or die!' She looked as quiet and happy as a child on its mother's breast; and so before he lost heart again, he heaved her up, and threw her as far as he could over into the glaring, dizzying water; and straight leaped after her. She came up with an involuntary look of terror on her face; but when she saw him by the red glare of the burning ship, close by her side, she shut her eyes, and looked as if peacefully going to sleep. He swam, guiding the spar.

'I think we are near Llandudno. I know we have passed the little Ormes' head.'* That was all he said; but she did not speak.

He swam out of the heat and fierce blaze of light into the quiet dark waters; and then into the moon's path. It might be half an hour before he got into that silver stream. When the beams fell down upon them, he looked at Maggie. Her head rested on the spar, quite still. He could not bear it. 'Maggie,—dear heart! speak!'

With a great effort she was called back from the borders of death by that voice, and opened her filmy eyes, which looked abroad as if she could see nothing nearer than the gleaming lights of Heaven. She let the lids fall softly again. He was as if alone in the wide world with God.

'A quarter of an hour more and all is over,' thought he. 'The people at Llandudno must see our burning ship, and will come out in their boats.' He kept in the line of light, although it did not lead him direct to the shore, in order that they might be seen. He swam with desperation. One moment he thought he had heard her last gasp rattle through the rush of the waters; and all strength was gone, and he lay on the waves as if he himself must die, and go with her spirit straight through that purple lift to heaven; the next he heard the splash of oars, and raised himself and cried aloud. The boatmen took them in,—and examined her by the lantern—and spoke in Welsh,—and shook their heads. Frank threw himself on his knees, and prayed them to take her to land. They did not know his words, but they understood his prayer. He kissed her lips,—he chafed her hands,—he wrung the water out of her hair,—he held her feet against his warm breast.

'She is not dead,' he kept saying to the men, as he saw their sorrowful pitying looks.

The kind people at Llandudno had made ready their own humble beds, with every appliance of comfort they could think of, as soon as they understood the nature of the calamity which had befallen the ship on their coasts. Frank walked, dripping, bareheaded, by the body of his Margaret, which was borne by some men along the rocky sloping shore.

'She is not dead!' he said. He stopped at the first house they came to. It belonged to a kind-hearted woman. They laid Maggie in her bed, and got the village doctor to come and see her.

'There is life still,' said he gravely.

'I knew it,' said Frank. But it felled him to the ground. He sank first in prayer, and then in insensibility. The doctor did everything. All that night long he passed to and fro from house to house; for several had swum to Llandudno. Others, it was thought, had gone to Abergele.*

In the morning Frank was recovered enough to write to his father, by Maggie's bedside. He sent the letter off to Conway* by a little bright-looking Welsh boy. Late in the afternoon she awoke.

In a moment or two she looked eagerly round her, as if gathering in her breath; and then she covered her head and sobbed.

'Where is Edward?' asked she.

'We do not know,' said Frank, gravely. 'I have been round the village, and seen every survivor here; he is not among them, but he may be at some other place along the coast.'

She was silent, reading in his eyes his fears,—his belief.

At last she asked again.

'I cannot understand it. My head is not clear. There are such rushing noises in it. How came you there?' She shuddered involuntarily as she recalled the terrible where.

For an instant he dreaded, for her sake, to recall the circumstances of the night before; but then he understood how her mind would dwell upon them until she was satisfied.

'You remember writing to me, love, telling me all. I got your letter—I don't know how long ago—yesterday, I think. Yes! in the evening. You could not think, Maggie, I would let you go alone to America. I won't speak against Edward, poor fellow! but we must both allow that he was not the person to watch over you, as such a treasure should be watched over. I thought I would go with you. I hardly know if I meant to make myself known to you all at once, for I had no wish to have much to do with your brother. I see now that it was selfish in me. Well! there was nothing to be done, after receiving your letter, but to set off for Liverpool straight, and join you. And after that decision was made, my spirits rose, for the old talks about Canada and Australia came to my mind, and this seemed like a realization of them. Besides, Maggie, I suspected—I even suspect now—that my father had something to do with your going with Edward?'

'Indeed, Frank!' said she earnestly, 'you are mistaken; I cannot tell you all now; but he was so good and kind at last. He never urged me to go; though, I believe, he did tell me it would be the saving of Edward.'

'Don't agitate yourself, love. I trust there will be time enough, some happy day at home, to tell me all. And till then, I will believe that my father did not in any way suggest this voyage. But you'll allow that, after all that has passed, it was not unnatural in me to suppose so. I only told Middleton I was obliged to leave him by the next train. It was not till I was fairly off, that I began to reckon up what money I had with me. I doubt even if I was sorry to find it was so little. I should have to put forth my energies and fight my way, as I had often wanted to do. I remember, I thought how happy you and I would be, striving together as poor people "in that new world which is the old."* Then you had told me you were going in the steerage; and that was all suitable to my desires for myself.'

'It was Erminia's kindness that prevented our going there. She asked your father to take us cabin places unknown to me.'

'Did she? Dear Erminia! it is just like her. I could almost laugh to remember the eagerness with which I doffed my signs of wealth, and put on those of poverty. I sold my watch when I got into Liverpool—yesterday, I believe—but it seems like months ago. And I rigged myself out at a slop-shop* with suitable clothes for a steerage passenger. Maggie! you never told me the name of the vessel you were going to sail in!'

'I did not know it till I got to Liverpool. All Mr Buxton said was, that some ship sailed on the 15th.'

'I concluded it must be the Anna-Maria (poor Anna-Maria!) and I had no time to lose. She had just heaved her anchor when I came on board. Don't you recollect a boat hailing her at the last moment? There were three of us in her.'

'No! I was below in my cabin—trying not to think,' said she, colouring a little.

'Well! as soon as I got on board it began to grow dark, or, perhaps, it was the fog on the river; at any rate, instead of being able to single out your figure at once, Maggie—it is one among a thousand—I had to go peering into every woman's face; and many were below. I went between decks, and by-and-by I was afraid I had mistaken the vessel; I sat down; I had no spirit to stand; and every time the door opened I roused up and looked,—but you never came. I was thinking what to do; whether to be put on shore in Ireland, or to go on to New York, and wait for you there;—it was the worst time of all, for I had nothing to do; and the suspense was horrible. I might have known,' said he, smiling, 'my little Emperor of Russia was not one to be a steerage passenger.'

But Maggie was too much shaken to smile; and the thought of Edward lay heavy upon her mind.

'Then the fire broke out; how, or why, I suppose, will never be ascertained. It was at our end of the vessel. I thanked God, then, that you were not there. The second mate wanted some one to go down with him to bring up the gunpowder, and throw it over-board. I had nothing to do, and I went. We wrapped it up in wet sails, but it was a ticklish piece of work, and took time. When we had got it overboard, the flames were gathering far and wide. I don't remember what I did until I heard Edward's voice speaking your name.'

It was decided that the next morning they should set off home-wards, striving on their way to obtain tidings of Edward. Frank would have given his only valuable (his mother's diamond-guard, which he wore constantly), as a pledge for some advance of money; but the kind Welsh people would not have it. They had not much spare cash, but what they had they readily lent to the survivors of the Anna-Maria. Dressed in the homely country garb of the people, Frank and Maggie set off in their car.* It was a clear, frosty morning; the first that winter. The road soon lay high up on the cliffs along the coast. They looked down on the sea rocking below. At every village they stopped, and Frank inquired, and made the driver inquire in Welsh; but no tidings gained they of Edward; though here and there Maggie watched Frank into some cottage or other, going to see a dead body, beloved by some one; and when he came out, solemn and grave, their sad eyes met, and she knew it was not he they sought, without needing words.

At Abergele they stopped to rest; and because, being a larger place, it would need a longer search, Maggie lay down on the sofa, for she was very weak, and shut her eyes, and tried not to see for ever and ever that mad struggling crowd lighted by the red flames.

Frank came back in an hour or so; and soft behind him,—laboriously treading on tiptoe,—Mr Buxton followed. He was evidently choking down his sobs; but when he saw the white wan figure of Maggie, he held out his arms.

'My dear! my daughter!' he said, 'God bless you!' He could not speak more,—he was fairly crying; but he put her hand in Frank's, and kept holding them both.

'My father,' said Frank, speaking in a husky voice, while his eyes filled with tears, 'had heard of it before he received my letter. I might have known that the lighthouse signals would take it fast to Liverpool. I had written a few lines to him saying I was going to you; happily they never reached,—that was spared to my dear father.'

Maggie saw the look of restored confidence that passed between father and son.

'My mother?' said she at last.

'She is here,' said they both at once, with sad solemnity.

'Oh, where? Why did not you tell me?' exclaimed she, starting up. But their faces told her why.

'Edward is drowned,—is dead,' said she, reading their looks.

There was no answer.

'Let me go to my mother.'

'Maggie, she is with him. His body was washed ashore last night. My father and she heard of it as they came along. Can you bear to see her? She will not leave him.'

'Take me to her,' Maggie answered.

They led her into a bed-room. Stretched on the bed lay Edward, but now so full of hope and worldly plans.

Mrs Browne looked round, and saw Maggie. She did not get up from her place by his head; nor did she long avert her gaze from his poor face. But she held Maggie's hand, as the girl knelt by her, and spoke to her in a hushed voice, undisturbed by tears. Her miserable heart could not find that relief.

'He is dead!—he is gone!—he will never come back again! If he had gone to America,—it might have been years first,—but he would have come back to me. But now he will never come back again; never,—never!'

Her voice died away, as the wailings of the night-wind die in the distance; and there was silence,—silence more sad and hopeless than any passionate words of grief.

And to this day it is the same. She prizes her dead son more than a thousand living daughters, happy and prosperous as is Maggie now,—rich in the love of many. If Maggie did not show such reverence to her mother's faithful sorrows, others might wonder at her refusal to be comforted by that sweet daughter. But Maggie treats her with such tender sympathy, never thinking of herself or her own claims, that Frank, Erminia, Mr Buxton, Nancy, and all, are reverent and sympathizing too.

Over both old and young the memory of one who is dead broods like a dove,—of one who could do but little during her lifetime; who was doomed only to 'stand and wait,'* who was meekly content to *be* gentle, holy, patient, and undefiled,—the memory of the invalid Mrs Buxton.

THE SEXTON'S HERO

THE afternoon sun shed down his glorious rays on the grassy churchyard, making the shadow, cast by the old yew-tree under which we sat, seem deeper and deeper by contrast. The everlasting hum of myriads of summer insects made luxurious lullaby.

Of the view that lay beneath our gaze, I cannot speak adequately. The foreground was the grey-stone wall of the vicarage-garden; rich in the colouring made by innumerable lichens, ferns, ivy of most tender green and most delicate tracery, and the vivid scarlet of the crane's-bill, which found a home in every nook and crevice— and at the summit of that old wall flaunted some unpruned tendrils of the vine, and long flower-laden branches of the climbing rose-tree, trained against the inner side. Beyond, lay meadow green, and mountain grey, and the blue dazzle of Morecambe Bay,* as it sparkled between us and the more distant view.

For a while we were silent, living in sight and murmuring sound. Then Jeremy took up our conversation where, suddenly feeling weariness, as we saw that deep green shadowy resting-place, we had ceased speaking a quarter of an hour before.

It is one of the luxuries of holiday-time that thoughts are not rudely shaken from us by outward violence of hurry and busy impatience, but fall maturely from our lips in the sunny leisure of our days. The stock may be bad, but the fruit is ripe.

'How would you then define a hero?' I asked.

There was a long pause, and I had almost forgotten my question in watching a cloud-shadow floating over the far-away hills, when Jeremy made answer:

'My idea of a hero is one who acts up to the highest idea of duty he has been able to form, no matter at what sacrifice. I think that by this definition, we may include all phases of character, even to the heroes of old, whose sole (and to us, low) idea of duty consisted in personal prowess.'

'Then you would even admit the military heroes?' asked I.

'I would; with a certain kind of pity for the circumstances which had given them no higher ideas of duty. Still, if they sacrificed self to do what they sincerely believed to be right, I do not think I could deny them the title of hero.'

'A poor, unchristian heroism, whose manifestation consists in injury to others!' I said.

We were both startled by a third voice.

'If I might make so bold, sir'—and then the speaker stopped.

It was the Sexton, whom, when we first arrived, we had noticed, as an accessory to the scene, but whom we had forgotten, as much as though he were as inanimate as one of the moss-covered head-stones.

'If I might be so bold,' said he again, waiting leave to speak. Jeremy bowed in deference to his white, uncovered head. And so encouraged, he went on.

'What that gentleman' (alluding to my last speech) 'has just now said, brings to my mind one who is dead and gone this many a year ago. I, may be, have not rightly understood your meaning, gentlemen, but as far as I could gather it, I think you'd both have given in to thinking poor Gilbert Dawson a hero. At any rate,' said he, heaving a long quivering sigh, 'I have reason to think him so.'

'Will you take a seat, sir, and tell us about him?' said Jeremy, standing up until the old man was seated. I confess I felt impatient at the interruption.

'It will be forty-five year come Martinmas,'* said the Sexton, sitting down on a grassy mound at our feet, 'since I finished my 'prenticeship, and settled down at Lindal. You can see Lindal, sir, at evenings and mornings across the bay; a little to the right of Grange;* at least, I used to see it, many a time and oft, afore my sight grew so dark: and I have spent many a quarter of an hour a-gazing at it far away, and thinking of the days I lived there, till the tears came so thick to my eyes, I could gaze no longer. I shall never look upon it again, either far-off or near, but you may see it, both ways, and a terrible bonny spot it is. In my young days, when I went to settle there, it was full of as wild a set of young fellows as ever were clapped eyes on; all for fighting, poaching, quarrelling, and such like work. I were startled myself when I first found what a set I were among, but soon I began to fall into their ways, and I ended by being as rough a chap as any on 'em. I'd been there a matter of two year, and were reckoned by most the cock of the village, when Gilbert Dawson, as I was speaking of, came to Lindal.

He were about as strapping a chap as I was (I used to be six feet high, though now I'm so shrunk and doubled up), and, as we were like in the same trade (both used to prepare osiers and wood for the Liverpool coopers,* who get a deal of stuff from the copses round the bay, sir) we were thrown together, and took mightily to each other. I put my best leg foremost to be equal with Gilbert, for I'd had some schooling, though since I'd been at Lindal I'd lost a good part of what I'd learnt; and I kept my rough ways out of sight for a time, I felt so ashamed of his getting to know them. But that did not last long. I began to think he fancied a girl I dearly loved, but who had always held off from me. Eh! but she was a pretty one in those days! There's none like her, now. I think I see her going along the road with her dancing tread, and shaking back her long yellow curls, to give me or any other young fellow a saucy word; no wonder Gilbert was taken with her, for all he was grave, and she so merry and light. But I began to think she liked him again; and then my blood was all afire. I got to hate him for everything he did. Afore-time I had stood by, admiring to see him, how he leapt, and what a quoiter and cricketer he was. And now I ground my teeth with hatred whene'er he did a thing which caught Letty's eye. I could read it in her look that she liked him, for all she held herself just as high with him as with all the rest. Lord God forgive me! how I hated that man.'

He spoke as if the hatred were a thing of yesterday, so clear within his memory were shown the actions and feelings of his youth. And then he dropped his voice, and said:

'Well! I began to look out to pick a quarrel with him, for my blood was up to fight him. If I beat him (and I were a rare boxer in those days), I thought Letty would cool towards him. So one evening at quoits (I'm sure I don't know how or why, but large doings grow out of small words) I fell out with him, and challenged him to fight. I could see he were very wroth by his colour coming and going—and, as I said before, he were a fine active young fellow. But all at once he drew in, and said he would not fight. Such a yell as the Lindal lads, who were watching us, set up! I hear it yet. I could na' help but feel sorry for him, to be so scorned, and I thought he'd not rightly taken my meaning, and I'd give him another chance; so I said it again, and dared him, as plain as words could speak, to fight out the quarrel. He told me then, he had no quarrel against me; that he might have said something to put me up; he did not know that he had, but that if he had, he asked pardon; but that he would not fight no-how.

'I was so full of scorn at his cowardliness, that I was vexed I'd given him the second chance, and I joined in the yell that was set up, twice as bad as before. He stood it out, his teeth set, and looking very white, and when we were silent for want of breath, he said out loud, but in a hoarse voice, quite different from his own—

' "I cannot fight, because I think it is wrong to quarrel, and use violence."

'Then he turned to go away; I were so beside myself with scorn and hate, that I called out,—

' "Tell truth, lad, at least; if thou dare not fight, dunnot go and tell a lie about it. Mother's moppet is afraid of a black eye, pretty dear. It shannot be hurt, but it munnot tell lies."

'Well, they laughed, but I could not laugh. It seemed such a thing for a stout young chap to be a coward, and afraid!

'Before the sun had set, it was talked of all over Lindal, how I had challenged Gilbert to fight, and how he'd denied me; and the folks stood at their doors, and looked at him going up the hill to his home, as if he'd been a monkey or a foreigner,—but no one wished him good e'en. Such a thing as refusing to fight had never been heard of afore at Lindal. Next day, however, they had found voice. The men muttered the word "coward" in his hearing, and kept aloof; the women tittered as he passed, and the little impudent lads and lasses shouted out, "How long is it sin' thou turned quaker?" "Good-by, Jonathan Broad-brim,"* and such like jests.

'That evening I met him, with Letty by his side, coming up from the shore. She was almost crying as I came upon them at the turn of the lane; and looking up in his face, as if begging him something. And so she was, she told me it after. For she did really like him; and could not abide to hear him scorned by every one for being a coward; and she, coy as she was, all but told him that very night that she loved him, and begged him not to disgrace himself, but fight me as I'd dared him to. When he still stuck to it he could not, for that it was wrong, she was so vexed and mad-like at the way she'd spoken, and the feelings she'd let out to coax him, that she said more stinging things about his being a coward than all the rest put together (according to what she told me, sir, afterwards), and ended by saying she'd never speak to him again, as long as she lived;—she did once again though,—her blessing was the last human speech that reached his ear in his wild death struggle.

'But much happened afore that time. From the day I met them walking, Letty turned towards me; I could see a part of it was to spite Gilbert, for she'd be twice as kind when he was near, or likely to hear of it; but by-and-by she get to like me for my own sake, and it was all settled for our marriage. Gilbert kept aloof from every one, and fell into a sad, careless way. His very gait was changed; his step used to be brisk and sounding, and now his foot lingered heavily on the ground. I used to try and daunt him with my eye, but he would always meet my look in a steady, quiet way, for all so much about him was altered; the lads would not play with him; and as soon as he found he was to be slighted by them whenever he came to quoiting or cricket, he just left off coming.

'The old clerk was the only one he kept company with; or perhaps, rightly to speak, the only one who would keep company with him. They got so thick at last, that old Jonas would say, Gilbert had gospel on his side, and did no more than gospel told him to do; but we none of us gave much credit to what he said, more by token our vicar had a brother, a colonel in the army; and as we threeped* it many a time to Jonas, would he set himself up to know the gospel better than the vicar? that would be putting the cart afore the horse, like the French radicals.* And if the vicar had thought quarrelling and fighting wicked, and again the Bible, would he have made so much work about all the victories, that were as plenty as blackberries at that time of day, and kept the little bell of Lindal church for ever ringing; or would he have thought so much of "my brother the colonel," as he was always talking on?

'After I was married to Letty I left off hating Gilbert. I even kind of pitied him—he was so scorned and slighted; and for all he'd a bold look about him, as if he were not ashamed, he seemed pining and shrunk. It's a wearying thing to be kept at arm's length by one's kind; and so Gilbert found it, poor fellow. The little children took to him, though; they'd be round about him like a swarm of bees—them as was too young to know what a coward was, and only felt that he was ever ready to love and to help them, and was never loud or cross, however naughty they might be. After a while we had our little one too; such a blessed darling she was, and dearly did we love her; Letty in especial, who seemed to get all the thought I used to think sometimes she wanted, after she had her baby to care for.

'All my kin lived on this side the bay, up above Kellet.* Jane (that's her that lies buried near yon white rose-tree) was to be married, and nought would serve her but that Letty and I must come to the wedding; for all my sisters loved Letty, she had such winning ways with her. Letty did not like to leave her baby, nor yet did I want her to take it: so, after a talk, we fixed to leave it with Letty's mother for the afternoon. I could see her heart ached a bit, for she'd never left it till then, and she seemed to fear all manner of evil, even to the French coming and taking it away.* Well! we borrowed a shandry,* and harnessed my old grey mare, as I used in th' cart, and set off as grand as King George* across the Sands about three o'clock, for you see it were high water about twelve, and we'd to go and come back same tide, as Letty could not leave her baby for long. It were a merry afternoon, were that; last time I ever saw Letty laugh heartily; and for that matter, last time I ever laughed downright hearty myself. The latest crossing time fell about nine o'clock, and we were late at starting. Clocks were wrong; and we'd a piece of work chasing a pig father had given Letty to take home; we bagged him at last, and he screeched and screeched in the back part o' th' shandry, and we laughed and they laughed; and in the midst of all the merriment the sun set, and that sober'd us a bit, for then we knew what time it was. I whipped the old mare, but she was a deal beener* than she was in the morning, and would neither go quick up nor down the brows, and they're not a few 'twixt Kellet and the shore. On the sands it were worse. They were very heavy, for the fresh* had come down after the rains we'd had. Lord! how I did whip the poor mare, to make the most of the red light as yet lasted. You, maybe, don't know the Sands, gentlemen. From Bolton side,* where we started from, it is better than six mile to Cart-lane, and two channels to cross, let alone holes and quick-sands. At the second channel from us the guide waits, all during crossing time from sunrise to sunset;—but for the three hours on each side high water he's not there, in course. He stays after sunset if he's forespoken, not else. So now you know where we were that awful night. For we'd crossed the first channel about two mile, and it were growing darker and darker above and around us, all but one red line of light above the hills, when we came to a hollow (for all the Sands look so flat, there's many a hollow in them where you lose all sight of the shore). We were longer than we should ha' been in crossing the hollow, the sand was so quick;* and when we came up again, there, again the blackness, was the white line of the rushing tide coming up the bay! It looked not a mile from us; and when the wind blows up the bay, it comes swifter than a galloping horse. "Lord help us!" said I; and then I were sorry I'd spoken, to frighten Letty, but the words were crushed out of my heart by the terror. I felt her shiver up by my side, and clutch my coat. And as if the pig (as had screeched himself hoarse some time ago) had found out the danger we were all in, he took to squealing again, enough to bewilder any man. I cursed him between my teeth for his noise; and yet it was God's answer to my prayer, blind sinner as I was. Ay! you may smile, sir, but God can work through many a scornful thing, if need be.

'By this time the mare were all in a lather, and trembling and panting, as if in mortal fright; for though we were on the last bank afore the second channel, the water was gathering up her legs; and she so tired out! When we came close to the channel she stood still, and not all my flogging could get her to stir; she fairly groaned aloud, and shook in a terrible quaking way. Till now Letty had not spoken; only held my coat tightly. I heard her say something, and bent down my head.

' "I think, John—I think—I shall never see baby again!"

'And then she sent up such a cry—so loud and shrill, and pitiful! It fairly maddened me. I pulled out my knife to spur on the old mare, that it might end one way or the other, for the water was stealing sullenly up to the very axle tree, let alone the white waves that knew no mercy in their steady advance. That one quarter of an hour, sir, seemed as long as all my life since. Thoughts, and fancies, and dreams, and memory, ran into each other. The mist, the heavy mist, that was like a ghastly curtain, shutting us in for death, seemed to bring with it the scents of the flowers that grew around our own threshold;—it might be, for it was falling on them like blessed dew, though to us it was a shroud. Letty told me at after, she heard her baby crying for her, above the gurgling of the rising waters, as plain as ever she heard anything; but the sea-birds were skirling, and the pig shrieking; I never caught it; it was miles away, at any rate.

'Just as I'd gotten my knife out, another sound was close upon us, blending with the gurgle of the near waters, and the roar of the distant; (not so distant though) we could hardly see, but we thought we saw something black against the deep lead colour of wave, and mist, and sky. It neared, and neared: with slow, steady motion, it came across the channel right to where we were.

'O God! it was Gilbert Dawson on his strong bay horse.

'Few words did we speak, and little time had we to say them in. I had no knowledge at that moment of past or future—only of one present thought—how to save Letty, and, if I could, myself. I only remembered afterwards that Gilbert said he had been guided by an animal's shriek of terror; I only heard when all was over, that he had been uneasy about our return, because of the depth of fresh, and had borrowed a pillion,* and saddled his horse early in the evening, and ridden down to Cart-lane to watch for us. If all had gone well, we should ne'er have heard of it. As it was, old Jonas told it, the tears down-dropping from his withered cheeks.

'We fastened his horse to the shandry. We lifted Letty to the pillion. The waters rose every instant with sullen sound. They were all but in the shandry. Letty clung to the pillion handles, but drooped her head as if she had yet no hope of life. Swifter than thought (and yet he might have had time for thought and for temptation, sir:—if he had ridden off with Letty, he would have been saved not me), Gilbert was in the shandry by my side.

' "Quick!" said he, clear and firm. "You must ride before her, and keep her up. The horse can swim. By God's mercy I will follow. I can cut the traces, and if the mare is not hampered with the shandry, she'll carry me safely through. At any rate, you are a husband and a father. No one cares for me."

'Do not hate me, gentlemen. I often wish that night was a dream. It has haunted my sleep ever since like a dream, and yet it was no dream. I took his place on the saddle, and put Letty's arms around me, and felt her head rest on my shoulder. I trust in God I spoke some word of thanks; but I can't remember. I only recollect Letty raising her head, and calling out,—

' "God bless you, Gilbert Dawson, for saving my baby from being an orphan this night." And then she fell against me, as if unconscious.

'I bore her through; or, rather, the strong horse swam bravely through the gathering waves. We were dripping wet when we reached the banks in-shore; but we could have but one thought— where was Gilbert? Thick mists and heaving waters compassed us round. Where was he? We shouted. Letty, faint as she was, raised her voice and shouted, clear and shrill. No answer came, the sea boomed on with ceaseless sullen beat. I rode to the guide's house. He was a-bed, and would not get up, though I offered him more than I was worth. Perhaps he knew it, the cursed old villain! At any rate I'd have paid it if I'd toiled my life long. He said I might take his horn and welcome. I did, and blew such a blast through the still, black night, the echoes came back upon the heavy air: but no human voice or sound was heard; that wild blast could not awaken the dead.

'I took Letty home to her baby, over whom she wept the live-long night. I rode back to the shore about Cart-lane; and to and fro, with weary march, did I pace along the brink of the waters, now and then shouting out into the silence a vain cry for Gilbert. The waters went back and left no trace. Two days afterwards he was washed ashore near Flukeborough. The shandry and poor old mare were found half-buried in a heap of sand by Arnside Knot.* As far as we could guess, he had dropped his knife while trying to cut the traces, and so had lost all chance of life. Any rate, the knife was found in a cleft of the shaft.

'His friends came over from Garstang to his funeral. I wanted to go chief mourner, but it was not my right, and I might not; though I've never done mourning him to this day. When his sister packed up his things, I begged hard for something that had been his. She would give me none of his clothes (she was a right-down having woman), as she had boys of her own, who might grow up into them. But she threw me his Bible, as she said they'd gotten one already, and his were but a poor used-up thing. It was his, and so I cared for it. It were a black leather one, with pockets at the sides, old-fashioned-wise; and in one were a bunch of wild flowers, Letty said she could almost be sure were some she had once given him.

'There were many a text in the Gospel, marked broad with his carpenter's pencil, which more than bore him out in his refusal to fight. Of a surety, sir, there's call enough for bravery in the service of God, and to show love to man, without quarrelling and fighting.

'Thank you, gentlemen, for listening to me. Your words called up the thoughts of him, and my heart was full to speaking. But I must make up; I've to dig a grave for a little child, who is to be buried to-morrow morning, just when his playmates are trooping off to school.'

'But tell us of Letty; is she yet alive?' asked Jeremy.

The old man shook his head, and struggled against a choking sigh. After a minute's pause he said,—

'She died in less than two year at after that night. She was never like the same again. She would sit thinking, on Gilbert, I guessed; but I could not blame her. We had a boy, and we named it Gilbert Dawson Knipe; he that's stoker on the London railway. Our girl was carried off in teething, and Letty just quietly drooped, and died in less than a six week. They were buried here; so I came to be near them, and away from Lindal, a place I could never abide after Letty was gone.'

He turned to his work, and we, having rested sufficiently, rose up, and came away.

CHRISTMAS STORMS
AND SUNSHINE

IN the town of ——(no matter where) there circulated two local newspapers (no matter when). Now the *Flying Post* was long established and respectable—alias bigoted and Tory; the *Examiner* was spirited and intelligent—alias new-fangled and democratic. Every week these newspapers contained articles abusing each other; as cross and peppery as articles could be, and evidently the production of irritated minds, although they seemed to have one stereotyped commencement,—'Though the article appearing in last week's *Post* (or *Examiner*) is below contempt, yet we have been induced,' &c., &c., and every Saturday the Radical shopkeepers shook hands together, and agreed that the *Post* was done for, by the slashing, clever *Examiner*; while the more dignified Tories began by regretting that Johnson* should think that low paper, only read by a few of the vulgar, worth wasting his wit upon; however the *Examiner* was at its last gasp.

It was not though. It lived and flourished; at least it paid its way, as one of the heroes of my story could tell. He was chief compositor, or whatever title may be given to the head-man of the mechanical part of a newspaper. He hardly confined himself to that department. Once or twice, unknown to the editor, when the manuscript had fallen short, he had filled up the vacant space by compositions of his own; announcements of a forthcoming crop of green peas in December; a grey thrush having been seen, or a white hare, or such interesting phenomena; invented for the occasion, I must confess; but what of that? His wife always knew when to expect a little specimen of her husband's literary talent by a peculiar cough, which served as prelude; and, judging from this encouraging sign, and the high-pitched and emphatic voice in which he read them, she was inclined to think, that an 'Ode to an early Rose-bud,' in the corner devoted to original poetry, and a letter in the correspondence department, signed 'Pro Bono Publico,'* were her husband's writing, and to hold up her head accordingly.

I never could find out what it was that occasioned the Hodgsons to lodge in the same house as the Jenkinses. Jenkins held the same office in the Tory paper as Hodgson did in the *Examiner*, and, as I said before, I leave you to give it a name. But Jenkins had a proper sense of his position, and a proper reverence for all in authority, from the king down to the editor and sub-editor. He would as soon have thought of borrowing the king's crown for a nightcap, or the king's sceptre for a walking-stick, as he would have thought of filling up any spare corner with any production of his own; and I think it would have even added to his contempt of Hodgson (if that were possible), had he known of the 'productions of his brain,' as the latter fondly alluded to the paragraphs he inserted, when speaking to his wife.

Jenkins had his wife too. Wives were wanting to finish the completeness of the quarrel, which existed one memorable Christmas week, some dozen years ago, between the two neighbours, the two compositors. And with wives, it was a very pretty, a very complete quarrel. To make the opposing parties still more equal, still more well-matched, if the Hodgsons had a baby ('such a baby!—a poor, puny little thing'), Mrs Jenkins had a cat ('such a cat! a great, nasty, miowling tom-cat, that was always stealing the milk put by for little Angel's supper'). And now, having matched Greek with Greek, I must proceed to the tug of war.* It was the day before Christmas; such a cold east wind! such an inky sky! such a blue-black look in people's faces, as they were driven out more than usual, to complete their purchases for the next day's festival.

Before leaving home that morning, Jenkins had given some money to his wife to buy the next day's dinner.

'My dear, I wish for turkey and sausages. It may be a weakness, but I own I am partial to sausages. My deceased mother was. Such tastes are hereditary. As to the sweets—whether plum-pudding or mince-pies—I leave such considerations to you; I only beg you not to mind expense. Christmas comes but once a year.'

And again he had called out from the bottom of the first flight of stairs, just close to the Hodgsons' door ('such ostentatiousness,' as Mrs Hodgson observed), 'You will not forget the sausages, my dear?'

'I should have liked to have had something above common, Mary,' said Hodgson, as they too made their plans for the next day, 'but I think roast beef must do for us. You see, love, we've a family.'

'Only one, Jem! I don't want more than roast beef, though, I'm sure. Before I went to service, mother and me would have thought roast beef a very fine dinner.'

'Well, let's settle it then, roast beef and a plum-pudding; and now, good-by. Mind and take care of little Tom. I thought he was a bit hoarse this morning.'

And off he went to his work.

Now, it was a good while since Mrs Jenkins and Mrs Hodgson had spoken to each other, although they were quite as much in possession of the knowledge of events and opinions as though they did. Mary knew that Mrs Jenkins despised her for not having a real lace cap, which Mrs Jenkins had; and for having been a servant, which Mrs Jenkins had not; and the little occasional pinchings which the Hodgsons were obliged to resort to, to make both ends meet, would have been very patiently endured by Mary, if she had not winced under Mrs Jenkins's knowledge of such economy. But she had her revenge. She had a child, and Mrs Jenkins had none. To have had a child, even such a puny baby as little Tom, Mrs Jenkins would have worn commonest caps, and cleaned grates, and drudged her fingers to the bone. The great unspoken disappointment of her life soured her temper, and turned her thoughts inward, and made her morbid and selfish.

'Hang that cat! he's been stealing again! he's gnawed the cold mutton in his nasty mouth till it's not fit to set before a Christian; and I've nothing else for Jem's dinner. But I'll give it him now I've caught him, that I will!'

So saying, Mary Hodgson caught up her husband's Sunday cane, and despite pussy's cries and scratches, she gave him such a beating as she hoped might cure him of his thievish propensities; when lo! and behold, Mrs Jenkins stood at the door with a face of bitter wrath.

'Aren't you ashamed of yourself, ma'am, to abuse a poor dumb animal, ma'am, as knows no better than to take food when he sees it, ma'am? He only follows the nature which God has given, ma'am; and it's a pity your nature, ma'am, which I've heard, is of the stingy saving species, does not make you shut your cupboard-door a little closer. There is such a thing as law for brute animals.* I'll ask Mr Jenkins, but I don't think them Radicals has done away with that law yet, for all their Reform Bill,* ma'am. My poor precious love of a Tommy, is he hurt? and is his leg broke for taking a mouthful of scraps, as most people would give away to a beggar,—if he'd take 'em?' wound up Mrs Jenkins, casting a contemptuous look on the remnant of a scrag end of mutton.

Mary felt very angry and very guilty. For she really pitied the poor limping animal as he crept up to his mistress, and there lay down to bemoan himself; she wished she had not beaten him so hard, for it certainly was her own careless way of never shutting the cupboard-door that had tempted him to his fault. But the sneer at her little bit of mutton turned her penitence to fresh wrath, and she shut the door in Mrs Jenkins's face, as she stood caressing her cat in the lobby, with such a bang, that it wakened little Tom, and he began to cry.

Everything was to go wrong with Mary to-day. Now baby was awake, who was to take her husband's dinner to the office? She took the child in her arms, and tried to hush him off to sleep again, and as she sung she cried, she could hardly tell why,—a sort of reaction from her violent angry feelings. She wished she had never beaten the poor cat; she wondered if his leg was really broken. What would her mother say if she knew how cross and cruel her little Mary was getting? If she should live to beat her child in one of her angry fits?

It was of no use lullabying while she sobbed so; it must be given up, and she must just carry her baby in her arms, and take him with her to the office, for it was long past dinner-time. So she pared the mutton carefully, although by so doing she reduced the meat to an infinitesimal quantity, and taking the baked potatoes out of the oven, she popped them piping hot into her basket with the et-ceteras of plate, butter, salt, and knife and fork.

It was, indeed, a bitter wind. She bent against it as she ran, and the flakes of snow were sharp and cutting as ice. Baby cried all the way, though she cuddled him up in her shawl. Then her husband had made his appetite up for a potato pie, and (literary man as he was) his body got so much the better of his mind, that he looked rather black at the cold mutton. Mary had no appetite for her own dinner when she arrived at home again. So, after she had tried to feed baby, and he had fretfully refused to take his bread and milk, she laid him down as usual on his quilt, surrounded by play-things, while she sided away, and chopped suet for the next day's pudding.

Early in the afternoon a parcel came, done up first in brown paper, then in such a white, grass-bleached, sweet-smelling towel, and a note from her dear, dear mother; in which quaint writing she endeavoured to tell her daughter that she was not forgotten at Christmas time; but that learning that Farmer Burton was killing his pig, she had made interest for some of his famous pork, out of which she had manufactured some sausages, and flavoured them just as Mary used to like when she lived at home.

'Dear, dear mother!' said Mary to herself. 'There never was any one like her for remembering other folk. What rare sausages she used to make! Home things have a smack with 'em, no bought things can ever have. Set them up with their sausages! I've a notion if Mrs Jenkins had ever tasted mother's she'd have no fancy for them town-made things Fanny took in just now.'

And so she went on thinking about home, till the smiles and the dimples came out again at the remembrance of that pretty cottage, which would look green even now in the depth of winter, with its pyracanthus,* and its holly-bushes, and the great Portugal laurel that was her mother's pride. And the back path through the orchard to Farmer Burton's; how well she remembered it. The bushels of unripe apples she had picked up there, and distributed among his pigs, till he had scolded her for giving them so much green trash.

She was interrupted—her baby (I call him a baby, because his father and mother did, and because he was so little of his age, but I rather think he was eighteen months old) had fallen asleep some time before among his playthings; an uneasy, restless sleep; but of which Mary had been thankful, as his morning's nap had been too short, and as she was so busy. But now he began to make such a strange crowing noise, just like a chair drawn heavily and gratingly along a kitchen-floor! His eyes were open, but expressive of nothing but pain.

'Mother's darling!' said Mary, in terror, lifting him up. 'Baby, try not to make that noise. Hush, hush, darling; what hurts him?' But the noise came worse and worse.

'Fanny! Fanny!' Mary called in mortal fright, for her baby was almost black with his gasping breath, and she had no one to ask for aid or sympathy but her landlady's daughter, a little girl of twelve or thirteen, who attended to the house in her mother's absence, as daily cook in gentlemen's families. Fanny was more especially considered the attendant of the upstairs lodgers (who paid for the use of the kitchen, 'for Jenkins could not abide the smell of meat cooking'), but just now she was fortunately sitting at her afternoon's work of darning stockings, and hearing Mrs Hodgson's cry of terror, she ran to her sitting-room, and understood the case at a glance.

'He's got the croup!* Oh, Mrs Hodgson, he'll die as sure as fate. Little brother had it, and he died in no time. The doctor said he could do nothing for him—it had gone too far. He said if we'd put him in a warm bath at first, it might have saved him; but, bless you! he was never half so bad as your baby.' Unconsciously there mingled in her statement some of a child's love of producing an effect; but the increasing danger was clear enough.

'Oh, my baby! my baby! Oh, love, love! don't look so ill; I cannot bear it. And my fire so low! There, I was thinking of home, and picking currants, and never minding the fire. Oh, Fanny! what is the fire like in the kitchen? Speak.'

'Mother told me to screw it up, and throw some slack on* as soon as Mrs Jenkins had done with it, and so I did. It's very low and black. But, oh, Mrs Hodgson! let me run for the doctor—I cannot abear to hear him, it's so like little brother.'

Through her streaming tears Mary motioned her to go; and trembling, sinking, sick at heart, she laid her boy in his cradle, and ran to fill her kettle.

Mrs Jenkins, having cooked her husband's snug little dinner, to which he came home; having told him her story of pussy's beating, at which he was justly and dignifiedly (?) indignant, saying it was all of a piece with that abusive *Examiner*; having received the sausages, and turkey, and mince pies, which her husband had ordered; and cleaned up the room, and prepared everything for tea, and coaxed and duly bemoaned her cat (who had pretty nearly forgotten his beating, but very much enjoyed the petting); having done all these and many other things, Mrs Jenkins sat down to get up the real lace cap. Every thread was pulled out separately, and carefully stretched: when, what was that? Outside, in the street, a chorus of piping children's voices sang the old carol she had heard a hundred times in the days of her youth:—

As Joseph was a walking he heard an angel sing,
'This night shall be born our heavenly King.
He neither shall be born in housen nor in hall,
Nor in the place of Paradise, but in an ox's stall.
He neither shall be clothed in purple nor in pall,
But all in fair linen, as were babies all:
He neither shall be rocked in silver nor in gold,
But in a wooden cradle that rocks on the mould,' &c.*

She got up and went to the window. There, below, stood the group of grey black little figures, relieved against the snow, which now enveloped everything. 'For old sake's sake,' as she phrased it, she counted out a halfpenny apiece for the singers, out of the copper bag, and threw them down below.

The room had become chilly while she had been counting out and throwing down her money, so she stirred her already glowing fire, and sat down right before it—but not to stretch her lace; like Mary Hodgson, she began to think over long-past days, on softening remembrances of the dead and gone, on words long forgotten, on holy stories heard at her mother's knee.

'I cannot think what's come over me to-night,' said she, half aloud, recovering herself by the sound of her own voice from her train of thought—'My head goes wandering on them old times. I'm sure more texts have come into my head with thinking on my mother within this last half hour, than I've thought on for years and years. I hope I'm not going to die. Folks say, thinking too much on the dead betokens we're going to join 'em; I should be loth to go just yet—such a fine turkey as we've got for dinner to-morrow, too!'

Knock, knock, knock, at the door, as fast as knuckles could go. And then, as if the comer could not wait, the door was opened, and Mary Hodgson stood there as white as death.

'Mrs Jenkins!—oh, your kettle is boiling, thank God! Let me have the water for my baby, for the love of God! He's got croup, and is dying!'

Mrs Jenkins turned on her chair with a wooden inflexible look on her face, that (between ourselves) her husband knew and dreaded for all his pompous dignity.

'I'm sorry I can't oblige you, ma'am; my kettle is wanted for my husband's tea. Don't be afeared, Tommy, Mrs Hodgson won't venture to intrude herself where she's not desired. You'd better send for the doctor, ma'am, instead of wasting your time in wring-ing your hands, ma'am—my kettle is engaged.'

Mary clasped her hands together with passionate force, but spoke no word of entreaty to that wooden face—that sharp, determined voice; but, as she turned away, she prayed for strength to bear the coming trial, and strength to forgive Mrs Jenkins.

Mrs Jenkins watched her go away meekly, as one who has no hope, and then she turned upon herself as sharply as she ever did on any one else.

'What a brute I am, Lord forgive me! What's my husband's tea to a baby's life? In croup, too, where time is everything. You crabbed old vixen, you!—any one may know you never had a child!'

She was down stairs (kettle in hand) before she had finished her self-upbraiding; and when in Mrs Hodgson's room, she rejected all thanks (Mary had not the voice for many words), saying, stiffly, 'I do it for the poor babby's sake, ma'am, hoping he may live to have mercy to poor dumb beasts, if he does forget to lock his cupboards.'

But she did everything, and more than Mary, with her young inexperience, could have thought of. She prepared the warm bath, and tried it with her husband's own thermometer (Mr Jenkins was as punctual as clockwork in noting down the temperature of every day). She let his mother place her baby in the tub, still preserving the same rigid, affronted aspect, and then she went upstairs with-out a word. Mary longed to ask her to stay, but dared not; though, when she left the room, the tears chased each other down her cheeks faster than ever. Poor young mother! how she counted the minutes till the doctor should come. But, before he came, down again stalked Mrs Jenkins, with something in her hand.

'I've seen many of these croup-fits, which, I take it, you've not, ma'am. Mustard plaisters* is very sovereign, put on the throat; I've been up and made one, ma'am, and, by your leave, I'll put it on the poor little fellow.'

Mary could not speak, but she signed her grateful assent.

It began to smart while they still kept silence; and he looked up to his mother as if seeking courage from her looks to bear the stinging pain; but she was softly crying, to see him suffer, and her want of courage reacted upon him, and he began to sob aloud. Instantly Mrs Jenkins's apron was up, hiding her face: 'Peep-bo, baby,' said she, as merrily as she could. His little face brightened, and his mother having once got the cue, the two women kept the little fellow amused, until his plaister had taken effect.

'He's better,—oh, Mrs Jenkins, look at his eyes! how different! And he breathes quite softly—'

As Mary spoke thus, the doctor entered. He examined his patient. Baby was really better.

'It has been a sharp attack, but the remedies you have applied have been worth all the Pharmacopoeia* an hour later.—I shall send a powder,' &c. &c.

Mrs Jenkins stayed to hear this opinion; and (her heart wonderfully more easy) was going to leave the room, when Mary seized her hand and kissed it; she could not speak her gratitude.

Mrs Jenkins looked affronted and awkward, and as if she must go upstairs and wash her hand directly.

But, in spite of these sour looks, she came softly down an hour or so afterwards to see how baby was.

The little gentleman slept well after the fright he had given his friends; and on Christmas morning, when Mary awoke and looked at the sweet little pale face lying on her arm, she could hardly realize the danger he had been in.

When she came down (later than usual), she found the household in a commotion. What do you think had happened? Why, pussy had been a traitor to his best friend, and eaten up some of Mr Jenkins's own especial sausages; and gnawed and tumbled the rest so, that they were not fit to be eaten! There were no bounds to that cat's appetite! he would have eaten his own father if he had been tender enough. And now Mrs Jenkins stormed and cried—'Hang the cat!'

Christmas Day, too! and all the shops shut! 'What was turkey without sausages?' gruffly asked Mr Jenkins.

'Oh, Jem!' whispered Mary, 'hearken what a piece of work he's making about sausages,—I should like to take Mrs Jenkins up some of mother's; they're twice as good as bought sausages.'

'I see no objection, my dear. Sausages do not involve intimacies, else his politics are what I can no ways respect.'

'But, oh, Jem, if you had seen her last night about baby! I'm sure she may scold me for ever, and I'll not answer. I'd even make her cat welcome to the sausages.' The tears gathered to Mary's eyes as she kissed her boy.

'Better take 'em upstairs, my dear, and give them to the cat's mistress.' And Jem chuckled at his saying.

Mary put them on a plate, but still she loitered.

'What must I say, Jem? I never know.'

'Say—I hope you'll accept of these sausages, as my mother—no, that's not grammar;—say what comes uppermost, Mary, it will be sure to be right.'

So Mary carried them upstairs and knocked at the door; and when told to 'come in,' she looked very red, but went up to Mrs Jenkins, saying, 'Please take these. Mother made them.' And was away before an answer could be given.

Just as Hodgson was ready to go to church, Mrs Jenkins came downstairs, and called Fanny. In a minute, the latter entered the Hodgsons' room, and delivered Mr and Mrs Jenkins's compliments and they would be particular glad if Mr and Mrs Hodgson would eat their dinner with them.

'And carry baby upstairs in a shawl, be sure,' added Mrs Jenkins's voice in the passage, close to the door, whither she had followed her messenger. There was no discussing the matter, with the certainty of every word being overheard.

Mary looked anxiously at her husband. She remembered his saying he did not approve of Mr Jenkins's politics.

'Do you think it would do for baby?' asked he.

'Oh, yes,' answered she, eagerly; 'I would wrap him up so warm.'

'And I've got our room up to sixty-five already, for all it's so frosty,' added the voice outside.

Now, how do you think they settled the matter? The very best way in the world. Mr and Mrs Jenkins came down into the Hodgsons' room, and dined there. Turkey at the top, roast beef at the bottom, sausages at one side, potatoes at the other. Second course, plum-pudding at the top, and mince pies at the bottom.

And after dinner, Mrs Jenkins would have baby on her knee; and he seemed quite to take to her; she declared he was admiring the real lace on her cap, but Mary thought (though she did not say so) that he was pleased by her kind looks and coaxing words. Then he was wrapped up and carried carefully upstairs to tea, in Mrs Jenkins's room. And after tea, Mrs Jenkins, and Mary, and her husband, found out each other's mutual liking for music, and sat singing old glees and catches, till I don't know what o'clock, without one word of politics or newspapers.

Before they parted, Mary had coaxed pussy on to her knee; for Mrs Jenkins would not part with baby, who was sleeping on her lap.

'When you're busy, bring him to me. Do, now, it will be a real favour. I know you must have a deal to do, with another coming; let him come up to me. I'll take the greatest of cares of him; pretty darling, how sweet he looks when he's asleep!'

When the couples were once more alone, the husbands unburdened their minds to their wives.

Mr Jenkins said to his—'Do you know, Burgess tried to make me believe Hodgson was such a fool as to put paragraphs into the *Examiner* now and then; but I see he knows his place, and has got too much sense to do any such thing.'

Hodgson said—'Mary, love, I almost fancy from Jenkins's way of speaking (so much civiler than I expected), he guesses I wrote that "Pro Bono" and the "Rose-bud,"—at any rate, I've no objection to your naming it, if the subject should come uppermost; I should like him to know I'm a literary man.'

Well! I've ended my tale; I hope you don't think it too long; but, before I go, just let me say one thing.

If any of you have any quarrels, or misunderstandings, or coolnesses, or cold shoulders, or shynesses, or tiffs, or miffs, or huffs, with any one else, just make friends before Christmas,—you will be so much merrier if you do.

I ask it of you for the sake of that old angelic song, heard so many years ago by the shepherds, keeping watch by night, on Bethlehem Heights.*

THE WELL OF PEN-MORFA

CHAPTER I

OF a hundred travellers who spend a night at Trê-Madoc, in North Wales, there is not one, perhaps, who goes to the neighbouring village of Pen-Morfa. The new town, built by Mr Maddocks, Shelley's friend, has taken away all the importance of the ancient village—formerly, as its name imports, 'the head of the marsh;' that marsh which Mr Maddocks drained and dyked, and reclaimed from the Traeth Mawr, till Pen-Morfa, against the walls of whose cottages the winter tides lashed in former days, has come to stand, high and dry, three miles from the sea, on a disused road to Caernarvon.* I do not think there has been a new cottage built in Pen-Morfa this hundred years, and many an old one has dates in some obscure corner which tell of the fifteenth century. The joists of timber, where they meet overhead, are blackened with the smoke of centuries. There is one large room, round which the beds are built like cupboards, with wooden doors to open and shut, somewhat in the old Scotch fashion, I imagine; and below the bed (at least in one instance I can testify that this was the case, and I was told it was not uncommon) is a great wide wooden drawer, which contained the oat-cake, baked for some months' consumption by the family. They call the promontory of Llyn (the point at the end of Caernarvonshire), *Welsh* Wales.* I think they might call Pen-Morfa a Welsh Welsh village; it is so national in its ways, and buildings, and inhabitants, and so different from the towns and hamlets into which the English throng in summer. How these said inhabitants of Pen-Morfa ever are distinguished by their names, I, uninitiated, cannot tell. I only know for a fact, that in a family there with which I am acquainted, the eldest son's name is John Jones, because his father's was John Thomas; that the second son is called David Williams, because his grandfather was William Wynn; and that the girls are called indiscriminately by the names of Thomas and Jones. I have heard some of the Welsh chuckle over the way in which they have baffled the barristers at Caernarvon assizes, denying the name under which they had been subpoenaed to give evidence, if they were unwilling witnesses.* I could tell you of a great deal which is peculiar and wild in these true Welsh people, who are what I suppose we English were a century ago; but I must hasten on to my tale.

I have received great, true, beautiful kindness from one of the members of the family of whom I just now spoke as living at Pen-Morfa; and when I found that they wished me to drink tea with them, I gladly did so, though my friend was the only one in the house who could speak English at all fluently. After tea, I went with them to see some of their friends; and it was then I saw the interiors of the houses of which I have spoken. It was an autumn evening: we left mellow sunset-light in the open air when we entered the houses, in which all seemed dark, save in the ruddy sphere of the firelight, for the windows were very small, and deep-set in the thick walls. Here were an old couple, who welcomed me in Welsh; and brought forth milk and oat-cake with patriarchal hospitality. Sons and daughters had married away from them; they lived alone; he was blind, or nearly so; and they sat one on each side of the fire, so old and so still (till we went in and broke the silence) that they seemed to be listening for death. At another house lived a woman stern and severe-looking. She was busy hiving a swarm of bees, alone and unassisted. I do not think my companion would have chosen to speak to her; but seeing her out in her hill-side garden, she made some inquiry in Welsh, which was answered in the most mournful tone I ever heard in my life; a voice of which the freshness and 'timbre' had been choked up by tears long years ago. I asked who she was. I dare say the story is common enough; but the sight of the woman and her few words had impressed me. She had been the beauty of Pen-Morfa; had been in service; had been taken to London by the family whom she served; had come down, in a year or so, back to Pen-Morfa, her beauty gone into that sad, wild, despairing look which I saw; and she about to become a mother. Her father had died during her absence, and left her a very little money; and after her child was born, she took the little cottages where I saw her, and made a scanty living by the produce of her bees. She associated with no one. One event had made her savage and distrustful to her kind. She kept so much aloof that it was some time before it became known that her child was deformed, and had lost the use of its lower limbs. Poor thing! When I saw the mother, it had been for fifteen years bedridden. But go past when you would, in the night, you saw a light burning; it was often that of the watching mother, solitary and friendless, soothing the moaning child; or you might hear her crooning some old Welsh air, in hopes to still the pain with the loud monotonous music. Her sorrow was so dignified, and her mute endurance and her patient love won her such respect, that the neighbours would fain have been friends; but she kept alone and solitary. This a most true story. I hope that woman and her child are dead now, and their souls above.

Another story which I heard of these old primitive dwellings I mean to tell at somewhat greater length:—

There are rocks high above Pen-Morfa; they are the same that hang over Trê-Madoc, but near Pen-Morfa they sweep away, and are lost in the plain. Everywhere they are beautiful. The great, sharp ledges, which would otherwise look hard and cold, are adorned with the brightest-coloured moss, and the golden lichen. Close to, you see the scarlet leaves of the crane's-bill, and the tufts of purple heather, which fill up every cleft and cranny; but, in the distance, you see only the general effect of infinite richness of colour, broken, here and there, by great masses of ivy. At the foot of these rocks come a rich, verdant meadow or two; and then you are at Pen-Morfa. The village well is sharp down under the rocks. There are one or two large sloping pieces of stone in that last field, on the road leading to the well, which are always slippery; slippery in the summer's heat, almost as much as in the frost of winter, when some little glassy stream that runs over them is turned into a thin sheet of ice. Many, many years back—a lifetime ago—there lived in Pen-Morfa a widow and her daughter. Very little is required in those out-of-the-way Welsh villages. The wants of the people are very simple. Shelter, fire, a little oat-cake and buttermilk, and garden produce; perhaps some pork and bacon from the pig in winter; clothing, which is principally of home manufacture, and of the most enduring kind: these take very little money to purchase, especially in a district into which the large capitalists have not yet come, to buy up two or three acres of the peasants; and nearly every man about Pen-Morfa owned, at the time of which I speak, his dwelling and some land beside.

Eleanor Gwynn inherited the cottage (by the roadside, on the left hand as you go from Trê-Madoc to Pen-Morfa) in which she and her husband had lived all their married life, and a small garden sloping southwards, in which her bees lingered before winging their way to the more distant heather. She took rank among her neighbours as the possessor of a moderate independence—not rich, and not poor. But the young men of Pen-Morfa thought her very rich in the possession of a most lovely daughter. Most of us know how very pretty Welsh women are; but, from all accounts Nest Gwynn (Nest, or Nesta, is the Welsh for Agnes)* was more regularly beautiful than any one for miles round. The Welsh are still fond of triads, and 'as beautiful as a summer's morning at sunrise, as a white seagull on the green sea wave, and as Nest Gwynn,' is yet a saying in that district.* Nest knew she was beautiful, and delighted in it. Her mother sometimes checked her in her happy pride, and sometimes reminded her that beauty was a great gift of God (for the Welsh are a very pious people); but when she began her little homily, Nest came dancing to her, and knelt down before her, and put her face up to be kissed, and so, with a sweet interruption, she stopped her mother's lips. Her high spirits made some few shake their heads, and some called her a flirt and a coquette; for she could not help trying to please all, both old and young, both men and women. A very little from Nest sufficed for this; a sweet, glittering smile, a word of kindness, a merry glance, or a little sympathy; all these pleased and attracted: she was like the fairy-gifted child, and dropped inestimable gifts.* But some, who had interpreted her smiles and kind words rather as their wishes led them, than as they were really warranted, found that the beautiful, beaming Nest could be decided and saucy enough; and so they revenged them-selves by calling her a flirt. Her mother heard it, and sighed; but Nest only laughed.

It was her work to fetch water for the day's use from the well I told you about. Old people say it was the prettiest sight in the world to see her come stepping lightly and gingerly over the stones with the pail of water balanced on her head; she was too adroit to need to steady it with her hand. They say, now that they can afford to be charitable and speak the truth, that in all her changes to other people, there never was a better daughter to a widowed mother than Nest. There is a picturesque old farmhouse under

Moel Gwynn, on the road from Trê-Madoc to Criccaeth, called by some Welsh name which I now forget; but its meaning in English is 'The End of Time;'* a strange, boding, ominous name. Perhaps, the builder meant his work to endure till the end of time. I do not know; but there the old house stands, and will stand for many a year. When Nest was young, it belonged to one Edward Williams; his mother was dead, and people said he was on the look-out for a wife. They told Nest so, but she tossed her head and reddened, and said she thought he might look long before he got one; so it was not strange that one morning when she went to the well, one autumn morning when the dew lay heavy on the grass, and the thrushes were busy among the mountain-ash berries, Edward Williams happened to be there, on his way to the coursing match* near, and somehow his greyhounds threw her pail of water over in their romping play, and she was very long in filling it again; and when she came home she threw her arms round her mother's neck, and, in a passion of joyous tears, told her that Edward Williams, of 'The End of Time,' had asked her to marry him, and that she had said 'Yes.'

Eleanor Gwynn shed her tears too; but they fell quietly when she was alone. She was thankful Nest had found a protector—one suitable in age and apparent character, and above her in fortune; but she knew she should miss her sweet daughter in a thousand household ways; miss her in the evenings by the fireside; miss her when at night she wakened up with a start from a dream of her youth, and saw her fair face lying calm in the moonlight, pillowed by her side. Then she forgot her dream, and blessed her child, and slept again. But who could be so selfish as to be sad when Nest was so supremely happy; she danced and sang more than ever; and then sat silent, and smiled to herself: if spoken to, she started and came back to the present with a scarlet blush, which told what she had been thinking of.

That was a sunny, happy, enchanted autumn. But the winter was nigh at hand; and with it came sorrow. One fine frosty morning, Nest went out with her lover—she to the well, he to some farming business, which was to be transacted at the little inn of Pen-Morfa. He was late for his appointment; so he left her at the entrance of the village, and hastened to the inn; and she, in her best cloak and new hat (put on against her mother's advice; but they were a recent purchase, and very becoming), went through the Dol Mawr,* radiant with love and happiness. One who lived until lately, met her going down towards the well that morning, and said he turned round to look after her—she seemed unusually lovely. He wondered at the time at her wearing her Sunday clothes; for the pretty, hooded blue-cloth cloak is kept among the Welsh women as a church and market garment, and not commonly used, even on the coldest days of winter, for such household errands as fetching water from the well. However, as he said, 'It was not possible to look in her face, and "fault" anything she wore.' Down the sloping stones the girl went blithely with her pail. She filled it at the well; and then she took off her hat, tied the strings together, and slung it over her arm. She lifted the heavy pail and balanced it on her head. But, alas! in going up the smooth, slippery, treacherous rock, the encumbrance of her cloak—it might be such a trifle as her slung hat—something, at any rate, took away her evenness of poise; the freshet* had frozen on the slanting stone, and was one coat of ice; poor Nest fell, and put out her hip. No more flushing rosy colour on that sweet face; no more look of beaming innocent happiness; instead, there was deadly pallor, and filmy eyes, over which dark shades seemed to chase each other as the shoots of agony grew more and more intense. She screamed once or twice; but the exertion (involuntary, and forced out of her by excessive pain) overcame her, and she fainted. A child, coming an hour or two afterwards, on the same errand, saw her lying there, ice-glued to the stone, and thought she was dead. It flew crying back.

'Nest Gwynn is dead! Nest Gwynn is dead!' and, crazy with fear, it did not stop until it had hid its head in its mother's lap. The village was alarmed, and all who were able went in haste towards the well. Poor Nest had often thought she was dying in that dreary hour; had taken fainting for death, and struggled against it; and prayed that God would keep her alive till she could see her lover's face once more; and when she did see it, white with terror, bending over her, she gave a feeble smile, and let herself faint away into unconsciousness.

Many a month she lay on her bed unable to move. Sometimes she was delirious, sometimes worn-out into the deepest depression. Through all, her mother watched her with tenderest care. The neighbours would come and offer help. They would bring presents of country dainties; and I do not suppose that there was a better dinner than ordinary cooked in any household in Pen-Morfa parish, but a portion of it was sent to Eleanor Gwynn, if not for her sick daughter, to try and tempt her herself to eat and be strengthened; for to no one would she delegate the duty of watching over her child. Edward Williams was for a long time most assiduous in his inquiries and attentions; but by-and-by (ah! you see the dark fate of poor Nest now), he slackened, so little at first that Eleanor blamed herself for her jealousy on her daughter's behalf, and chid her suspicious heart. But as spring ripened into summer, and Nest was still bedridden, Edward's coolness was visible to more than the poor mother. The neighbours would have spoken to her about it, but she shrunk from the subject as if they were probing a wound. 'At any rate,' thought she, 'Nest shall be strong before she is told about it. I will tell lies—I shall be forgiven—but I must save my child; and when she is stronger, perhaps I may be able to comfort her. Oh! I wish she would not speak to him so tenderly and trustfully, when she is delirious. I could curse him when she does.' And then Nest would call for her mother, and Eleanor would go and invent some strange story about the summonses Edward had had to Caernarvon assizes, or to Harlech cattle market. But at last she was driven to her wits' end; it was three weeks since he had even stopped at the door to inquire, and Eleanor, mad with anxiety about her child, who was silently pining off to death for want of tidings of her lover, put on her cloak, when she had lulled her daughter to sleep one fine June evening, and set off to 'The End of Time.' The great plain which stretches out like an amphitheatre, in the half-circle of hills formed by the ranges of Moel Gwynn and the Trê-Madoc Rocks, was all golden-green in the mellow light of sunset. To Eleanor it might have been black with winter frost—she never noticed outward things till she reached 'The End of Time;' and there, in the little farm-yard, she was brought to a sense of her present hour and errand by seeing Edward. He was examining some hay, newly stacked; the air was scented by its fragrance, and by the lingering sweetness of the breath of the cows. When Edward turned round at the footstep and saw Eleanor, he coloured and looked confused; however, he came forward to meet her in a cordial manner enough.

'It's a fine evening,' said he. 'How is Nest? But, indeed, your

being here is a sign she is better. Won't you come in and sit down?'
He spoke hurriedly, as if affecting a welcome which he did not feel.

'Thank you. I'll just take this milking-stool and sit down here.
The open air is like balm, after being shut up so long.'

'It is a long time,' he replied, 'more than five months.'

Mrs Gwynn was trembling at heart. She felt an anger which she
did not wish to show; for, if by any manifestations of temper or
resentment she lessened or broke the waning thread of attachment
which bound him to her daughter, she felt she should never forgive
herself. She kept inwardly saying, 'Patience, patience! he may be
true, and love her yet;' but her indignant convictions gave her
words the lie.

'It's a long time, Edward Williams, since you've been near us to
ask after Nest,' said she. 'She may be better, or she may be worse,
for aught you know.' She looked up at him reproachfully, but spoke
in a gentle, quiet tone.

'I—you see the hay has been a long piece of work. The weather
has been fractious—and a master's eye is needed. Besides,' said he,
as if he had found the reason for which he sought to account for
his absence, 'I have heard of her from Rowland Jones. I was at
the surgery for some horse-medicine—he told me about her:' and a
shade came over his face, as he remembered what the doctor had
said. Did he think that shade would escape the mother's eye?

'You saw Rowland Jones! Oh, man-alive, tell me what he said
of my girl! He'll say nothing to me, but just hems and haws
the more I pray him. But you will tell me. You *must* tell me.' She
stood up and spoke in a tone of command, which his feeling
of independence, weakened just then by an accusing conscience,
did not enable him to resist. He strove to evade the question,
however.

'It was an unlucky day that ever she went to the well!'

'Tell me what the doctor said of my child,' repeated Mrs Gwynn.
'Will she live, or will she die?' He did not dare to disobey the
imperious tone in which this question was put.

'Oh, she will live, don't be afraid. The doctor said she would live.'
He did not mean to lay any peculiar emphasis on the word 'live,'
but somehow he did, and she, whose every nerve vibrated with
anxiety, caught the word.

'She will live!' repeated she. 'But there is something behind. Tell me, for I will know. If you won't say, I'll go to Rowland Jones to-night, and make him tell me what he has said to you.'

There had passed something in this conversation between himself and the doctor, which Edward did not wish to have known; and Mrs Gwynn's threat had the desired effect. But he looked vexed and irritated.

'You have such impatient ways with you, Mrs Gwynn,' he remonstrated.

'I am a mother asking news of my sick child,' said she. 'Go on. What did he say? She'll live—' as if giving the clue.

'She'll live, he has no doubt of that. But he thinks—now don't clench your hands so—I can't tell you if you look in that way; you are enough to frighten a man.'

'I'm not speaking,' said she, in a low, husky tone. 'Never mind my looks: she'll live——'

'But she'll be a cripple for life. There! you would have it out,' said he, sulkily.

'A cripple for life,' repeated she, slowly. 'And I'm one-and-twenty years older than she is!' She sighed heavily.

'And, as we're about it, I'll just tell you what is in my mind,' said he, hurried and confused. 'I've a deal of cattle; and the farm makes heavy work, as much as an able healthy woman can do. So you see——' He stopped, wishing her to understand his meaning without words. But she would not. She fixed her dark eyes on him, as if reading his soul, till he flinched under her gaze.

'Well,' said she, at length, 'say on. Remember, I've a deal of work in me yet, and what strength is mine is my daughter's.'

'You're very good. But, altogether, you must be aware, Nest will never be the same as she was.'

'And you've not yet sworn in the face of God to take her for better, for worse;* and, as she is worse'—she looked in his face, caught her breath, and went on—'as she is worse, why, you cast her off, not being church-tied to her. Though her body may be crippled, her poor heart is the same—alas!—and full of love for you. Edward, you don't mean to break it off because of our sorrows. You're only trying me, I know,' said she, as if begging him to assure her that her fears were false. 'But, you see, I'm a foolish woman—a poor, foolish woman—and ready to take fright at a few words.' She smiled up in his face; but it was a forced, doubting smile, and his face still retained its sullen, dogged aspect.

'Nay, Mrs Gwynn,' said he, 'you spoke truth at first. Your own good sense told you Nest would never be fit to be any man's wife—unless, indeed, she could catch Mr Griffiths of Tynwnty-rybwlch;* he might keep her a carriage, maybe.' Edward really did not mean to be unfeeling; but he was obtuse, and wished to carry off his embarrassment by a kind of friendly joke, which he had no idea would sting the poor mother as it did. He was startled at her manner.

'Put it in words like a man. Whatever you mean by my child, say it for yourself, and don't speak as if my good sense had told me anything. I stand here, doubting my own thoughts, cursing my own fears. Don't be a coward. I ask you whether you and Nest are troth-plight?'

'I am not a coward. Since you ask me, I answer, Nest and I *were* troth-plight; but we *are* not. I cannot—no one would expect me to wed a cripple. It's your own doing I've told you now; I had made up my mind, but I should have waited a bit before telling you.'

'Very well,' said she, and she turned to go away; but her wrath burst the flood-gates, and swept away discretion and forethought. She moved, and stood in the gateway. Her lips parted, but no sound came; with an hysterical motion, she threw her arms suddenly up to heaven, as if bringing down lightning towards the grey old house to which she pointed as they fell, and then she spoke—

'The widow's child is unfriended. As surely as the Saviour brought the son of a widow from death to life,* for her tears and cries, so surely will God and His angels watch over my Nest, and avenge her cruel wrongs.' She turned away weeping, and wringing her hands.

Edward went in-doors; he had no more desire to reckon his stores; he sat by the fire, looking gloomily at the red ashes. He might have been there half an hour or more, when some one knocked at the door. He would not speak. He wanted no one's company. Another knock, sharp and loud. He did not speak. Then the visitor opened the door, and, to his surprise—almost to his affright—Eleanor Gwynn came in.

'I knew you were here. I knew you could not go out into the clear, holy night as if nothing had happened. Oh! did I curse you? If I did,

I beg you to forgive me; and I will try and ask the Almighty to bless you, if you will but have a little mercy—a very little. It will kill my Nest if she knows the truth now—she is so very weak. Why, she cannot feed herself, she is so low and feeble. You would not wish to kill her, I think, Edward!' She looked at him, as if expecting an answer; but he did not speak. She went down on her knees on the flags by him.

'You will give me a little time, Edward, to get her strong, won't you, now? I ask it on my bended knees! Perhaps, if I promise never to curse you again, you will come sometimes to see her, till she is well enough to know how all is over, and her heart's hopes crushed. Only say you'll come for a month or so, as if you still loved her—the poor cripple, forlorn of the world. I'll get her strong, and not tax you long.' Her tears fell too fast for her to go on.

'Get up, Mrs Gwynn,' Edward said. 'Don't kneel to me. I have no objection to come and see Nest, now and then, so that all is clear between you and me. Poor thing! I'm sorry, as it happens, she's so taken up with the thought of me.'

'It was likely, was not it? and you to have been her husband before this time, if—oh, miserable me! to let my child go and dim her bright life! But you'll forgive me, and come sometimes, just for a little quarter of an hour, once or twice a week. Perhaps she'll be asleep sometimes when you call, and then, you know, you need not come in. If she were not so ill, I'd never ask you.'

So low and humble was the poor widow brought, through her exceeding love for her daughter.

CHAPTER II

NEST revived during the warm summer weather. Edward came to see her, and stayed the allotted quarter of an hour; but he dared not look her in the face. She was, indeed, a cripple: one leg was much shorter than the other, and she halted on a crutch. Her face, formerly so brilliant in colour, was wan and pale with suffering; the bright roses were gone, never to return. Her large eyes were sunk deep down in their hollow, cavernous sockets; but the light was in them still, when Edward came. Her mother dreaded her returning strength—dreaded, yet desired it; for the heavy burden of her secret was most oppressive at times, and she thought Edward was beginning to weary of his enforced attentions. One October evening she told her the truth. She even compelled her rebellious heart to take the cold, reasoning side of the question; and she told her child that her disabled frame was a disqualification for ever becoming a farmer's wife. She spoke hardly, because her inner agony and sympathy was such, she dared not trust herself to express the feelings that were rending her. But Nest turned away from cold reason; she revolted from her mother; she revolted from the world. She bound her sorrow tight up in her breast, to corrode and fester there.

Night after night, her mother heard her cries and moans—more pitiful, by far, than those wrung from her by bodily pain a year before; and night after night, if her mother spoke to soothe, she proudly denied the existence of any pain but what was physical, and consequent upon her accident.

'If she would but open her sore heart to me—to me, her mother,' Eleanor wailed forth in prayer to God, 'I would be content. Once it was enough to have my Nest all my own. Then came love, and I knew it would never be as before; and then I thought the grief I felt, when Edward spoke to me, was as sharp a sorrow as could be; but this present grief, O Lord, my God, is worst of all; and Thou only, Thou, canst help!'

When Nest grew as strong as she was ever likely to be on earth, she was anxious to have as much labour as she could bear. She would not allow her mother to spare her anything. Hard work—bodily fatigue—she seemed to crave. She was glad when she was stunned by exhaustion into a dull insensibility of feeling. She was almost fierce when her mother, in those first months of convalescence, performed the household tasks which had formerly been hers; but she shrank from going out of doors. Her mother thought that she was unwilling to expose her changed appearance to the neighbours' remarks, but Nest was not afraid of that; she was afraid of their pity, as being one deserted and cast off. If Eleanor gave way before her daughter's imperiousness, and sat by while Nest 'tore' about her work with the vehemence of a bitter heart, Eleanor could have cried, but she durst not; tears, or any mark of commiseration, irritated the crippled girl so much, she even drew away from caresses. Everything was to go on as it had been before she had known Edward; and so it did, outwardly; but they trod carefully, as if the ground on which they moved was hollow—deceptive. There was no more careless ease, every word was guarded, and every action planned. It was a dreary life to both. Once, Eleanor brought in a little baby, a neighbour's child, to try and tempt Nest out of herself, by her old love of children. Nest's pale face flushed as she saw the innocent child in her mother's arms; and, for a moment, she made as if she would have taken it; but then she turned away, and hid her face behind her apron, and murmured, 'I shall never have a child to lie in my breast, and call me mother!' In a minute she arose, with compressed and tightened lips, and went about her household work, without her noticing the cooing baby again, till Mrs Gwynn, heart-sick at the failure of her little plan, took it back to its parents.

One day the news ran through Pen-Morfa that Edward Williams was about to be married. Eleanor had long expected this intelligence. It came upon her like no new thing, but it was the filling-up of her cup of woe. She could not tell Nest. She sat listlessly in the house, and dreaded that each neighbour who came in would speak about the village news. At last some one did. Nest looked round from her employment, and talked of the event with a kind of cheerful curiosity as to the particulars, which made her informant go away, and tell others that Nest had quite left off caring for Edward Williams. But when the door was shut, and Eleanor and she were left alone, Nest came and stood before her weeping mother like a stern accuser.

'Mother, why did not you let me die? Why did you keep me alive for this?' Eleanor could not speak, but she put her arms out towards her girl. Nest turned away, and Eleanor cried aloud in her soreness of spirit. Nest came again.

'Mother, I was wrong. You did your best. I don't know how it is I am so hard and cold. I wish I had died when I was a girl, and had a feeling heart.'

'Don't speak so, my child. God has afflicted you sore, and your hardness of heart is but for a time. Wait a little. Don't reproach yourself, my poor Nest. I understand your ways. I don't mind them, love. The feeling heart will come back to you in time. Anyways, don't think you're grieving me; because, love, that may sting you when I'm gone; and I'm not grieved, my darling. Most times, we're very cheerful, I think.'

After this, mother and child were drawn more together. But Eleanor had received her death from these sorrowful, hurrying events. She did not conceal the truth from herself; nor did she pray to live, as some months ago she had done, for her child's sake; she had found out that she had no power to console the poor wounded heart. It seemed to her as if her prayers had been of no avail; and then she blamed herself for this thought.

There are many Methodist preachers in this part of Wales. There was a certain old man, named David Hughes, who was held in peculiar reverence because he had known the great John Wesley.* He had been captain of a Caernarvon slate-vessel;* he had traded in the Mediterranean, and had seen strange sights. In those early days (to use his own expression) he had lived without God in the world; but he went to mock John Wesley, and was converted by the white-haired patriarch, and remained to pray. Afterwards he became one of the earnest, self-denying, much-abused band of itinerant preachers who went forth under Wesley's direction, to spread abroad a more earnest and practical spirit of religion. His rambles and travels were of use to him. They extended his knowledge of the circumstances in which men are sometimes placed, and enlarged his sympathy with the tried and tempted. His sympathy, combined with the thoughtful experience of fourscore years, made him cognizant of many of the strange secrets of humanity; and when younger preachers upbraided the hard hearts they met with, and despaired of the sinners, he 'suffered long, and was kind.'*

When Eleanor Gwynn lay low on her death-bed, David Hughes came to Pen-Morfa. He knew her history, and sought her out. To him she imparted the feelings I have described.

'I have lost my faith, David. The tempter has come, and I have yielded. I doubt if my prayers have been heard. Day and night have I prayed that I might comfort my child in her great sorrow; but God has not heard me. She has turned away from me, and refused my poor love. I wish to die now; but I have lost my faith, and have no more pleasure in the thought of going to God. What must I do, David?'

She hung upon his answer; and it was long in coming.

'I am weary of earth,' said she, mournfully, 'and can I find rest in death even, leaving my child desolate and broken-hearted?'

'Eleanor,' said David, 'where you go, all things will be made clear; and you will learn to thank God for the end of what now seems grievous and heavy to be borne. Do you think your agony has been greater than the awful agony in the Garden*—or your prayers more earnest than that which He prayed in that hour when the great drops of blood ran down his face like sweat?* We know that God heard Him, although no answer came to Him through the dread silence of that night. God's times are not our times. I have lived eighty and one years, and never yet have I known an earnest prayer fall to the ground unheeded. In an unknown way, and when no one looked for it, maybe, the answer came; a fuller, more satisfying answer than heart could conceive of, although it might be different to what was expected. Sister, you are going where in His light you will see light; you will learn there that in very faithfulness he has afflicted you!'

'Go on—you strengthen me,' said she.

After David Hughes left that day, Eleanor was calm as one already dead, and past mortal strife. Nest was awed by the change. No more passionate weeping—no more sorrow in the voice; though it was low and weak, it sounded with a sweet composure. Her last look was a smile; her last word a blessing.

Nest, tearless, streeked the poor worn body. She laid a plate with salt upon it on the breast, and lighted candles for the head and feet.* It was an old Welsh custom; but when David Hughes came in, the sight carried him back to the time when he had seen the chapels in some old Catholic cathedral. Nest sat gazing on the dead with dry, hot eyes.

'She is dead,' said David, solemnly; 'she died in Christ. Let us bless God, my child. He giveth and He taketh away.'*

'She is dead,' said Nest, 'my mother is dead. No one loves me now.'

She spoke as if she were thinking aloud, for she did not look at David, or ask him to be seated.

'No one loves you now? No human creature, you mean. You are not yet fit to be spoken to concerning God's infinite love. I, like you, will speak of love for human creatures. I tell you if no one loves you, it is time for you to begin to love.' He spoke almost severely (if David Hughes ever did); for, to tell the truth, he was repelled by her hard rejection of her mother's tenderness, about which the neighbours had told him.

'Begin to love!' said she, her eyes flashing. 'Have I not loved? Old man, you are dim, and worn-out. You do not remember what love is.' She spoke with a scornful kind of pitying endurance. 'I will tell you how I have loved by telling you the change it has wrought in me. I was once the beautiful Nest Gwynn; I am now a cripple, a poor, wan-faced cripple, old before my time. That is a change, at least people think so.' She paused and then spoke lower. 'I tell you, David Hughes, that outward change is as nothing compared to the change in my nature caused by the love I have felt—and have had rejected. I was gentle once, and if you spoke a tender word, my heart came towards you as natural as a little child goes to its mammy. I never spoke roughly, even to the dumb creatures, for I had a kind feeling for all. Of late (since I loved, old man), I have been cruel in my thoughts to every one. I have turned away from tenderness with bitter indifference. Listen!' she spoke in a hoarse whisper. 'I will own it. I have spoken hardly to her,' pointing towards the corpse,—'her who was ever patient, and full of love for me. She did not know,' she muttered, 'she is gone to the grave without knowing how I loved her—I had such strange, mad, stubborn pride in me.'

'Come back, mother! Come back,' said she, crying wildly to the still, solemn corpse; 'come back as a spirit or a ghost—only come back, that I may tell you how I have loved you.'

But the dead never come back.

The passionate adjuration ended in tears—the first she had shed. When they ceased, or were absorbed into long quivering sobs, David knelt down. Nest did not kneel, but bowed her head. He prayed, while his own tears fell fast. He rose up. They were both calm.

'Nest,' said he, 'your love has been the love of youth—passionate, wild, natural to youth. Henceforward, you must love like Christ, without thought of self, or wish for return. You must take the sick and the weary to your heart, and love them. That love will lift you up above the storms of the world into God's own peace. The very vehemence of your nature proves that you are capable of this. I do not pity you. You do not require pity. You are powerful enough to trample down your own sorrows into a blessing for others; and to others you will be a blessing. I see it before you, I see in it the answer to your mother's prayer.'

The old man's dim eyes glittered as if they saw a vision; the fire-light sprang up, and glinted on his long white hair. Nest was awed as if she saw a prophet, and a prophet he was to her.

When next David Hughes came to Pen-Morfa, he asked about Nest Gwynn, with a hovering doubt as to the answer. The inn-folk told him she was living still in the cottage, which was now her own.

'But would you believe it, David,' said Mrs Thomas, 'she has gone and taken Mary Williams to live with her? You remember Mary Williams, I'm sure.'

No! David Hughes remembered no Mary Williams at Pen-Morfa.

'You must have seen her, for I know you've called at John Griffiths', where the parish boarded her?'

'You don't mean the half-witted woman—the poor crazy creature?'

'But I do!' said Mrs Thomas.

'I have seen her sure enough, but I never thought of learning her name. And Nest Gwynn has taken her to live with her.'

'Yes! I thought I should surprise you. She might have had many a decent girl for companion. My own niece, her that is an orphan, would have gone, and been thankful. Besides, Mary Williams is a regular savage at times: John Griffiths says there were days when he used to beat her till she howled again, and yet she would not do as he told her. Nay, once, he says, if he had not seen her eyes glare like a wild beast, from under the shadow of the table where she had taken shelter, and got pretty quickly out of her way, she would have flown upon him, and throttled him. He gave Nest fair warning of what she must expect, and he thinks some day she will be found murdered.'

David Hughes thought a while. 'How came Nest to take her to live with her?' asked he.

'Well! Folk say John Griffiths did not give her enough to eat. Half-wits, they tell me, take more to feed them than others, and Eleanor Gwynn had given her oat-cake, and porridge a time or two, and most likely spoken kindly to her (you know Eleanor spoke kind to all), so some months ago, when John Griffiths had been beating her, and keeping her without food to try and tame her, she ran away, and came to Nest's cottage in the dead of night, all shivering and starved, for she did not know Eleanor was dead, and thought to meet with kindness from her, I've no doubt; and Nest remembered how her mother used to feed and comfort the poor idiot, and made her some gruel, and wrapped her up by the fire. And, in the morning, when John Griffiths came in search of Mary, he found her with Nest, and Mary wailed so piteously at the sight of him, that Nest went to the parish officers, and offered to take her to board with her for the same money they gave to him. John says he was right glad to be off his bargain.'

David Hughes knew there was a kind of remorse which sought relief in the performance of the most difficult and repugnant tasks. He thought he could understand how, in her bitter repentance for her conduct towards her mother, Nest had taken in the first helpless creature that came seeking shelter in her name. It was not what he would have chosen, but he knew it was God that had sent the poor wandering idiot there.

He went to see Nest the next morning. As he drew near the cottage—it was summer time, and the doors and windows were all open—he heard an angry passionate kind of sound that was scarcely human. That sound prevented his approach from being heard; and, standing at the threshold, he saw poor Mary Williams pacing backwards and forwards in some wild mood. Nest, cripple as she was, was walking with her, speaking low soothing words, till the pace was slackened, and time and breathing was given to put her arm around the crazy woman's neck, and soothe her by this tender caress into the quiet luxury of tears—tears which give the hot brain relief. Then David Hughes came in. His first words, as he took off his hat, standing on the lintel, were—'The peace of God be upon this house.' Neither he nor Nest recurred to the past, though solemn recollections filled their minds. Before he went, all three knelt and prayed; for, as Nest told him, some mysterious influence of peace came over the poor half-wit's mind, when she heard the holy words of prayer; and often when she felt a paroxysm coming on, she would kneel and repeat a homily rapidly over, as if it were a charm to scare away the Demon in possession; sometimes, indeed, the control over herself requisite for this effort was enough to dispel the fluttering burst. When David rose up to go, he drew Nest to the door.

'You are not afraid, my child?' asked he.

'No,' she replied. 'She is often very good and quiet. When she is not, I can bear it.'

'I shall see your face on earth no more,' said he. 'God bless you!' He went on his way. Not many weeks after, David Hughes was borne to his grave.

The doors of Nest's heart were opened—opened wide by the love she grew to feel for crazy Mary, so helpless, so friendless, so dependent upon her. Mary loved her back again, as a dumb animal loves its blind master. It was happiness enough to be near her. In general, she was only too glad to do what she was bidden by Nest. But there were times when Mary was overpowered by the glooms and fancies of her poor disordered brain. Fearful times! No one knew how fearful. On those days, Nest warned the little children who loved to come and play around her, that they must not visit the house. The signal was a piece of white linen hung out of a side window. On those days, the sorrowful and sick waited in vain for the sound of Nest's lame approach. But what she had to endure was only known to God, for she never complained. If she had given up the charge of Mary, or if the neighbours had risen, out of love and care for her life, to compel such a step, she knew what hard curses and blows, what starvation and misery, would await the poor creature.

She told of Mary's docility, and her affection, and her innocent, little sayings; but she never told the details of the occasional days of wild disorder, and driving insanity.

Nest grew old before her time, in consequence of her accident. She knew that she was as old at fifty as many are at seventy. She knew it partly by the vividness with which the remembrance of the days of her youth came back to her mind, while the events of yesterday were dim and forgotten. She dreamt of her girlhood and youth. In sleep, she was once more the beautiful Nest Gwynn, the admired of all beholders, the light-hearted girl, beloved by her mother. Little circumstances connected with those early days, forgotten since the very time when they occurred, came back to her mind, in her waking hours. She had a scar on the palm of her left hand, occasioned by the fall of a branch of a tree, when she was a child. It had not pained her since the first two days after the accident; but now it began to hurt her slightly; and clear in her ears was the crackling sound of the treacherous, rending wood; distinct before her rose the presence of her mother, tenderly binding up the wound. With these remembrances came a longing desire to see the beautiful, fatal well once more before her death. She had never gone so far since the day when, by her fall there, she lost love and hope, and her bright glad youth. She yearned to look upon its waters once again. This desire waxed as her life waned.* She told it to poor crazy Mary.

'Mary!' said she, 'I want to go to the Rock Well. If you will help me, I can manage it. There used to be many a stone in the Dol Mawr on which I could sit and rest. We will go to-morrow morning before folks are astir.'

Mary answered briskly, 'Up, up! To the Rock Well. Mary will go. Mary will go.' All day long she kept muttering to herself, 'Mary will go.'

Nest had the happiest dream that night. Her mother stood beside her—not in the flesh, but in the bright glory of a blessed spirit. And Nest was no longer young—neither was she old—'they reckon not by days, nor years, where she was gone to dwell;'* and her mother stretched out her arms to her with a calm, glad look of welcome. She awoke; the woodlark was singing in the near copse— the little birds were astir, and rustling in their leafy nests. Nest arose, and called Mary. The two set out through the quiet lane. They went along slowly and silently. With many a pause they crossed the broad Dol Mawr, and carefully descended the sloping stones, on which no trace remained of the hundreds of feet that had passed over them since Nest was last there. The clear water sparkled and quivered in the early sunlight, the shadows of the birch-leaves were stirred on the ground; the ferns—Nest could have believed that they were the very same ferns which she had seen thirty years before—hung wet and dripping where the water overflowed—a thrush chanted matins* from a hollybush near—and the running stream made a low, soft, sweet accompaniment. All was the same. Nature was as fresh and young as ever. It might have been yesterday that Edward Williams had overtaken her, and told her his love— the thought of his words—his handsome looks—(he was a gray, hard-featured man by this time), and then she recalled the fatal wintry morning when joy and youth had fled; and as she remembered that faintness of pain, a new, a real faintness—no echo of the memory—came over her. She leant her back against a rock, without a moan or sigh, and died! She found immortality by the well-side, instead of her fragile, perishing youth. She was so calm and placid that Mary (who had been dipping her fingers in the well, to see the waters drop off in the gleaming sunlight), thought she was asleep, and for some time continued her amusement in silence. At last, she turned, and said,—

'Mary is tired. Mary wants to go home.' Nest did not speak, though the idiot repeated her plaintive words. She stood and looked till a strange terror came over her—a terror too mysterious to be borne.

'Mistress, wake! Mistress, wake!' she said, wildly, shaking the form.

But Nest did not awake. And the first person who came to the well that morning found crazy Mary sitting, awestruck, by the poor dead Nest. They had to get the poor creature away by force, before they could remove the body.

Mary is in Trê-Madoc workhouse. They treat her pretty kindly, and, in general, she is good and tractable. Occasionally, the old paroxysms come on; and, for a time, she is unmanageable. But some one thought of speaking to her about Nest. She stood arrested at the name; and, since then, it is astonishing to see what efforts she makes to curb her insanity; and when the dread time is past, she creeps up to the matron, and says, 'Mary has tried to be good. Will God let her go to Nest now?'

THE HEART OF
JOHN MIDDLETON

I WAS born at Sawley, where the shadow of Pendle Hill falls at sunrise. I suppose Sawley sprang up into a village in the time of the monks, who had an abbey there. Many of the cottages are strange old places; others, again, are built of the abbey stones, mixed up with the shale from the neighbouring quarries; and you may see many a quaint bit of carving worked into the walls, or forming the lintels of the doors. There is a row of houses, built still more recently, where one Mr Peel came to live there for the sake of the water-power,* and gave the place a fillip into something like life; though a different kind of life, as I take it, from the grand, slow ways folks had when the monks were about.

Now it was—six o'clock, ring the bell, throng to the factory; sharp home at twelve; and even at night, when work was done, we hardly knew how to walk slowly, we had been so bustled all day long. I can't recollect the time when I did not go to the factory. My father used to drag me there when I was quite a little fellow, in order to wind reels for him. I never remember my mother. I should have been a better man than I have been, if I had only had a notion of the sound of her voice, or the look on her face.

My father and I lodged in the house of a man who also worked in the factory. We were sadly thronged in Sawley, so many people came from different parts of the country to earn a livelihood at the new work; and it was some time before the row of cottages I have spoken of could be built. While they were building, my father was turned out of his lodgings for drinking and being disorderly, and he and I slept in the brick-kiln; that is to say, when we did sleep o' nights; but, often and often, we went poaching; and many a hare and pheasant have I rolled up in clay, and roasted in the embers of the kiln. Then, as followed to reason, I was drowsy next day over my work; but father had no mercy on me for sleeping, for all he knew the cause of it, but kicked me where I lay, a heavy lump on the factory floor, and cursed and swore at me till I got up for very fear, and to my winding again. But, when his back was turned, I paid him off with heavier curses than he had given me, and longed to be a man, that I might be revenged on him. The words I then spoke I would not now dare to repeat; and worse than hating words, a hating heart went with them. I forget the time when I did not know how to hate. When I first came to read, and learnt about Ishmael, I thought I must be of his doomed race, for my hand was against every man, and every man's against me.* But I was seventeen or more before I cared for my book enough to learn to read.

After the row of works was finished, father took one, and set up for himself, in letting lodgings. I can't say much for the furnishing; but there was plenty of straw, and we kept up good fires; and there is a set of people who value warmth above everything. The worst lot about the place lodged with us. We used to have a supper in the middle of the night; there was game enough, or if there was not game, there was poultry to be had for the stealing. By day, we all made a show of working in the factory. By night, we feasted and drank.

Now this web of my life was black enough, and coarse enough; but, by-and-by, a little golden, filmy thread began to be woven in; the dawn of God's mercy was at hand.

One blowy October morning, as I sauntered lazily along to the mill, I came to the little wooden bridge over a brook that falls into the Bribble. On the plank there stood a child, balancing the pitcher on her head, with which she had been to fetch water. She was so light on her feet that, had it not been for the weight of the pitcher, I almost believe the wind would have taken her up, and wafted her away as it carries off a blow-ball* in seed-time; her blue cotton dress was blown before her, as if she were spreading her wings for a flight; she turned her face round, as if to ask me for something, but when she saw who it was, she hesitated, for I had a bad name in the village, and I doubt not she had been warned against me. But her heart was too innocent to be distrustful; so she said to me, timidly,—

'Please, John Middleton, will you carry me this heavy jug just over the bridge?'

It was the very first time I had ever been spoken to gently. I was ordered here and there by my father and his rough companions; I was abused, and cursed by them if I failed in doing what they wished; if I succeeded, there came no expression of thanks or gratitude. I was informed of facts necessary for me to know. But the gentle words of request or entreaty were aforetime unknown to me, and now their tones fell on my ear soft and sweet as a distant peal of bells. I wished that I knew how to speak properly in reply; but though we were of the same standing as regarded worldly circumstances, there was some mighty difference between us, which made me unable to speak in her language of soft words and modest entreaty. There was nothing for me but to take up the pitcher in a kind of gruff, shy silence, and carry it over the bridge, as she had asked me. When I gave it her back again, she thanked me and tripped away, leaving me, wordless, gazing after her like an awkward lout as I was. I knew well enough who she was. She was grandchild to Eleanor Hadfield, an aged woman, who was reputed as a witch by my father and his set, for no other reason, that I can make out, than her scorn, dignity, and fearlessness of rancour. It was true we often met her in the grey dawn of the morning, when we returned from poaching, and my father used to curse her, under his breath, for a witch, such as were burnt long ago on Pendle Hill top; but I had heard that Eleanor was a skilful sick nurse, and ever ready to give her services to those who were ill; and I believe that she had been sitting up through the night (the night that we had been spending under the wild heavens, in deeds as wild), with those who were appointed to die. Nelly was her orphan granddaughter; her little hand-maiden; her treasure; her one ewe lamb. Many and many a day have I watched by the brook-side, hoping that some happy gust of wind, coming with opportune bluster down the hollow of the dale, might make me necessary once more to her. I longed to hear her speak to me again. I said the words she had used to myself, trying to catch her tone; but the chance never came again. I do not know that she ever knew how I watched for her there. I found out that she went to school, and nothing would serve me but that I must go too. My father scoffed at me; I did not care. I knew nought of what reading was, nor that it was likely that I should be laughed at; I, a great hulking lad of seventeen or upwards, for going to learn my A, B, C, in the midst of a crowd of little ones. I stood just this way in my mind. Nelly was at school; it was the best place for seeing her, and hearing her voice again. Therefore I would go too. My father talked, and swore, and threatened, but I stood to it. He said I should leave school, weary of it in a month. I swore a deeper oath than I like to remember, that I would stay a year, and come out a reader and a writer. My father hated the notion of folks learning to read, and said it took all the spirit out of them; besides, he thought he had a right to every penny of my wages, and though, when he was in good humour, he might have given me many a jug of ale, he grudged my twopence a week for schooling. However, to school I went. It was a different place to what I had thought it before I went inside. The girls sat on one side, and the boys on the other; so I was not near Nelly. She, too, was in the first class; I was put with the little toddling things that could hardly run alone. The master sat in the middle, and kept pretty strict watch over us. But I could see Nelly, and hear her read her chapter; and even when it was one with a long list of hard names, such as the master was very fond of giving her, to show how well she could hit them off without spelling, I thought I had never heard a prettier music. Now and then she read other things. I did not know what they were, true or false; but I listened because she read; and, by-and-by, I began to wonder. I remember the first word I ever spoke to her was to ask her (as we were coming out of school) who was the Father of whom she had been reading, for when she said the words 'Our Father,' her voice dropped into a soft, holy kind of low sound, which struck me more than any loud reading, it seemed so loving and tender. When I asked her this, she looked at me with her great blue wondering eyes, at first shocked; and then, as it were, melted down into pity and sorrow, she said in the same way, below her breath, in which she read the words, 'Our Father,'—

'Don't you know? It is God.'

'God?'

'Yes; the God that grandmother tells me about.'

'Tell me what she says, will you?' So we sat down on the hedge-bank, she a little above me, while I looked up into her face, and she told me all the holy texts her grandmother had taught her, as explaining all that could be explained of the Almighty. I listened in silence, for indeed I was overwhelmed with astonishment. Her knowledge was principally rote-knowledge; she was too young for much more; but we, in Lancashire, speak a rough kind of Bible language, and the texts seemed very clear to me. I rose up, dazed and overpowered. I was going away in silence, when I bethought me of my manners, and turned back, and said, 'Thank you,' for the first time I ever remember saying it in my life. That was a great day for me, in more ways than one.

I was always one who could keep very steady to an object when once I had set it before me. My object was to know Nelly. I was conscious of nothing more. But it made me regardless of all other things. The master might scold, the little ones might laugh; I bore it all without giving it a second thought. I kept to my year, and came out a reader and writer; more, however, to stand well in Nelly's good opinion, than because of my oath. About this time, my father committed some bad, cruel deed, and had to fly the country. I was glad he went; for I had never loved or cared for him, and wanted to shake myself clear of his set. But it was no easy matter. Honest folk stood aloof; only bad men held out their arms to me with a welcome. Even Nelly seemed to have a mixture of fear now with her kind ways towards me. I was the son of John Middleton, who, if he were caught, would be hung at Lancaster Castle. I thought she looked at me sometimes with a sort of sorrowful horror. Others were not forbearing enough to keep their expression of feeling confined to looks. The son of the overlooker at the mill never ceased twitting me with my father's crime; he now brought up his poaching against him, though I knew very well how many a good supper he himself had made on game which had been given him to make him and his father wink at late hours in the morning. And how were such as my father to come honestly by game?

This lad, Dick Jackson, was the bane of my life. He was a year or two older than I was, and had much power over the men who worked at the mill, as he could report to his father what he chose. I could not always hold my peace when he 'threaped'* me with my father's sins, but gave it him back sometimes in a storm of passion. It did me no good; only threw me farther from the company of better men, who looked aghast and shocked at the oaths I poured out—blasphemous words learnt in my childhood, which I could not forget now that I would fain have purified myself of them; while all the time Dick Jackson stood by, with a mocking smile of intelligence; and when I had ended, breathless and weary with spent passion, he would turn to those whose respect I longed to earn, and ask if I were not a worthy son of my father, and likely to tread in his steps. But this smiling indifference of his to my miserable vehemence was not all, though it was the worst part of his conduct, for it made the rankling hatred grow up in my heart, and overshadow it like the great gourd-tree of the prophet Jonah.* But his was a merciful shade, keeping out the burning sun; mine blighted what it fell upon.

What Dick Jackson did besides, was this. His father was a skilful overlooker, and a good man. Mr Peel valued him so much, that he was kept on, although his health was failing; and when he was unable, through illness, to come to the mill, he deputed his son to watch over, and report the men. It was too much power for one so young—I speak it calmly now. Whatever Dick Jackson became, he had strong temptations when he was young, which will be allowed for hereafter. But at the time of which I am telling, my hate raged like a fire. I believed that he was the one sole obstacle to my being received as fit to mix with good and honest men. I was sick of crime and disorder, and would fain have come over to a different kind of life, and have been industrious, sober, honest, and right-spoken (I had no idea of higher virtue then), and at every turn Dick Jackson met me with his sneers. I have walked the night through, in the old abbey field, planning how I could outwit him, and win men's respect in spite of him. The first time I ever prayed, was underneath the silent stars, kneeling by the old abbey walls, throwing up my arms, and asking God for the power of revenge upon him.

I had heard that if I prayed earnestly, God would give me what I asked for, and I looked upon it as a kind of chance for the fulfilment of my wishes. If earnestness would have won the boon for me, never were wicked words so earnestly spoken. And oh, later on, my prayer was heard, and my wish granted! All this time I saw little of Nelly. Her grandmother was failing, and she had much to do in-doors. Besides, I believed I had read her looks aright, when I took them to speak of aversion; and I planned to hide myself from her sight, as it were, until I could stand upright before men, with fearless eyes, dreading no face of accusation. It was possible to acquire a good character; I would do it—I did it: but no one brought up among respectable untempted people can tell the unspeakable hardness of the task. In the evenings I would not go forth among the village throng; for the acquaintances that claimed me were my father's old associates, who would have been glad enough to enlist a strong young man like me in their projects; and the men who would have shunned me and kept aloof, were the steady and orderly. So I stayed in-doors, and practised myself in reading. You will say, I should have found it easier to earn a good character away from Sawley, at some place where neither I nor my father was known. So I should; but it would not have been the same thing to my mind. Besides, representing all good men, all goodness to me, in Sawley Nelly lived. In her sight I would work out my life, and fight my way upwards to men's respect. Two years passed on. Every day I strove fiercely; every day my struggles were made fruitless by the son of the overlooker; and I seemed but where I was—but where I must ever be esteemed by all who knew me—but as the son of the criminal—wild, reckless, ripe for crime myself. Where was the use of my reading and writing? These acquirements were disregarded and scouted by those among whom I was thrust back to take my portion. I could have read any chapter in the Bible now; and Nelly seemed as though she would never know it. I was driven in upon my books; and few enough of them I had. The pedlars brought them round in their packs, and I bought what I could. I had the *Seven Champions*,* and the *Pilgrim's Progress*,* and both seemed to me equally wonderful, and equally founded on fact. I got Byron's *Narrative*,* and Milton's *Paradise Lost*;* but I lacked the knowledge which would give a clue to all. Still they afforded me pleasure, because they took me out of myself, and made me forget my miserable position, and made me unconscious (for the time at least) of my one great passion of hatred against Dick Jackson.

When Nelly was about seventeen her grandmother died. I stood aloof in the churchyard, behind the great yew-tree, and watched the funeral. It was the first religious service that ever I heard; and, to my shame, as I thought, it affected me to tears. The words seemed so peaceful and holy that I longed to go to church, but I durst not, because I had never been. The parish church was at Bolton, far enough away to serve as an excuse for all who did not care to go. I heard Nelly's sobs filling up every pause in the clergyman's voice; and every sob of hers went to my heart. She passed me on her way out of the churchyard; she was so near I might have touched her; but her head was hanging down, and I durst not speak to her. Then the question arose, what was to become of her? She must earn her living! was it to be as a farm-servant, or by working at the mill? I knew enough of both kinds of life to make me tremble for her. My wages were such as to enable me to marry, if I chose; and I never thought of woman, for my wife, but Nelly. Still, I would not have married her now, if I could; for, as yet, I had not risen up to the character which I determined it was fit that Nelly's husband should have. When I was rich in good report, I would come forwards, and take my chance, but until then I would hold my peace. I had faith in the power of my long-continued dogged breasting of opinion. Sooner or later it must, it should, yield, and I be received among the ranks of good men. But, meanwhile, what was to become of Nelly? I reckoned up my wages; I went to inquire what the board of a girl would be who should help her in her household work, and live with her as a daughter, at the house of one of the most decent women of the place; she looked at me suspiciously. I kept down my temper, and told her I would never come near the place; that I would keep away from that end of the village, and that the girl for whom I made the inquiry should never know but what the parish paid for her keep. It would not do; she suspected me; but I know I had power over myself to have kept my word; and besides, I would not for worlds have had Nelly put under any obligation to me, which should speck the purity of her love, or dim it by a mixture of gratitude,—the love that I craved to earn, not for my money, not for my kindness, but for myself. I heard that Nelly had met with a place in Bolland; and I could see no reason why I might not speak to her once before she left our neighbourhood. I meant it to be a quiet friendly telling her of my sympathy in her sorrow. I felt I could command myself. So, on the Sunday before she was to leave Sawley, I waited near the wood-path, by which I knew that she would return from afternoon church. The birds made such a melodious warble, such a busy sound among the leaves, that I did not hear approaching footsteps till they were close at hand; and then there were sounds of two persons' voices. The wood was near that part of Sawley where Nelly was staying with friends; the path through it led to their house, and theirs only, so I knew it must be she, for I had watched her setting out to church alone.

But who was the other?

The blood went to my heart and head, as if I were shot, when I saw that it was Dick Jackson. Was this the end of it all? In the steps of sin which my father had trod, I would rush to my death and my doom. Even where I stood I longed for a weapon to slay him. How dared he come near my Nelly? She too,—I thought her faithless, and forgot how little I had ever been to her in outward action; how few words, and those how uncouth, I had ever spoken to her; and I hated her for a traitress. These feelings passed through me before I could see, my eyes and head were so dizzy and blind. When I looked I saw Dick Jackson holding her hand, and speaking quick and low and thick, as a man speaks in great vehemence. She seemed white and dismayed; but all at once, at some word of his (and what it was she never would tell me), she looked as though she defied a fiend, and wrenched herself out of his grasp. He caught hold of her again, and began once more the thick whisper that I loathed. I could bear it no longer, nor did I see why I should. I stepped out from behind the tree where I had been lying. When she saw me, she lost her look of one strung up to desperation, and came and clung to me; and I felt like a giant in strength and might. I held her with one arm, but I did not take my eyes off him; I felt as if they blazed down into his soul, and scorched him up. He never spoke, but tried to look as though he defied me. At last, his eyes fell before mine, I dared not speak; for the old horrid oaths thronged up to my mouth; and I dreaded giving them way, and terrifying my poor, trembling Nelly.

At last, he made to go past me: I drew her out of the pathway. By instinct she wrapped her garments round her, as if to avoid his accidental touch; and he was stung by this, I suppose—I believe— to the mad, miserable revenge he took. As my back was turned to him, in an endeavour to speak some words to Nelly that might soothe her into calmness, she, who was looking after him, like one fascinated with terror, saw him take a sharp, shaley stone, and aim it at me. Poor darling! she clung round me as a shield, making her sweet body into a defence for mine. It hit her, and she spoke no word, kept back her cry of pain, but fell at my feet in a swoon. He—the coward!—ran off as soon as he saw what he had done. I was with Nelly alone in the green gloom of the wood. The quivering and leaf-tinted light made her look as if she were dead. I carried her, not knowing if I bore a corpse or not, to her friend's house. I did not stay to explain, but ran madly for the doctor.

Well! I cannot bear to recur to that time again. Five weeks I lived in the agony of suspense; from which my only relief was in laying savage plans for revenge. If I hated him before, what think ye I did now? It seemed as if earth could not hold us twain, but that one of us must go down to Gehenna.* I could have killed him; and would have done it without a scruple, but that seemed too poor and bold a revenge. At length—oh! the weary waiting—oh! the sickening of my heart—Nelly grew better; as well as she was ever to grow. The bright colour had left her cheek; the mouth quivered with re-pressed pain, the eyes were dim with tears that agony had forced into them; and I loved her a thousand times better and more than when she was bright and blooming! What was best of all, I began to perceive that she cared for me. I know her grandmother's friends warned her against me, and told her I came of a bad stock; but she had passed the point where remonstrance from bystanders can take effect—she loved me as I was, a strange mixture of bad and good, all unworthy of her. We spoke together now, as those do whose lives are bound up in each other. I told her I would marry her as soon as she had recovered her health. Her friends shook their heads; but they saw she would be unfit for farm-service or heavy work, and they perhaps thought, as many a one does, that a bad husband was better than none at all. Anyhow, we were married; and I learnt to bless God for my happiness, so far beyond my deserts. I kept her like a lady. I was a skilful workman, and earned good wages; and every want she had I tried to gratify. Her wishes were few and simple enough, poor Nelly! If they had been ever so fanciful, I should have had my reward in the new feeling of the holiness of home. She could lead me as a little child, with the charm of her gentle voice, and her ever-kind words. She would plead for all when I was full of anger and passion; only Dick Jackson's name passed never between our lips during all that time. In the evening she lay back in her beehive chair,* and read to me. I think I see her now, pale and weak, with her sweet, young face, lighted by her holy, earnest eyes, telling me of the Saviour's life and death, till they were filled with tears. I longed to have been there, to have avenged him on the wicked Jews. I liked Peter* the best of all the disciples. But I got the Bible myself, and read the mighty act of God's vengeance, in the Old Testament,* with a kind of triumphant faith that, sooner or later, He would take my cause in hand, and revenge me on mine enemy.

In a year or so, Nelly had a baby—a little girl, with eyes just like hers, that looked, with a grave openness, right into yours. Nelly recovered but slowly. It was just before winter, the cotton-crop had failed,* and master had to turn off many hands. I thought I was sure of being kept on, for I had earned a steady character, and did my work well; but once again it was permitted that Dick Jackson should do me wrong. He induced his father to dismiss me among the first in my branch of the business; and there was I, just before winter set in, with a wife and new-born child, and a small enough store of money to keep body and soul together, till I could get to work again. All my savings had gone by Christmas Eve, and we sat in the house, foodless for the morrow's festival. Nelly looked pinched and worn; the baby cried for a larger supply of milk than its poor, starving mother could give it. My right hand had not forgot its cunning,* and I went out once more to my poaching. I knew where the gang met; and I knew what a welcome back I should have,—a far warmer and more hearty welcome than good men had given me when I tried to enter their ranks. On the road to the meeting-place I fell in with an old man,—one who had been a companion to my father in his early days.

'What, lad!' said he, 'art thou turning back to the old trade? It's the better business, now that cotton has failed.'

'Ay,' said I, 'cotton is starving us outright. A man may bear a deal himself, but he'll do aught bad and sinful to save his wife and child.'

'Nay, lad,' said he, 'poaching is not sinful; it goes against man's laws, but not against God's.'

I was too weak to argue or talk much. I had not tasted food for two days. But I murmured, 'At any rate, I trusted to have been clear of it for the rest of my days. It led my father wrong at first. I have tried and I have striven. Now I give all up. Right or wrong shall be the same to me. Some are fore-doomed; and so am I.' And as I spoke, some notion of the futurity that would separate Nelly, the pure and holy, from me, the reckless and desperate one, came over me with an irrepressible burst of anguish. Just then the bells of Bolton-in-Bolland struck up a glad peal, which came over the woods, in the solemn midnight air, like the sons of the morning shouting for joy—they seemed so clear and jubilant. It was Christmas Day: and I felt like an outcast from the gladness and the salvation. Old Jonah spoke out:—

'Yon's the Christmas bells. I say, Johnny, my lad, I've no notion of taking such a spiritless chap as thou into the thick of it, with thy rights and thy wrongs. We don't trouble ourselves with such fine lawyer's stuff, and we bring down the "varmint"* all the better. Now, I'll not have thee in our gang, for thou art not up to the fun, and thou'd hang fire when the time came to be doing. But I've a shrewd guess that plaguy wife and child of thine are at the bottom of thy half-and-half joining. Now, I was thy father's friend afore he took to them helter-skelter ways, and I've five shillings and a neck of mutton at thy service. I'll not list* a fasting man; but if thou'lt come to us with a full stomach, and say, "I like your life, my lads, and I'll make one of you with pleasure, the first shiny night," why, we'll give you a welcome and a half; but, to-night, make no more ado, but turn back with me for the mutton and the money.'

I was not proud: nay, I was most thankful. I took the meat, and boiled some broth for my poor Nelly. She was in a sleep, or a faint, I know not which; but I roused her, and held her up in bed, and fed her with a teaspoon, and the light came back to her eyes, and the faint, moonlight smile to her lips; and when she had ended, she said her innocent grace, and fell asleep, with her baby on her breast. I sat over the fire, and listened to the bells, as they swept past my cottage on the gusts of the wind. I longed and yearned for the second coming of Christ, of which Nelly had told me. The world seemed cruel, and hard, and strong—too strong for me; and I prayed to cling to the hem of His garment,* and be borne over the rough places when I fainted, and bled, and found no man to pity or help me, but poor old Jonah, the publican and sinner.* All this time my own woes and my own self were uppermost in my mind, as they are in the minds of most who have been hardly used. As I thought of my wrongs, and my sufferings, my heart burned against Dick Jackson; and as the bells rose and fell, so my hopes waxed and waned, that in those mysterious days, of which they were both the remembrance and the prophecy, he would be purged from off the earth. I took Nelly's Bible, and turned, not to the gracious story of the Saviour's birth, but to the records of the former days, when the Jews took such wild revenge upon all their opponents. I was a Jew,—a leader among the people. Dick Jackson was as Pharaoh, as the King Agag,* who walked delicately, thinking the bitterness of death was past,—in short, he was the conquered enemy, over whom

I gloated, with my Bible in my hand—that Bible which contained our Saviour's words on the Cross. As yet, those words seemed faint and meaningless to me, like a tract of country seen in the starlight haze; while the histories of the Old Testament were grand and distinct in the blood-red colour of sunset. By-and-by that night passed into day, and little piping voices came round, carol-singing. They wakened Nelly. I went to her as soon as I heard her stirring.

'Nelly,' said I, 'there's money and food in the house; I will be off to Padiham seeking work, while thou hast something to go upon.'

'Not to-day,' said she; 'stay to-day with me. If thou wouldst only go to church with me this once'—for you see I had never been inside a church but when we were married, and she was often praying me to go; and now she looked at me, with a sigh just creeping forth from her lips, as she expected a refusal. But I did not refuse. I had been kept away from church before because I dared not go; and now I was desperate, and dared do anything. If I did look like a heathen in the face of all men, why, I was a heathen in my heart; for I was falling back into all my evil ways. I had resolved if my search of work at Padiham should fail, I would follow my father's footsteps, and take with my own right hand and by my strength of arm what it was denied me to obtain honestly. I had resolved to leave Sawley, where a curse seemed to hang over me; so, what did it matter if I went to church, all unbeknowing what strange ceremonies were there performed? I walked thither as a sinful man—sinful in my heart. Nelly hung on my arm, but even she could not get me to speak. I went in; she found my places, and pointed to the words, and looked up into my eyes with hers, so full of faith and joy. But I saw nothing but Richard Jackson—I heard nothing but his loud nasal voice, making response, and desecrating all the holy words. He was in broadcloth of the best—I in my fustian* jacket. He was prosperous and glad—I was starving and desperate. Nelly grew pale, as she saw the expression in my eyes; and she prayed ever, and ever more fervently as the thought of me tempted by the Devil even at that very moment came more fully before her.

By-and-by she forgot even me, and laid her soul bare before God, in a long, silent, weeping prayer, before we left the church. Nearly all had gone; and I stood by her, unwilling to disturb her, unable to join her. At last she rose up, heavenly calm. She took my arm, and we went home through the woods, where all the birds seemed tame and familiar. Nelly said she thought all living creatures knew it was Christmas Day, and rejoiced, and were loving together. I believed it was the frost that had tamed them; and I felt the hatred that was in me, and knew that whatever else was loving, I was full of malice and uncharitableness, nor did I wish to be otherwise. That afternoon I bade Nelly and our child farewell, and tramped to Padiham. I got work—* how I hardly know; for stronger and stronger came the force of the temptation to lead a wild, free life of sin; legions seemed whispering evil thoughts to me, and only my gentle, pleading Nelly to pull me back from the great gulf. However, as I said before, I got work, and set off homewards to move my wife and child to that neighbourhood. I hated Sawley, and yet I was fiercely indignant to leave it, with my purposes unaccomplished. I was still an outcast from the more respectable, who stood afar off from such as I; and mine enemy lived and flourished in their regard. Padiham, however, was not so far away for me to despair—to relinquish my fixed determination. It was on the eastern side of the great Pendle Hill, ten miles away—maybe. Hate will overleap a greater obstacle. I took a cottage on the Fell,* high up on the side of the hill. We saw a long black moorland slope before us, and then the grey stone houses of Padiham, over which a black cloud hung, different from the blue wood or turf smoke about Sawley. The wild winds came down and whistled round our house many a day when all was still below. But I was happy then. I rose in men's esteem. I had work in plenty. Our child lived and throve. But I forgot not our country proverb—'Keep a stone in thy pocket for seven years: turn it, and keep it seven years more; but have it ever ready to cast at thine enemy when the time comes.'*

One day a fellow-workman asked me to go to a hill-side preaching. Now, I never cared to go to church; but there was something newer and freer in the notion of praying to God right under His great dome; and the open air had had a charm to me ever since my wild boyhood. Besides, they said, these ranters had strange ways with them, and I thought it would be fun to see their way of setting about it; and this ranter of all others had made himself a name in our parts. Accordingly we went; it was a fine summer's evening, after work was done. When we got to the place we saw such a crowd as I never saw before—men, women, and children; all ages were gathered together, and sat on the hill-side. They were care-worn, diseased, sorrowful, criminal; all that was told on their faces, which were hard and strongly marked. In the midst, standing in a cart, was the ranter. When I first saw him, I said to my companion, 'Lord! what a little man to make all this pother! I could trip him up with one of my fingers,' and then I sat down, and looked about me a bit. All eyes were fixed on the preacher; and I turned mine upon him too. He began to speak; it was in no fine-drawn language, but in words such as we heard every day of our lives, and about things we did every day of our lives. He did not call our shortcomings pride or worldliness, or pleasure-seeking, which would have given us no clear notion of what he meant, but he just told us outright what we did, and then he gave it a name, and said that it was accursed, and that we were lost if we went on so doing.

By this time the tears and sweat were running down his face; he was wrestling for our souls. We wondered how he knew our innermost lives as he did, for each one of us saw his sin set before him in plain-spoken words. Then he cried out to us to repent; and spoke first to us, and then to God, in a way that would have shocked many—but it did not shock me. I liked strong things; and I liked the bare, full truth: and I felt brought nearer to God in that hour—the summer darkness creeping over us, and one after one the stars coming out above us, like the eyes of the angels watching us—than I had ever done in my life before. When he had brought us to our tears and sighs, he stopped his loud voice of upbraiding, and there was a hush, only broken by sobs and quivering moans, in which I heard through the gloom the voices of strong men in anguish and supplication, as well as the shriller tones of women. Suddenly he was heard again; by this time we could not see him; but his voice was now tender as the voice of an angel, and he told us of Christ, and implored us to come to Him. I never heard such passionate entreaty. He spoke as if he saw Satan hovering near us in the dark, dense night, and as if our only safety lay in a very present coming to the Cross; I believe he did see Satan; we know he haunts the desolate old hills, awaiting his time, and now or never it was with many a soul. At length there was a sudden silence; and by the cries of those nearest to the preacher, we heard that he had fainted. We had all crowded round him, as if he were our safety and our guide; and he was overcome by the heat and the fatigue, for we were the fifth set of people whom he had addressed that day. I left the crowd who were leading him down, and took a lonely path myself.

Here was the earnestness I needed. To this weak and weary fainting man, religion was a life and a passion. I look back now, and wonder at my blindness as to what was the root of all my Nelly's patience and long-suffering; for I thought, now I had found out what religion was, and that hitherto it had been all an unknown thing to me.

Henceforward, my life was changed. I was zealous and fanatical. Beyond the set to whom I had affiliated myself, I had no sympathy. I would have persecuted all who differed from me, if I had only had the power. I became an ascetic in all bodily enjoyments. And, strange and inexplicable mystery, I had some thoughts that by every act of self-denial I was attaining to my unholy end, and that, when I had fasted and prayed long enough, God would place my vengeance in my hands. I have knelt by Nelly's bedside, and vowed to live a self-denying life, as regarded all outward things, if so that God would grant my prayer. I left it in His hands. I felt sure He would trace out the token and the word; and Nelly would listen to my passionate words, and lie awake sorrowful and heart-sore through the night; and I would get up and make her tea, and rearrange her pillows, with a strange and wilful blindness that my bitter words and blasphemous prayers had cost her miserable, sleepless nights. My Nelly was suffering yet from that blow. How or where the stone had hurt her, I never understood; but in consequence of that one moment's action, her limbs became numb and dead, and, by slow degrees, she took to her bed, from whence she was never carried alive. There she lay, propped up by pillows, her meek face ever bright, and smiling forth a greeting; her white, pale hands ever busy with some kind of work; and our little Grace was as the power of motion to her. Fierce as I was away from her, I never could speak to her but in my gentlest tones. She seemed to me as if she had never wrestled for salvation as I had; and when away from her, I resolved many a time and oft, that I would rouse her up to her state of danger when I returned home that evening—even if strong reproach were required I would rouse her up to her soul's need. But I came in and heard her voice singing softly some holy word of patience, some psalm which, maybe, had comforted the martyrs, and when I saw her face like the face of an angel, full of patience and happy faith, I put off my awakening speeches till another time.

One night, long ago, when I was yet young and strong, although my years were past forty, I sat alone in my houseplace.* Nelly was always in bed, as I have told you, and Grace lay in a cot by her side. I believed them to be both asleep; though how they could sleep I could not conceive, so wild and terrible was the night. The wind came sweeping down from the hill-top in great beats, like the pulses of heaven; and, during the pauses, while I listened for the coming roar, I felt the earth shiver beneath me. The rain beat against windows and doors, and sobbed for entrance. I thought the Prince of the Air* was abroad; and I heard, or fancied I heard, shrieks come on the blast, like the cries of sinful souls given over to his power.

The sounds came nearer and nearer. I got up and saw to the fastenings of the door, for though I cared not for mortal man, I did care for what I believed was surrounding the house, in evil might and power. But the door shook as though it, too, were in deadly terror, and I thought the fastenings would give way. I stood facing the entrance, lashing my heart up to defy the spiritual enemy that I looked to see, every instant, in bodily presence; and the door did burst open; and before me stood—what was it? man or demon? a grey-haired man, with poor, worn clothes all wringing wet, and he himself battered and piteous to look upon, from the storm he had passed through.

'Let me in!' he said. 'Give me shelter. I am poor, or I would reward you. And I am friendless, too,' he said, looking up in my face, like one seeking what he cannot find. In that look, strangely changed, I knew that God had heard me; for it was the old cowardly look of my life's enemy. Had he been a stranger, I might not have welcomed him; but as he was mine enemy, I gave him welcome in a lordly dish.* I sat opposite to him. 'Whence do you come?' said I. 'It is a strange night to be out on the fells.'

He looked up at me sharp; but in general he held his head down like a beast or hound.

'You won't betray me. I'll not trouble you long. As soon as the storm abates, I'll go.'

'Friend!' said I, 'what have I to betray?' and I trembled lest he should keep himself out of my power and not tell me. 'You come for shelter, and I give you of my best. Why do you suspect me?'

'Because,' said he, in his abject bitterness, 'all the world is against me. I never met with goodness or kindness; and now I am hunted like a wild beast. I'll tell you——I'm a convict returned before my time. I was a Sawley man' (as if I, of all men, did not know it!), 'and I went back, like a fool, to the old place. They've hunted me out where I would fain have lived rightly and quietly, and they'll send me back to that hell upon earth, if they catch me. I did not know it would be such a night. Only let me rest and get warm once more, and I'll go away. Good, kind man, have pity upon me!' I smiled all his doubts away; I promised him a bed on the floor, and I thought of Jael and Sisera.* My heart leaped up like a war-horse at the sound of the trumpet, and said, 'Ha, ha, the Lord hath heard my prayer and supplication; I shall have vengeance at last!'

He did not dream who I was. He was changed; so that I, who had learned his features with all the diligence of hatred, did not, at first, recognize him; and he thought not of me, only of his own woe and affright. He looked into the fire with the dreamy gaze of one whose strength of character, if he had any, is beaten out of him, and cannot return at any emergency whatsoever. He sighed and pitied himself, yet could not decide on what to do. I went softly about my business, which was to make him up a bed on the floor, and, when he was lulled to sleep and security, to make the best of my way to Padiham, and summon the constable, into whose hands I would give him up, to be taken back to his 'hell upon earth.' I went into Nelly's room. She was awake and anxious. I saw she had been listening to the voices.

'Who is there?' said she. 'John, tell me; it sounded like a voice I knew. For God's sake, speak!'

I smiled a quiet smile. 'It is a poor man, who has lost his way. Go to sleep, my dear——I shall make him up on the floor. I may not come for some time. Go to sleep;' and I kissed her. I thought she was soothed, but not fully satisfied. However, I hastened away before there was any further time for questioning. I made up the bed, and Richard Jackson, tired out, lay down and fell asleep. My contempt for him almost equalled my hate. If I were avoiding return to a place which I thought to be a hell upon earth, think you I would have taken a quiet sleep under any man's roof till, somehow or another, I was secure. Now comes this man, and, with incontinence of tongue, blabs out the very thing he most should conceal, and then lies down to a good, quiet, snoring sleep. I looked again. His face was old, and worn, and miserable. So should mine enemy look. And yet it was sad to gaze upon him, poor, hunted creature!

I would gaze no more, lest I grew weak and pitiful. Thus I took my hat, and softly opened the door. The wind blew in, but did not disturb him, he was so utterly weary. I was out in the open air of night. The storm was ceasing, and, instead of the black sky of doom that I had seen when I last looked forth, the moon was come out, wan and pale, as if wearied with the fight in the heavens, and her white light fell ghostly and calm on many a well-known object. Now and then, a dark, torn cloud was blown across her home in the sky; but they grew fewer and fewer, and at last she shone out steady and clear. I could see Padiham down before me. I heard the noise of the watercourses down the hill-side. My mind was full of one thought, and strained upon that one thought, and yet my senses were most acute and observant. When I came to the brook, it was swollen to a rapid, tossing river; and the little bridge, with its handrail, was utterly swept away. It was like the bridge at Sawley, where I had first seen Nelly; and I remembered that day even then in the midst of my vexation at having to go round. I turned away from the brook, and there stood a little figure facing me. No spirit from the dead could have affrighted me as it did; for I saw it was Grace, whom I had left in bed by her mother's side.

She came to me, and took my hand. Her bare feet glittered white in the moonshine, and sprinkled the light upwards, as they plashed through the pool.

'Father,' said she, 'mother bade me say this.' Then pausing to gather breath and memory, she repeated these words, like a lesson of which she feared to forget a syllable:—

'Mother says, "There is a God in heaven; and in His house are many mansions.* If you hope to meet her there, you will come back and speak to her; if you are to be separate for ever and ever, you will go on, and may God have mercy on her and on you!" Father, I have said it right—every word.'

I was silent. At last, I said,—

'What made mother say this? How came she to send you out?'

'I was asleep, father, and I heard her cry. I wakened up, and I think you had but just left the house, and that she was calling for you. Then she prayed, with the tears rolling down her cheeks, and kept saying—"Oh, that I could walk!—oh, that for one hour I could run and walk!" So I said, "Mother, I can run and walk. Where must I go?" And she clutched at my arm, and bade God bless me, and told me not to fear, for that He would compass me about, and taught me my message: and now, father, dear father, you will meet mother in heaven, won't you, and not be separate for ever and ever?' She clung to my knees, and pleaded once more in her mother's words. I took her up in my arms, and turned homewards.

'Is yon man there, on the kitchen floor?' asked I.

'Yes!' she answered. At any rate, my vengeance was not out of my power yet.

When we got home I passed him, dead asleep.

In our room, to which my child guided me, was Nelly. She sat up in bed, a most unusual attitude for her, and one of which I thought she had been incapable of attaining to without help. She had her hands clasped, and her face rapt, as if in prayer; and when she saw me, she lay back with a sweet ineffable smile. She could not speak at first; but when I came near, she took my hand and kissed it, and then she called Grace to her, and made her take off her cloak and her wet things, and dressed in her short scanty nightgown, she slipped in to her mother's warm side; and all this time my Nelly never told me why she summoned me: it seemed enough that she should hold my hand, and feel that I was there. I believed she had read my heart; and yet I durst not speak to ask her. At last, she looked up. 'My husband,' said she, 'God has saved you and me from a great sorrow this night.' I would not understand, and I felt her look die away into disappointment.

'That poor wanderer in the house-place is Richard Jackson, is it not?'

I made no answer. Her face grew white and wan.

'Oh,' said she, 'this is hard to bear. Speak what is in your mind, I beg of you. I will not thwart you harshly; dearest John, only speak to me.'

'Why need I speak? You seem to know all.'

'I do know that his is a voice I can never forget; and I do know the awful prayers you have prayed; and I know how I have lain awake, to pray that your words might never be heard; and I am a powerless cripple. I put my cause in God's hands. You shall not do the man any harm. What you have it in your thoughts to do, I cannot tell. But I know that you cannot do it. My eyes are dim with a strange mist; but some voice tells me that you will forgive even Richard Jackson. Dear husband—dearest John, it is so dark, I cannot see you: but speak once to me.'

I moved the candle; but when I saw her face, I saw what was drawing the mist over those loving eyes—how strange and woeful that she could die! Her little girl lying by her side looked in my face, and then at her; and the wild knowledge of death shot through her young heart, and she screamed aloud.

Nelly opened her eyes once more. They fell upon the gaunt, sorrow-worn man who was the cause of all. He roused him from his sleep, at that child's piercing cry, and stood at the doorway, looking in. He knew Nelly, and understood where the storm had driven him to shelter. He came towards her—

'Oh, woman—dying woman—you have haunted me in the loneliness of the Bush far away—you have been in my dreams for ever—the hunting of men has not been so terrible as the hunting of your spirit,—that stone—that stone!' He fell down by her bedside in an agony; above which her saint-like face looked on us all, for the last time, glorious with the coming light of heaven. She spoke once again:—

'It was a moment of passion; I never bore you malice for it. I forgive you; and so does John, I trust.'

Could I keep my purpose there? It faded into nothing. But, above my choking tears, I strove to speak clear and distinct, for her dying ear to hear, and her sinking heart to be gladdened.

'I forgive you, Richard; I will befriend you in your trouble.'

She could not see; but, instead of the dim shadow of death stealing over her face, a quiet light came over it, which we knew was the look of a soul at rest.

That night I listened to his tale for her sake; and I learned that it is better to be sinned against than to sin.* In the storm of the night mine enemy came to me; in the calm of the grey morning I led him forth, and bade him 'God speed.' And a woe had come upon me, but the burning burden of a sinful, angry heart was taken off. I am old now, and my daughter is married. I try to go about preaching and teaching in my rough, rude way; and what I teach is, how Christ lived and died, and what was Nelly's faith of love.

MORTON HALL

CHAPTER I

OUR old Hall is to be pulled down, and they are going to build streets on the site. I said to my sister, 'Ethelinda! if they really pull down Morton Hall, it will be a worse piece of work than the Repeal of the Corn Laws.'* And, after some consideration, she replied, that if she must speak what was on her mind, she would own that she thought the Papists had something to do with it; that they had never forgiven the Morton who had been with Lord Monteagle when he discovered the Gunpowder Plot;* for we knew that, somewhere in Rome, there was a book kept, and which had been kept for generations, giving an account of the secret private history of every English family of note, and registering the names of those to whom the Papists owed either grudges or gratitude.

We were silent for some time; but I am sure the same thought was in both our minds; our ancestor, a Sidebotham, had been a follower of the Morton of that day; it had always been said in the family that he had been with his master when he went with the Lord Monteagle, and found Guy Fawkes and his dark lantern under the Parliament House; and the question flashed across our minds, were the Sidebothams marked with a black mark in that terrible mysterious book which was kept under lock and key by the Pope and the Cardinals in Rome? It was terrible, yet, somehow, rather pleasant to think of. So many of the misfortunes which had happened to us through life, and which we had called 'mysterious dispensations,' but which some of our neighbours had attributed to our want of prudence and foresight, were accounted for at once, if we were objects of the deadly hatred of such a powerful order as the Jesuits,* of whom we had lived in dread ever since we had read the *Female Jesuit*.* Whether this last idea suggested what my sister said next I can't tell; we did know the female Jesuit's second cousin, so might be said to have literary connections, and from that the startling thought might spring up in my sister's mind, for, said she, 'Biddy!' (my name is Bridget, and no one but my sister calls me Biddy) 'suppose you write some account of Morton Hall; we have known much in our time of the Mortons, and it will be a shame if they pass away completely from men's memories while we can speak or write.' I was pleased with the notion, I confess; but I felt ashamed to agree to it all at once, though even, as I objected for modesty's sake, it came into my mind how much I had heard of the old place in its former days, and how it was, perhaps, all I could now do for the Mortons, under whom our ancestors had lived as tenants for more than three hundred years. So at last I agreed; and, for fear of mistakes, I showed it to Mr Swinton, our young curate, who has put it quite in order for me.

Morton Hall is situated about five miles from the centre of Drumble.* It stands on the outskirts of a village, which, when the Hall was built, was probably as large as Drumble in those days; and even I can remember when there was a long piece of rather lonely road, with high hedges on either side, between Morton village and Drumble. Now, it is all street, and Morton seems but a suburb of the great town near. Our farm stood where Liverpool Street* runs now; and people used to come snipe-shooting just where the Baptist chapel is built. Our farm must have been older than the Hall, for we had a date of 1460 on one of the cross-beams. My father was rather proud of this advantage, for the Hall had no date older than 1554; and I remember his affronting Mrs Dawson, the house-keeper, by dwelling too much on this circumstance one evening when she came to drink tea with my mother, when Ethelinda and I were mere children. But my mother, seeing that Mrs Dawson would never allow that any house in the parish could be older than the Hall, and that she was getting very warm, and almost insinuat-ing that the Sidebothams had forged the date to disparage the squire's family, and set themselves up as having the older blood, asked Mrs Dawson to tell us the story of old Sir John Morton before we went to bed. I slily reminded my father that Jack, our man, was not always so careful as might be in housing the Alderney* in good time in the autumn evenings. So he started up, and went off to see after Jack; and Mrs Dawson and we drew nearer the fire to hear the story about Sir John.

Sir John Morton had lived some time about the Restoration. The Mortons had taken the right side; so when Oliver Cromwell came into power, he gave away their lands to one of his Puritan followers—a man who had been but a praying, canting, Scotch pedlar till the war broke out; and Sir John had to go and live with his royal master at Bruges. The upstart's name was Carr, who came to live at Morton Hall; and, I'm proud to say, we—I mean our ancestors—led him a pretty life. He had hard work to get any rent at all from the tenantry, who knew their duty better than to pay it to a Roundhead. If he took the law to them, the law officers fared so badly, that they were shy of coming out to Morton—all along that lonely road I told you of—again. Strange noises were heard about the Hall, which got the credit of being haunted; but, as those noises were never heard before or since that Richard Carr lived there, I leave you to guess if the evil spirits did not know well over whom they had power—over schismatic rebels, and no one else. They durst not trouble the Mortons, who were true and loyal, and were faithful followers of King Charles in word and deed. At last, Old Oliver died;* and folks did say that, on that wild and stormy night, his voice was heard high up in the air, where you hear the flocks of wild geese skirl, crying out for his true follower Richard Carr to accompany him in the terrible chase the fiends were giving him before carrying him down to hell. Anyway, Richard Carr died within a week—summoned by the dead or not, he went his way down to his master, and his master's master.

Then his daughter Alice came into possession. Her mother was somehow related to General Monk,* who was beginning to come into power about that time. So when Charles the Second came back to his throne, and many of the sneaking Puritans had to quit their ill-gotten land, and turn to the right about, Alice Carr was still left at Morton Hall to queen it there. She was taller than most women, and a great beauty, I have heard. But, for all her beauty, she was a stern, hard woman. The tenants had known her to be hard in her father's lifetime, but now that she was the owner, and had the power, she was worse than ever. She hated the Stuarts* worse than ever her father had done; had calves' head for dinner every thirtieth of January;* and when the first twenty-ninth of May* came round, and every mother's son in the village gilded his oak-leaves, and wore them in his hat, she closed the windows of the great hall with her own hands, and sat throughout the day in darkness and mourning. People did not like to go against her by force, because she was a young and beautiful woman. It was said the King got her cousin,

the Duke of Albemarle,* to ask her to court, just as courteously as
if she had been the Queen of Sheba, and King Charles, Solomon,
praying her to visit him in Jerusalem.* But she would not go; not
she! She lived a very lonely life, for now the King had got his own
again, no servant but her nurse would stay with her in the Hall; and
none of the tenants would pay her any money for all that her father
had purchased the lands from the Parliament, and paid the price
down in good red gold.*

All this time, Sir John was somewhere in the Virginian plantations;* and the ships sailed from thence only twice a year: but
his royal master had sent for him home; and home he came, that
second summer after the restoration. No one knew if Mistress
Alice had heard of his landing in England or not; all the villagers
and tenantry knew, and were not surprised, and turned out in their
best dresses, and with great branches of oak, to welcome him as he
rode into the village one July morning, with many gay-looking
gentlemen by his side, laughing, and talking, and making merry,
and speaking gaily and pleasantly to the village people. They came
in on the opposite side to the Drumble Road; indeed Drumble was
nothing of a place then, as I have told you. Between the last cottage
in the village and the gates to the old Hall, there was a shady part
of the road, where the branches nearly met overhead, and made a
green gloom. If you'll notice, when many people are talking merrily out of doors in sunlight, they will stop talking for an instant,
when they come into the cool green shade, and either be silent for
some little time, or else speak graver, and slower, and softer. And
so old people say those gay gentlemen did; for several people
followed to see Alice Carr's pride taken down. They used to tell
how the cavaliers had to bow their plumed hats in passing under
the unlopped and drooping boughs. I fancy Sir John expected that
the lady would have rallied her friends, and got ready for a sort of
battle to defend the entrance to the house; but she had no friends.
She had no nearer relations than the Duke of Albemarle, and he was
mad with her for having refused to come to court, and so save her
estate, according to his advice.

Well, Sir John rode on in silence; the tramp of the many horses'
feet, and the clumping sound of the clogs of the village people were
all that was heard. Heavy as the great gate was, they swung it wide
on its hinges, and up they rode to the Hall steps, where the lady

stood, in her close, plain, Puritan dress, her cheeks one crimson flush, her great eyes flashing fire, and no one behind her, or with her, or near her, or to be seen, but the old trembling nurse, catching at her gown in pleading terror. Sir John was taken aback; he could not go out with swords and warlike weapons against a woman; his very preparations for forcing an entrance made him ridiculous in his own eyes, and, he well knew, in the eyes of his gay, scornful comrades too; so he turned him round about, and bade them stay where they were, while he rode close to the steps, and spoke to the young lady; and there they saw him, hat in hand, speaking to her; and she, lofty and unmoved, holding her own as if she had been a sovereign queen with an army at her back. What they said, no one heard; but he rode back, very grave and much changed in his look, though his grey eye showed more hawk-like than ever, as if seeing the way to his end, though as yet afar off. He was not one to be jested with before his face; so when he professed to have changed his mind, and not to wish to disturb so fair a lady in possession, he and his cavaliers rode back to the village inn, and roystered there all day, and feasted the tenantry, cutting down the branches that had incommoded them in their morning's ride, to make a bonfire of on the village green, in which they burnt a figure, which some called Old Noll,* and others Richard Carr: and it might do for either, folks said, for unless they had given it the name of a man, most people would have taken it for a forked log of wood.

But the lady's nurse told the villagers afterwards that Mistress Alice went in from the sunny Hall steps into the chill house shadow, and sat her down and wept as her poor faithful servant had never seen her do before, and could not have imagined her proud young lady ever doing. All through that summer's day she cried; and if for very weariness she ceased for a time, and only sighed as if her heart was breaking, they heard through the upper windows— which were open because of the heat—the village bells ringing merrily through the trees, and bursts of choruses to gay cavalier songs, all in favour of the Stuarts. All the young lady said was once or twice, 'Oh God! I am very friendless!'—and the old nurse knew it was true, and could not contradict her; and always thought, as she said long after, that such weary weeping showed there was some great sorrow at hand.

I suppose it was the dreariest sorrow that ever a proud woman

had; but it came in the shape of a gay wedding. How, the village
never knew. The gay gentlemen rode away from Morton the next
day as lightly and carelessly as if they had attained their end, and
Sir John had taken possession; and, by-and-by, the nurse came
timorously out to market in the village, and Mistress Alice was met
in the wood walks just as grand and as proud as ever in her ways,
only a little more pale, and a little more sad. The truth was, as I
have been told, that she and Sir John had each taken a fancy to each
other in that parley they held on the Hall steps; she, in the deep,
wild way in which she took the impressions of her whole life, deep
down, as if they were burnt in. Sir John was a gallant-looking man,
and had a kind of foreign grace and courtliness about him. The way
he fancied her was very different—a man's way, they tell me. She
was a beautiful woman to be tamed, and made to come to his beck
and call; and perhaps he read in her softening eyes that she might
be won, and so all legal troubles about the possession of the estate
come to an end in an easy, pleasant manner. He came to stay with
friends in the neighbourhood; he was met in her favourite walks,
with his plumed hat in his hand, pleading with her, and she
looking softer and far more lovely than ever; and lastly, the tenants
were told of the marriage then nigh at hand.

After they were wedded, he stayed for a time with her at the Hall,
and then off back to court. They do say that her obstinate refusal to
go with him to London was the cause of their first quarrel; but such
fierce, strong wills would quarrel the first day of their wedded life.
She said that the court was no place for an honest woman; but
surely Sir John knew best, and she might have trusted him to take
care of her. However, he left her all alone; and at first she cried most
bitterly, and then she took to her old pride, and was more haughty
and gloomy than ever. By-and-by she found out hidden conventicles;* and, as Sir John never stinted her of money, she gathered
the remnants of the old Puritan party about her, and tried to
comfort herself with long prayers, snuffled through the nose, for
the absence of her husband, but it was of no use. Treat her as he
would, she loved him still with a terrible love. Once, they say, she
put on her waiting-maid's dress, and stole up to London to find out
what kept him there; and something she saw or heard that changed
her altogether, for she came back as if her heart was broken. They
say that the only person she loved with all the wild strength of her

heart, had proved false to her; and if so, what wonder! At the best of times she was but a gloomy creature, and it was a great honour for her father's daughter to be wedded to a Morton. She should not have expected too much.

After her despondency came her religion. Every old Puritan preacher in the country was welcome at Morton Hall. Surely that was enough to disgust Sir John. The Mortons had never cared to have much religion, but what they had, had been good of its kind hitherto. So, when Sir John came down wanting a gay greeting and a tender show of love, his lady exhorted him, and prayed over him, and quoted the last Puritan text she had heard at him; and he swore at her, and at her preachers; and made a deadly oath that none of them should find harbour or welcome in any house of his. She looked scornfully back at him, and said she had yet to learn in what county of England the house he spoke of was to be found; but in the house her father purchased, and she inherited, all who preached the Gospel should be welcome, let kings make what laws, and kings' minions swear what oaths they would. He said nothing to this—the worst sign for her; but he set his teeth at her; and in an hour's time he rode away back to the French witch that had beguiled him.

Before he went away from Morton he set his spies. He longed to catch his wife in his fierce clutch, and punish her for defying him. She had made him hate her with her Puritanical ways. He counted the days till the messenger came, splashed up to the top of his deep leather boots, to say that my lady had invited the canting Puritan preachers of the neighbourhood to a prayer-meeting, and a dinner, and a night's rest at her house. Sir John smiled as he gave the messenger five gold pieces for his pains; and straight took post-horses,* and rode long days till he got to Morton; and only just in time; for it was the very day of the prayer-meeting. Dinners were then at one o'clock in the country. The great people in London might keep late hours, and dine at three in the afternoon or so; but the Mortons they always clung to the good old ways, and as the church bells were ringing twelve when Sir John came riding into the village, he knew he might slacken bridle; and, casting one glance at the smoke which came hurrying up as if from a newly-mended fire, just behind the wood, where he knew the Hall kitchen chimney stood, Sir John stopped at the smithy, and pretended to question the smith about his horse's shoes; but he took little heed of the answers, being more occupied by an old serving-man from the Hall, who had been loitering about the smithy half the morning, as folk thought afterwards to keep some appointment with Sir John. When their talk was ended, Sir John lifted himself straight in his saddle; cleared his throat, and spoke out aloud:—

'I grieve to hear your lady is so ill.' The smith wondered at this, for all the village knew of the coming feast at the Hall; the spring-chickens had been bought up, and the cade-lambs* killed; for the preachers in those days, if they fasted they fasted, if they fought they fought, if they prayed they prayed, sometimes for three hours at a standing; and if they feasted they feasted, and knew what good eating was, believe me.

'My lady ill?' said the smith, as if he doubted the old prim serving-man's word. And the latter would have chopped in with an angry asseveration (he had been at Worcester* and fought on the right side), but Sir John cut him short.

'My lady is very ill, good Master Fox. It touches her here,' continued he, pointing to his head. 'I am come down to take her to London, where the King's own physician shall prescribe for her.' And he rode slowly up to the hall.

The lady was as well as ever she had been in her life, and happier than she had often been; for in a few minutes some of those whom she esteemed so highly would be about her, some of those who had known and valued her father—her dead father, to whom her sorrowful heart turned in its woe, as the only true lover and friend she had ever had on earth. Many of the preachers would have ridden far,—was all in order in their rooms, and on the table in the great dining parlour? She had got into restless hurried ways of late. She went round below, and then she mounted the great oak staircase to see if the tower bed-chamber was all in order for old Master Hilton, the oldest among the preachers. Meanwhile, the maidens below were carrying in mighty cold rounds of spiced beef, quarters of lamb, chicken pies, and all such provisions, when, suddenly, they knew not how, they found themselves each seized by strong arms, their aprons thrown over their heads, after the manner of a gag, and themselves borne out of the house on to the poultry green behind, where, with threats of what worse might befall them, they were sent with many a shameful word (Sir John could not always command his men, many of whom had been soldiers in the French wars) back into the village. They scudded away like frightened hares. My lady was strewing the white-headed preacher's room with the last year's lavender, and stirring up the sweet-pot on the dressing-table, when she heard a step on the echoing stairs. It was no measured tread of any Puritan; it was the clang of a man of war coming nearer and nearer, with loud rapid strides. She knew the step; her heart stopped beating, not for fear, but because she loved Sir John even yet; and she took a step forward to meet him, and then stood still and trembled, for the flattering false thought came before her that he might have come yet in some quick impulse of reviving love, and that his hasty step might be prompted by the passionate tenderness of a husband. But when he reached the door, she looked as calm and indifferent as ever.

'My lady,' said he, 'you are gathering your friends to some feast. May I know who are thus invited to revel in my house? Some graceless fellows, I see, from the store of meat and drink below—wine-bibbers and drunkards, I fear.'

But, by the working glance of his eye, she saw that he knew all; and she spoke with a cold distinctness.

'Master Ephraim Dixon, Master Zerubbabel Hopkins, Master Help-me-or-I-perish Perkins, and some other godly ministers, come to spend the afternoon in my house.'

He went to her, and in his rage he struck her. She put up no arm to save herself, but reddened a little with the pain, and then drawing her neckerchief on one side, she looked at the crimson mark on her white neck.

'It serves me right,' she said. 'I wedded one of my father's enemies; one of those who would have hunted the old man to death. I gave my father's enemy house and lands, when he came as a beggar to my door; I followed my wicked, wayward heart in this, instead of minding my dying father's words. Strike again, and avenge him yet more!'

But he would not, because she bade him. He unloosed his sash, and bound her arms tight,—tight together, and she never struggled or spoke. Then pushing her so that she was obliged to sit down on the bed side,—

'Sit there,' he said, 'and hear how I will welcome the old hypocrites you have dared to ask to my house—my house and my ancestors' house, long before your father—a canting pedlar—hawked his goods about, and cheated honest men.'

And, opening the chamber window right above those Hall steps where she had awaited him in her maiden beauty scarce three short years ago, he greeted the company of preachers as they rode up to the Hall with such terrible hideous language (my lady had provoked him past all bearing, you see), that the old men turned round aghast, and made the best of their way back to their own places.

Meanwhile, Sir John's serving-men below had obeyed their master's orders. They had gone through the house, closing every window, every shutter, and every door, but leaving all else just as it was—the cold meats on the table, the hot meats on the spit, the silver flagons on the side-board, all just as if it were ready for a feast; and then Sir John's head-servant, he that I spoke of before, came up and told his master all was ready.

'Is the horse and the pillion* all ready? Then you and I must be my lady's tire-women;'* and as it seemed to her in mockery, but in reality with a deep purpose, they dressed the helpless woman in her riding things all awry, and strange and disorderly, Sir John carried her down stairs; and he and his man bound her on the pillion; and Sir John mounted before. The man shut and locked the great house-door, and the echoes of the clang went through the empty Hall with an ominous sound. 'Throw the key,' said Sir John, 'deep into the mere* yonder. My lady may go seek it if she lists,* when next I set her arms at liberty. Till then I know whose house Morton Hall shall be called.'

'Sir John! it shall be called the Devil's House, and you shall be his steward.'

But the poor lady had better have held her tongue; for Sir John only laughed, and told her to rave on. As he passed through the village, with his serving-men riding behind, the tenantry came out and stood at their doors, and pitied him for having a mad wife, and praised him for his care of her, and of the chance he gave her of amendment by taking her up to be seen by the King's physician. But, somehow, the Hall got an ugly name; the roast and boiled meats, the ducks, the chickens had time to drop into dust, before any human being now dared to enter in; or, indeed, had any right to enter in, for Sir John never came back to Morton; and as for my lady, some said she was dead, and some said she was mad, and shut up in London, and some said Sir John had taken her to a convent abroad.

'And what did become of her?' asked we, creeping up to Mrs Dawson.

'Nay, how should I know?'

'But what do you think?' we asked pertinaciously.

'I cannot tell. I have heard that after Sir John was killed at the battle of the Boyne* she got loose, and came wandering back to Morton, to her old nurse's house; but, indeed, she was mad then, out and out, and I've no doubt Sir John had seen it coming on. She used to have visions and dream dreams: and some thought her a prophetess, and some thought her fairly crazy. What she said about the Mortons was awful. She doomed them to die out of the land, and their house to be razed to the ground, while pedlars and huxters,* such as her own people, her father, had been, should dwell where the knightly Mortons had once lived. One winter's night she strayed away, and the next morning they found the poor crazy woman frozen to death in Drumble meeting-house yard; and the Mr Morton who had succeeded to Sir John had her decently buried where she was found, by the side of her father's grave.'

We were silent for a time. 'And when was the old Hall opened, Mrs Dawson, please?'

'Oh! when the Mr Morton, our Squire Morton's grandfather, came into possession. He was a distant cousin of Sir John's, a much quieter kind of man. He had all the old rooms opened wide, and aired, and fumigated; and the strange fragments of musty food were collected and burnt in the yard; but somehow that old dining-parlour had always a charnel-house* smell, and no one ever liked making merry in it—thinking of the grey old preachers, whose ghosts might be even then scenting the meats afar off, and trooping unbidden to a feast, that was not that of which they were baulked. I was glad for one when the squire's father built another dining-room; and no servant in the house will go an errand into the old dining-parlour after dark, I can assure ye.'

'I wonder if the way the last Mr Morton had to sell his land to the people at Drumble had anything to do with old Lady Morton's prophecy,' said my mother, musingly.

'Not at all,' said Mrs Dawson, sharply. 'My lady was crazy, and her words not to be minded. I should like to see the cotton-spinners of Drumble offer to purchase land from the squire. Besides, there's a strict entail* now. They can't purchase the land if they would. A set of trading pedlars, indeed!'

I remember Ethelinda and I looked at each other at this word 'pedlars;' which was the very word she had put into Sir John's mouth when taunting his wife with her father's low birth and calling. We thought, 'We shall see.'

Alas! we have seen.

Soon after that evening our good old friend Mrs Dawson died. I remember it well, because Ethelinda and I were put into mourning for the first time in our lives. A dear little brother of ours had died only the year before, and then my father and mother had decided that we were too young; that there was no necessity for their incurring the expense of black frocks. We mourned for the little delicate darling in our hearts, I know; and to this day I often wonder what it would have been to have had a brother. But when Mrs Dawson died it became a sort of duty we owed to the squire's family to go into black, and very proud and pleased Ethelinda and I were with our new frocks. I remember dreaming Mrs Dawson was alive again, and crying, because I thought my new frock would be taken away from me. But all this has nothing to do with Morton Hall.

When I first became aware of the greatness of the squire's station in life, his family consisted of himself, his wife (a frail, delicate lady), his only son, 'little master,' as Mrs Dawson was allowed to call him, 'the young squire,' as we in the village always termed him. His name was John Marmaduke. He was always called John; and after Mrs Dawson's story of the old Sir John, I used to wish he might not bear that ill-omened name. He used to ride through the village in his bright scarlet coat, his long fair curling hair falling over his lace collar, and his broad black hat and feather shading his merry blue eyes. Ethelinda and I thought then, and I always shall think, there never was such a boy. He had a fine high spirit, too, of his own, and once horsewhipped a groom twice as big as himself who had thwarted him. To see him and Miss Phillis go tearing through the village on their pretty Arabian horses, laughing as they met the west wind, and their long golden curls flying behind them, you would have thought them brother and sister, rather than nephew and aunt; for Miss Phillis was the squire's sister, much younger than himself; indeed, at the time I speak of, I don't think she could have been above seventeen, and the young squire, her nephew, was nearly ten. I remember Mrs Dawson sending for my mother and me up to the Hall that we might see Miss Phillis dressed ready to go with her brother to a ball given at some great lord's house to Prince William of Gloucester, nephew to good old George the Third.*

When Mrs Elizabeth, Mrs Morton's maid, saw us at tea in Mrs Dawson's room, she asked Ethelinda and me if we would not like to come into Miss Phillis's dressing-room, and watch her dress; and then she said, if we would promise to keep from touching anything, she would make interest for us to go. We would have promised to stand on our heads, and would have tried to do so too, to earn such a privilege. So in we went, and stood together, hand-in-hand, up in a corner out of the way, feeling very red, and shy, and hot, till Miss Phillis put us at our case by playing all manner of comical tricks, just to make us laugh, which at last we did outright, in spite of all our endeavours to be grave, lest Mrs Elizabeth should complain of us to my mother. I recollect the scent of the *maréchale* powder* with which Miss Phillis's hair was just sprinkled; and how she shook her head, like a young colt, to work the hair loose which Mrs Elizabeth was straining up over a cushion. Then Mrs Elizabeth would try a little of Mrs Morton's rouge; and Miss Phillis would wash it off with a wet towel, saying that she liked her own paleness better than any performer's colour; and when Mrs Elizabeth wanted just to touch her cheeks once more, she hid herself behind the great arm-chair, peeping out, with her sweet, merry face, first at one side and then at another, till we all heard the squire's voice at the door, asking her, if she was dressed, to come and show herself to madam, her sister-in-law; for, as I said, Mrs Morton was a great invalid, and unable to go out to any grand parties like this. We were all silent in an instant; and even Mrs Elizabeth thought no more of the rouge, but how to get Miss Phillis's beautiful blue dress on quick enough. She had cherry-coloured knots in her hair, and her breast-knots were of the same ribbon. Her gown was open in front, to a quilted white silk skirt. We felt very shy of her as she stood there fully dressed—she looked so much grander than anything we had ever seen; and it was like a relief when Mrs Elizabeth told us to go down to Mrs Dawson's parlour, where my mother was sitting all this time.

Just as we were telling how merry and comical Miss Phillis had been, in came a footman. 'Mrs Dawson,' said he, 'the squire bids me ask you to go with Mrs Sidebotham into the west parlour, to have a look at Miss Morton before she goes.' We went, too, clinging to my mother. Miss Phillis looked rather shy as we came in, and stood just by the door. I think we all must have shown her that we had never seen anything so beautiful as she was in our lives before; for she went very scarlet at our fixed gaze of admiration, and, to relieve herself, she began to play all manner of antics— whirling round, and making cheeses* with her rich silk petticoat; unfurling her fan (a present from madam, to complete her dress), and peeping first on one side and then on the other, just as she had done upstairs; and then catching hold of her nephew, and insisting that he should dance a minuet with her until the carriage came; which proposal made him very angry, as it was an insult to his manhood (at nine years old) to suppose he could dance. 'It was all very well for girls to make fools of themselves,' he said, 'but it did not do for men.' And Ethelinda and I thought we had never heard so fine a speech before. But the carriage came before we had half feasted our eyes enough; and the squire came from his wife's room to order the little master to bed, and hand his sister to the carriage.

I remember a good deal of talk about royal dukes and unequal marriages that night. I believe Miss Phillis did dance with Prince William; and I have often heard that she bore away the bell at the ball, and that no one came near her for beauty and pretty, merry ways. In a day or two after I saw her scampering through the village, looking just as she did before she had danced with a royal duke. We all thought she would marry some one great, and used to look out for the lord who was to take her away. But poor madam died, and there was no one but Miss Phillis to comfort her brother, for the young squire was gone away to some great school down south; and Miss Phillis grew grave, and reined in her pony to keep by the squire's side, when he rode out on his steady old mare in his lazy, careless way.

We did not hear so much of the doings at the Hall now Mrs Dawson was dead; so I cannot tell how it was; but, by-and-by, there was a talk of bills that were once paid weekly, being now allowed to run to quarter-day; and then, instead of being settled every quarter-day, they were put off to Christmas; and many said they had hard enough work to get their money then. A buzz went through the village that the young squire played high at college, and that he made away with more money than his father could afford. But when he came down to Morton, he was as handsome as ever; and I, for one, never believed evil of him; though I'll allow others might cheat him, and he never suspect it. His aunt was as fond of him as ever; and he of her. Many is the time I have seen them out walking together, sometimes sad enough, sometimes merry as ever. By-and-by, my father heard of sales of small pieces of land, not included in the entail; and, at last, things got so bad, that the very crops were sold yet green upon the ground, for any price folks would give, so that there was but ready money paid. The squire at length gave way entirely, and never left the house; and the young master in London; and poor Miss Phillis used to go about trying to see after the workmen and labourers, and save what she could. By this time she would be above thirty; Ethelinda and I were nineteen and twenty-one when my mother died, and that was some years before this. Well, at last the squire died; they do say of a broken heart at his son's extravagance; and, though the lawyers kept it very close, it began to be rumoured that Miss Phillis's fortune had gone too. Any way, the creditors came down on the estate like wolves. It was entailed, and it could not be sold; but they put it into the hands of a lawyer, who was to get what he could out of it, and have no pity for the poor young squire, who had not a roof for his head. Miss Phillis went to live by herself in a little cottage in the village, at the end of the property, which the lawyer allowed her to have because he could not let it to any one, it was so tumble-down and old. We never knew what she lived on, poor lady; but she said she was well in health, which was all we durst ask about. She came to see my father just before he died, and he seemed made bold with the feeling that he was a dying man; so he asked, what I had longed to know for many a year, where was the young squire? he had never been seen in Morton since his father's funeral. Miss Phillis said he was gone abroad; but in what part he was then, she herself hardly knew; only she had a feeling that, sooner or later, he would come back to the old place; where she should strive to keep a home for him whenever he was tired of wandering about, and trying to make his fortune.

'Trying to make his fortune still?' asked my father, his

questioning eyes saying more than his words. Miss Phillis shook her head, with a sad meaning in her face; and we understood it all. He was at some French gaming-table, if he was not at an English one. But when he came down to Morton, he was at hand once

Miss Phillis was right. It might be a year after my father's death when he came back, looking old and grey and worn. He came to our door just after we had barred it one winter's evening. Ethelinda and I still lived at the farm, trying to keep it up, and make it pay; but it was hard work. We heard a step coming up the straight pebble walk; and then it stopped right at our door, under the very porch, and we heard a man's breathing, quick and short.

'Shall I open the door?' said I.

'No, wait!' said Ethelinda; for we lived alone, and there was no cottage near us. We held our breaths. There came a knock.

'Who's there?' I cried.

'Where does Miss Morton live—Miss Phillis?'

We were not sure if we would answer him; for she, like us, lived alone.

'Who's there?' again said I.

'Your master,' he answered, proud and angry. 'My name is John Morton. Where does Miss Phillis live?'

We had the door unbarred in a trice, and begged him to come in; to pardon our rudeness. We would have given him of our best, as was his due from us; but he only listened to the directions we gave him to his aunt's, and took no notice of our apologies.

CHAPTER II

UP to this time we had felt it rather impertinent to tell each other of our individual silent wonder as to what Miss Phillis lived on; but I know in our hearts we each thought about it, with a kind of respectful pity for her fallen low estate. Miss Phillis—that we remembered like an angel for beauty, and like a little princess for the imperious sway she exercised, and which was such sweet compulsion that we had all felt proud to be her slaves—Miss Phillis was now a worn, plain woman, in homely dress, tending towards old age; and looking—(at that time I dared not have spoken so insolent a thought, not even to myself)—but she did look as if she had hardly the proper nourishing food she required. One day, I remember Mrs Jones, the butcher's wife (she was a Drumble person) saying, in her saucy way, that she was not surprised to see Miss Morton so bloodless and pale, for she only treated herself to a Sunday's dinner of meat, and lived on slop and bread-and-butter all the rest of the week. Ethelinda put on her severe face—a look that I am afraid of to this day—and said, 'Mrs Jones, do you suppose Miss Morton can eat your half-starved meat? You do not know how choice and dainty she is, as becomes one born and bred like her. What was it we had to bring for her only last Saturday from the grand new butcher's, in Drumble, Biddy?'—(We took our eggs to market in Drumble every Saturday, for the cotton-spinners would give us a higher price than the Morton people: the more fools they!)

I thought it rather cowardly of Ethelinda to put the story-telling on me; but she always thought a great deal of saving her soul; more than I did, I am afraid, for I made answer, as bold as a lion, 'Two sweet breads, at a shilling a-piece; and a forequarter of house-lamb, at eighteen-pence a pound.' So off went Mrs Jones, in a huff, saying, 'their meat was good enough for Mrs Donkin, the great mill-owner's widow, and might serve a beggarly Morton any day.' When we were alone, I said to Ethelinda, 'I'm afraid we shall have to pay for our lies at the great day of account;' and Ethelinda answered, very sharply—(she's a good sister in the main)—'Speak for yourself, Biddy. I never said a word. I only asked questions. How could I help it if you told lies? I'm sure I wondered at you, how glib you spoke out what was not true.' But I knew she was glad I told the lies, in her heart.

After the poor squire came to live with his aunt, Miss Phillis, we ventured to speak a bit to ourselves. We were sure they were pinched. They looked like it. He had a bad hacking cough at times; though he was so dignified and proud he would never cough when any one was near. I have seen him up before it was day, sweeping the dung off the roads, to try and get enough to manure the little plot of ground behind the cottage, which Miss Phillis had let alone, but which her nephew used to dig in and till; for, said he, one day, in his grand, slow way, 'he was always fond of experiments in agriculture.' Ethelinda and I do believe that the two or three score of cabbages he raised were all they had to live on that winter, besides the bit of meal and tea they got at the village shop.

One Friday night I said to Ethelinda, 'It is a shame to take these eggs to Drumble to sell, and never to offer one to the squire, on whose lands we were born.' She answered, 'I have thought so many a time; but how can we do it? I, for one, dare not offer them to the squire; and as for Miss Phillis, it would seem like impertinence.' 'I'll try at it,' said I.

So that night I took some eggs—fresh yellow eggs from our own pheasant hen, the like of which there were not for twenty miles round—and I laid them softly after dusk on one of the little stone seats in the porch of Miss Phillis's cottage. But, alas! when we went to market at Drumble, early the next morning, there were my eggs all shattered and splashed, making an ugly yellow pool in the road just in front of the cottage. I had meant to have followed it up by a chicken or so; but I saw now that it would never do. Miss Phillis came now and then to call on us; she was a little more high and distant than she had been when a girl, and we felt we must keep our place. I suppose we had affronted the young squire, for he never came near our house.

Well, there came a hard winter, and provisions rose; and Ethelinda and I had much ado to make ends meet. If it had not been for my sister's good management, we should have been in debt, I know; but she proposed that we should go without dinner, and only have a breakfast and a tea, to which I agreed, you may be sure.

One baking day I had made some cakes for tea—potato-cakes we called them. They had a savoury, hot smell about them; and, to tempt Ethelinda, who was not quite well, I cooked a rasher of bacon. Just as we were sitting down, Miss Phillis knocked at our door. We let her in. God only knows how white and haggard she looked. The heat of our kitchen made her totter, and for a while she could not speak. But all the time she looked at the food on the table as if she feared to shut her eyes lest it should all vanish away. It was an eager stare like that of some animal, poor soul! 'If I durst,' said Ethelinda, wishing to ask her to share our meal, but being afraid to speak out. I did not speak, but handed her the good, hot, buttered cake; on which she seized, and putting it up to her lips as if to taste it, she fell back in her chair, crying.

We had never seen a Morton cry before; and it was something

awful. We stood silent and aghast. She recovered herself, but did not taste the food; on the contrary, she covered it up with both her hands, as if afraid of losing it. 'If you'll allow me,' said she, in a stately kind of way, to make up for our having seen her crying, 'I'll take it to my nephew.' And she got up to go away; but she could hardly stand for very weakness, and had to sit down again; she smiled at us, and said she was a little dizzy, but it would soon go off; but as she smiled, the bloodless lips were drawn far back over her teeth, making her face seem somehow like a death's head. 'Miss Morton,' said I, 'do honour us by taking tea with us this once. The squire, your father, once took a luncheon with my father, and we are proud of it to this day.' I poured her out some tea, which she drank; the food she shrank away from as if the very sight of it turned her sick again. But when she rose to go, she looked at it with her sad, wolfish eyes, as if she could not leave it; and at last she broke into a low cry, and said, 'Oh, Bridget, we are starving! we are starving for want of food! I can bear it; I don't mind; but he suffers—oh, how he suffers! Let me take him food for this one night.'

We could hardly speak; our hearts were in our throats, and the tears ran down our cheeks like rain. We packed up a basket, and carried it to her very door, never venturing to speak a word, for we knew what it must have cost her to say that. When we left her at the cottage, we made her our usual deep courtesy, but she fell upon our necks, and kissed us. For several nights after she hovered round our house about dusk; but she would never come in again, and face us in candle or fire light, much less meet us by daylight. We took out food to her as regularly as might be, and gave it to her in silence, and with the deepest courtesies we could make, we felt so honoured. We had many plans now she had permitted us to know of her distress. We hoped she would allow us to go on serving her in some way as became us as Sidebothams. But one night she never came; we stayed out in the cold, bleak wind, looking into the dark for her thin, worn figure; all in vain. Late the next afternoon, the young squire lifted the latch, and stood right in the middle of our houseplace.* The roof was low overhead, and made lower by the deep beams supporting the floor above; he stooped as he looked at us, and tried to form words, but no sound came out of his lips. I never saw such gaunt woe; no, never! At last he took me by the shoulder, and led me out of the house.

'Come with me!' he said, when we were in the open air, as if that gave him strength to speak audibly. I needed no second word. We entered Miss Phillis's cottage; a liberty I had never taken before. What little furniture was there, it was clear to be seen were cast-off fragments of the old splendour of Morton Hall. No fire. Grey wood ashes lay on the hearth. An old settee, once white and gold, now doubly shabby in its fall from its former estate. On it lay Miss Phillis, very pale; very still; her eyes shut.

'Tell me!' he gasped. 'Is she dead? I think she is asleep; but she looks so strange—as if she might be—' He could not say the awful word again. I stooped, and felt no warmth; only a cold chill atmosphere seemed to surround her.

'She is dead!' I replied at length. 'Oh, Miss Phillis! Miss Phillis!' and, like a fool, I began to cry. But he sat down without a tear, and looked vacantly at the empty hearth. I dared not cry any more when I saw him so stony sad. I did not know what to do. I could not leave him; and yet I had no excuse for staying. I went up to Miss Phillis, and softly arranged the grey ragged locks about her face.

'Ay!' said he. 'She must be laid out. Who so fit to do it as you and your sister, children of good old Robert Sidebotham?'

'Oh, my master,' I said, 'this is no fit place for you. Let me fetch my sister to sit up with me all night; and honour us by sleeping at our poor little cottage.'

I did not expect he would have done it; but after a few minutes' silence he agreed to my proposal. I hastened home, and told Ethelinda, and both of us crying, we heaped up the fire, and spread the table with food, and made up a bed in one corner of the floor. While I stood ready to go, I saw Ethelinda open the great chest in which we kept our treasures; and out she took a fine Holland shift that had been one of my mother's wedding shifts; and, seeing what she was after, I went upstairs and brought down a piece of rare old lace, a good deal darned to be sure, but still old Brussels point, bequeathed to me long ago by my god-mother, Mrs Dawson. We huddled these things under our cloaks, locked the door behind us, and set out to do all we could now for poor Miss Phillis. We found the squire sitting just as we left him; I hardly knew if he understood me when I told him how to unlock our door, and gave him the key, though I spoke as distinctly as ever I could for the choking in my throat. At last he rose and went; and Ethelinda and

I composed her poor thin limbs to decent rest, and wrapped her in the fine Holland shift; and then I plaited up my lace into a close cap to tie up the wasted features. When all was done we looked upon her from a little distance.

'A Morton to die of hunger!' said Ethelinda solemnly. 'We should not have dared to think that such a thing was within the chances of life. Do you remember that evening, when you and I were little children, and she a merry young lady peeping at us from behind her fan?'

We did not cry any more; we felt very still and awestruck. After a while I said, 'I wonder if, after all, the young squire did go to our house. He had a strange look about him. If I dared I would go and see.' I opened the door; the night was black as pitch; the air very still. 'I'll go,' said I; and off I went, not meeting a creature, for it was long past eleven. I reached our house; the window was long and low, and the shutters were old and shrunk. I could peep between them well, and see all that was going on. He was there, sitting over the fire, never shedding a tear; but seeming as if he saw his past life in the embers. The food we had prepared was untouched. Once or twice, during my long watch (I was more than an hour away), he turned towards the food, and made as though he would have eaten it, and then shuddered back; but at last he seized it, and tore it with his teeth, and laughed and rejoiced over it like some starved animal. I could not keep from crying then. He gorged himself with great morsels; and when he could eat no more, it seemed as if his strength for suffering had come back. He threw himself on the bed, and such a passion of despair I never heard of, much less ever saw. I could not bear to witness it. The dead Miss Phillis lay calm and still. Her trials were over. I would go back and watch with Ethelinda.

When the pale grey morning dawn stole in, making us shiver and shake after our vigil, the squire returned. We were both mortal afraid of him, we knew not why. He looked quiet enough—the lines were worn deep before—no new traces were there. He stood and looked at his aunt for a minute or two. Then he went up into the loft above the room where we were; he brought a small paper parcel down; bade us keep on our watch yet a little time. First one and then the other of us went home to get some food. It was a bitter black frost; no one was out who could stop indoors; and those who were out cared not to stop to speak. Towards afternoon the air darkened, and a great snow-storm came on. We durst not be left only one alone; yet, at the cottage where Miss Phillis had lived, there was neither fire nor fuel. So we sat and shivered and shook till morning. The squire never came that night nor all next day.

'What must we do?' asked Ethelinda, broken down entirely. 'I shall die if I stop here another night. We must tell the neighbours and get help for the watch.'

'So we must,' said I, very low and grieved. I went out and told the news at the nearest house, taking care, you may be sure, never to speak of the hunger and cold Miss Phillis must have endured in silence. It was bad enough to have them come in, and make their remarks on the poor bits of furniture; for no one had known their bitter straits even as much as Ethelinda and me, and we had been shocked at the bareness of the place. I did hear that one or two of the more ill-conditioned had said, it was not for nothing we had kept the death to ourselves for two nights; that, to judge from the lace on her cap, there must have been some pretty pickings. Ethelinda would have contradicted this, but I bade her let it alone; it would save the memory of the proud Mortons from the shame that poverty is thought to be; and as for us, why we could live it down. But, on the whole, people came forward kindly; money was not wanting to bury her well, if not grandly, as became her birth; and many a one was bidden to the funeral who might have looked after her a little more in her life-time. Among others was Squire Hargreaves from Bothwick Hall over the moors. He was some kind of far-away cousin to the Morton's; so when he came he was asked to go chief mourner in Squire Morton's strange absence, which I should have wondered at the more if I had not thought him almost crazy when I watched his ways through the shutter that night. Squire Hargreaves started when they paid him the compliment of asking him to take the head of the coffin.

'Where is her nephew?' asked he.

'No one has seen him since eight o'clock last Thursday morning.'

'But I saw him at noon on Thursday,' said Squire Hargreaves, with a round oath. 'He came over the moors to tell me of his aunt's death, and to ask me to give him a little money to bury her, on the pledge of his gold shirt-buttons. He said I was a cousin, and could pity a gentleman in such sore need; that the buttons were his mother's first gift to him; and that I was to keep them safe, for some day he would make his fortune, and come back to redeem them. He had not known his aunt was so ill, or he would have parted with these buttons sooner, though he held them as more precious than he could tell me. I gave him money; but I could not find in my heart to take the buttons. He bade me not tell of all this; but when a man is missing it is my duty to give all the clue I can.'

And so their poverty was blazoned abroad! But folk forgot it all in the search for the squire on the moor-side. Two days they searched in vain; the third, upwards of a hundred men turned out, hand-in-hand, step to step, to leave no foot of ground unsearched. They found him stark and stiff, with Squire Hargreaves' money, and his mother's gold buttons, safe in his waistcoat pocket.

And we laid him down by the side of his poor aunt Phillis.

After the squire, John Marmaduke Morton, had been found dead in that sad way, on the dreary moors, the creditors seemed to lose all hold on the property; which indeed, during the seven years they had had it, they had drained as dry as a sucked orange. But for a long time no one seemed to know who rightly was the owner of Morton Hall and lands. The old house fell out of repair; the chimneys were full of starlings' nests; the flags in the terrace in front were hidden by the long grass; the panes in the windows were broken, no one knew how or why, for the children of the village got up a tale that the house was haunted. Ethelinda and I went some-times in the summer mornings, and gathered some of the roses that were being strangled by the bindweed that spread over all; and we used to try and weed the old flower-garden a little; but we were no longer young, and the stooping made our backs ache. Still we always felt happier if we cleared but ever such a little space. Yet we did not go there willingly in the afternoons, and left the garden always long before the first slight shade of dusk.

We did not choose to ask the common people—many of them were weavers for the Drumble manufacturers, and no longer decent hedgers and ditchers—we did not choose to ask them, I say, who was squire now, or where he lived. But one day, a great London lawyer came to the Morton Arms, and made a pretty stir. He came on behalf of a General Morton, who was squire now, though he was far away in India. He had been written to, and they had proved him heir, though he was a very distant cousin, farther back than Sir

John, I think. And now he had sent word they were to take money of his that was in England, and put the house in thorough repair; for that three maiden sisters of his, who lived in some town in the north, would come and live at Morton Hall till his return. So the lawyer sent for a Drumble builder, and gave him directions. We thought it would have been prettier if he had hired John Cobb, the Morton builder and joiner, he that had made the squire's coffin, and the squire's father's before that. Instead, came a troop of Drumble men, knocking and tumbling about in the Hall, and making their jests up and down all those stately rooms. Ethelinda and I never went near the place till they were gone, bag and baggage. And then what a change! The old casement windows, with their heavy leaded panes half overgrown with vines and roses, were taken away, and great staring sash windows were in their stead. New grates inside; all modern, new-fangled, and smoking, instead of the brass dogs which held the mighty logs of wood in the old squire's time. The little square Turkey carpet under the dining-table, which had served Miss Phillis, was not good enough for these new Mortons; the dining-room was all carpeted over. We peeped into the old dining-parlour—that parlour where the dinner for the Puritan preachers had been laid out; the flag parlour, as it had been called of late years. But it had a damp, earthy smell, and was used as a lumber-room. We shut the door quicker than we had opened it. We came away disappointed. The Hall was no longer like our own honoured Morton Hall.

'After all, these three ladies are Mortons,' said Ethelinda to me. 'We must not forget that: we must go and pay our duty to them as soon as they have appeared in church.'

Accordingly we went. But we had heard and seen a little of them before we paid our respects at the Hall. Their maid had been down in the village; their maid, as she was called now; but a maid-of-all-work she had been until now, as she very soon let out when we questioned her. However, we were never proud; and she was a good honest farmer's daughter out of Northumberland. What work she did make with the Queen's English! The folk in Lancashire are said to speak broad, but I could always understand our own kindly tongue; whereas, when Mrs Turner told me her name, both Ethelinda and I could have sworn she said Donagh, and were afraid she was an Irishwoman.* Her ladies were what you may call past the bloom of youth; Miss Sophronia—Miss Morton, properly—was just sixty; Miss Annabella, three years younger; and Miss Dorothy (or Baby, as they called her when they were by themselves), was two years younger still. Mrs Turner was very confidential to us, partly because, I doubt not, she had heard of our old connection with the family, and partly because she was an arrant talker, and was glad of anybody who would listen to her. So we heard the very first week how each of the ladies had wished for the east bed-room— that which faced the north-east—which no one slept in in the old squire's days; but there were two steps leading up into it, and, said Miss Sophronia, she would never let a younger sister have a room more elevated than she had herself. She was the eldest, and she had a right to the steps. So she bolted herself in for two days, while she unpacked her clothes, and then came out, looking like a hen that has laid an egg, and defies any one to take that honour from her.

But her sisters were very deferential to her in general; that must be said. They never had more than two black feathers in their bonnets; while she had always three. Mrs Turner said that once, when they thought Miss Annabella had been going to have an offer of marriage made her, Miss Sophronia had not objected to her wearing three that winter; but when it all ended in smoke, Miss Annabella had to pluck it out as became a younger sister. Poor Miss Annabella! She had been a beauty (Mrs Turner said), and great things had been expected of her. Her brother, the general, and her mother had both spoilt her, rather than cross her unnecessarily, and so spoil her good looks; which old Mrs Morton had always expected would make the fortune of the family. Her sisters were angry with her for not having married some great rich gentleman; though, as she used to say to Mrs Turner, how could she help it? She was willing enough, but no rich gentleman came to ask her. We agreed that it really was not her fault; but her sisters thought it was; and now, that she had lost her beauty, they were always casting it up what they would have done if they had had her gifts. There were some Miss Burrells they had heard of, each of whom had married a lord; and these Miss Burrells had not been such great beauties. So Miss Sophronia used to work the question by the rule of three;* and put it in this way—If Miss Burrell, with a tolerable pair of eyes, a snub nose, and a wide mouth, married a baron, what rank of peer ought our pretty Annabella to have espoused? And the worst was, Miss Annabella—who had never had any ambition—wanted to have married a poor curate in her youth; but was pulled up by her mother and sisters, reminding her of the duty she owed to her family. Miss Dorothy had done her best—Miss Morton always praised her for it. With not half the good looks of Miss Annabella, she had danced with an honourable* at Harrogate three times running; and, even now, she persevered in trying; which was more than could be said of Miss Annabella, who was very broken-spirited.

I do believe Mrs Turner told us all this before we had ever seen the ladies. We had let them know, through Mrs Turner, of our wish to pay them our respects; so we ventured to go up to the front door, and rap modestly. We had reasoned about it before, and agreed that if we were going in our every-day clothes, to offer a little present of eggs, or to call on Mrs Turner (as she had asked us to do), the back door would have been the appropriate entrance for us. But going, however humbly, to pay our respects, and offer our reverential welcome to the Miss Mortons, we took rank as their visitors, and should go to the front door. We were shown up the wide stairs, along the gallery, up two steps, into Miss Sophronia's room. She put away some papers hastily as we came in. We heard afterwards that she was writing a book, to be called *The Female Chesterfield; or, Letters from a Lady of Quality to her Niece.** And the little niece sat there in a high chair, with a flat board tied to her back, and her feet in stocks on the rail of the chair; so that she had nothing to do but listen to her aunt's letters; which were read aloud to her as they were written, in order to mark their effect on her manners. I was not sure whether Miss Sophronia liked our interruption; but I know little Miss Cordelia Mannisty did.

'Is the young lady crooked?' asked Ethelinda, during a pause in our conversation. I had noticed that my sister's eyes would rest on the child; although, by an effort, she sometimes succeeded in looking at something else occasionally.

'No! indeed, ma'am,' said Miss Morton. 'But she was born in India, and her backbone has never properly hardened. Besides, I and my two sisters each take charge of her for a week; and their systems of education—I might say non-education—differ so totally and entirely from my ideas, that when Miss Mannisty comes to me, I consider myself fortunate if I can undo the—hem!—that has been done during a fortnight's absence. Cordelia, my dear, repeat to these good ladies the geography lesson you learnt this morning.'

Poor little Miss Mannisty began to tell us a great deal about some river in Yorkshire of which we had never heard, though I dare say we ought to, and then a great deal more about the towns that it passed by, and what they were famous for; and all I can remember—indeed, could understand at the time—was that Pomfret was famous for Pomfret cakes;* which I knew before. But Ethelinda gasped for breath before it was done, she was so nearly choked up with astonishment; and when it was ended, she said, 'Pretty dear; it's wonderful!' Miss Morton looked a little displeased, and replied, 'Not at all. Good little girls can learn anything they choose, even French verbs. Yes, Cordelia, they can. And to be good is better than to be pretty. We don't think about looks here. You may get down, child, and go into the garden; and take care you put your bonnet on, or you'll be all over freckles.' We got up to take leave at the same time, and followed the little girl out of the room. Ethelinda fumbled in her pocket.

'Here's a sixpence, my dear, for you. Nay, I am sure you may take it from an old woman like me, to whom you've told over more geography than I ever thought there was out of the Bible.' For Ethelinda always maintained that the long chapters in the Bible which were all names, were geography; and though I knew well enough they were not, yet I had forgotten what the right word was, so I let her alone; for one hard word did as well as another. Little miss looked as if she was not sure if she might take it; but I suppose we had two kindly old faces, for at last the smile came into her eyes—not to her mouth, she had lived too much with grave and quiet people for that—and, looking wistfully at us, she said,—

'Thank you. But won't you go and see aunt Annabella?' We said we should like to pay our respects to both her other aunts if we might take that liberty; and perhaps she would show us the way. But, at the door of a room, she stopped short, and said, sorrowfully, 'I mayn't go in; it is not my week for being with aunt Annabella;' and then she went slowly and heavily towards the garden-door.

'That child is cowed by somebody,' said I to Ethelinda.

'But she knows a deal of geography'—Ethelinda's speech was cut short by the opening of the door in answer to our knock. The once beautiful Miss Annabella Morton stood before us, and bade us enter. She was dressed in white, with a turned-up velvet hat, and two or three short drooping black feathers in it. I should not like to say she rouged, but she had a very pretty colour in her cheeks; that much can do neither good nor harm. At first she looked so unlike anybody I had ever seen, that I wondered what the child could have found to like in her; for like her she did, that was very clear. But, when Miss Annabella spoke, I came under the charm. Her voice was very sweet and plaintive, and suited well with the kind of things she said; all about charms of nature, and tears, and grief, and such sort of talk, which reminded me rather of poetry—very pretty to listen to, though I never could understand it as well as plain, comfortable prose. Still I hardly know why I liked Miss Annabella. I think I was sorry for her; though whether I should have been if she had not put it in my head, I don't know. The room looked very comfortable; a spinnet* in a corner to amuse herself with, and a good sofa to lie down upon. By-and-by, we got her to talk of her little niece, and she, too, had her system of education. She said she hoped to develop the sensibilities and to cultivate the tastes. While with her, her darling niece read works of imagination, and acquired all that Miss Annabella could impart of the fine arts. We neither of us quite knew what she was hinting at, at the time; but afterwards, by dint of questioning little miss, and using our own eyes and ears, we found that she read aloud to her aunt while she lay on the sofa. *Santo Sebastiano; or, the Young Protector,** was what they were deep in at this time; and, as it was in five volumes and the heroine spoke broken English—which required to be read twice over to make it intelligible—it lasted them a long time. She also learned to play on the spinnet; not much, for I never heard above two tunes, one of which was God save the King,* and the other was not. But I fancy the poor child was lectured by one aunt, and frightened by the other's sharp ways and numerous fancies. She might well be fond of her gentle, pensive (Miss Annabella told me she was pensive, so I know I am right in calling her so) aunt, with her soft voice, and her never-ending novels, and the sweet scents that hovered about the sleepy room.

No one tempted us towards Miss Dorothy's apartment when we left Miss Annabella; so we did not see the youngest Miss Morton this first day. We had each of us treasured up many little mysteries to be explained by our dictionary, Mrs Turner.

'Who is little Miss Mannisty?' we asked in one breath, when we saw our friend from the Hall. And then we learnt that there had been a fourth—a younger Miss Morton, who was no beauty, and no wit, and no anything; so Miss Sophronia, her eldest sister, had allowed her to marry a Mr Mannisty, and ever after spoke of her as 'my poor sister Jane.' She and her husband had gone out to India, and both had died there; and the general had made it a sort of condition with his sisters that they should take charge of the child, or else none of them liked children except Miss Annabella.

'Miss Annabella likes children,' said I. 'Then that's the reason children like her.'

'I can't say she likes children; for we never have any in our house but Miss Cordelia; but her she does like dearly.'

'Poor little miss!' said Ethelinda, 'does she never get a game of play with other little girls?' And I am sure from that time Ethelinda considered her in a diseased state from this very circumstance, and that her knowledge of geography was one of the symptoms of the disorder; for she used often to say, 'I wish she did not know so much geography! I'm sure it is not quite right.'

Whether or not her geography was right, I don't know; but the child pined for companions. A very few days after we had called—and yet long enough to have passed her into Miss Annabella's week—I saw Miss Cordelia in a corner of the church green, playing, with awkward humility, along with some of the rough village girls, who were as expert at the game as she was unapt and slow. I hesitated a little, and at last I called to her.

'How do you, my dear?' I said. 'How come you here, so far from home?'

She reddened, and then looked up at me with her large, serious eyes.

'Aunt Annabel sent me into the wood to meditate—and—and—it was very dull—and I heard these little girls playing and laughing—and I had my sixpence with me, and—it was not wrong, was it, ma'am?—I came to them, and told one of them I would give it to her if she would ask the others to let me play with them.'

'But, my dear, they are—some of them—very rough little children, and not fit companions for a Morton.'

'But I am a Mannisty, ma'am!' she pleaded, with so much entreaty in her ways, that if I had not known what naughty, bad girls some of them were, I could not have resisted her longing for companions of her own age. As it was, I was angry with them for having taken her sixpence; but, when she had told me which it was, and saw that I was going to reclaim it, she clung to me, and said,—

'Oh! don't, ma'am—you must not. I gave it to her quite of my own self.'

So I turned away; for there was truth in what the child said. But to this day I have never told Ethelinda what became of her sixpence. I took Miss Cordelia home with me while I changed my dress to be fit to take her back to the Hall. And on the way, to make up for her disappointment, I began talking of my dear Miss Phillis, and her bright, pretty youth. I had never named her name since her death to any one but Ethelinda—and that only on Sundays and quiet times. And I could not have spoken of her to a grown-up person; but somehow to Miss Cordelia it came out quite natural. Not of her latter days, of course; but of her pony, and her little black King Charles's dogs, and all the living creatures that were glad in her presence when first I knew her. And nothing would satisfy the child but I must go into the Hall garden and show her where Miss Phillis's garden had been. We were deep in our talk, and she was stooping down to clear the plot from weeds, when I heard a sharp voice cry out, 'Cordelia! Cordelia! Dirtying your frock with kneeling on the wet grass! It is not my week; but I shall tell your aunt Annabella of you.'

And the window was shut down with a jerk. It was Miss Dorothy. And I felt almost as guilty as poor little Miss Cordelia; for I had heard from Mrs Turner that we had given great offence to Miss Dorothy by not going to call on her in her room that day on which we had paid our respects to her sisters; and I had a sort of an idea that seeing Miss Cordelia with me was almost as much of a fault as the kneeling down on the wet grass. So I thought I would take the bull by the horns.

'Will you take me to your aunt Dorothy, my dear?' said I.

The little girl had no longing to go into her aunt Dorothy's room, as she had so evidently had at Miss Annabella's door. On the contrary, she pointed it out to me at a safe distance, and then went away in the measured step she was taught to use in that house; where such things as running, going upstairs two steps at a time, or jumping down three, were considered undignified and vulgar.

Miss Dorothy's room was the least prepossessing of any. Somehow it had a north-east look about it, though it did face direct south; and as for Miss Dorothy herself, she was more like a 'cousin Betty' than anything else; if you know what a cousin Betty is, and perhaps it is too old-fashioned a word to be understood by any one who has learnt the foreign languages: but when I was a girl, there used to be poor crazy women rambling about the country, one or two in a district. They never did any harm that I know of; they might have been born idiots, poor creatures! or crossed in love, who knows? But they roamed the country, and were well known at the farm-houses, where they often got food and shelter for as long a time as their restless minds would allow them to stay in any one place; and the farmer's wife would, maybe, rummage up a ribbon, or a feather, or a smart old breadth of silk, to please the harmless vanity of these poor crazy women; and they would go about so bedizened some-times that, as we called them always 'cousin Betty,' we made it into a kind of proverb for any one dressed in a fly-away, showy style, and said they were like a cousin Betty. So now you know what I mean that Miss Dorothy was like. Her dress was white, like Miss Anna-bella's; but, instead of the black velvet hat her sister wore, she had on, even in the house, a small black silk bonnet. This sounds as if it should be less like a cousin Betty than a hat; but wait till I tell you how it was lined—with strips of red silk, broad near the face, narrow near the brim; for all the world like the rays of the rising sun, as they are painted on the public-house sign. And her face was like the sun; as round as an apple; and with rouge on, without any doubt: indeed, she told me once, a lady was not dressed unless she had put her rouge on. Mrs Turner told us she studied reflections a great deal; not that she was a thinking woman in general, I should say; and that this rayed lining was the fruit of her study. She had her hair pulled together, so that her forehead was quite covered with it; and I won't deny that I rather wished myself at home, as I stood facing her in the doorway. She pretended she did not know who I was, and made me tell all about myself; and then it turned out she knew all about me, and she hoped I had recovered from my fatigue the other day.

'What fatigue?' asked I, immovably. Oh! she had understood I was very much tired after visiting her sisters; otherwise, of course, I should not have felt it too much to come on to her room. She kept hinting at me in so many ways, that I could have asked her gladly to slap my face and have done with it, only I wanted to make Miss Cordelia's peace with her for kneeling down and dirtying her frock. I did say what I could to make things straight; but I don't know if I did any good. Mrs Turner told me how suspicious and jealous she was of everybody, and of Miss Annabella in particular, who had been set over her in her youth because of her beauty; but since it had faded, Miss Morton and Miss Dorothy had never ceased peck-ing at her; and Miss Dorothy worst of all. If it had not been for little Miss Cordelia's love, Miss Annabella might have wished to die; she did often wish she had had the small-pox as a baby. Miss Morton was stately and cold to her, as one who had not done her duty to her family, and was put in the corner for her bad behaviour. Miss Dorothy was continually talking at her, and particularly dwelling on the fact of her being the older sister. Now she was but two years older; and was still so pretty and gentle-looking, that I should have forgotten it continually but for Miss Dorothy.

The rules that were made for Miss Cordelia! She was to eat her meals standing, that was one thing! Another was, that she was to drink two cups of cold water before she had any pudding; and it just made the child loathe cold water. Then there were ever so many words she might not use; each aunt had her own set of words which were ungenteel or improper for some reason or another. Miss Dorothy would never let her say 'red;' it was always to be pink, or crimson, or scarlet. Miss Cordelia used at one time to come to us, and tell us she had a 'pain at her chest' so often, that Ethelinda and I began to be uneasy, and questioned Mrs Turner to know if her mother had died of consumption;* and many a good pot of currant jelly have I given her, and only made her pain at the chest worse; for—would you believe it?—Miss Morton told her never to say she had got a stomach-ache, for that it was not proper to say so. I had heard it called by a worse name still in my youth, and so had Ethelinda; and we sat and wondered to ourselves how it was that some kinds of pain were genteel and others were not. I said that old families, like the Mortons, generally thought it showed good blood to have their complaints as high in the body as they could—brain-fevers and headaches had a better sound, and did perhaps belong more to the aristocracy. I thought I had got the right view in saying this, when Ethelinda would put in that she had often heard of Lord

Toffey having the gout* and being lame, and that nonplussed me. If there is one thing I do dislike more than another, it is a person saying something on the other side when I am trying to make up my mind—how can I reason if I am to be disturbed by another person's arguments?

But though I tell all these peculiarities of the Miss Mortons, they were good women in the main: even Miss Dorothy had her times of kindness, and really did love her little niece, though she was always laying traps to catch her doing wrong. Miss Morton I got to respect, if I never liked her. They would ask us up to tea; and we would put on our best gowns; and taking the house-key in my pocket, we used to walk slowly through the village, wishing that people who had been living in our youth could have seen us now, going by invitation to drink tea with the family at the Hall—not in the housekeeper's room, but with the family, mind you. But since they began to weave in Morton, everybody seemed too busy to notice us; so we were fain to be content with reminding each other how we should never have believed it in our youth that we could have lived to this day. After tea, Miss Morton would set us to talk of the real old family, whom they had never known; and you may be sure we told of all their pomp and grandeur and stately ways: but Ethelinda and I never spoke of what was to ourselves like the memory of a sad, terrible dream. So they thought of the squire in his coach-and-four as high sheriff, and madam lying in her morning-room in her Genoa velvet wrapping-robe, all over pea-cock's eyes (it was a piece of velvet the squire brought back from Italy, when he had been the grand tour), and Miss Phillis going to a ball at a great lord's house and dancing with a royal duke. The three ladies were never tired of listening to the tale of the splendour that had been going on here, while they and their mother had been starving in genteel poverty up in Northumberland; and as for Miss Cordelia, she sat on a stool at her aunt Annabella's knee, her hand in her aunt's, and listened, open-mouthed and unnoticed, to all we could say.

One day, the child came crying to our house. It was the old story; aunt Dorothy had been so unkind to aunt Annabella! The little girl said she would run away to India, and tell her uncle the general, and seemed in such a paroxysm of anger, and grief, and despair, that a sudden thought came over me. I thought I would try and teach her something of the deep sorrow that lies awaiting all at some part of their lives, and of the way in which it ought to be borne, by telling her of Miss Phillis's love and endurance for her wasteful, handsome nephew. So from little, I got to more, and I told her all; the child's great eyes filling slowly with tears, which brimmed over and came rolling down her cheeks unnoticed as I spoke. I scarcely needed to make her promise not to speak about all this to any one. She said, 'I could not—no! not even to aunt Annabella.' And to this day she never has named it again, not even to me; but she tried to make herself more patient, and more silently helpful in the strange household among whom she was cast.

By-and-by, Miss Morton grew pale, and grey, and worn, amid all her stiffness. Mrs Turner whispered to us that for all her stern, unmoved looks, she was ill unto death; that she had been secretly to see the great doctor at Drumble; and he had told her she must set her house in order. Not even her sisters knew this; but it preyed upon Mrs Turner's mind and she told us. Long after this, she kept up her week of discipline with Miss Cordelia; and walked in her straight, soldier-like way about the village, scolding people for having too large families, and burning too much coal, and eating too much butter. One morning she sent Mrs Turner for her sisters; and, while she was away, she rummaged out an old locket made of the four Miss Mortons' hair when they were all children; and, threading the eye of the locket with a piece of brown ribbon, she tied it round Cordelia's neck, and kissing her, told her she had been a good girl, and had cured herself of stooping; that she must fear God and honour the king;* and that now she might go and have a holiday. Even while the child looked at her in wonder at the unusual tenderness with which this was said, a grim spasm passed over her face, and Cordelia ran in affright to call Mrs Turner. But when she came, and the other two sisters came, she was quite herself again. She had her sisters in her room alone when she wished them good-by; so no one knows what she said, or how she told them (who were thinking of her as in health) that the signs of near-approaching death, which the doctor had foretold, were upon her. One thing they both agreed in saying—and it was much that Miss Dorothy agreed in anything—that she bequeathed her sitting-room, up the two steps, to Miss Annabella as being next in age. Then they left her room crying, and went both together into

Miss Annabella's room, sitting hand in hand (for the first time since childhood I should think), listening for the sound of the little hand-bell which was to be placed close by her, in case, in her agony, she required Mrs Turner's presence. But it never rang. Noon became twilight. Miss Cordelia stole in from the garden with its long, black, green shadows, and strange eerie sounds of the night wind through the trees, and crept to the kitchen fire. At last Mrs Turner knocked at Miss Morton's door, and hearing no reply, went in and found her cold and dead in her chair.

I suppose that some time or other we had told them of the funeral the old squire had; Miss Phillis's father, I mean. He had had a procession of tenantry half-a-mile long to follow him to the grave. Miss Dorothy sent for me to tell her what tenantry of her brother's could follow Miss Morton's coffin; but what with people working in mills, and land having passed away from the family, we could but muster up twenty people, men and women and all; and one or two were dirty enough to be paid for their loss of time.

Poor Miss Annabella did not wish to go into the room up two steps; nor yet dared she stay behind; for Miss Dorothy, in a kind of spite for not having had it bequeathed to her, kept telling Miss Annabella it was her duty to occupy it; that it was Miss Sophronia's dying wish, and that she should not wonder if Miss Sophronia were to haunt Miss Annabella, if she did not leave her warm room, full of ease and sweet scent, for the grim north-east chamber. We told Mrs Turner we were afraid Miss Dorothy would lord it sadly over Miss Annabella, and she only shook her head; which, from so talkative a woman, meant a great deal. But, just as Miss Cordelia had begun to droop, the general came home, without any one knowing he was coming. Sharp and sudden was the word with him. He sent Miss Cordelia off to school; but not before she had had time to tell us that she loved her uncle dearly, in spite of his quick, hasty ways. He carried his sisters off to Cheltenham; and it was astonishing how young they made themselves look before they came back again. He was always here, there, and everywhere: and very civil to us into the bargain; leaving the key of the Hall with us whenever they went from home. Miss Dorothy was afraid of him, which was a blessing, for it kept her in order, and really I was rather sorry when she died; and, as for Miss Annabella, she fretted after her till she injured her health, and Miss Cordelia had to leave school to come and keep her company. Miss Cordelia was not pretty; she had too sad and grave a look for that; but she had winning ways, and was to have her uncle's fortune some day, so I expected to hear of her being soon snapped up. But the general said her husband was to take the name of Morton; and what did my young lady do but begin to care for one of the great mill-owners at Drumble, as if there were not all the lords and commons to choose from besides? Mrs Turner was dead; and there was no one to tell us about it; but I could see Miss Cordelia growing thinner and paler every time they came back to Morton Hall; and I longed to tell her to pluck up a spirit, and be above a cotton-spinner. One day, not half a year before the general's death, she came to see us, and told us, blushing like a rose, that her uncle had given his consent; and so, although 'he' had refused to take the name of Morton, and had wanted to marry her without a penny, and without her uncle's leave, it had all come right at last, and they were to be married at once; and their house was to be a kind of home for her aunt Annabella, who was getting tired of being perpetually on the ramble with the general.

'Dear old friends!' said our young lady, 'you must like him. I am sure you will; he is so handsome, and brave, and good. Do you know, he says a relation of his ancestors lived at Morton Hall in the time of the Commonwealth.'

'His ancestors,' said Ethelinda. 'Has he got ancestors? That's one good point about him, at any rate. I didn't know cotton-spinners had ancestors.'

'What is his name?' asked I.

'Mr Marmaduke Carr,' said she, sounding each r with the old Northumberland burr,* which was softened into a pretty pride and effort to give distinctness to each letter of the beloved name.

'Carr,' said I, 'Carr and Morton! Be it so! It was prophesied of old!' But she was too much absorbed in the thought of her own secret happiness to notice my poor sayings.

He was and is a good gentleman; and a real gentleman, too. They never lived at Morton Hall. Just as I was writing this, Ethelinda came in with two pieces of news. Never again say I am superstitious! There is no one living in Morton that knows the tradition of Sir John Morton and Alice Carr; yet the very first part of the Hall the Drumble builder has pulled down is the old stone dining-parlour where the great dinner for the preachers mouldered away—

flesh from flesh, crumb from crumb! And the street they are going to build right through the rooms through which Alice Carr was dragged in her agony of despair at her husband's loathing hatred, is to be called Carr Street.

And Miss Cordelia has got a baby; a little girl; and writes in pencil two lines at the end of her husband's note, to say she means to call it Phillis.

Phillis Carr! I am glad he did not take the name of Morton. I like to keep the name of Phillis Morton in my memory very still and unspoken.

MY FRENCH MASTER

CHAPTER I

MY father's house was in the country, seven miles away from the nearest town. He had been an officer in the navy; but as he had met with some accident that would disable him from ever serving again, he gave up his commission, and his half-pay.* He had a small private fortune, and my mother had not been penniless; so he purchased a house, and ten or twelve acres of land, and set himself up as an amateur farmer on a very small scale. My mother rejoiced over the very small scale of his operations; and when my father regretted, as he did very often, that no more land was to be purchased in the neighbourhood, I could see her setting herself a sum in her head, 'If on twelve acres he manages to lose a hundred pounds a year, what would be our loss on a hundred and fifty?' But when my father was pushed hard on the subject of the money he spent in his sailor-like farming, he had one constant retreat:

'Think of the health, and the pleasure we all of us take in the cultivation of the fields around us! It is something for us to do, and to look forward to every day.' And this was so true that, as long as my father confined himself to these arguments, my mother left him unmolested: but to strangers he was still apt to enlarge on the returns his farm brought him in; and he had often to pull up in his statements when he caught the warning glance of my mother's eye, showing him that she was not so much absorbed in her own conversation as to be deaf to his voice. But as for the happiness that arose out of our mode of life, that was not to be calculated by tens or hundreds of pounds. There were only two of us, my sister and myself; and my mother undertook the greater part of our education. We helped her in her household cares during part of the morning; then came an old-fashioned routine of lessons, such as she herself had learnt when a girl—Goldsmith's *History of England*, Rollins's *Ancient History*, Lindley Murray's Grammar,* and plenty of sewing, and stitching.

My mother used sometimes to sigh, and wish that she could buy us a piano, and teach us what little music she knew; but many of my dear father's habits were expensive; at least, for a person possessed of no larger an income than he had. Besides the quiet and unsuspected drain of his agricultural pursuits, he was of a social turn; enjoying the dinners to which he was invited by his more affluent neighbours; and especially delighted in returning them the compliment, and giving them choice little entertainments, which would have been yet more frequent in their recurrence than they were, if it had not been for my mother's prudence. But we never were able to purchase the piano; it required a greater outlay of ready money than we ever possessed. I daresay we should have grown up ignorant of any language but our own if it had not been for my father's social habits, which led to our learning French in a very unexpected manner. He and my mother went to dine with General Ashburton, one of the forest rangers; and there they met with an emigrant* gentleman, a Monsieur de Chalabre, who had escaped in a wonderful manner, and at terrible peril to his life; and was, consequently, in our small forest-circle, a great lion,* and a worthy cause of a series of dinner parties. His first entertainer, General Ashburton, had known him in France, under very different circumstances; and he was not prepared for the quiet and dignified request made by his guest, one afternoon after M. de Chalabre had been about a fortnight in the forest, that the general would recommend him as a French teacher, if he could conscientiously do so.

To the general's remonstrances, M. de Chalabre smilingly replied, by an assurance that his assumption of his new occupation could only be for a short time; that the good cause would—*must* triumph. It was before the fatal 21st of January, 1793;* and then, still smiling, he strengthened his position by quoting innumerable instances out of the classics, of heroes and patriots, generals and commanders, who had been reduced by Fortune's frolics to adopt some occupation far below their original one. He closed his speech with informing the general that, relying upon his kindness in acting as referee, he had taken lodgings for a few months at a small farm which was in the centre of our forest circle of acquaintances. The general was too thoroughly a gentleman to say anything more than that he should be most happy to do whatever he could to forward M. de Chalabre's plans, and as my father was the first person whom he met with after this conversation, it was announced to us, on the very evening of the day on which it had taken place, that we were forthwith to learn French; and I verily believe that, if my father could have persuaded my mother to join him, we should have formed a French class of father, mother, and two head of daughters, so touched had my father been by the general's account of M. de Chalabre's present desires, as compared with the high estate from which he had fallen. Accordingly, we were installed in the dignity of his first French pupils. My father was anxious that we should have a lesson every other day, ostensibly that we might get on all the more speedily, but really that he might have a larger quarterly bill to pay; at any rate, until M. de Chalabre had more of his time occupied with instruction. But my mother gently interfered, and calmed her husband down into two lessons a week, which was, she said, as much as we could manage. Those happy lessons! I remember them now, at the distance of more than fifty years. Our house was situated on the edge of the forest; our fields were, in fact, cleared out of it. It was not good land for clover; but my father would always sow one particular field with clover seed, because my mother was so fond of the fragrant scent in her evening walks, and through this a footpath ran which led into the forest.

A quarter of a mile beyond—a walk on the soft, fine, springy turf, and under the long, low branches of the beech-trees—and we arrived at the old red-brick farm where M. de Chalabre was lodging. Not that we went there to take our lessons; that would have been an offence to his spirit of politeness; but as my father and mother were his nearest neighbours, there was a constant interchange of small messages and notes, which we little girls were only too happy to take to our dear M. de Chalabre. Moreover, if our lessons with my mother were ended pretty early, she would say—'You have been good girls; now you may run to the high point in the clover-field, and see if M. de Chalabre is coming; and if he is, you may walk with him; but take care and give him the cleanest part of the path, for you know he does not like to dirty his boots.'

This was all very well in theory; but, like many theories, the difficulty was to put it in practice. If we slipped to the side of the path where the water lay longest, he bowed and retreated behind us to a still wetter place, leaving the clean part for us; yet when we got home, his polished boots would be without a speck, while our shoes were covered with mud.

Another little ceremony which we had to get accustomed to, was his habit of taking off his hat as we approached, and walking by us holding it in his hand. To be sure, he wore a wig, delicately powdered, frizzed, and tied in a queue* behind; but we had always a feeling that he would catch cold, and that he was doing us too great an honour, and that he did not know how old or rather how young we were, until one day we saw him (far away from our house) hand a countrywoman over a stile with the same kind of dainty, courteous politeness, lifting her basket of eggs over first; and then, taking up the silk-lined lapel of his coat, he spread it on the palm of his hand for her to rest her fingers upon; instead of which, she took his small white hand in her plump, vigorous gripe, and leant her full weight upon him. He carried her basket for her as far as their roads lay together; and from that time we were less shy in receiving his courtesies, perceiving that he considered them as deference due to our sex, however old or young, or rich or poor. So, as I said, we came down from the clover-field in rather a stately manner, and through the wicket-gate that opened into our garden, which was as rich in its scents of varied kinds as the clover-field had been in its one pure fragrance. My mother would meet us here; and somehow—our life was passed as much out of doors as in-doors, both winter and summer—we seemed to have our French lessons more frequently in the garden than in the house; for there was a sort of arbour on the lawn near the drawing-room window, to which we always found it easy to carry a table and chairs, and all the rest of the lesson paraphernalia, if my mother did not prohibit a lesson al fresco.

M. de Chalabre wore, as a sort of morning costume, a coat, waistcoat, and breeches, all made of a kind of coarse grey cloth, which he had bought in the neighbourhood. His three-cornered hat was brushed to a nicety, his wig sat as no one else's did. (My father's was always awry.) And the only thing wanting to his costume when he came was a flower. Sometimes I fancied he purposely omitted gathering one of the roses that clustered up the farm-house in which he lodged, in order to afford my mother the pleasure of culling her choicest carnations and roses to make him up his nosegay, or 'posy,' as he liked to call it. He had picked up that pretty country word, and adopted it as an especial favourite, dwelling on the first syllable with all the languid softness of an Italian accent. Many a time have Mary and I tried to say it like him, we did so admire his way of speaking.

Once seated round the table, whether in the house or out of it, we were bound to attend to our lessons; and somehow he made us perceive that it was a part of the same chivalrous code that made him so helpful to the helpless, to enforce the slightest claim of duty to the full. No half-prepared lessons for him! The patience, and the resource with which he illustrated and enforced every precept; the untiring gentleness with which he made our stubborn English tongues pronounce, and mis-pronounce, and re-pronounce certain words; above all, the sweetness of temper which never varied, were such as I have never seen equalled. If we wondered at these qualities when we were children, how much greater has been our surprise at their existence since we have been grown up, and have learnt that, until his emigration, he was a man of rapid and impulsive action, with the imperfect education implied in the circumstance, that at fifteen he was a sous-lieutenant* in the Queen's regiment, and must, consequently, have had to apply himself hard and conscientiously to master the language which he had in after-life to teach.

Twice we had holidays to suit his sad convenience. Holidays with us were not at Christmas, and Midsummer, Easter, and Michaelmas.* If my mother was unusually busy, we had what we called a holiday, though, in reality, it involved harder work than our regular lessons; but we fetched, and carried, and ran errands, and became rosy, and dusty, and sang merry songs in the gaiety of our hearts. If the day was remarkably fine, my dear father—whose spirits were rather apt to vary with the weather—would come bursting in with his bright, kind, bronzed face, and carry the day by storm with my mother. 'It was a shame to coop such young things up in a house,' he would say, 'when every other young animal was frolicking in the air and sunshine. Grammar!—what was that but the art of arranging words?—and he never knew a woman but could do that fast enough. Geography!—he would undertake to teach us more geography in one winter evening, telling us of the countries where he had been, with just a map before him, than we could learn in ten years with that stupid book, all full of hard words. As for the French—why, that must be learnt; for he should not like M. de Chalabre to think we slighted the lessons he took so much pains to give us; but surely we could get up the earlier to learn our French.' We promised by acclamation; and my mother— sometimes smilingly, sometimes reluctantly—was always compelled to yield. And these were the usual occasions for our holidays. But twice we had a fortnight's entire cessation of French lessons: once in January, and once in October. Nor did we even see our dear French master during those periods. We went several times to the top of the clover-field, to search the dark green outskirts of the forest with our busy eyes; and if we could have seen his figure in that shade, I am sure we should have scampered to him, forgetful of the prohibition which made the forest forbidden ground. But we did not see him.

It was the fashion in those days to keep children much less informed than they are now on the subjects which interest their parents. A sort of hieroglyphic or cypher talk was used in order to conceal the meaning of much that was said if children were present. My mother was a proficient in this way of talking, and took, we fancied, a certain pleasure in perplexing my father by inventing a new cypher, as it were, every day. For instance, for some time, I was called Martia,* because I was very tall of my age; and, just as my father began to understand the name—and, it must be owned, a good while after I had learnt to prick up my ears whenever Martia was named—my mother suddenly changed me into the 'buttress,' from the habit I had acquired of leaning my languid length against a wall. I saw my father's perplexity about this 'buttress' for some days, and could have helped him out of it, but I durst not. And so, when the unfortunate Louis the Sixteenth was executed, the news was too terrible to be put into plain English, and too terrible also to be made known to us children, nor could we at once find the clue to the cypher in which it was spoken about. We heard about 'the Iris being blown down;'* and saw my father's honest loyal excitement about it, and the quiet reserve which always betokened some secret grief on my mother's part.

We had no French lessons; and somehow the poor, battered, storm-torn Iris was to blame for this. It was many weeks after this before we knew the full reason of M. de Chalabre's deep depression when he again came amongst us; why he shook his head when my mother timidly offered him some snowdrops on that first morning on which we began lessons again; why he wore the deep mourning of that day, when all of the dress that could be black was black, and the white muslin frills and ruffles were unstarched and limp, as if to bespeak the very abandonment of grief. We knew well enough the meaning of the next hieroglyphic announcement—'The wicked, cruel boys had broken off the White Lily's head!'* That beautiful queen, whose portrait once had been shown to us, with her blue eyes, and her fair resolute look, her profusion of lightly-powdered hair, her white neck adorned with strings of pearls. We could have cried, if we had dared, when we heard the transparent mysterious words. We did cry at night, sitting up in bed, with our arms round each other's necks, and vowing, in our weak, passionate, childish way, that if we lived long enough, that lady's death avenged should be. No one who cannot remember that time can tell the shudder of horror that thrilled through the country at hearing of this last execution. At the moment, there was no time for any consideration of the silent horrors endured for centuries by the people, who at length rose in their madness against their rulers. This last blow changed our dear M. de Chalabre. I never saw him again in quite the same gaiety of heart as before this time. There seemed to be tears very close behind his smiles for ever after. My father went to see him when he had been about a week absent from us—no reason given, for did not we, did not every one, know the horror the sun had looked upon! As soon as my father had gone, my mother gave it in charge to us to make the dressing-room belonging to our guest-chamber as much like a sitting-room as possible. My father hoped to bring back M. de Chalabre for a visit to us; but he would probably like to be a good deal alone; and we might move any article of furniture we liked, if we only thought it would make him comfortable.

I believe General Ashburton had been on a somewhat similar errand to my father's before; but he had failed. My father gained his point, as I afterwards learnt, in a very unconscious and characteristic manner. He had urged his invitation on M. de Chalabre, and received such a decided negative that he was hopeless, and quitted the subject. Then M. de Chalabre began to relieve his heart by telling him all the details; my father held his breath to listen—at last, his honest heart could contain itself no longer, and the tears ran down his face. His unaffected sympathy touched M. de

Chalabre inexpressibly; and in an hour after we saw our dear French master coming down the clover-field slope, leaning on my father's arm, which he had involuntarily offered as a support to one in trouble—although he was slightly lame, and ten or fifteen years older than M. de Chalabre.

For a year after that time, M. de Chalabre never wore any flowers; and after that, to the day of his death, no gay or coloured rose or carnation could tempt him. We secretly observed his taste, and always took care to bring him white flowers for his posy. I noticed, too, that on his left arm, under his coat sleeve (sleeves were made very open then), he always wore a small band of black crape.* He lived to be eighty-one, but he had the black crape band on when he died.

M. de Chalabre was a favourite in all the forest circle. He was a great acquisition to the sociable dinner parties that were perpetually going on; and though some of the families piqued themselves on being aristocratic, and turned up their noses at any one who had been engaged in trade, however largely, M. de Chalabre, in right of his good blood, his loyalty, his daring *preux chevalier** actions, was ever an honoured guest. He took his poverty, and the simple habits it enforced, so naturally and gaily, as a mere trifling accident of his life, about which neither concealment nor shame could be necessary, that the very servants—often so much more pseudo-aristocratic than their masters—loved and respected the French gentleman, who, perhaps, came to teach in the mornings, and in the evenings made his appearance dressed with dainty neatness as a dinner guest. He came lightly prancing through the forest mire; and, in our little hall, at any rate, he would pull out a neat minute case containing a blacking-brush and blacking, and repolish his boots, speaking gaily, in his broken English, to the footman all the time. That blacking-case was his own making; he had a genius for using his fingers. After our lessons were over, he relaxed into the familiar house friend, the merry play-fellow. We lived far from any carpenter or joiner; if a lock was out of order, M. de Chalabre made it right for us.* If any box was wanted, his ingenious fingers had made it before our lesson day. He turned silk-winders* for my mother, made a set of chessmen for my father, carved an elegant watch-case out of a rough beef-bone, dressed up little cork dolls for us—in short, as he said, his heart would have been broken but for his joiner's tools. Nor were his ingenious gifts employed for us alone. The farmer's wife where he lodged had numerous contrivances in her house which he had made. One particularly which I remember was a paste-board,* made after a French pattern, which would not slip about on a dresser, as he had observed her English paste-board do. Susan, the farmer's ruddy daughter, had her work-box, too, to show us; and her cousin-lover had a wonderful stick, with an extraordinary demon head carved upon it;—all by M. de Chalabre. Farmer, farmer's wife, Susan, Robert, and all were full of his praises.

We grew from children into girls—from girls into women; and still M. de Chalabre taught on in the forest; still he was beloved and honoured; still no dinner-party within five miles was thought complete without him, and ten miles' distance strove to offer him a bed sooner than miss his company. The pretty, merry Susan of sixteen had been jilted by the faithless Robert, and was now a comely, demure damsel of thirty-one or two; still waiting upon M. de Chalabre, and still constant in respectfully singing his praises. My own poor mother was dead; my sister was engaged to be married to a young lieutenant, who was with his ship in the Mediterranean. My father was as youthful as ever in heart, and, indeed, in many of his ways; only his hair was quite white, and the old lameness was more frequently troublesome than it had been. An uncle of his had left him a considerable fortune, so he farmed away to his heart's content, and lost an annual sum of money with the best grace and the lightest heart in the world. There were not even the gentle reproaches of my mother's eyes to be dreaded now.

Things were in this state when the peace of 1814* was declared. We had heard so many and such contradictory rumours that we were inclined to doubt even the *Gazette** at last, and were discussing probabilities with some vehemence, when M. de Chalabre entered the room unannounced and breathless:

'My friends, give me joy!' he said. 'The Bourbons'*—he could not go on; his features, nay, his very fingers, worked with agitation, but he could not speak. My father hastened to relieve him.

'We have heard the good news (you see, girls, it is quite true this time). I do congratulate you, my dear friend. I *am* glad.' And he seized M. de Chalabre's hand in his own hearty gripe, and brought the nervous agitation of the latter to a close by unconsciously administering a pretty severe dose of wholesome pain.

'I go to London. I go straight this afternoon to see my sovereign. My sovereign holds a court to-morrow at Grillon's Hotel;* I go to pay him my *devoirs*.* I put on my uniform of Gardes du Corps,* which have lain by these many years; a little old, a little worm-eaten, but never mind; they have been seen by Marie Antoinette, which gives them a grace for ever.' He walked about the room in a nervous, hurried way. There was something on his mind, and we signed to my father to be silent for a moment or two, and let it come out. 'No!' said M. de Chalabre, after a moment's pause. 'I cannot say adieu; for I shall return to say, dear friends, my adieux. I did come a poor emigrant; noble Englishmen took me for their friend, and welcomed me to their houses. Chalabre is one large mansion, and my English friends will not forsake me; they will come and see me in my own country; and, for their sakes, not an English beggar shall pass the doors of Chalabre without being warmed and clothed and fed. I will not say adieu. I go now but for two days.'

CHAPTER II

MY father insisted upon driving M. de Chalabre in his gig to the nearest town through which the London mail* passed; and, during the short time that elapsed before my father was ready, he told us something more about Chalabre. He had never spoken of his ancestral home to any of us before; we knew little of his station in his own country. General Ashburton had met with him in Paris, in a set where a man was judged of by his wit and talent for society, and general brilliance of character, rather than by his wealth and hereditary position. Now we learned for the first time that he was heir to considerable estates in Normandy; to an old Château Chalabre; all of which he had forfeited by his emigration, it was true, but that was under another régime.

'Ah! if my dear friend, your poor mother, were alive now, I could send her such slips of rare and splendid roses from Chalabre. Often when I did see her nursing up some poor little specimen, I longed in secret for my rose garden at Chalabre. And the orangerie!* Ah! Miss Fanny,* the bride must come to Chalabre who wishes for a beautiful wreath.'* This was an allusion to my sister's engagement; a fact well known to him, as the faithful family friend.

My father came back in high spirits; and began to plan that very evening how to arrange his crops for the ensuing year, so as best to spare time for a visit to Château Chalabre; and as for us, I think we believed that there was no need to delay our French journey beyond the autumn of the present year.

M. de Chalabre came back in a couple of days; a little damped, we girls fancied, though we hardly liked to speak about it to my father. However, M. de Chalabre explained it to us by saying that he had found London more crowded and busy than he had expected; that it was smoky and dismal after leaving the country, where the trees were already coming into leaf; and, when we pressed him a little more respecting the reception at Grillon's, he laughed at himself for having forgotten the tendency of the Count de Provence in former days to become stout, and so being dismayed at the mass of corpulence which Louis the Eighteenth* presented, as he toiled up the long drawing-room of the hotel.

'But what did he say to you?' Fanny asked. 'How did he receive you when you were presented?'

A flash of pain passed over his face; but it was gone directly.

'Oh! his majesty did not recognize my name. It was hardly to be expected he would; though it is a name of note in Normandy; and I have—well! that is worth nothing. The Duc de Duras* reminded him of a circumstance or two, which I had almost hoped his majesty would not have forgotten; but I myself forgot the pressure of long years of exile; it was no wonder he did not remember me. He said he hoped to see me at the Tuileries.* His hopes are my laws. I go to prepare for my departure. If his majesty does not need my sword, I turn it into a ploughshare* at Chalabre. Ah! my friend, I will not forget there all the agricultural science I have learned from you.'

A gift of a hundred pounds would not have pleased my father so much as this last speech. He began forthwith to inquire about the nature of the soil, &c., in a way which made our poor M. de Chalabre shrug his shoulders in despairing ignorance.

'Never mind!' said my father. 'Rome was not built in a day.* It was a long time before I learnt all that I know now. I was afraid I could not leave home this autumn, but I perceive you'll need some one to advise you about laying out the ground for next year's crops.'

So M. de Chalabre left our neighbourhood, with the full understanding that we were to pay him a visit in his Norman château in the following September; nor was he content until he had persuaded every one who had shown him kindness to promise him a visit at some appointed time. As for his old landlord at the farm, the comely dame and buxom Susan—they, we found, were to be franked* there and back, under the pretence that the French dairy-maids had no notion of cleanliness, any more than that the French farming men were judges of stock; so it was absolutely necessary to bring over some one from England to put the affairs of the Château Chalabre in order; and Farmer Dobson and his wife considered the favour quite reciprocal.

For some time we did not hear from our friend. The war had made the post between France and England very uncertain; so we were obliged to wait, and we tried to be patient; but, somehow, our autumn visit to France was silently given up; and my father gave us long expositions of the disordered state of affairs in a country which had suffered so much as France, and lectured us severely on the folly of having expected to hear so soon. We knew, all the while, that the exposition was repeated to soothe his own impatience, and that the admonition to patience was what he felt that he himself was needing.

At last the letter came. There was a brave attempt at cheerfulness in it, which nearly made me cry, more than any complaints would have done. M. de Chalabre had hoped to retain his commission as sous-lieutenant in the Gardes du Corps—a commission signed by Louis the Sixteenth himself, in 1791. But the regiment was to be remodelled, or re-formed, I forget which; and M. de Chalabre assured us that his was not the only case where applicants had been refused. He had then tried for a commission in the Cent Suisses, the Gardes du Porte, the Mousquetaires*—but all were full. 'Was it not a glorious thing for France to have so many brave sons ready to fight on the side of honour and loyalty?' To which question Fanny replied 'that it was a shame;' and my father, after a grunt or two, comforted himself by saying, 'that M. de Chalabre would have the more time to attend to his neglected estate.'

That winter was full of incidents in our home. As it often

happens when a family has seemed stationary, and secure from change for years, and then at last one important event happens, another is sure to follow. Fanny's lover returned, and they were married, and left us alone—my father and I. Her husband's ship was stationed in the Mediterranean, and she was to go and live at Malta, with some of his relations there. I know not if it was the agitation of parting with her, but my father was stricken down from health into confirmed invalidism, by a paralytic stroke, soon after her departure, and my interests were confined to the fluctuating reports of a sick room. I did not care for the foreign intelligence which was shaking Europe with an universal tremor. My hopes, my fears were centred in one frail human body—my dearly beloved, my most loving father. I kept a letter in my pocket for days from M. de Chalabre, unable to find the time to decipher his French hieroglyphics; at last I read it aloud to my poor father, rather as a test of his power of enduring interest, than because I was impatient to know what it contained. The news in it was depressing enough, as everything else seemed to be that gloomy winter. A rich manufacturer of Rouen had bought the Château Chalabre; forfeited to the nation by its former possessor's emigration. His son, M. du Fay, was well-affected towards Louis the Eighteenth—at least as long as his government was secure and promised to be stable, so as not to affect the dyeing and selling of Turkey-red wools; and so the natural legal consequence was, that M. du Fay, Fils,* was not to be disturbed in his purchased and paid-for property. My father cared to hear of this disappointment to our poor friend—cared just for one day, and forgot all about it the next. Then came the return from Elba—the hurrying events of that spring—the battle of Waterloo;* and to my poor father, in his second childhood, the choice of a daily pudding was far more important than all.

One Sunday, in that August of 1815, I went to church. It was many weeks since I had been able to leave my father for so long a time before. Since I had been last there to worship, it seemed as if my youth had passed away—gone without a warning—leaving no trace behind. After service, I went through the long grass to the unfrequented part of the churchyard where my dear mother lay buried. A garland of brilliant yellow immortelles* lay on her grave; and the unwonted offering took me by surprise. I knew of the foreign custom, although I had never seen the kind of wreath before. I took it up, and read one word in the black floral letters; it was simply 'Adieu.' I knew, from the first moment I saw it, that M. de Chalabre must have returned to England. Such a token of regard was like him, and could spring from no one else. But I wondered a little that we had never heard or seen anything of him; nothing, in fact, since Lady Ashburton had told me that her husband had met with him in Belgium, hurrying to offer himself as a volunteer to one of the eleven generals appointed by the Duc de Feltre* to receive such applications. General Ashburton himself had since this died at Brussels, in consequence of wounds received at Waterloo. As the recollection of all these circumstances gathered in my mind, I found I was drawing near the field-path which led out of the direct road home, to farmer Dobson's; and thither I suddenly determined to go, and hear if they had learnt anything respecting their former lodger. As I went up the garden-walk leading to the house, I caught M. de Chalabre's eye; he was gazing abstractedly out of the window of what used to be his sitting-room. In an instant he had joined me in the garden. If my youth had flown, his youth, and middle-age as well, had vanished altogether. He looked older by at least twenty years than when he had left us twelve months ago. How much of this was owing to the change in the arrangement of his dress, I cannot tell. He had formerly been remarkably dainty in all these things; now he was careless, even to the verge of slovenliness. He asked after my sister, after my father, in a manner which evinced the deepest, most respectful interest; but, somehow, it appeared to me as if he hurried question after question, rather to stop any inquiries which I, in my turn, might wish to make.

'I return here to my duties; to my only duties. The good God has not seen me fit to undertake any higher. Henceforth I am the faithful French teacher; the diligent, punctual French teacher: nothing more. But I do hope to teach the French language as becomes a gentleman and a Christian; to do my best. Henceforth the grammar and the syntax are my estate, my coat of arms.' He said this with a proud humility which prevented any reply. I could only change the subject, and urge him to come and see my poor sick father. He replied,—

'To visit the sick, that is my duty as well as my pleasure. For the mere society—I renounce all that. That is now beyond my position, to which I accommodate myself with all my strength.'

Accordingly, when he came to spend an hour with my father, he brought a small bundle of printed papers, announcing the terms on which M. Chalabre (the 'de' was dropped* now and for evermore) was desirous of teaching French, and a little paragraph at the bottom of the page solicited the patronage of schools. Now this was a great coming-down. In former days, non-teaching at schools had been the line which marked that M. de Chalabre had taken up teaching rather as an amateur profession, than with any intention of devoting his life to it. He respectfully asked me to distribute these papers where I thought fit. I say 'respectfully' advisedly; there was none of the old deferential gallantry, as offered by a gentleman to a lady, his equal in birth and fortune—instead, there was the matter-of-fact request and statement which a workman offers to his employer. Only in my father's room, he was the former M. de Chalabre; he seemed to understand how vain would be all attempts to recount or explain the circumstances which had led him so decidedly to take a lower level in society. To my father, to the day of his death, M. de Chalabre maintained the old easy footing; assumed a gaiety which he never even pretended to feel anywhere else; listened to my father's childish interests with a true and kindly sympathy for which I ever felt grateful, although he purposely put a deferential reserve between him and me, as a barrier to any expression of such feeling on my part.

His former lessons had been held in such high esteem by those who were privileged to receive them, that he was soon sought after on all sides. The schools of the two principal county towns put forward their claims, and considered it a favour to receive his instructions. Morning, noon, and night he was engaged; even if he had not proudly withdrawn himself from all merely society engagements, he would have had no leisure for them. His only visits were paid to my father, who looked for them with a kind of childish longing. One day, to my surprise, he asked to be allowed to speak to me for an instant alone. He stood silent for a moment, turning his hat in his hand.

'You have a right to know—you, my first pupil; next Tuesday, I marry myself to Miss Susan Dobson, good, respectable woman, to whose happiness I mean to devote my life, or as much of it as is not occupied with the duties of instruction.' He looked up at me, expecting congratulations, perhaps; but I was too much stunned with my surprise: the buxom, red-armed, apple-cheeked Susan, who, when she blushed, blushed the colour of beet-root; who did not know a word of French; who regarded the nation (always excepting the gentleman before me) as frog-eating Mounseers, the national enemies of England! I afterwards thought that perhaps this very ignorance constituted one of her charms. No word, nor allusion, nor expressive silence, nor regretful sympathetic sighs, could remind M. de Chalabre of the bitter past, which he was evidently striving to forget. And, most assuredly, never man had a more devoted and admiring wife than poor Susan made M. de Chalabre. She was a little awed by him, to be sure; never quite at her ease before him; but I imagine husbands do not dislike such a tribute to their Jupiter-ship.* Madame Chalabre received my call, after their marriage, with a degree of sober, rustic, happy dignity, which I could not have foreseen in Susan Dobson. They had taken a small cottage on the borders of the forest; it had a garden round it; and the cow, pigs, and poultry, which were to be her charge, found their keep in the forest. She had a rough country servant to assist her in looking after them; and in what scanty leisure he had, her husband attended to the garden and the bees. Madame Chalabre took me over the neatly furnished cottage with evident pride. 'Moussire,' as she called him, had done this; Moussire had fitted up that. Moussire was evidently a man of resource. In a little closet of a dressing-room belonging to Moussire, there hung a pencil drawing, elaborately finished to the condition of a bad pocket-book engraving. It caught my eye, and I lingered to look at it. It represented a high, narrow house, of considerable size, with four pepper-box turrets at each corner; and a stiff avenue formed the foreground.

'Château Chalabre?' said I, inquisitively.

'I never asked,' my companion replied. 'Moussire does not always like to be asked questions. It is the picture of some place he is very fond of, for he won't let me dust it for fear I should smear it.'

M. de Chalabre's marriage did not diminish the number of his visits to my father. Until that beloved parent's death, he was faithful in doing all he could to lighten the gloom of the sick-room. But a chasm, which he had opened, separated any present intercourse with him from the free, unreserved friendship that had existed formerly. And yet for his sake I used to go and see his wife. I could not forget early days, nor the walks to the top of the clover-field, nor the daily posies, nor my mother's dear regard for the emigrant gentleman; nor a thousand little kindnesses which he had shown to my absent sister and myself. He did not forget either in the closed and sealed chambers of his heart. So, for his sake, I tried to become a friend to his wife; and she learned to look upon me as such. It was my employment in the sick chamber to make clothes for the little expected Chalabre baby; and its mother would fain (as she told me) have asked me to carry the little infant to the font, but that her husband somewhat austerely reminded her that they ought to seek a *marraine** among those of their own station in society. But I regarded the pretty little Susan as my god-child nevertheless in my heart; and secretly pledged myself always to take an interest in her. Not two months after my father's death, a sister was born; and the human heart in M. de Chalabre subdued his pride; the child was to bear the pretty name of his French mother, although France could find no place for him, and had cast him out. That youngest little girl was called Aimée.

When my father died, Fanny and her husband urged me to leave Brookfield, and come and live with them at Valetta.* The estate was left to us; but an eligible tenant offered himself; and my health, which had suffered materially during my long nursing, did render it desirable for me to seek some change to a warmer climate. So I went abroad, ostensibly for a year's residence only; but, somehow, that year has grown into a lifetime. Malta and Genoa have been my dwelling-places ever since. Occasionally, it is true, I have paid visits to England, but I have never looked upon it as my home since I left it thirty years ago. During these visits I have seen the Chalabres. He had become more absorbed in his occupation than ever; had published a French grammar on some new principle, of which he presented me with a copy, taking some pains to explain how it was to be used. Madame looked plump and prosperous; the farm, which was under her management, had thriven; and as for the two daughters, behind their English shyness, they had a good deal of French piquancy and *esprit*.* I induced them to take some walks with me, with a view of asking them some questions which should make our friendship an individual reality, not merely an hereditary feeling; but the little monkeys put me through my catechism,* and asked me innumerable questions about France, which they evidently regarded as their country. 'How do you know all about French habits and customs?' asked I. 'Does Monsieur de——does your father talk to you much about France?'

'Sometimes, when we are alone with him——never when any one is by,' answered Susan, the elder, a grave, noble-looking girl, of twenty or thereabouts. 'I think he does not speak about France before my mother, for fear of hurting her.'

'And I think,' said little Aimée, 'that he does not speak at all, when he can help it; it is only when his heart gets too full with recollections, that he is obliged to talk to us, because many of the thoughts could not be said in English.'

'Then, I suppose, you are two famous French scholars?'

'Oh, yes! Papa always speaks to us in French; it is our own language.'

But with all their devotion to their father and to his country, they were most affectionate, dutiful daughters to their mother. They were her companions, her comforts in the pleasant household labours; most practical, useful young women. But in a privacy not the less sacred, because it was understood rather than prescribed, they kept all the enthusiasm, all the romance of their nature, for their father. They were the confidantes of that poor exile's yearnings for France; the eager listeners for what he chose to tell them of his early days. His words wrought up Susan to make the resolution that, if ever she felt herself free from home duties and responsibilities, she would become a Sister of Charity,* like Anne-Marguérite de Chalabre, her father's great-aunt, and model of woman's sanctity. As for Aimée, come what might, she never would leave her father; and that was all she was clear about in picturing her future.

Three years ago I was in Paris.* An English friend of mine who lives there——English by birth, but married to a German professor, and very French in manners and ways*——asked me to come to her house one evening. I was far from well, and disinclined to stir out.

'Oh, but come!' said she. 'I have a good reason; really a tempting reason. Perhaps this very evening a piece of poetical justice will be done in my *salon*.* A living romance! Now, can you resist?'

'What is it?' said I; for she was rather in the habit of exaggerating trifles into romances.

'A young lady is coming; not in the first youth, but still young, very pretty; daughter of a French *émigré*, whom my husband knew in Belgium, and who has lived in England ever since.'

'I beg your pardon, but what is her name?' interrupted I, roused to interest.

'De Chalabre. Do you know her?'

'Yes; I am much interested in her. I will gladly come to meet her. How long has she been in Paris? Is it Susan or Aimée?'

'Now I am not to be baulked of the pleasure of telling you my romance; my hoped-for bit of poetical justice. You must be patient, and you will have answers to all your questions.'

I sank back in my easy chair. Some of my friends are rather long-winded, and it is as well to be settled in a comfortable position before they begin to talk.

'I told you a minute ago, that my husband had become acquainted with M. de Chalabre in Belgium, in 1815. They have kept up a correspondence ever since; not a very brisk one, it is true, for M. de Chalabre was a French master in England, and my husband a professor in Paris; but still they managed to let each other know how they were going on, and what they were doing, once, if not twice every year. For myself, I never saw M. de Chalabre.'

'I know him well,' said I. 'I have known him all my life.'

'A year ago his wife died (she was an English-woman); she had had a long and suffering illness; and his eldest daughter had devoted herself to her with the patient sweetness of an angel, as he told us, and I can well believe. But after her mother's death, the world, it seems, became distasteful to her: she had been inured to the half-lights, the hushed voices, the constant thought for others required in a sick-room, and the noise and rough bustle of healthy people jarred upon her. So she pleaded with her father to allow her to become a Sister of Charity. She told him that he would have given a welcome to any suitor who came to offer to marry her, and bear her away from her home, and her father and sister; and now, when she was called by religion, would he grudge to part with her? He gave his consent, if not his full approbation; and he wrote to my husband to beg me to receive her here, while we sought out a convent into which she could be received. She has been with me two months, and endeared herself to me unspeakably; she goes home next week unless—'

'But, I beg your pardon; did you not say she wished to become a Sister of Charity?'

'It is true; but she was too old to be admitted into their order. She is eight-and-twenty. It has been a grievous disappointment to her; she has borne it very patiently and meekly, but I can see how deeply she has felt it. And now for my romance. My husband had a pupil some ten years ago, a M. du Fay, a clever, scientific young man, one of the first merchants of Rouen. His grandfather purchased M. de Chalabre's ancestral estate. The present M. du Fay came on business to Paris two or three days ago, and invited my husband to a little dinner; and somehow this story of Suzette Chalabre came out, in consequence of inquiries my husband was making for an escort to take her to England. M. du Fay seemed interested with the story; and asked my husband if he might pay his respects to me, some evening when Suzette should be in, and so is coming to-night, he, and a friend of his, who was at the dinner party the other day; will you come?'

I went, more in the hope of seeing Susan Chalabre, and hearing some news about my early home, than with any expectation of 'poetical justice.' And in that I was right; and yet I was wrong. Susan Chalabre was a grave, gentle woman, of an enthusiastic and devoted appearance, not unlike that portrait of his daughter which arrests every eye in Ary Scheffer's sacred pictures.* She was silent and sad; her cherished plan of life was uprooted. She talked to me a little in a soft and friendly manner, answering any questions I asked; but, as for gentlemen, her indifference and reserve made it impossible for them to enter into any conversation with her; and the meeting was indisputably 'flat.'

'Oh! my romance! my poetical justice! Before the evening was half over, I would have given up all my castles in the air for one well-sustained conversation of ten minutes long. Now don't laugh at me, for I can't bear it to-night.' Such was my friend's parting speech. I did not see her again for two days. The third she came in glowing with excitement.

'You may congratulate me after all; if it was not poetical justice, it is prosaic justice; and, except for the empty romance, that is a better thing!'

'What do you mean?' said I. 'Surely M. du Fay has not proposed for Susan?'

'No! but that charming M. de Frez, his friend, has; that is to say, not proposed but spoken; no, not spoken, but it seems he asked M. du Fay—whose confidant he was—if he was intending to proceed in his idea of marrying Suzette; and on hearing that he was not, M. de Frez said that he should come to us, and ask us to put him in the way of prosecuting the acquaintance, for that he had been charmed with her; looks, voice, silence, he admires them all; and we have arranged that he is to be the escort to England; he has business there, he says; and as for Suzette (she knows nothing of all this, of course, for who dared tell her?), all her anxiety is to return home, and the first person travelling to England will satisfy her, if it does us. And, after all, M. de Frez lives within five leagues of the Château Chalabre, so she can go and see the old place whenever she will.'

When I went to bid Susan good-by, she looked as unconscious and dignified as ever. No idea of a lover had ever crossed her mind. She considered M. de Frez as a kind of necessary incumbrance for the journey. I had not much hopes for him; and yet he was an agreeable man enough, and my friends told me that his character stood firm and high.

In three months, I was settled for the winter in Rome. In four, I heard that the marriage of Susan Chalabre had taken place. What were the intermediate steps between the cold, civil indifference with which I had last seen her regarding her travelling companion, and the full love with which such a woman as Suzette Chalabre must love a man before she could call him husband, I never learnt. I wrote to my old French master to congratulate him, as I believed I honestly might, on his daughter's marriage. It was some months before I received his answer. It was—

'Dear friend, dear old pupil, dear child of the beloved dead, I am an old man of eighty, and I tremble towards the grave. I cannot write many words; but my own hand shall bid you come to the home of Aimée and her husband. They tell me to ask you to come and see the old father's birth-place, while he is yet alive to show it to you. I have the very apartment in Château Chalabre that was mine when I was a boy, and my mother came in to bless me every night. Susan lives near us. The good God bless my sons-in-law, Bertrand de Frez and Alphonse du Fay, as He has blessed me all my life long. I think of your father and mother, my dear; and you must think no harm when I tell you I have had masses said for the repose of their souls. If I make a mistake, God will forgive.'

My heart could have interpreted this letter, even without the pretty letter of Aimée and her husband which accompanied it; and which told how, when M. du Fay came over to his friend's wedding, he had seen the younger sister, and in her seen his fate. The soft caressing, timid Aimée was more to his taste than the grave and stately Susan. Yet little Aimée managed to rule imperiously at Château Chalabre; or, rather, her husband was delighted to indulge her every wish; while Susan, in her grand way, made rather a pomp of her conjugal obedience. But they were both good wives, good daughters.

This last summer, you might have seen an old, old man, dressed in grey, with white flowers in his button-hole (gathered by a grand-child as fair as they), leading an elderly lady about the grounds of Château Chalabre, with tottering, unsteady eagerness of gait.

'Here!' said he to me, 'just here my mother bade me adieu when first I went to join my regiment. I was impatient to go. I mounted—I rode to yonder great chestnut, and then, looking back, I saw my mother's sorrowful countenance. I sprang off, threw the reins to the groom, and ran back for one more embrace. "My brave boy!" she said; "my own! Be faithful to God and your king!" I never saw her more; but I shall see her soon; and I think I may tell her I have been faithful both to my God and my king.'

Before now, he has told his mother all.

THE MANCHESTER MARRIAGE

MR and Mrs Openshaw came from Manchester to settle in London. He had been, what is called in Lancashire, a Salesman for a large manufacturing firm, who were extending their business, and opening a warehouse in the city; where Mr Openshaw was now to superintend their affairs. He rather enjoyed the change; having a kind of curiosity about London, which he had never yet been able to gratify in his brief visits to the metropolis. At the same time, he had an odd, shrewd, contempt for the inhabitants; whom he always pictured to himself as fine, lazy people; caring nothing but for fashion and aristocracy, and lounging away their days in Bond Street,* and such places; ruining good English, and ready in their turn to despise him as a provincial. The hours that the men of business kept in the city scandalized him too, accustomed as he was to the early dinners of Manchester folk and the consequently far longer evenings. Still, he was pleased to go to London; though he would not for the world have confessed it, even to himself, and always spoke of the step to his friends as one demanded of him by the interests of his employers, and sweetened to him by a considerable increase of salary. This, indeed, was so liberal that he might have been justified in taking a much larger house than the one he did, had he not thought himself bound to set an example to Londoners of how little a Manchester man of business cared for show. Inside, however, he furnished it with an unusual degree of comfort, and, in the winter-time, he insisted on keeping up as large fires as the grates would allow, in every room where the temperature was in the least chilly. Moreover, his northern sense of hospitality was such, that, if he were at home, he could hardly suffer a visitor to leave the house without forcing meat and drink upon him. Every servant in the house was well warmed, well fed, and kindly treated; for their master scorned all petty saving in aught that conduced to comfort; while he amused himself by following out all his accustomed habits and individual ways, in defiance of what any of his new neighbours might think.

His wife was a pretty, gentle woman, of suitable age and

character. He was forty-two, she thirty-five. He was loud and decided; she soft and yielding. They had two children; or rather, I should say, she had two; for the elder, a girl of eleven, was Mrs Openshaw's child by Frank Wilson, her first husband. The younger was a little boy, Edwin, who could just prattle, and to whom his father delighted to speak in the broadest and most unintelligible Lancashire dialect, in order to keep up what he called the true Saxon accent.*

Mrs Openshaw's Christian-name was Alice, and her first husband had been her own cousin. She was the orphan niece of a sea-captain in Liverpool; a quiet, grave little creature, of great personal attraction when she was fifteen or sixteen, with regular features and a blooming complexion. But she was very shy, and believed herself to be very stupid and awkward; and was frequently scolded by her aunt, her own uncle's second wife. So when her cousin, Frank Wilson, came home from a long absence at sea, and first was kind and protective to her; secondly, attentive, and thirdly, desperately in love with her, she hardly knew how to be grateful enough to him. It is true, she would have preferred his remaining in the first or second stages of behaviour; for his violent love puzzled and frightened her. Her uncle neither helped nor hindered the love affair; though it was going on under his own eyes. Frank's step-mother had such a variable temper, that there was no knowing whether what she liked one day she would like the next, or not. At length she went to such extremes of crossness, that Alice was only too glad to shut her eyes and rush blindly at the chance of escape from domestic tyranny offered her by a marriage with her cousin; and, liking him better than any one in the world, except her uncle (who was at this time at sea), she went off one morning and was married to him; her only bridesmaid being the housemaid at her aunt's. The consequence was, that Frank and his wife went into lodgings, and Mrs Wilson refused to see them, and turned away Norah, the warm-hearted housemaid, whom they accordingly took into their service. When Captain Wilson returned from his voyage, he was very cordial with the young couple, and spent many an evening at their lodgings, smoking his pipe, and sipping his grog; but he told them that, for quietness' sake, he could not ask them to his own house; for his wife was bitter against them. They were not, however, very unhappy about this.

The seed of future unhappiness lay rather in Frank's vehement, passionate disposition; which led him to resent his wife's shyness and want of demonstrativeness as failures in conjugal duty. He was already tormenting himself, and her too, in a slighter degree, by apprehensions and imaginations of what might befall her during his approaching absence at sea. At last, he went to his father and urged him to insist upon Alice's being once more received under his roof; the more especially as there was now a prospect of her confinement while her husband was away on his voyage. Captain Wilson was, as he himself expressed it, 'breaking up,'* and unwilling to undergo the excitement of a scene; yet he felt that what his son said was true. So he went to his wife. And before Frank set sail, he had the comfort of seeing his wife installed in her old little garret in his father's house. To have placed her in the one best spare room, was a step beyond Mrs Wilson's powers of submission or generosity. The worst part about it, however, was that the faithful Norah had to be dismissed. Her place as housemaid had been filled up; and, even if it had not, she had forfeited Mrs Wilson's good opinion for ever. She comforted her young master and mistress by pleasant prophecies of the time when they would have a household of their own; of which, whatever service she might be in meanwhile, she should be sure to form a part. Almost the last action Frank did, before setting sail, was going with Alice to see Norah once more at her mother's house; and then he went away.

Alice's father-in-law grew more and more feeble as winter advanced. She was of great use to her stepmother in nursing and amusing him; and, although there was anxiety enough in the household, there was, perhaps, more of peace than there had been for years; for Mrs Wilson had not a bad heart, and was softened by the visible approach of death to one whom she loved, and, touched by the lonely condition of the young creature, expecting her first confinement in her husband's absence. To this relenting mood Norah owed the permission to come and nurse Alice when her baby was born, and to remain to attend on Captain Wilson.

Before one letter had been received from Frank (who had sailed for the East Indies and China), his father died. Alice was always glad to remember that he had held her baby in his arms, and kissed and blessed it before his death. After that, and the consequent examination into the state of his affairs, it was found that he had left far less property than people had been led by his style of living to expect; and what money there was, was all settled upon his wife, and at her disposal after her death. This did not signify much to Alice, as Frank was now first mate of his ship, and, in another voyage or two, would be captain. Meanwhile he had left her rather more than two hundred pounds (all his savings) in the bank.

It became time for Alice to hear from her husband. One letter from the Cape* she had already received. The next was to announce his arrival in India. As week after week passed over, and no intelligence of the ship having got there reached the office of the owners, and the Captain's wife was in the same state of ignorant suspense as Alice herself, her fears grew most oppressive. At length the day came when, in reply to her inquiry at the Shipping Office, they told her that the owners had given up hope of ever hearing more of the 'Betsy-Jane,' and had sent in their claim upon the Underwriters.* Now that he was gone for ever, she first felt a yearning, longing love for the kind cousin, the dear friend, the sympathizing protector, whom she should never see again;—first felt a passionate desire to show him his child, whom she had hitherto rather craved to have all to herself—her own sole possession. Her grief was, however, noiseless, and quiet—rather to the scandal of Mrs Wilson; who bewailed her stepson as if he and she had always lived together in perfect harmony, and who evidently thought it her duty to burst into fresh tears at every strange face she saw; dwelling on his poor young widow's desolate state, and the helplessness of the fatherless child, with an unction, as if she liked the excitement of the sorrowful story.

So passed away the first days of Alice's widowhood. By-and-by things subsided into their natural and tranquil course. But, as if this young creature was always to be in some heavy trouble, her ewe-lamb began to be ailing, pining, and sickly. The child's mysterious illness turned out to be some affection of the spine, likely to affect health, but not to shorten life—at least, so the doctors said. But the long, dreary suffering of one whom a mother loves as Alice loved her only child, is hard to look forward to. Only Norah guessed what Alice suffered; no one but God knew.

And so it fell out, that when Mrs Wilson, the elder, came to her one day, in violent distress, occasioned by a very material diminution in the value of the property that her husband had left her,—a diminution which made her income barely enough to support herself, much less Alice—the latter could hardly understand how anything which did not touch health or life could cause such grief; and she received the intelligence with irritating composure. But when, that afternoon, the little sick child was brought in, and the grandmother—who after all loved it well—began a fresh moan over her losses to its unconscious ears—saying how she had planned to consult this or that doctor, and to give it this or that comfort or luxury in after years, but that now all chance of this had passed away—Alice's heart was touched, and she drew near to Mrs Wilson with unwonted caresses, and, in a spirit not unlike to that of Ruth,* entreated that, come what would, they might remain together. After much discussion in succeeding days, it was arranged that Mrs Wilson should take a house in Manchester, furnishing it partly with what furniture she had, and providing the rest with Alice's remaining two hundred pounds. Mrs Wilson was herself a Manchester woman, and naturally longed to return to her native town; some connections of her own, too, at that time required lodgings, for which they were willing to pay pretty handsomely. Alice undertook the active superintendence and superior work of the household; Norah, willing, faithful Norah, offered to cook, scour, do anything in short, so that she might but remain with them.

The plan succeeded. For some years, their first lodgers remained with them, and all went smoothly,—with the one sad exception of the little girl's increasing deformity. How that mother loved that child, it is not for words to tell!

Then came a break of misfortune. Their lodgers left, and no one succeeded to them. After some months, it became necessary to remove to a smaller house; and Alice's tender conscience was torn by the idea that she ought not to be a burden to her mother-in-law, but to go out and seek her own maintenance. And leave her child! The thought came like the sweeping boom of a funeral bell over her heart.

By-and-by, Mr Openshaw came to lodge with them. He had started in life as the errand-boy and sweeper-out of a warehouse; had struggled up through all the grades of employment in it, fighting his way through the hard striving Manchester life with strong, pushing energy of character. Every spare moment of time had been sternly given up to self-teaching. He was a capital accountant, a good French and German scholar, a keen, far-seeing, tradesman,—understanding markets, and the bearing of events, both near and distant, on trade: and yet, with such vivid attention to present details, that I do not think he ever saw a group of flowers in the fields without thinking whether their colours would, or would not, form harmonious contrasts in the coming spring muslins and prints. He went to debating societies, and threw himself with all his heart and soul into politics; esteeming, it must be owned, every man a fool or a knave who differed from him, and overthrowing his opponents rather by the loud strength of his language than the calm strength of his logic. There was something of the Yankee in all this. Indeed, his theory ran parallel to the famous Yankee motto—'England flogs creation, and Manchester flogs England.'* Such a man, as may be fancied, had had no time for falling in love, or any such nonsense. At the age when most young men go through their courting and matrimony, he had not the means of keeping a wife, and was far too practical to think of having one. And now that he was in easy circumstances, a rising man, he considered women almost as incumbrances to the world, with whom a man had better have as little to do as possible. His first impression of Alice was indistinct, and he did not care enough about her to make it distinct. 'A pretty yea-nay kind of woman,' would have been his description of her, if he had been pushed into a corner. He was rather afraid, in the beginning, that her quiet ways arose from a listlessness and laziness of character, which would have been exceedingly discordant to his active, energetic nature. But, when he found out the punctuality with which his wishes were attended to, and her work was done; when he was called in the morning at the very stroke of the clock, his shaving-water scalding hot, his fire bright, his coffee made exactly as his peculiar fancy dictated (for he was a man who had his theory about everything based upon what he knew of science, and often perfectly original)— then he began to think: not that Alice had any peculiar merit, but that he had got into remarkably good lodgings; his restlessness wore away, and he began to consider himself as almost settled for life in them.

Mr Openshaw had been too busy, all his days, to be introspective. He did not know that he had any tenderness in his nature; and if he had become conscious of its abstract existence, he would have considered it as a manifestation of disease in some part of him. But he was decoyed into pity unawares; and pity led on to tenderness. That little helpless child—always carried about by one of the three busy women of the house, or else patiently threading coloured beads in the chair from which, by no effort of its own, could it ever move,—the great grave blue eyes, full of serious, not uncheerful, expression, giving to the small delicate face a look beyond its years,—the soft plaintive voice dropping out but few words, so unlike the continual prattle of a child,—caught Mr Openshaw's attention in spite of himself. One day—he half scorned himself for doing so—he cut short his dinner-hour to go in search of some toy, which should take the place of those eternal beads. I forget what he bought; but, when he gave the present (which he took care to do in a short, abrupt manner, and when no one was by to see him), he was almost thrilled by the flash of delight that came over that child's face, and he could not help, all through that afternoon, going over and over again the picture left on his memory, by the bright effect of unexpected joy on the little girl's face. When he returned home, he found his slippers placed by his sitting-room fire; and even more careful attention paid to his fancies than was habitual in those model lodgings. When Alice had taken the last of his tea-things away—she had been silent as usual till then—she stood for an instant with the door in her hand. Mr Openshaw looked as if he were deep in his book, though in fact he did not see a line; but was heartily wishing the woman would go, and not make any palaver of gratitude. But she only said:

'I am very much obliged to you, sir. Thank you very much,' and was gone, even before he could send her away with a 'There, my good woman, that's enough!'

For some time longer he took no apparent notice of the child. He even hardened his heart into disregarding her sudden flush of colour and little timid smile of recognition, when he saw her by chance. But, after all, this could not last for ever; and, having a second time given way to tenderness, there was no relapse. The insidious enemy having thus entered his heart, in the guise of compassion to the child, soon assumed the more dangerous form of interest in the mother. He was aware of this change of feeling,— despised himself for it,—struggled with it; nay, internally yielded to it and cherished it, long before he suffered the slightest expression of it, by word, action, or look to escape him. He watched Alice's docile, obedient ways to her stepmother; the love which she had inspired in the rough Norah (roughened by the wear and tear of sorrow and years); but, above all, he saw the wild, deep, passionate affection existing between her and her child. They spoke little to any one else, or when any one else was by; but, when alone together, they talked, and murmured, and cooed, and chattered so continually, that Mr Openshaw first wondered what they could find to say to each other, and next became irritated because they were always so grave and silent with him. All this time he was perpetually devising small new pleasures for the child. His thoughts ran, in a pertinacious way, upon the desolate life before her; and often he came back from his day's work loaded with the very thing Alice had been longing for, but had not been able to procure. One time, it was a little chair for drawing the little sufferer along the streets; and, many an evening that following summer, Mr Openshaw drew her along himself, regardless of the remarks of his acquaintances. One day in autumn, he put down his newspaper, as Alice came in with the breakfast, and said, in as indifferent a voice as he could assume:—

'Mrs Frank, is there any reason why we two should not put up our horses together?'

Alice stood still in perplexed wonder. What did he mean? He had resumed the reading of his newspaper, as if he did not expect any answer; so she found silence her safest course, and went on quietly arranging his breakfast, without another word passing between them. Just as he was leaving the house, to go to the warehouse as usual, he turned back and put his head into the bright, neat, tidy kitchen, where all the women breakfasted in the morning:—

'You'll think of what I said, Mrs Frank' (this was her name with the lodgers), 'and let me have your opinion upon it to-night.'

Alice was thankful that her mother and Norah were too busy talking together to attend much to this speech. She determined not to think about it at all through the day; and, of course, the effort not to think, made her think all the more. At night she sent up Norah with his tea. But Mr Openshaw almost knocked Norah down as she was going out at the door, by pushing past her and calling out, 'Mrs Frank!' in an impatient voice, at the top of the stairs.

Alice went up, rather than seem to have affixed too much meaning to his words.

'Well, Mrs Frank,' he said, 'what answer? Don't make it too long; for I have lots of office work to get through to-night.'

'I hardly know what you meant, sir,' said truthful Alice.

'Well! I should have thought you might have guessed. You're not new at this sort of work, and I am. However, I'll make it plain this time. Will you have me to be thy wedded husband, and serve me, and love me, and honour me,* and all that sort of thing? Because, if you will, I will do as much by you, and be a father to your child—and that's more than is put in the Prayer-book. Now, I'm a man of my word; and what I say, I feel; and what I promise, I'll do. Now, for your answer!'

Alice was silent. He began to make the tea, as if her reply was a matter of perfect indifference to him; but, as soon as that was done, he became impatient.

'Well?' said he.

'How long, sir, may I have to think over it?'

'Three minutes!' (looking at his watch). 'You've had two already—that makes five. Be a sensible woman, say Yes, and sit down to tea with me, and we'll talk it over together; for, after tea, I shall be busy; say No' (he hesitated a moment to try and keep his voice in the same tone), 'and I shan't say another word about it, but pay up a year's rent for my rooms to-morrow, and be off. Time's up! Yes or no?'

'If you please, sir,—you have been so good to little Ailsie—'

'There, sit down comfortably by me on the sofa, and let us have our tea together. I am glad to find you are as good and sensible as I took you for.'

And this was Alice Wilson's second wooing.

Mr Openshaw's will was too strong, and his circumstances too good, for him not to carry all before him. He settled Mrs Wilson in a comfortable house of her own, and made her quite independent of lodgers. The little that Alice said with regard to future plans was in Norah's behalf.

'No,' said Mr Openshaw. 'Norah shall take care of the old lady as long as she lives; and, after that, she shall either come and live with us, or, if she likes it better, she shall have a provision for life—for your sake, missus. No one who has been good to you or the child shall go unrewarded. But even the little one will be better for some fresh stuff about her. Get her a bright, sensible girl as a nurse: one who won't go rubbing her with calf's-foot jelly as Norah does; wasting good stuff outside that ought to go in, but will follow doctors' directions; which, as you must see pretty clearly by this time, Norah won't; because they give the poor little wench pain. Now, I'm not above being nesh* for other folks myself. I can stand a good blow, and never change colour; but, set me in the operating-room in the Infirmary, and I turn as sick as a girl. Yet, if need were, I would hold the little wench on my knees while she screeched with pain, if it were to do her poor back good. Nay, nay, wench! keep your white looks for the time when it comes—I don't say it ever will. But this I know, Norah will spare the child and cheat the doctor, if she can. Now, I say, give the bairn a year or two's chance, and then, when the pack of doctors have done their best—and, maybe, the old lady has gone—we'll have Norah back, or do better for her.'

The pack of doctors could do no good to little Ailsie. She was beyond their power. But her father (for so he insisted on being called, and also on Alice's no longer retaining the appellation of Mamma, but becoming henceforward Mother), by his healthy cheerfulness of manner, his clear decision of purpose, his odd turns and quirks of humour, added to his real strong love for the help-less little girl, infused a new element of brightness and confidence into her life; and, though her back remained the same, her general health was strengthened, and Alice—never going beyond a smile herself—had the pleasure of seeing her child taught to laugh.

As for Alice's own life, it was happier than it had ever been before. Mr Openshaw required no demonstration, no expressions of affection from her. Indeed, these would rather have disgusted him. Alice could love deeply, but could not talk about it. The perpetual requirement of loving words, looks, and caresses, and miscon-struing their absence into absence of love, had been the great trial of her former married life. Now, all went on clear and straight, under the guidance of her husband's strong sense, warm heart, and powerful will. Year by year, their worldly prosperity increased. At Mrs Wilson's death, Norah came back to them, as nurse to the newly-born little Edwin; into which post she was not installed without a pretty strong oration on the part of the proud and happy father; who declared that if he found out that Norah ever tried to screen the boy by a falsehood, or to make him nesh either in body or mind, she should go that very day. Norah and Mr Openshaw were not on the most thoroughly cordial terms; neither of them fully recognizing or appreciating the other's best qualities.

This was the previous history of the Lancashire family who had now removed to London.

They had been there about a year, when Mr Openshaw suddenly informed his wife that he had determined to heal long-standing feuds, and had asked his uncle and aunt Chadwick to come and pay them a visit and see London. Mrs Openshaw had never seen this uncle and aunt of her husband's. Years before she had married him, there had been a quarrel. All she knew was, that Mr Chadwick was a small manufacturer in a country town in South Lancashire. She was extremely pleased that the breach was to be healed, and began making preparations to render their visit pleasant.

They arrived at last. Going to see London was such an event to them, that Mrs Chadwick had made all new linen fresh for the occasion—from nightcaps downwards; and as for gowns, ribbons, and collars, she might have been going into the wilds of Canada where never a shop is, so large was her stock. A fortnight before the day of her departure for London, she had formally called to take leave of all her acquaintance; saying she should need every bit of the intermediate time for packing up. It was like a second wedding in her imagination; and, to complete the resemblance which an entirely new wardrobe made between the two events, her husband brought her back from Manchester, on the last market-day before they set off, a gorgeous pearl and amethyst brooch, saying, 'Lunnon should see that Lancashire folks knew a handsome thing when they saw it.'

For some time after Mr and Mrs Chadwick arrived at the Openshaws' there was no opportunity for wearing this brooch; but at length they obtained an order to see Buckingham Palace, and the spirit of loyalty demanded that Mrs Chadwick should wear her best clothes in visiting the abode of her sovereign. On her return, she hastily changed her dress; for Mr Openshaw had planned that they should go to Richmond,* drink tea, and return by moonlight.

Accordingly, about five o'clock, Mr and Mrs Openshaw and Mr and Mrs Chadwick set off.

The housemaid and cook sat below, Norah hardly knew where. She was always engrossed in the nursery, in tending her two children, and in sitting by the restless, excitable Ailsie till she fell asleep. By-and-by, the housemaid Bessy tapped gently at the door. Norah went to her, and they spoke in whispers.

'Nurse! there's some one down stairs wants you.'

'Wants me! Who is it?'

'A gentleman—'

'A gentleman? Nonsense!'

'Well! a man, then, and he asks for you, and he rang at the front-door bell, and has walked into the dining-room.'

'You should never have let him,' exclaimed Norah, 'master and missus out—'

'I did not want him to come in; but, when he heard you lived here, he walked past me, and sat down on the first chair, and said, "Tell her to come and speak to me." There is no gas lighted in the room, and supper is all set out.'

'He'll be off with the spoons!' exclaimed Norah, putting the housemaid's fear into words, and preparing to leave the room, first, however, giving a look to Ailsie, sleeping soundly and calmly.

Down stairs she went, uneasy fears stirring in her bosom. Before she entered the dining-room she provided herself with a candle, and, with it in her hand, she went in, looking around her in the darkness for her visitor.

He was standing up, holding by the table. Norah and he looked at each other; gradual recognition coming into their eyes.

'Norah?' at length he asked.

'Who are you?' asked Norah, with the sharp tones of alarm and incredulity. 'I don't know you:' trying, by futile words of disbelief, to do away with the terrible fact before her.

'Am I so changed?' he said, pathetically. 'I dare say I am. But, Norah, tell me!' he breathed hard, 'where is my wife? Is she—is she alive?'

He came nearer to Norah, and would have taken her hand; but she backed away from him; looking at him all the time with staring eyes, as if he were some horrible object. Yet he was a handsome, bronzed, good-looking fellow, with beard and moustache, giving him a foreign-looking aspect; but his eyes! there was no mistaking those eager, beautiful eyes—the very same that Norah had watched not half an hour ago, till sleep stole softly over them.

'Tell me, Norah—I can bear it—I have feared it so often. Is she dead?' Norah still kept silence. 'She is dead!' He hung on Norah's words and looks, as if for confirmation or contradiction.

'What shall I do?' groaned Norah. 'O, sir! why did you come? how did you find me out? where have you been? We thought you dead, we did indeed!' She poured out words and questions to gain time, as if time would help her.

'Norah! answer me this question straight, by yes or no—Is my wife dead?'

'No, she is not!' said Norah, slowly and heavily.

'O, what a relief! Did she receive my letters? But perhaps you don't know. Why did you leave her? Where is she? O, Norah, tell me all quickly!'

'Mr Frank!' said Norah at last, almost driven to bay by her terror lest her mistress should return at any moment, and find him there—unable to consider what was best to be done or said—rushing at something decisive, because she could not endure her present state: 'Mr Frank! we never heard a line from you, and the shipowners said you had gone down, you and every one else. We thought you were dead, if ever man was, and poor Miss Alice and her little sick, helpless child! O, sir, you must guess it,' cried the poor creature at last, bursting out into a passionate fit of crying, 'for indeed I cannot tell it. But it was no one's fault. God help us all this night!'

Norah had sat down. She trembled too much to stand. He took her hands in his. He squeezed them hard, as if, by physical pressure, the truth could be wrung out.

'Norah.' This time his tone was calm, stagnant as despair. 'She has married again!'

Norah shook her head sadly. The grasp slowly relaxed. The man had fainted.

There was brandy in the room. Norah forced some drops into Mr Frank's mouth, chafed his hands, and—when mere animal life returned, before the mind poured in its flood of memories and thoughts—she lifted him up, and rested his head against her knees. Then she put a few crumbs of bread taken from the supper-table, soaked in brandy, into his mouth. Suddenly he sprang to his feet.

'Where is she? Tell me this instant.' He looked so wild, so mad, so desperate, that Norah felt herself to be in bodily danger; but her time of dread had gone by. She had been afraid to tell him the truth, and then she had been a coward. Now, her wits were sharpened by the sense of his desperate state. He must leave the house. She would pity him afterwards; but now she must rather command and upbraid; for he must leave the house before her mistress came home. That one necessity stood clear before her.

'She is not here: that is enough for you to know. Nor can I say exactly where she is' (which was true to the letter if not to the spirit). 'Go away, and tell me where to find you to-morrow, and I will tell you all. My master and mistress may come back at any minute, and then what would become of me, with a strange man in the house?'

Such an argument was too petty to touch his excited mind.

'I don't care for your master and mistress. If your master is a man, he must feel for me—poor shipwrecked sailor that I am—kept for years a prisoner amongst savages, always, always, always thinking of my wife and my home—dreaming of her by night, talking to her, though she could not hear, by day. I loved her more than all heaven and earth put together. Tell me where she is, this instant, you wretched woman, who salved over her wickedness to her, as you to do to me!'

The clock struck ten. Desperate positions require desperate measures.

'If you will leave the house now, I will come to you to-morrow and tell you all. What is more, you shall see your child now. She lies sleeping up-stairs. O, sir, you have a child, you do not know that as yet—a little weakly girl—with just a heart and soul beyond her years. We have reared her up with such care! We watched her, for we thought for many a year she might die any day, and we tended her, and no hard thing has come near her, and no rough word has ever been said to her. And now you come and will take her life into your hand, and will crush it. Strangers to her have been kind to her; but her own father—Mr Frank, I am her nurse, and I love her, and I tend her, and I would do anything for her that I could. Her mother's heart beats as hers beats; and, if she suffers a pain, her mother trembles all over. If she is happy, it is her mother that smiles and is glad. If she is growing stronger, her mother is healthy: if she dwindles, her mother languishes. If she dies—well,

I don't know: it is not every one can lie down and die when they wish it. Come up stairs, Mr Frank, and see your child. Seeing her will do good to your poor heart. Then go away, in God's name, just this one night;—to-morrow, if need be, you can do anything—kill us all if you will, or show yourself a great, grand man, whom God will bless for ever and ever. Come, Mr Frank, the look of a sleeping child is sure to give peace.'

She led him up-stairs; at first almost helping his steps, till they came near the nursery door. She had well-nigh forgotten the existence of little Edwin. It struck upon her with affright as the shaded light fell over the other cot; but she skilfully threw that corner of the room into darkness, and let the light fall on the sleeping Ailsie. The child had thrown down the coverings, and her deformity, as she lay with her back to them, was plainly visible through her slight night-gown. Her little face, deprived of the lustre of her eyes, looked wan and pinched, and had a pathetic expression in it, even as she slept. The poor father looked and looked with hungry, wistful eyes, into which the big tears came swelling up slowly and dropped heavily down, as he stood trembling and shaking all over. Norah was angry with herself, for growing impatient of the length of time that long lingering gaze lasted. She thought that she waited for full half an hour before Frank stirred. And then—instead of going away—he sank down on his knees by the bedside, and buried his face in the clothes. Little Ailsie stirred uneasily. Norah pulled him up in terror. She could afford no more time, even for prayer, in her extremity of fear; for surely the next moment would bring her mistress home. She took him forcibly by the arm: but, as he was going, his eye lighted on the other bed: he stopped. Intelligence came back into his face. His hands clenched.

'His child?' he asked.

'Her child,' replied Norah. 'God watches over him,' said she instinctively; for Frank's looks excited her fears, and she needed to remind herself of the Protector of the helpless.

'God has not watched over me,' he said, in despair; his thoughts apparently recoiling on his own desolate, deserted state. But Norah had no time for pity. To-morrow she would be as compassionate as her heart prompted. At length she guided him down-stairs, and shut the outer door, and bolted it—as if by bolts to keep out facts.

Then she went back into the dining-room, and effaced all traces of his presence, as far as she could. She went up-stairs to the nursery and sat there, her head on her hand, thinking what was to come of all this misery. It seemed to her very long before her master and mistress returned; yet it was hardly eleven o'clock. She heard the loud, hearty Lancashire voices on the stairs; and, for the first time, she understood the contrast of the desolation of the poor man who had so lately gone forth in lonely despair.

It almost put her out of patience to see Mrs Openshaw come in, calmly smiling, handsomely dressed, happy, easy, to inquire after her children.

'Did Ailsie go to sleep comfortably?' she whispered to Norah.

'Yes.'

Her mother bent over her, looking at her slumbers with the soft eyes of love. How little she dreamed who had looked on her last! Then she went to Edwin, with perhaps less wistful anxiety in her countenance, but more of pride. She took off her things, to go down to supper. Norah saw her no more that night.

Beside having a door into the passage, the sleeping-nursery opened out of Mr and Mrs Openshaw's room, in order that they might have the children more immediately under their own eyes. Early the next summer morning, Mrs Openshaw was awakened by Ailsie's startled call of 'Mother! mother!' She sprang up, put on her dressing-gown, and went to her child. Ailsie was only half awake, and in a not unusual state of terror.

'Who was he mother? Tell me!'

'Who, my darling? No one is here. You have been dreaming, love. Waken up quite. See, it is broad daylight.'

'Yes,' said Ailsie, looking round her; then clinging to her mother, 'but a man was here in the night, mother.'

'Nonsense, little goose. No man has ever come near you!'

'Yes, he did. He stood there. Just by Norah. A man with hair and a beard. And he knelt down and said his prayers. Norah knows he was here, mother' (half angrily, as Mrs Openshaw shook her head in smiling incredulity).

'Well! we will ask Norah when she comes,' said Mrs Openshaw, soothingly. 'But we won't talk any more about him now. It is not five o'clock; it is too early for you to get up. Shall I fetch you a book and read to you?'

'Don't leave me, mother,' said the child, clinging to her. So Mrs

Openshaw sat on the bedside talking to Ailsie, and telling her of what they had done at Richmond the evening before, until the little girl's eyes slowly closed and she once more fell asleep.

'What was the matter?' asked Mr Openshaw, as his wife returned to bed.

'Ailsie wakened up in a fright, with some story of a man having been in the room to say his prayers,—a dream, I suppose.' And no more was said at the time.

Mrs Openshaw had almost forgotten the whole affair when she got up about seven o'clock. But, by-and-by, she heard a sharp altercation going on in the nursery—Norah speaking angrily to Ailsie, a most unusual thing. Both Mr and Mrs Openshaw listened in astonishment.

'Hold your tongue, Ailsie! let me hear none of your dreams; never let me hear you tell that story again!' Ailsie began to cry.

Mr Openshaw opened the door of communication, before his wife could say a word.

'Norah, come here!'

The nurse stood at the door, defiant. She perceived she had been heard, but she was desperate.

'Don't let me hear you speak in that manner to Ailsie again,' he said sternly, and shut the door.

Norah was infinitely relieved; for she had dreaded some questioning; and a little blame for sharp speaking was what she could well bear, if cross examination was let alone.

Down-stairs they went, Mr Openshaw carrying Ailsie; the sturdy Edwin coming step by step, right foot foremost, always holding his mother's hand. Each child was placed in a chair by the breakfast-table, and then Mr and Mrs Openshaw stood together at the window, awaiting their visitors' appearance and making plans for the day. There was a pause. Suddenly Mr Openshaw turned to Ailsie, and said:

'What a little goosy somebody is with her dreams, wakening up poor, tired mother in the middle of the night, with a story of a man being in the room.'

'Father! I'm sure I saw him,' said Ailsie, half crying. 'I don't want to make Norah angry; but I was not asleep, for all she says I was. I had been asleep,—and I wakened up quite wide awake, though I was so frightened. I kept my eyes nearly shut, and I saw the man quite plain. A great brown man with a beard. He said his prayers. And then he looked at Edwin. And then Norah took him by the arm and led him away, after they had whispered a bit together.'

'Now, my little woman must be reasonable,' said Mr Openshaw, who was always patient with Ailsie. 'There was no man in the house last night at all. No man comes into the house, as you know, if you think; much less goes up into the nursery. But sometimes we dream something has happened, and the dream is so like reality, that you are not the first person, little woman, who has stood out that the thing has really happened.'

'But, indeed it was not a dream!' said Ailsie, beginning to cry.

Just then Mr and Mrs Chadwick came down, looking grave and discomposed. All during breakfast time, they were silent and uncomfortable. As soon as the breakfast things were taken away, and the children had been carried up-stairs, Mr Chadwick began, in an evidently preconcerted manner, to inquire if his nephew was certain that all his servants were honest; for, that Mrs Chadwick had that morning missed a very valuable brooch, which she had worn the day before. She remembered taking it off when she came home from Buckingham Palace. Mr Openshaw's face contracted into hard lines: grew like what it was before he had known his wife and her child. He rang the bell, even before his uncle had done speaking. It was answered by the housemaid.

'Mary, was any one here last night, while we were away?'

'A man, sir, came to speak to Norah.'

'To speak to Norah! Who was he? How long did he stay?'

'I'm sure I can't tell, sir. He came—perhaps about nine. I went up to tell Norah in the nursery, and she came down to speak to him. She let him out, sir. She will know who he was, and how long he stayed.'

She waited a moment to be asked any more questions, but she was not, so she went away.

A minute afterwards, Mr Openshaw made as though he were going out of the room; but his wife laid her hand on his arm:

'Do not speak to her before the children,' she said, in her low, quiet voice. 'I will go up and question her.'

'No! I must speak to her. You must know,' said he, turning to his uncle and aunt, 'my missus has an old servant, as faithful as ever woman was, I do believe, as far as love goes,—but at the same time, who does not always speak truth, as even the missus must allow. Now, my notion is, that this Norah of ours has been come over by some good-for-nothing chap (for she's at the time o' life when they say women pray for husbands—"any, good Lord, any"*) and has let him into our house, and the chap has made off with your brooch, and m'appen many another thing beside. It's only saying that Norah is soft-hearted, and doesn't stick at a white lie—that's all, missus.'

It was curious to notice how his tone, his eyes, his whole face was changed, as he spoke to his wife; but he was the resolute man through all. She knew better than to oppose him; so she went up-stairs, and told Norah her master wanted to speak to her, and that she would take care of the children in the meanwhile.

Norah rose to go, without a word. Her thoughts were these: 'If they tear me to pieces, they shall never know through me. He may come,—and then, just Lord have mercy upon us all! for some of us are dead folk to a certainty. But *he* shall do it; not me.'

You may fancy, now, her look of determination, as she faced her master alone in the dining-room; Mr and Mrs Chadwick having left the affair in their nephew's hands, seeing that he took it up with such vehemence.

'Norah! Who was that man that came to my house last night?'

'Man, sir!' As if infinitely surprised; but it was only to gain time.

'Yes; the man that Mary let in; that she went up-stairs to the nursery to tell you about; that you came down to speak to; the same chap, I make no doubt, that you took into the nursery to have your talk out with; the one Ailsie saw, and afterwards dreamed about; thinking, poor wench! she saw him say his prayers, when nothing, I'll be bound, was further from his thoughts; the one that took Mrs Chadwick's brooch, value ten pounds. Now, Norah! Don't go off. I'm as sure, as my name's Thomas Openshaw, that you knew nothing of this robbery. But I do think you've been imposed on, and that's the truth. Some good-for-nothing chap has been making up to you, and you've been just like all other women, and have turned a soft place in your heart to him; and he came last night a-lovyering, and you had him up in the nursery, and he made use of his opportunities, and made off with a few things on his way down! Come, now, Norah: it's no blame to you, only you must not be such a fool again! Tell us,' he continued, 'what name he gave you, Norah. I'll be bound, it was not the right one; but it will be a clue for the police.'

Norah drew herself up. 'You may ask that question, and taunt me with my being single, and with my credulity, as you will, Master Openshaw. You'll get no answer from me. As for the brooch, and the story of theft and burglary; if any friend ever came to see me (which I defy you to prove, and deny), he'd be just as much above doing such a thing as you yourself, Mr Openshaw—and more so too; for I'm not at all sure as everything you have is rightly come by, or would be yours long, if every man had his own.' She meant, of course, his wife; but he understood her to refer to his property in goods and chattels.

'Now, my good woman,' said he, 'I'll just tell you truly, I never trusted you out and out; but my wife liked you, and I thought you had many a good point about you. If you once begin to sauce me, I'll have the police to you, and get out the truth in a court of justice, if you'll not tell it me quietly and civilly here. Now, the best thing you can do, is quietly to tell me who the fellow is. Look here! a man comes to my house; asks for you; you take him up-stairs; a valuable brooch is missing next day; we know that you, and Mary, and cook, are honest; but you refuse to tell us who the man is. Indeed, you've told one lie already about him, saying no one was here last night. Now, I just put it to you, what do you think a policeman would say to this, or a magistrate? A magistrate would soon make you tell the truth, my good woman.'

'There's never the creature born that should get it out of me,' said Norah. 'Not unless I choose to tell.'

'I've a great mind to see,' said Mr Openshaw, growing angry at the defiance. Then, checking himself, he thought before he spoke again:

'Norah, for your missus's sake I don't want to go to extremities. Be a sensible woman, if you can. It's no great disgrace, after all, to have been taken in. I ask you once more—as a friend—who was this man that you let into my house last night?'

No answer. He repeated the question in an impatient tone. Still no answer. Norah's lips were set in determination not to speak.

'Then there is but one thing to be done. I shall send for a policeman.'

'You will not,' said Norah, starting forward. 'You shall not, sir!

No policeman shall touch me. I know nothing of the brooch, but I know this: ever since I was four-and-twenty, I have thought more of your wife than of myself: ever since I saw her, a poor motherless girl, put upon in her uncle's house, I have thought more of serving her than of serving myself! I have cared for her and her child, as nobody ever cared for me. I don't cast blame on you, sir, but I say it's ill giving up one's life to any one; for, at the end, they will turn round upon you, and forsake you. Why does not my missus come herself to suspect me? Maybe, she is gone for the police? But I don't stay here, either for police, or magistrate, or master. You're an unlucky lot. I believe there's a curse on you. I'll leave you this very day. Yes! I'll leave that poor Ailsie, too. I will! No good will ever come to you!'

Mr Openshaw was utterly astonished at this speech; most of which was completely unintelligible to him, as may easily be supposed. Before he could make up his mind what to say, or what to do, Norah had left the room. I do not think he had ever really intended to send for the police to this old servant of his wife's; for he had never for a moment doubted her perfect honesty. But he had intended to compel her to tell him who the man was, and in this he was baffled. He was, consequently, much irritated. He returned to his uncle and aunt in a state of great annoyance and perplexity, and told them he could get nothing out of the woman; that some man had been in the house the night before; but that she refused to tell who he was. At this moment his wife came in, greatly agitated, and asked what had happened to Norah; for that she had put on her things in passionate haste, and left the house.

'This looks suspicious,' said Mr Chadwick. 'It is not the way in which an honest person would have acted.'

Mr Openshaw kept silence. He was sorely perplexed. But Mrs Openshaw turned round on Mr Chadwick, with a sudden fierceness no one ever saw in her before.

'You don't know Norah, uncle! She is gone because she is deeply hurt at being suspected. Oh, I wish I had seen her—that I had spoken to her myself. She would have told me anything.' Alice wrung her hands.

'I must confess,' continued Mr Chadwick to his nephew, in a lower voice, 'I can't make you out. You used to be a word and a blow, and oftenest the blow first; and now, when there is every cause for suspicion, you just do nought. Your missus is a very good woman, I grant; but she may have been put upon as well as other folk, I suppose. If you don't send for the police, I shall.'

'Very well,' replied Mr Openshaw, surlily. 'I can't clear Norah. She won't clear herself, as I believe she might if she would. Only I wash my hands of it; for I am sure the woman herself is honest, and she's lived a long time with my wife, and I don't like her to come to shame.'

'But she will then be forced to clear herself. That, at any rate, will be a good thing.'

'Very well, very well! I am heart-sick of the whole business. Come, Alice, come up to the babies; they'll be in a sore way. I tell you, uncle,' he said, turning round once more to Mr Chadwick, suddenly and sharply, after his eye had fallen on Alice's wan, tearful, anxious face; 'I'll have no sending for the police, after all. I'll buy my aunt twice as handsome a brooch this very day; but I'll not have Norah suspected, and my missus plagued. There's for you!'

He and his wife left the room. Mr Chadwick quietly waited till he was out of hearing, and then said to his wife, 'For all Tom's heroics, I'm just quietly going for a detective, wench. Thou need'st know nought about it.'

He went to the police-station, and made a statement of the case. He was gratified by the impression which the evidence against Norah seemed to make. The men all agreed in his opinion, and steps were to be immediately taken to find out where she was. Most probably, as they suggested, she had gone at once to the man, who, to all appearance, was her lover. When Mr Chadwick asked how they would find her out, they smiled, shook their heads, and spoke of mysterious but infallible ways and means. He returned to his nephew's house with a very comfortable opinion of his own sagacity. He was met by his wife with a penitent face:

'O master, I've found my brooch! It was just sticking by its pin in the flounce of my brown silk, that I wore yesterday. I took it off in a hurry, and it must have caught in it: and I hung up my gown in the closet. Just now, when I was going to fold it up, there was the brooch! I'm very vexed, but I never dreamt but what it was lost!'

Her husband muttering something very like 'Confound thee and thy brooch too! I wish I'd never given it thee,' snatched up his hat, and rushed back to the station, hoping to be in time to stop the police from searching for Norah. But a detective was already gone off on the errand.

Where was Norah? Half mad with the strain of the fearful secret, she had hardly slept through the night for thinking what must be done. Upon this terrible state of mind had come Ailsie's questions, showing that she had seen the Man, as the unconscious child called her father. Lastly came the suspicion of her honesty. She was little less than crazy as she ran up stairs and dashed on her bonnet and shawl; leaving all else, even her purse, behind her. In that house she would not stay. That was all she knew or was clear about. She would not even see the children again, for fear it should weaken her. She dreaded above everything Mr Frank's return to claim his wife. She could not tell what remedy there was for a sorrow so tremendous, for her to stay to witness. The desire of escaping from the coming event was a stronger motive for her departure, than her soreness about the suspicions directed against her; although this last had been the final goad to the course she took. She walked away almost at headlong speed; sobbing as she went, as she had not dared to do during the past night for fear of exciting wonder in those who might hear her. Then she stopped. An idea came into her mind that she would leave London altogether, and betake herself to her native town of Liverpool. She felt in her pocket for her purse, as she drew near the Euston Square station with this intention. She had left it at home. Her poor head aching, her eyes swollen with crying, she had to stand still, and think, as well as she could, where next she should bend her steps. Suddenly the thought flashed into her mind, that she would go and find out poor Mr Frank. She had been hardly kind to him the night before, though her heart had bled for him ever since. She remembered his telling her, when she inquired for his address, almost as she had pushed him out of the door, of some hotel in a street not far distant from Euston Square. Thither she went: with what intention she scarcely knew, but to assuage her conscience by telling him how much she pitied him. In her present state she felt herself unfit to counsel, or restrain, or assist, or do aught else but sympathize and weep. The people of the inn said such a person had been there; had arrived only the day before; had gone out soon after his arrival, leaving his luggage in their care; but had never come back. Norah asked for leave to sit down, and await the gentleman's return. The landlady—pretty secure in the deposit of luggage against any probable injury—showed her into a room, and quietly locked the door on the outside. Norah was utterly worn out, and fell asleep—a shivering, starting, uneasy slumber, which lasted for hours.

The detective, meanwhile, had come up with her some time before she entered the hotel, into which he followed her. Asking the landlady to detain her for an hour or so, without giving any reason beyond showing his authority (which made the landlady applaud herself a good deal for having locked her in), he went back to the police-station to report his proceedings. He could have taken her directly; but his object was, if possible, to trace out the man who was supposed to have committed the robbery. Then he heard of the discovery of the brooch; and consequently did not care to return.

Norah slept till even the summer evening began to close in. Then started up. Some one was at the door. It would be Mr Frank; and she dizzily pushed back her ruffled grey hair, which had fallen over her eyes, and stood looking to see him. Instead, there came in Mr Openshaw and a policeman.

'This is Norah Kennedy,' said Mr Openshaw.

'O, sir,' said Norah, 'I did not touch the brooch; indeed I did not. O, sir, I cannot live to be thought so badly of;' and very sick and faint, she suddenly sank down on the ground. To her surprise, Mr Openshaw raised her up very tenderly. Even the policeman helped to lay her on the sofa; and, at Mr Openshaw's desire, he went for some wine and sandwiches; for the poor gaunt woman lay there almost as if dead with weariness and exhaustion.

'Norah,' said Mr Openshaw, in his kindest voice, 'the brooch is found. It was hanging to Mrs Chadwick's gown. I beg your pardon. Most truly I beg your pardon, for having troubled you about it. My wife is almost broken-hearted. Eat, Norah,—or, stay, first drink this glass of wine,' said he, lifting her head, and pouring a little down her throat.

As she drank, she remembered where she was, and who she was waiting for. She suddenly pushed Mr Openshaw away, saying, 'O, sir, you must go. You must not stop a minute. If he comes back, he will kill you.'

'Alas, Norah! I do not know who "he" is. But some one is gone away who will never come back: some one who knew you, and whom I am afraid you cared for.'

'I don't understand you, sir,' said Norah, her master's kind and sorrowful manner bewildering her yet more than his words. The policeman had left the room at Mr Openshaw's desire, and they two were alone.

'You know what I mean, when I say some one is gone who will never come back. I mean that he is dead!'

'Who?' said Norah, trembling all over.

'A poor man has been found in the Thames this morning— drowned.'

'Did he drown himself?' asked Norah, solemnly.

'God only knows,' replied Mr Openshaw, in the same tone. 'Your name and address at our house were found in his pocket: that, and his purse, were the only things that were found upon him. I am sorry to say it, my poor Norah; but you are required to go and identify him.'

'To what?' asked Norah.

'To say who it is. It is always done, in order that some reason may be discovered for the suicide—if suicide it was.—I make no doubt, he was the man who came to see you at our house last night.—It is very sad, I know.' He made pauses between each little clause, in order to try and bring back her senses, which he feared were wandering—so wild and sad was her look.

'Master Openshaw,' said she, at last, 'I've a dreadful secret to tell you—only you must never breathe it to any one, and you and I must hide it away for ever. I thought to have done it all by myself, but I see I cannot. You poor man—yes! the dead, drowned creature is, I fear, Mr Frank, my mistress's first husband!'

Mr Openshaw sat down, as if shot. He did not speak; but, after a while, he signed to Norah to go on.

'He came to me the other night—when—God be thanked! you were all away at Richmond. He asked me if his wife was dead or alive. I was a brute, and thought more of your all coming home than of his sore trial: I spoke out sharp, and said she was married again, and very content and happy: I all but turned him away: and now he lies dead and cold.'

'God forgive me!' said Mr Openshaw.

'God forgive us all!' said Norah. 'Yon poor man needs forgive-ness, perhaps, less than any one among us. He had been among the savages—shipwrecked—I know not what—and he had written letters which had never reached my poor missus.'

'He saw his child!'

'He saw her—yes! I took him up, to give his thoughts another start; for I believed he was going mad on my hands. I came to seek him here, as I more than half promised. My mind misgave me when I heard he never came in. O, sir! it must be him!'

Mr Openshaw rang the bell. Norah was almost too much stunned to wonder at what he did. He asked for writing materials, wrote a letter, and then said to Norah:

'I am writing to Alice, to say I shall be unavoidably absent for a few days; that I have found you; that you are well, and send her your love, and will come home to-morrow. You must go with me to the Police Court; you must identify the body; I will pay high to keep names and details out of the papers.'

'But where are you going, sir?'

He did not answer her directly. Then he said:

'Norah! I must go with you, and look on the face of the man whom I have so injured,—unwittingly, it is true; but it seems to me as if I had killed him. I will lay his head in the grave, as if he were my only brother: and how he must have hated me! I cannot go home to my wife till all that I can do for him is done. Then I go with a dreadful secret on my mind. I shall never speak of it again, after these days are over. I know you will not, either.' He shook hands with her: and they never named the subject again, the one to the other.

Norah went home to Alice the next day. Not a word was said on the cause of her abrupt departure a day or two before. Alice had been charged by her husband, in his letter, not to allude to the supposed theft of the brooch; so she, implicitly obedient to those whom she loved both by nature and habit, was entirely silent on the subject, only treated Norah with the most tender respect, as if to make up for unjust suspicion.

Nor did Alice inquire into the reason why Mr Openshaw had been absent during his uncle and aunt's visit, after he had once said that it was unavoidable. He came back grave and quiet; and from that time forth was curiously changed. More thoughtful, and perhaps less active; quite as decided in conduct, but with new and different rules for the guidance of that conduct. Towards Alice he could hardly be more kind than he had always been; but he now seemed to look upon her as some one sacred, and to be treated with reverence, as well as tenderness. He throve in business, and made a large fortune, one half of which was settled upon her.

Long years after these events—a few months after her mother died—Ailsie and her 'father' (as she always called Mr Openshaw), drove to a cemetery a little way out of town, and she was carried to a certain mound by her maid, who was then sent back to the carriage. There was a head-stone, with F. W. and a date upon it. That was all. Sitting by the grave, Mr Openshaw told her the story; and for the sad fate of that poor father whom she had never seen,* he shed the only tears she ever saw fall from his eyes.

CROWLEY CASTLE

SIR Mark Crowley was the last baronet of his name, and it is now nearly a century since he died. Last year I visited the ruins of his great old Norman castle; and loitered in the village near, where I heard some of the particulars of the following tale from old inhabitants, who had heard them from their fathers; no further back.

We drove from our little sea-bathing place, in Sussex, to see the massive ruins of Crowley Castle, which is the show-excursion of Merton.* We had to alight at a field gate: the road further on being too bad for the slightly-built carriage, or the poor tired Merton horse: and we walked for about a quarter of a mile through uneven ground, which had once been an Italian garden; and then we came to a bridge over a dry moat, and went over the groove of a portcullis* that had once closed the massive entrance, into an empty space surrounded by thick walls, draperied with ivy, unroofed, and open to the sky. We could judge of the beautiful tracery that had been in the windows, by the remains of the stonework here and there; and an old man—'ever so old,' he called himself when we inquired his exact age—who scrambled and stumbled out of some lair in the least devastated part of the ruins at our approach, and who established himself as our guide, showed us a scrap of glass yet lingering in what was the window of the great drawing-room not above seventy years ago. After he had done his duty, he hobbled with us to the neighbouring church, where the knightly Crowleys lie buried: some commemorated by ancient brasses, some by altar-tombs, some by fine Latin epitaphs, bestowing upon them every virtue under the sun. He had to take the church-key back to the adjoining parsonage at the entrance of the long straggling street which forms the village of Crowley. The castle and the church were on the summit of a hill, from which we could see the distant line of sea beyond the misty marshes. The village fell away from the church and parsonage, down the hill. The aspect of the place was little, if at all, changed, from its aspect in the year 1772.

But I must begin a little earlier. From one of the Latin epitaphs I learnt that Amelia Lady Crowley died in 1756, deeply regretted

by her loving husband, Sir Mark. He never married again, though
his wife had left him no heir to his name or his estate—only a little
tiny girl—Theresa Crowley. This child would inherit her mother's
fortune, and all that Sir Mark was free to leave; but this little was
not much; the castle and all the lands going to his sister's son,
Marmaduke, or as he was usually called Duke, Brownlow. Duke's
parents were dead, and his uncle was his guardian, and his
guardian's house was his home. The lad was some seven or eight
years older than his cousin; and probably Sir Mark thought it not
unlikely that his daughter and his heir might make a match.
Theresa's mother had had some foreign blood in her, and had been
brought up in France—not so far away but that its shores might be
seen by any one who chose to take an easy day's ride from Crowley
Castle for the purpose.

   Lady Crowley had been a delicate elegant creature, but no great
beauty, judging from all accounts; Sir Mark's family were famous
for their good looks; Theresa, an unusually lucky child, inherited
the outward graces of both her parents. A portrait which I saw of
her, degraded to a station over the parlour chimney-piece in the
village inn, showed me black hair, soft yet arch grey eyes with
brows and lashes of the same tint as her hair, a full pretty pouting
passionate mouth, and a round slender throat. She was a wilful
little creature, and her father's indulgence made her more wayward.
She had a nurse, too, a French bonne,* whose mother had been
about my lady from her youth, who had followed my lady to
England, and who had died there. Victorine had been in attendance
on the young Theresa from her earliest infancy, and almost took the
place of a parent in power and affection—in power, as to ordering
and arranging almost what she liked, concerning the child's management—in love, because they speak to this day of the black year
when virulent smallpox was rife in Crowley, and when, Sir Mark
being far away on some diplomatic mission—in Vienna, I fancy—
Victorine shut herself up with Miss Theresa when the child was
taken ill with the disease, and nursed her night and day. She only
succumbed to the dreadful illness when all danger to the child was
over. Theresa came out of it with unblemished beauty; Victorine
barely escaped with life, and was disfigured for life.

   This disfigurement put a stop to much unfounded scandal which
had been afloat respecting the French servant's great influence over

Sir Mark. He was, in fact, an easy and indolent man, rarely excited to any vehemence of emotion, and who felt it to be a point of honour to carry out his dead wife's wish that Victorine should never leave Theresa, and that the management of the child should be confided to her. Only once had there been a struggle for power between Sir Mark and the bonne, and then she had won the victory. And no wonder, if the old butler's account were true; for he had gone into the room unawares, and had found Sir Mark and Victorine at high words; and he said that Victorine was white with rage, that her eyes were blazing with passionate fire, that her voice was low, and her words were few, but that, although she spoke in French, and he the butler only knew his native English, he would rather have been sworn at by a drunken grenadier* with a sword in his hand, than have had those words of Victorine's addressed to him.

Even the choice of Theresa's masters was left to Victorine. A little reference was occasionally made to Madam Hawtrey, the parson's wife and a distant relation of Sir Mark's, but, seeing that, if Victorine chose so to order it, Madam Hawtrey's own little daughter Bessy would have been deprived of the advantages resulting from gratuitous companionship in all Theresa's lessons, she was careful how she opposed or made an enemy of Mademoiselle Victorine. Bessy was a gentle quiet child, and grew up to be a sensible sweet-tempered girl, with a very fair share of English beauty; fresh-complexion, brown-eyed round-faced, with a stiff though well-made figure, as different as possible from Theresa's slight lithe graceful form. Duke was a young man to these two maidens, while they to him were little more than children. Of course he admired his cousin Theresa the most—who would not?—but he was establishing his first principles of morality for himself, and her conduct towards Bessy sometimes jarred against his ideas of right. One day, after she had been tyrannizing over the self-contained and patient Bessy so as to make the latter cry—and both the amount of the tyranny and the crying were unusual circumstances, for Theresa was of a generous nature when not put out of the way—Duke spoke to his cousin:

'Theresa! You had no right to blame Bessy as you did. It was as much your fault as hers. You were as much bound to remember Mr Dawson's directions about the sums you were to do for him, as she was.'

The girl opened her great grey eyes in surprise. She to blame!

'What does Bessy come to the castle for, I wonder? They pay nothing—we pay all. The least she can do, is to remember for me what we are told. I shan't trouble myself with attending to Mr Dawson's directions; and if Bessy does not like to do so, she can stay away. She already knows enough to earn her bread as a maid: which I suppose is what she'll have to come to.'

The moment Theresa had said this, she could have bitten her tongue out for the meanness and rancour of the speech. She saw pain and disappointment clearly expressed on Duke's face; and, in another moment, her impulses would have carried her to the opposite extreme, and she would have spoken out her self-reproach. But Duke thought it his duty to remonstrate with her, and to read her a homily, which, however true and just, weakened the effect of the look of distress on his face. Her wits were called into play to refute his arguments; her head rather than her heart took the prominent part in the controversy; and it ended unsatisfactorily to both; he, going away with dismal though unspoken prognostics touching what she would become as a woman if she were so super-cilious and unfeeling as a girl; she, the moment his back was turned, throwing herself on the floor and sobbing as if her heart would break. Victorine heard her darling's passionate sobs, and came in.

'What hast thou, my angel! Who has been vexing thee,—tell me, my cherished?'

She tried to raise the girl, but Theresa would not be raised; neither would she speak till she chose, in spite of Victorine's entreaties. When she chose, she lifted herself up, still sitting on the floor, and putting her tangled hair off her flushed tear-stained face, said:

'Never mind, it was only something Duke said; I don't care for it now.' And refusing Victorine's aid, she got up, and stood thought-fully looking out of the window.

'That Duke!' exclaimed Victorine. 'What business has that Mr Duke to go vex my darling? He is not your husband yet, that he should scold you, or that you should mind what he says.'

Theresa listened and gained a new idea; but she gave no outward sign of attention, or of her now hearing for the first time how that she was supposed to be intended for her cousin's wife. She made no reply to Victorine's caresses and speeches; one might almost say she shook her off. As soon as she was left to herself, she took her hat, and going out alone, as she was wont, in the pleasure-grounds, she went down the terrace steps, crossed the bowling-green, and opened a little wicket-gate which led into the garden of the parsonage. There, were Bessy and her mother, gathering fruit. It was Bessy whom Theresa sought; for there was something in Madam Hawtrey's silky manner that was always rather repugnant to her. However, she was not going to shrink from her resolution because Madam Hawtrey was there. So she went up to the startled Bessy, and said to her, as if she were reciting a prepared speech: 'Bessy, I behaved very crossly to you; I had no business to have spoken to you as I did.'—'Will you forgive me?' was the pre-determined end of this confession; but somehow, when it came to that, she could not say it with Madam Hawtrey standing by, ready to smile and to curtsey as soon as she could catch Theresa's eye. There was no need to ask forgiveness though; for Bessy had put down her half filled basket, and came softly up to Theresa, stealing her brown soil-stained little hand into the young lady's soft white one, and looking up at her with loving brown eyes.

'I am so sorry, but I think it was the sums on page 108. I have been looking and looking, and I am almost sure.'

Her exculpatory tone caught her mother's ear, although her words did not.

'I am sure, Miss Theresa, Bessy is so grateful for the privileges of learning with you! It is such an advantage to her! I often tell her, "Take pattern by Miss Theresa, and do as she does, and try and speak as she does, and there'll not be a parson's daughter in all Sussex to compare with you." Don't I, Bessy?'

Theresa shrugged her shoulders—a trick she had caught from Victorine—and, turning to Bessy, asked her what she was going to do with those gooseberries she was gathering? And as Theresa spoke, she lazily picked the ripest out of the basket, and ate them.

'They are for a pudding,' said Bessy. 'As soon as we have gathered enough, I am going in to make it.'

'I'll come and help you,' said Theresa, eagerly. 'I should so like to make a pudding. Our Monsieur Antoine never makes gooseberry puddings.'

Duke came past the parsonage an hour or so afterwards: and,

looking in by chance through the open casement windows of the kitchen, saw Theresa pinned up in a bib and apron, her arms all over flour, flourishing a rolling-pin, and laughing and chattering with Bessy similarly attired. Duke had spent his morning ostensibly in fishing; but in reality in weighing in his own mind what he could do or say to soften the obdurate heart of his cousin. And here it was, all inexplicably right, as if by some enchanter's wand!

The only conclusion Duke could come to was the same that many a wise (and foolish) man had come to before his day:

'Well! Women are past my comprehension, that's all!'

When all this took place, Theresa was about fifteen; Bessy was perhaps six months older; Duke was just leaving Oxford. His uncle, Sir Mark, was excessively fond of him; yes! and proud, too, for he had distinguished himself at college, and every one spoke well of him. And he, for his part, loved Sir Mark, and, unspoiled by the fame and reputation he had gained at Christ Church, paid respectful deference to Sir Mark's opinions.

As Theresa grew older, her father supposed that he played his cards well in singing Duke's praises on every possible occasion. She tossed her head, and said nothing. Thanks to Victorine's revelations, she understood the tendency of her father's speeches. She intended to make her own choice of a husband when the time came; and it might be Duke, or it might be some one else. When Duke did not lecture or prose, but was sitting his horse so splendidly at the meet,* before the huntsman gave the blast, 'Found;' when Duke was holding his own in discourse with other men; when Duke gave her a short sharp word of command on any occasion; then she decided that she would marry him, and no one else. But when he found fault, or stumbled about awkwardly in a minuet, or talked moralities against duelling, then she was sure that Duke should never be her husband. She wondered if he knew about it; if any one had told him, as Victorine had told her; if her father had revealed his thoughts and wishes to his nephew, as plainly as he had done to his daughter? This last query made her cheeks burn; and, on days when the suspicion had been brought by any chance prominently before her mind, she was especially rude and disagreeable to Duke.

He was to go abroad on the grand tour of Europe, to which young men of fortune usually devoted three years. He was to have a tutor, because all young men of his rank had tutors; else he was quite wise enough, and steady enough, to have done without one, and probably knew a good deal more about what was best to be observed in the countries they were going to visit, than Mr Roberts, his appointed bear-leader.* He was to come back full of historical and political knowledge, speaking French and Italian like a native, and having a smattering of barbarous German, and he was to enter the House as a county member, if possible—as a borough member* at the worst; and was to make a great success; and then, as every one understood, he was to marry his cousin Theresa.

He spoke to her father about it, before starting on his travels. It was after dinner in Crowley Castle. Sir Mark and Duke sat alone, each pensive at the thought of the coming parting.

'Theresa is but young,' said Duke, breaking into speech after a long silence, 'but if you have no objection, uncle, I should like to speak to her before I leave England, about my—my hopes.'

Sir Mark played with his glass, poured out some more wine, drank it off at a draught, and then replied:

'No, Duke, no. Leave her in peace with me. I have looked forward to having her for my companion through these three years; they'll soon pass away' (to age, but not to youth), 'and I should like to have her undivided heart till you come back. No, Duke! Three years will soon pass away, and then we'll have a royal wedding.'

Duke sighed, but said no more. The next day was the last. He wanted Theresa to go with him to take leave of the Hawtreys at the Parsonage, and of the villagers; but she was wilful, and would not. He remembered, years afterwards, how Bessy's gentle peaceful manner had struck him as contrasted with Theresa's, on that last day. Both girls regretted his departure. He had been so uniformly gentle and thoughtful in his behaviour to Bessy, that, without any idea of love, she felt him to be her pattern of noble chivalrous manhood; the only person, except her father, who was steadily kind to her. She admired his sentiments, she esteemed his principles, she considered his long evolvement of his ideas as the truest eloquence. He had lent her books, he had directed her studies; all the advice and information which Theresa had rejected had fallen to Bessy's lot, and she had received it thankfully.

Theresa burst into a passion of tears as soon as Duke and his suite were out of sight. She had refused the farewell kiss her father had told her to give him, but had waved her white handkerchief out of the great drawing-room window (that very window in which the old guide showed me the small piece of glass still lingering). But Duke had ridden away with slack rein and downcast head, without looking back.

His absence was a great blank in Sir Mark's life. He had never sought London much as a place of residence; in former days he had been suspected of favouring the Stuarts;* but nothing could be proved against him, and he had subsided into a very tolerably faithful subject of King George the Third.* Still, a cold shoulder having been turned to him by the court party at one time, he had become prepossessed against the English capital. On the contrary, his wife's predilections and his own tendencies had always made Paris a very agreeable place of residence to him. To Paris he at length resorted again, when the blank in his life oppressed him; and from Paris, about two years after Duke's departure, he returned after a short absence from home, and suddenly announced to his daughter and the household that he had taken an apartment in the Rue Louis le Grand for the coming winter, to which there was to be an immediate removal of his daughter, Victorine, and certain other personal attendants and servants.

Nothing could exceed Theresa's mad joy at this unexpected news. She sprang upon her father's neck, and kissed him till she was tired—whatever he was. She ran to Victorine, and told her to guess what 'heavenly bliss' was going to befall them, dancing round the middle-aged woman until she, in her spoilt impatience, was becoming angry, when, kissing her, she told her, and ran off to the Parsonage, and thence to the church, bursting in upon morning prayers—for it was All Saints' Day,* although she had forgotten it—and filliping* a scrap of paper on which she had hastily written, 'We are going to Paris for the winter—all of us,' rolled into a ball, from the castle pew to that of the parson. She saw Bessy redden as she caught it, put it into her pocket unread, and, after an apologetic glance at the curtained seat in which Theresa was, go on with her meek responses. Theresa went out by the private door in a momentary fit of passion. 'Stupid cold-blooded creature!' she said to herself. But that afternoon Bessy came to the castle, so sorry—and so losing her own sorrow in sympathy with her friend's gladness, that Theresa took her into favour again. The girls parted with promises of correspondence, and with some regret: the greatest on Bessy's side. Some grand promises of Paris fashion, and presents of dress, Theresa made in her patronizing way; but Bessy did not seem to care much for them—which was fortunate, for they were never fulfilled.

Sir Mark had an idea in his head of perfecting Theresa's accomplishments and manners by Parisian masters and Parisian society. English residents in Venice, Florence, Rome, wrote to their friends at home about Duke. They spoke of him as of what we should, at the present day, call a 'rising young man.' His praises ran so high, that Sir Mark began to fear lest his handsome nephew, fêted by princes, courted by ambassadors, made love to by lovely Italian ladies, might find Theresa too country-bred for his taste.

Thus had come about, the engaging of the splendid apartment in the Rue Louis le Grand. The street itself is narrow, and now-a-days we are apt to think the situation close; but in those days it was the height of fashion; for, the great arbiter of fashion, the Duc de Richelieu,* lived there, and, to inhabit an apartment in that street, was in itself a mark of bon ton.* Victorine seemed almost crazy with delight when they took possession of their new abode. 'This dear Paris! This lovely France! And now I see my young lady, my darling, my angel, in a room suited to her beauty and her rank: such as my lady her mother would have planned for her, if she had lived.' Any allusion to her dead mother always touched Theresa to the quick. She was in her bed, under the blue silk curtains of an alcove, when Victorine said this,—being too much fatigued after her journey to respond to Victorine's rhapsodies; but now she put out her little hand and gave Victorine's a pressure of gratitude and pleasure. Next day she wandered about the rooms and admired their splendour almost to Victorine's content. Her father, Sir Mark, found a handsome carriage and horses for his darling's use; and also found that not less necessary article—a married lady of rank who would take his girl under her wing. When all these preliminary arrangements were made, who so wildly happy as Theresa! Her carriage was of the newest fashion, fit to vie with any on the Cours de la Reine, the then fashionable drive. The box at the Grand Opéra, and at the Français,* which she shared with Madame la Duchesse de G., was the centre of observation; Victorine was in her best humour, Theresa's credit at her dressmaker's was unlimited, her indulgent father was charmed with all she did and said. She had masters, it is true; but, to a rich and beautiful young lady, masters were wonderfully complaisant, and with them as with all the world, she did what she pleased. Of Parisian society, she had enough and more than enough. The duchess went everywhere, and Theresa went too. So did a certain Count de la Grange: some relation or connection of the duchess: handsome, with a south of France handsomeness: with delicate features, marred by an over-softness of expression, from which (so men said) the tiger was occasionally seen to peep forth. But, for elegance of dress and demeanour he had not his fellow in Paris—which of course meant, not in the world.

Sir Mark heard rumours of this man's conduct, which were not pleasing to him; but when he accompanied his daughter into society, the count was only as deferential as it became a gentleman to be to so much beauty and grace. When Theresa was taken out by the duchess to the opera, to balls, to petits soupers,* without her father, then the count was more than deferential; he was adoring. It was a little intoxicating for a girl brought up in the solitude of an English village, to have so many worshippers at her feet all at once, in the great gay city; and the inbred coquetry of her nature came out, adding to her outward grace, if taking away from the purity and dignity of her character. It was Victorine's delight to send her darling out arrayed for conquest; her hair delicately powdered, and scented with *maréchale*;* her little 'mouches'* put on with skill; the tiny half-moon patch, to lengthen the already almond-shaped eye; the minute star to give the effect of a dimple at the corner of her scarlet lips; the silver gauze looped up over the petticoat of blue brocade, distended over a hoop, much as gowns are worn in our days; the coral ornaments of her silver dress, matching with the tint of the high heels to her shoes. And, at night, Victorine was never tired of listening and questioning; of triumphing in Theresa's triumphs; of invariably reminding her that she was bound to marry the absent cousin, and return to the half-feudal state of the old castle in Sussex.

Still, even now, if Duke had returned from Italy, all might have gone well; but when Sir Mark, alarmed by the various proposals he received for Theresa's hand from needy French noblemen, and by the admiration she was exciting everywhere, wrote to Duke, and urged him to join them in Paris on his return from his travels, Duke answered that three months were yet unexpired of the time allotted for the grand tour; and that he was anxious to avail himself of that interval to see something of Spain. Sir Mark read this letter aloud to Theresa, with many expressions of annoyance as he read. Theresa merely said, 'Of course, Duke does what he likes,' and turned away to see some new lace brought for her inspection. She heard her father sigh over a re-perusal of Duke's letter, and she set her teeth in the anger she would not show in acts or words. That day the Count de Grange met with gentler treatment from her than he had done for many days—than he had done since her father's letter to Duke had been sent off to Genoa. As ill fortune would have it, Sir Mark had occasion to return to England at this time, and he, guileless himself, consigned Theresa and her maid Victorine, and her man Felix, to the care of the duchess for three weeks. They were to reside at the Hôtel de G. during this time. The duchess welcomed them in her most caressing manner, and showed Theresa the suite of rooms, with the little private staircase, appropriated to her use.

The Count de Grange was an habitual visitor at the house of his cousin the duchess, who was a gay Parisian, absorbed in her life of giddy dissipation. The count found means of influencing Victorine in his favour; not by money; so coarse a bribe would have had no power over her; but by many presents, accompanied with senti-mental letters, breathing devotion to her charge, and extremest appreciation of the faithful friend whom Theresa looked upon as a mother, and whom for this reason he, the count, revered and loved. Intermixed, were wily allusions to his great possessions in Provence, and to his ancient lineage:—the one mortgaged, the other disgraced. Victorine, whose right hand had forgotten its cunning* in the length of her dreary vegetation at Crowley Castle, was deceived, and became a vehement advocate of the dissolute Adonis* of the Paris saloons, in his suit to her darling. When Sir Mark came back, he was dismayed and shocked beyond measure by finding the count and Theresa at his feet, entreating him to forgive their stolen marriage—a marriage which, though incomplete as to its legal forms, was yet too complete to be otherwise than sanc-tioned by Theresa's nearest friends. The duchess accused her cousin of perfidy and treason. Sir Mark said nothing. But his health failed from that time, and he sank into an old querulous grey-haired man.

There was some ado, I know not what, between Sir Mark and the count regarding the control and disposition of the fortune which Theresa inherited from her mother. The count gained the victory, owing to the different nature of the French laws from the English; and this made Sir Mark abjure the country and the city he had loved so long. Henceforward, he swore, his foot should never touch French soil; if Theresa liked to come and see him at Crowley Castle, she should be as welcome as a daughter of the house ought to be, and ever should be; but her husband should never enter the gates of the house in Sir Mark's lifetime.

For some months he was out of humour with Duke, because of his tardy return from his tour and his delay in joining them in Paris: through which, so Sir Mark fancied, Theresa's marriage had been brought about. But—when Duke came home, depressed in spirits and submissive to his uncle, even under unjust blame—Sir Mark restored him to favour in the course of a summer's day, and henceforth added another injury to the debtor side of the count's reckoning.

Duke never told his uncle of the woeful ill-report he had heard of the count in Paris, where he had found all the better part of the French nobility pitying the lovely English heiress who had been entrapped into a marriage with one of the most disreputable of their order, a gambler and a reprobate. He could not leave Paris without seeing Theresa, whom he believed to be as yet unacquainted with his arrival in the city, so he went to call upon her one evening. She was sitting alone, splendidly dressed, ravishingly beautiful; she made a step forward to meet him, hardly heeding the announcement of his name; for she had recognized a man's tread, and fancied it was her husband, coming to accompany her to some grand reception. Duke saw the quick change from hope to disappointment on her mobile face, and she spoke out at once her reason. 'Adolphe promised to come and fetch me; the princess receives to-night. I hardly expected a visit from you, cousin Duke,' recovering herself into a pretty proud reserve. 'It is a fortnight, I think, since I heard you were in Paris. I had given up all expectation of the honour of a visit from you!'

Duke felt that, as she had heard of his being there, it would be awkward to make excuses which both she and he must know to be false, or explanations the very truth of which would be offensive to the loving, trusting, deceived wife. So, he turned the conversation to his travels, his heart aching for her all the time, as he noticed her wandering attention when she heard any passing sound. Ten, eleven, twelve o'clock; he would not leave her. He thought his presence was a comfort and a pleasure to her. But when one o'clock struck, she said some unexpected business must have detained her husband, and she was glad of it, as she had all along felt too much tired to go out: and besides, the happy consequence of her husband's detention had been that long talk with Duke.

He did not see her again after this polite dismissal, nor did he see her husband at all. Whether through ill chance, or carefully disguised purpose, it did so happen that he called several times, he wrote several notes requesting an appointment when he might come with the certainty of finding the count and countess at home, in order to wish them farewell before setting out for England. All in vain. But he said nothing to Sir Mark of all this. He only tried to fill up the blank in the old man's life. He went between Sir Mark and the tenants to whom he was unwilling to show himself unaccompanied by the beautiful daughter, who had so often been his companion in his walks and rides, before that ill-omened winter in Paris. He was thankful to have the power of returning the long kindness his uncle had shown him in childhood; thankful to be of use to him in his desertion; thankful to atone in some measure for his neglect of his uncle's wish that he should have made a hasty return to Paris.

But it was a little dull after the long excitement of travel, after associating with all that was most cultivated and seeing all that was most famous, in Europe, to be shut up in that vast magnificent dreary old castle, with Sir Mark for a perpetual companion—Sir Mark, and no other. The parsonage was near at hand, and occasionally Mr Hawtrey came in to visit his parishioner in his trouble. But Sir Mark kept the clergyman at bay; he knew that his brother in age, his brother in circumstances (for had not Mr Hawtrey an only child and she a daughter?), was sympathizing with him in his sorrow, and he was too proud to bear it; indeed, sometimes he was so rude to his old neighbour, that Duke would go next morning to the parsonage, to soothe the smart.

And so—and so—gradually, imperceptibly, at last his heart was drawn to Bessy. Her mother angled and angled skilfully; at first scarcely daring to hope; then remembering her own descent from the same stock as Duke, she drew herself up, and set to work with fresh skill and vigour. To be sure, it was a dangerous game for a mother to play; for her daughter's happiness was staked on her success. How could simple country-bred Bessy help being attracted to the courtly handsome man, travelled and accomplished, good and gentle, whom she saw every day, and who treated her with the kind familiarity of a brother; while he was not a brother, but in some measure a disappointed man, as everybody knew? Bessy was a daisy of an English maiden; pure good to the heart's core and most hidden thought; sensible in all her accustomed daily ways, yet not so much without imagination as not to desire something beyond the narrow range of knowledge and experience in which her days had hitherto been passed. Add to this her pretty figure, a bright healthy complexion, lovely teeth, and quite enough of beauty in her other features to have rendered her the belle of a country town, if her lot had been cast in such a place; and it is not to be wondered at, that, after she had been secretly in love with Duke with all her heart for nearly a year, almost worshipping him, he should discover that, of all the women he had ever known—except perhaps the lost Theresa—Bessy Hawtrey had it in her power to make him the happiest of men.

Sir Mark grumbled a little; but now-a-days he grumbled at everything, poor disappointed, all but childless, old man! As to the vicar he stood astonished and almost dismayed. 'Have you thought enough about it, Mr Duke?' the parson asked. 'Young men are apt to do things in a hurry, that they repent at leisure.* Bessy is a good girl, a good girl, God bless her: but she has not been brought up as your wife should have been: at least as folks will say your wife should have been. Though I may say for her she has a very pretty sprinkling of mathematics. I taught her myself, Mr Duke.'

'May I go and ask her myself? I only want your permission,' urged Duke.

'Ay, go! But perhaps you'd better ask Madam first. She will like to be told everything as soon as me.'

But Duke did not care for Madam. He rushed through the open door of the parsonage, into the homely sitting-rooms, and softly called for Bessy. When she came, he took her by the hand and led her forth into the field-path at the back of the orchard, and there he won his bride to the full content of both their hearts.

All this time the inhabitants of Crowley Castle and the quiet people of the neighbouring village of Crowley, heard but little of 'The Countess,' as it was their fashion to call her. Sir Mark had his letters from her, it is true, and he read them over and over again, and moaned over them, and sighed, and put them carefully away in a bundle. But they were like arrows of pain to him. None knew their contents; none, even knowing them, would have dreamed, any more than he did, for all his moans and sighs, of the utter wretchedness of the writer. Love had long since vanished from the habitation of that pair; a habitation, not a home, even in its brightest days. Love had gone out of the window, long before poverty had come in at the door:* yet that grim visitant who never tarries in tracking a disreputable gambler, had now arrived. The count lost the last remnants of his character as a man who played honourably, and thenceforth—that being pretty nearly the only sin which banished men from good society in those days—he had to play where and how he could. Theresa's money went as her poor angry father had foretold. By-and-by, and without her consent, her jewel-box was rifled; the diamonds round the locket holding her mother's picture were wrenched and picked out by no careful hand. Victorine found Theresa crying over the poor relics;—crying at last, without disguise, as if her heart would break.

'Oh, mamma! mamma! mamma!' she sobbed out, holding up the smashed and disfigured miniature as an explanation of her grief. She was sitting on the floor, on which she had thrown herself in the first discovery of the theft. Victorine sat down by her, taking her head upon her breast, and soothing her. She did not ask who had done it; she asked Theresa no question which the latter would have shrunk from answering; she knew all in that hour, without the count's name having passed the lips of either of them. And from that time she watched him as a tiger watches his prey.

When the letters came from England, the three letters from Sir Mark and the affianced bride and bridegroom, announcing the approaching marriage of Duke and Bessy, Theresa took them straight to Victorine. Theresa's lips were tightened, her pale cheeks were paler. She waited for Victorine to speak. Not a word did the Frenchwoman utter; but she smoothed the letters one over the other, and tore them in two, throwing the pieces on the ground, and stamping on them.

'Oh, Victorine!' cried Theresa, dismayed at passion that went so far beyond her own, 'I never expected it—I never thought of it—but, perhaps, it was but natural.'

'It was not natural; it was infamous! To have loved you once, and not to wait for chances, but to take up with that mean poor girl at the parsonage. Pah! and *her* letter! Sir Mark is of my mind though, I can see. I am sorry I tore up his letter. He feels, he knows, that Mr Duke Brownlow ought to have waited, waited, waited. Some one waited fourteen years,* did he not? The count will not live for ever.'

Theresa did not see the face of wicked meaning as those last words were spoken.

Another year rolled heavily on its course of wretchedness to Theresa. That same revolution of time brought increase of peace and joy to the English couple, striving humbly, striving well, to do their duty as children to the unhappy and deserted Sir Mark. They had their reward in the birth of a little girl. Yet, close on the heels of this birth, followed a great sorrow. The good parson died, after a short sudden illness. Then came the customary trouble after the death of a clergyman. The widow had to leave the parsonage, the home of a lifetime, and seek a new resting-place for her declining years.

Fortunately for all parties, the new vicar was a bachelor; no other than the tutor who had accompanied Duke on his grand tour; and it was made a condition that he should allow the widow of his predecessor to remain at the parsonage as his housekeeper. Bessy would fain have had her mother at the castle, and this course would have been infinitely preferred by Madam Hawtrey, who, indeed, suggested the wish to her daughter. But Sir Mark was obstinately against it; nor did he spare his caustic remarks on Madam Hawtrey, even before her own daughter. He had never quite forgiven Duke's marriage, although he was personally exceedingly fond of Bessy. He referred this marriage, in some part, and perhaps to no greater extent than was true, to madam's good management in throwing the young people together; and he was explicit in the expression of his opinion.

Poor Theresa! Every day she more and more bitterly rued her ill-starred marriage. Often and often she cried to herself, when she was alone in the dead of the night, 'I cannot bear it—I cannot bear it!' But again in the daylight her pride would help her to keep her woe to herself. She could not bear the gaze of pitying eyes; she could not bear even Victorine's fierce sympathy. She might have gone home like a poor prodigal* to her father, if Duke and Bessy had not, as she imagined, reigned triumphant in her place, both in her father's heart and in her father's home. And all this while, that father almost hated the tender attentions which were rendered to him by those who were not his Theresa, his only child, for whose presence he yearned and longed in silent misery. Then again (to return to Theresa), her husband had his fits of kindness towards her. If he had been very fortunate in play, if he had heard other men admire her, he would come back for a few moments to his loyalty, and would lure back the poor tortured heart, only to crush it afresh. One day—after a short time of easy temper, caresses, and levity— she found out something, I know not what, in his life, which stung her to the quick. Her sharp wits and sharper tongue spoke out most cutting insults; at first he smiled, as if rather amused to see how she was ransacking her brain to find stabbing speeches; but at length she touched some sore; he scarcely lost the mocking smile upon his face, but his eyes flashed lurid fire, and his heavy closed hand fell on her white shoulder with a terrible blow!

She stood up, facing him, tearless, deadly white. 'The poor old man at home!' was all she said, trembling, shivering all over, but with her eyes fixed on his coward face. He shrank from her look, laughed aloud to hide whatever feeling might be hidden in his bosom, and left the room. She only said again, 'The poor old man—the poor old deserted, desolate man!' and felt about blindly for a chair.

She had not sat down a minute though, before she started up and rang her bell. It was Victorine's office to answer it; but Theresa looked almost surprised to see her. 'You!—I wanted the others—I want them all! They shall all see how their master treats his wife! Look here!' she pushed the gauze neckerchief from her shoulder— the mark was there red and swollen. 'Bid them all come here— Victorine, Amadée, Jean, Adèle, all—I will be justified by their testimony, whatever I do!' Then she fell to shaking and crying.

Victorine said nothing, but went to a certain cupboard where she kept medicines and drugs of which she alone knew the properties, and there she mixed a draught, which she made her mistress take. Whatever its nature was, it was soothing. Theresa leaned back in her chair, still sobbing heavily from time to time, until at last she dropped into a kind of doze. Then Victorine softly lifted the neckerchief, which had fallen into its place, and looked at the mark. She did not speak; but her whole face was a fearful threat. After she had looked her fill, she smiled a deadly smile. And then she touched the soft bruised flesh with her lips, much as though Theresa were the child she had been twenty years ago. Soft as the touch was Theresa shivered, and started and half awoke. 'Are they come?' she murmured; 'Amadée, Jean, Adèle?' but without waiting for an answer she fell asleep again.

Victorine went quietly back to the cupboard where she kept her drugs, and stayed there, mixing something noiselessly. When she had done what she wanted, she returned to her mistress's bedroom, and looked at her, still sleeping. Then she began to arrange the room. No blue silk curtains and silver mirrors, now, as in the Rue Louis le Grand. A washed-out faded Indian chintz, and an old battered toilette service of Japan-ware;* the disorderly signs of the count's late presence; an emptied flask of liqueur.

All the time Victorine arranged this room she kept saying to herself, 'At last! At last!' Theresa slept through the daylight, slept late into the evening, leaning back where she had fallen in her chair. She was so motionless that Victorine appeared alarmed. Once or twice she felt her pulse, and gazed earnestly into the tear-stained face. Once, she very carefully lifted one of the eyelids, and holding a lighted taper near, peered into the eye. Apparently satisfied, she went out and ordered a basin of broth to be ready when she asked for it. Again she sat in deep silence; nothing stirred in the closed chamber; but in the street the carriages began to roll, and the footmen and torch-bearers to cry aloud their masters' names and titles, to show what carriage in that narrow street below, was entitled to precedence. A carriage stopped at the hotel of which they occupied the third floor. Then the bell of their apartment rang loudly—rang violently. Victorine went out to see what it was that might disturb her darling—as she called Theresa to herself—her sleeping lady as she spoke of her to her servants.

She met those servants bringing in their master, the count, dead. Dead with a swordwound received in some infamous struggle.

Victorine stood and looked at him. 'Better so,' she muttered. 'Better so. But, monseigneur,* you shall take this with you, whithersoever your wicked soul is fleeing.' And she struck him a stroke on his shoulder, just where Theresa's bruise was. It was as light a stroke as well could be; but this irreverence to the dead called forth indignation even from the hardened bearers of the body. Little recked Victorine. She turned her back on the corpse, went to her cupboard, took out the mixture she had made with so much care, poured it out upon the bare wooden floor, and smeared it about with her foot.

A fortnight later, when no news had come from Theresa for many weeks, a poor chaise was seen from the castle windows lumbering slowly up the carriage road to the gate. No one thought much of it; perhaps it was some friend of the housekeeper's; perhaps it was some humble relation of Mrs Duke's (for many such had found out their cousin since her marriage). No one noticed the shabby carriage much, until the hall-porter was startled by the sound of the great bell pealing, and, on opening wide the hall-doors, saw standing before him the Mademoiselle Victorine of old days— thinner, sallower, in mourning. In the carriage sat Theresa, in the deep widow's weeds* of those days. She looked out of the carriage-window wistfully, in beyond Joseph, the hall-porter.

'My father!' she cried eagerly, before Victorine could speak. 'Is Sir Mark—well?' ('alive' was her first thought, but she dared not give the word utterance.)

'Call Mr. Duke!' said Joseph, speaking to some one unseen. Then he came forward. 'God bless you, Miss! God bless you! And this day of all days! Sir Mark is well—leastways he's sadly changed. Where's Mr Duke? Call him! My young lady's fainting!'

And this was Theresa's return home. None ever knew how much she had suffered since she had left home. If any one had known, Victorine would never have stood there dressed in that mourning. She put it on, sorely against her will, for the purpose of upholding the lying fiction of Theresa's having been a happy prosperous marriage. She was always indignant if any of the old servants fell back into the once familiar appellation of Miss Theresa. 'The countess,' she would say, in lofty rebuke.

What passed between Theresa and her father at that first interview no one ever knew. Whether she told him anything of her married life, or whether she only soothed the tears he shed on seeing her again, by sweet repetition of tender words and caresses—such as are the sugared pabulum* of age as well as of infancy—no one ever knew. Neither Duke nor his wife ever heard her allude to the time she had passed in Paris, except in the most cursory and superficial manner. Sir Mark was anxious to show her that all was forgiven, and would fain have displaced Bessy from her place as lady of the castle, and made Theresa take the headship of the house, and sit at table where the mistress ought to be. And Bessy would have given up her onerous dignities without a word; for Duke was always more jealous for his wife's position than she herself was, but Theresa declined to assume any such place in the household, saying, in the languid way which now seemed habitual to her, that English house-keeping, and all the domestic arrangements of an English country house were cumbrous and wearisome to her; that if Bessy would continue to act as she had done hitherto, and would so forestall what must be her natural duties at some future period, she, Theresa, should be infinitely obliged.

Bessy consented, and in everything tried to remember what Theresa liked, and how affairs were ordered in the old Theresa days. She wished the servants to feel that 'the countess' had equal rights with herself in the management of the house. But she, to whom the housekeeper takes her accounts—she in whose hands the power of conferring favours and privileges remains de facto*—will always be held by servants as the mistress; and Theresa's claims soon sank into the background. At first, she was too broken-spirited, too languid, to care for anything but quiet rest in her father's companionship. They sat sometimes for hours hand in hand; or they sauntered out on the terraces, hardly speaking, but happy; because they were once more together, and once more on loving terms. Theresa grew strong during this time of gentle brooding peace. The pinched pale face of anxiety lined with traces of suffering, relaxed into the soft oval; the light came into the eyes, the colour came into the cheeks.

But, in the autumn after Theresa's return, Sir Mark died; it had been a gradual decline of strength, and his last moments were passed in her arms. Her new misfortune threw her back into the wan worn creature she had been when she first came home, a widow, to Crowley Castle; she shut herself up in her rooms, and allowed no one to come near her but Victorine. Neither Duke nor

Bessy was admitted into the darkened rooms, which she had hung with black cloth in solemn funereal state.

Victorine's life since her return to the castle had been anything but peaceable. New powers had arisen in the housekeeper's room. Madam Brownlow had her maid, far more exacting than Madam Brownlow herself; and a new housekeeper reigned in the place of her who was formerly but an echo of Victorine's opinions. Victorine's own temper, too, was not improved by her four years abroad, and there was a general disposition among the servants to resist all her assumption of authority. She felt her powerlessness after a struggle or two, but treasured up her vengeance. If she had lost power over the household, however, there was no diminution of her influence over her mistress. It was her device at last that lured the countess out of her gloomy seclusion.

Almost the only creature Victorine cared for, besides Theresa, was the little Mary Brownlow. What there was of softness in her woman's nature, seemed to come out towards children; though, if the child had been a boy instead of a girl, it is probable that Victorine might not have taken it into her good graces. As it was, the French nurse and the English child were capital friends; and when Victorine sent Mary into the countess's room, and bade her not be afraid, but ask the lady in her infantine babble to come out and see Mary's snow-man, she knew that the little one, for her sake, would put her small hand into Theresa's, and thus plead with more success, because with less purpose, than any one else had been able to plead. Out came Theresa, colourless and sad, holding Mary by the hand. They went, unobserved as they thought, to the great gallery-window, and looked out into the court-yard; then Theresa returned to her rooms. But the ice was broken, and before the winter was over, Theresa fell into her old ways, and sometimes smiled, and sometimes even laughed, until chance visitors again spoke of her rare beauty and her courtly grace.

It was noticeable that Theresa revived first out of her lassitude to an interest in all Duke's pursuits. She grew weary of Bessy's small cares and domestic talk—now about the servants, now about her mother and the parsonage, now about the parish. She questioned Duke about his travels, and could enter into his appreciation and judgement of foreign nations; she perceived the latent powers of his mind; she became impatient of their remaining dormant in country seclusion. She had spoken of leaving Crowley Castle, and of finding some other home, soon after her father's death; but both Duke and Bessy had urged her to stay with them, Bessy saying, in the pure innocence of her heart, how glad she was that, in the probably increasing cares of her nursery, Duke would have a companion so much to his mind.

About a year after Sir Mark's death, the member for Sussex died, and Theresa set herself to stir up Duke to assume his place. With some difficulty (for Bessy was passive: perhaps even opposed to the scheme in her quiet way), Theresa succeeded, and Duke was elected. She was vexed at Bessy's torpor, as she called it, in the whole affair; vexed as she now often was with Bessy's sluggish interest in all things beyond her immediate ken. Once, when Theresa tried to make Bessy perceive how Duke might shine and rise in his new sphere, Bessy burst into tears, and said, 'You speak as if his presence here were nothing, and his fame in London everything. I cannot help fearing that he will leave off caring for all the quiet ways in which we have been so happy ever since we were married.'

'But when he is here,' replied Theresa, 'and when he wants to talk to you of politics, of foreign news, of great public interests, you drag him down to your level of woman's cares.'

'Do I?' said Bessy. 'Do I drag him down? I wish I was cleverer; but you know, Theresa, I was never clever in anything but house-wifery.'

Theresa was touched for a moment by this humility.

'Yet, Bessy, you have a great deal of judgement, if you will but exercise it. Try and take an interest in all he cares for, as well as making him try and take an interest in home affairs.'

But, somehow, this kind of conversation too often ended in dissatisfaction on both sides; and the servants gathered, from induction rather than from words, that the two ladies were not on the most cordial terms; however friendly they might wish to be, and might strive to appear. Madam Hawtrey, too, allowed her jealousy of Theresa to deepen into dislike. She was jealous because, in some unreasonable way, she had taken it into her head that Theresa's presence at the castle was the reason why she was not urged to take up her abode there on Sir Mark's death: as if there were not rooms and suites of rooms enough to lodge a wilderness of dowagers in the building, if the owner so wished. But Duke had certain ideas pretty strongly fixed in his mind; and one was a repugnance to his mother-in-law's constant company. But he greatly increased her income as soon as he had it in his power, and left it entirely to herself how she should spend it.*

Having now the means of travelling about, Madam Hawtrey betook herself pretty frequently to such watering-places as were in vogue at that day, or went to pay visits at the houses of those friends who occasionally came lumbering up in shabby vehicles to visit their cousin Bessy at the castle. Theresa cared little for Madam Hawtrey's coldness; perhaps, indeed, never perceived it. She gave up striving with Bessy, too; it was hopeless to try to make her an intellectual ambitious companion to her husband. He had spoken in the House; he had written a pamphlet that made much noise; the minister of the day had sought him out, and was trying to attach him to the government. Theresa, with her Parisian experience of the way in which women influenced politics, would have given anything for the Brownlows to have taken a house in London. She longed to see the great politicians, to find herself in the thick of the struggle for place and power, the brilliant centre of all that was worth hearing and seeing in the kingdom. There had been some talk of this same London house; but Bessy had pleaded against it earnestly while Theresa sat by in indignant silence, until she could bear the discussion no longer; going off to her own sitting-room, where Victorine was at work. Here her pent-up words found vent—not addressed to her servant, but not restrained before her:

'I cannot bear it—to see him cramped in by her narrow mind, to hear her weak selfish arguments, urged because she feels she would be out of place beside him. And Duke is hampered with this woman: he whose powers are unknown even to himself, or he would put her feeble nature on one side, and seek his higher atmosphere. How he would shine! How he does shine! Good Heaven! To think—'

And here she sank into silence, watched by Victorine's furtive eyes.

Duke had excelled all he had previously done by some great burst of eloquence, and the country rang with his words. He was to come down to Crowley Castle for a parliamentary recess, which occurred almost immediately after this. Theresa calculated the hours of each part of the complicated journey, and could have told to five minutes when he might be expected; but the baby was ill and absorbed all Bessy's attention. She was in the nursery by the cradle in which the child slept, when her husband came riding up to the castle gate. But Theresa was at the gate; her hair all out of powder, and blowing away into dishevelled curls, as the hood of her cloak fell back; her lips parted with a breathless welcome; her eyes shining out love and pride. Duke was but mortal. All London chanted his rising fame; and here in his home Theresa seemed to be the only person who appreciated him.

The servants clustered in the great hall; for it was now some length of time since he had been at home. Victorine was there, with some headgear for her lady; and when, in reply to his inquiry for his wife, the grave butler asserted that she was with young master, who was, they feared, very seriously ill, Victorine said, with the familiarity of an old servant, and as if to assuage Duke's anxiety: 'Madam fancies the child is ill, because she can think of nothing but him, and perpetual watching has made her nervous.' The child, however, was really ill; and after a brief greeting to her husband, Bessy returned to her nursery, leaving Theresa to question, to hear, to sympathize. That night she gave way to another burst of disparaging remarks on poor motherly homely Bessy, and that night Victorine thought she read a deeper secret in Theresa's heart.

The child was scarcely ever out of its mother's arms; but the illness became worse, and it was nigh unto death.* Some cream had been set aside for the little wailing creature, and Victorine had unwittingly used it for the making of a cosmetic for her mistress. When the servant in charge of it reproved her, a quarrel began as to their respective mistress's right to give orders in the household. Before the dispute ended, pretty strong things had been said on both sides.

The child died. The heir was lifeless; the servants were in whispering dismay, and bustling discussion of their mourning; Duke felt the vanity of fame, as compared to a baby's life. Theresa was full of sympathy, but dared not express it to him; so tender was her heart becoming. Victorine regretted the death in her own way. Bessy lay speechless, and tearless; not caring for loving voices, nor for gentle touches; taking neither food nor drink; neither sleeping nor weeping. 'Send for her mother,' the doctor said; for Madam Hawtrey was away on her visits, and the letters telling her of her grandchild's illness had not reached her in the slow-delaying cross-country posts of those days. So she was sent for; by a man riding express, as a quicker and surer means than the post.

Meanwhile, the nurses, exhausted by their watching, found the care of little Mary by day, quite enough. Madam's maid sat up with Bessy for a night or two; Duke striding in from time to time through the dark hours to look at the white motionless face, which would have seemed like the face of one dead, but for the long-quivering sighs that came up from the overladen heart. The doctor tried his drugs, in vain, and then he tried again. This night, Victorine at her own earnest request, sat up instead of the maid. As usual, towards midnight, Duke came stealing in with shaded light. 'Hush!' said Victorine, her finger on her lips. 'She sleeps at last.' Morning dawned faint and pale, and still she slept. The doctor came, and stole in on tip-toe, rejoicing in the effect of his drugs. They all stood round the bed; Duke, Theresa, Victorine. Suddenly the doctor—a strange change upon him, a strange fear in his face—felt the patient's pulse, put his ear to her open lips, called for a glass—a feather. The mirror was not dimmed, the delicate fibres stirred not. Bessy was dead.

I pass rapidly over many months. Theresa was again over-whelmed with grief, or rather, I should say, remorse; for now that Bessy was gone, and buried out of sight, all her innocent virtues, all her feminine homeliness, came vividly into Theresa's mind—not as wearisome, but as admirable, qualities of which she had been too blind to perceive the value. Bessy had been her own old compan-ion too, in the happy days of childhood, and of innocence. Theresa rather shunned than sought Duke's company now. She remained at the castle, it is true, and Madam Hawtrey, as Theresa's only condi-tion of continuing where she was, came to live under the same roof. Duke felt his wife's death deeply, but reasonably, as became his character. He was perplexed by Theresa's bursts of grief, knowing, as he dimly did, that she and Bessy had not lived together in perfect harmony. But he was much in London now; a rising statesman; and when, in autumn, he spent some time at the castle, he was full of admiration for the strangely patient way in which Theresa behaved

towards the old lady. It seemed to Duke that in his absence Madam
Hawtrey had assumed absolute power in his household, and that
the high-spirited Theresa submitted to her fantasies with even
more docility than her own daughter would have done. Towards
Mary, Theresa was always kind and indulgent.

Another autumn came; and before it went, old ties were renewed,
and Theresa was pledged to become her cousin's wife.

There were two people strongly affected by this news when it
was promulgated; one—and this was natural under the circumstances—was Madam Hawtrey; who chose to resent the marriage
as a deep personal offence to herself as well as to her daughter's
memory, and who sternly rejecting all Theresa's entreaties, and
Duke's invitation to continue her residence at the castle, went off
into lodgings in the village. The other person strongly affected by
the news, was Victorine.

From being a dry active energetic middle-aged woman, she now,
at the time of Theresa's engagement, sank into the passive languor
of advanced life. It seemed as if she felt no more need of effort, or
strain, or exertion. She sought solitude; liked nothing better than
to sit in her room adjoining Theresa's dressing-room, sometimes
sunk in a reverie, sometimes employed on an intricate piece of
knitting with almost spasmodic activity. But wherever Theresa
went, thither would Victorine go. Theresa had imagined that her
old nurse would prefer being left at the castle, in the soothing
tranquillity of the country, to accompanying her and her husband
to the house in Grosvenor-square, which they had taken for the
parliamentary season. But the mere offer of a choice seemed to
irritate Victorine inexpressibly. She looked upon the proposal as a
sign that Theresa considered her as superannuated—that her
nursling was weary of her, and wished to supplant her services by
those of a younger maid. It seemed impossible to dislodge this
idea when it had once entered into her head, and it led to frequent
bursts of temper, in which she violently upbraided Theresa for her
ingratitude towards so faithful a follower.

One day, Victorine went a little further in her expressions than
usual, and Theresa, usually so forbearing towards her, turned at
last. 'Really, Victorine!' she said, 'this is misery to both of us. You
say you never feel so wicked as when I am near you; that my
ingratitude is such as would be disowned by fiends; what can I,

what must I do? You say you are never so unhappy as when you are near me; must we, then, part? Would that be for your happiness?'

'And is that what it has come to!' exclaimed Victorine. 'In my country they reckon a building secure against wind and storm and all the ravages of time, if the first mortar used has been tempered with human blood. But not even our joint secret, though it was tempered well with blood, can hold our lives together! How much less all the care, all the love, that I lavished upon you in the days of my youth and strength!'

Theresa came close to the chair in which Victorine was seated. She took hold of her hand and held it fast in her own. 'Speak, Victorine,' said she, hoarsely, 'and tell me what you mean. *What* is our joint secret? And what do you mean by its being a secret of blood? Speak out. I *will* know.'

'As if you do not know!' replied Victorine, harshly. 'You don't remember my visits to Bianconi, the Italian chemist in the Marais,* long ago?' She looked into Theresa's face, to see if her words had suggested any deeper meaning than met the ear. No; Theresa's look was stern, but free and innocent.

'You told me you went there to learn the composition of certain unguents, and cosmetics, and domestic medicines.'

'Ay, and paid high for my knowledge, too,' said Victorine, with a low chuckle. 'I learned more than you have mentioned, my lady countess. I learnt the secret nature of many drugs—to speak plainly, I learnt the art of poisoning. And,' suddenly standing up, 'it was for your sake I learnt it. For your service—you—who would fain cast me off in my old age. For you!'

Theresa blanched to a deadly white. But she tried to move neither feature nor limb, nor to avert her eyes for one moment from the eyes that defied her. 'For my service, Victorine?'

'Yes! The quieting draught was all ready for your husband, when they brought him home dead.'

'Thank God his death does not lie at your door!'

'Thank God?' mocked Victorine. 'The wish for his death does lie at your door; and the intent to rid you of him does lie at my door. And I am not ashamed of it. Not I! It was not for myself I would have done it, but because you suffered so. He had struck you, whom I had nursed on my breast.'

'Oh, Victorine!' said Theresa, with a shudder. 'Those days are past. Do not let us recall them. I was so wicked because I was so miserable; and now I am so happy, so inexpressibly happy, that— do let me try to make you happy too!'

'You ought to try,' said Victorine, not yet pacified; 'can't you see how the incomplete action once stopped by Fate, was tried again, and with success; and how you are now reaping the benefit of my sin, if sin it was?'

'Victorine! I do not know what you mean!' But some terror must have come over her, she so trembled and so shivered.

'Do you not indeed? Madame Brownlow, the country girl from Crowley Parsonage, needed sleep, and would fain forget the little child's death that was pressing on her brain. I helped the doctor to his end. She sleeps now, and she has met her baby before this, if priests' tales are true. And you, my beauty, my queen, you reign in her stead! Don't treat the poor Victorine as if she were mad, and speaking in her madness. I have heard of tricks like that being played, when the crime was done, and the criminal of use no longer.'

That evening, Duke was surprised by his wife's entreaty and petition that she might leave him, and return with Victorine and her other personal servants to the seclusion of Crowley Castle. She, the great London toast, the powerful enchantress of society, and most of all, the darling wife and true companion, with this sudden fancy for this complete retirement, and for leaving her husband when he was first fully entering into the comprehension of all that a wife might be! Was it ill health? Only last night she had been in dazzling beauty, in brilliant spirits; this morning only, she had been so merry and tender. But Theresa denied that she was in any way indisposed; and seemed suddenly so unwilling to speak of herself, and so much depressed, that Duke saw nothing for it but to grant her wish and let her go. He missed her terribly. No more pleasant tête-à-tête breakfasts, enlivened by her sense and wit, and cheered by her pretty caressing ways. No gentle secretary now, to sit by his side through long long hours, never weary. When he went into society, he no longer found his appearance watched and waited for by the loveliest woman there. When he came home from the House at night, there was no one to take an interest in his speeches, to be indignant at all that annoyed him, and charmed and proud of all the admiration he had won. He longed for the time to come when he would be able to go down for a day or two to see his wife; for her letters appeared to him dull and flat after her bright companionship. No wonder that her letters came out of a heavy heart, knowing what she knew.

She scarcely dared to go near Victorine, whose moods were becoming as variable as though she were indeed the mad woman she had tauntingly defied Theresa to call her. At times she was miserable because Theresa looked so ill, and seemed so deeply unhappy. At other times she was jealous because she fancied Theresa shrank from her and avoided her. So, wearing her life out with passion, Victorine's health grew daily worse and worse during that summer.

Theresa's only comfort seemed to be little Mary's society. She seemed as though she could not lavish love enough upon the motherless child, who repaid Theresa's affection with all the pretty demonstrativeness of her age. She would carry the little three-year-old maiden in her arms when she went to see Victorine, or would have Mary playing about in her dressing-room, if the old French-woman, for some jealous freak, would come and arrange her lady's hair with her trembling hands. To avoid giving offence to Victorine, Theresa engaged no other maid; to shun over-much or over-frank conversation with Victorine, she always had little Mary with her when there was a chance of the French waiting-maid coming in. For, the presence of the child was a holy restraint even on Victorine's tongue; she would sometimes check her fierce temper, to caress the little creature playing at her knees; and would only dart a covert bitter sting at Theresa under the guise of a warning against ingratitude, to Mary.

Theresa drooped and drooped in this dreadful life. She sought out Madam Hawtrey, and prayed her to come on a long visit to the castle. She was lonely, she said, asking for madam's company as a favour to herself. Madam Hawtrey was difficult to persuade; but the more she resisted, the more Theresa entreated; and, when once madam was at the castle, her own daughter had never been so dutiful, so humble a slave to her slightest fancy as was the proud Theresa now.

Yet, for all this, the lady of the castle drooped and drooped, and when Duke came down to see his darling he was in utter dismay at her looks. Yet she said she was well enough, only tired. If she had anything more upon her mind, she refused him her confidence. He watched her narrowly, trying to forestall her smallest desires. He saw her tender affection for Mary, and thought he had never seen so lovely and tender a mother to another woman's child. He wondered at her patience with Madam Hawtrey, remembering how often his own stock had been exhausted by his mother-in-law, and how the brilliant Theresa had formerly scouted and flouted at the vicar's wife. With all this renewed sense of his darling's virtues and charms, the idea of losing her was too terrible to bear.

He would listen to no pleas, to no objections. Before he returned to town, where his presence was a political necessity, he sought the best medical advice that could be had in the neighbourhood. The doctors came; they could make but little out of Theresa, if her vehement assertion were true that she had nothing on her mind. Nothing.

'Humour him at least, my dear lady!' said the doctor, who had known Theresa from her infancy, but who, living at the distant county town, was only called in on the Olympian occasions of great state illnesses. 'Humour your husband, and perhaps do yourself some good too, by consenting to his desire that you should have change of air. Brighthelmstone* is a quiet village by the sea-side. Consent, like a gracious lady, to go there for a few weeks.'

So, Theresa, worn out with opposition, consented, and Duke made all the arrangements for taking her, and little Mary, and the necessary suite of servants, to Brighton, as we call it now. He resolved in his own mind that Theresa's personal attendant should be some woman young enough to watch and wait upon her mistress, and not Victorine, to whom Theresa was in reality a servant. But of this plan, neither Theresa nor Victorine knew anything until the former was in the carriage with her husband some miles distant from the castle. Then he, a little exultant in the good management by which he supposed he had spared his wife the pain and trouble of decision, told her that Victorine was left behind, and that a new accomplished London maid would await her at her journey's end.

Theresa only exclaimed, 'O! What will Victorine say?' and covered her face, and sat shivering and speechless.

What Victorine did say, when she found out the trick, as she esteemed it, that had been played upon her, was too terrible to repeat. She lashed herself up into an ungoverned passion; and then became so really and seriously ill that the servants went to fetch Madam Hawtrey in terror and dismay. But when that lady came, Victorine shut her eyes, and refused to look at her. 'She has got her daughter in her hand! I will not look!' Shaking all the time she uttered these awe-stricken words, as if she were in an ague-fit.* 'Bring the countess back to me. Let *her* face the dead woman standing there, I will not do it. They wanted her to sleep—and so did the countess, that she might step into her lawful place. Theresa, Theresa, where are you? You tempted me. What I did, I did in your service. And you have gone away, and left me alone with the dead woman! It was the same drug as the doctor gave, after all—only he gave little, and I gave much. My lady the countess spent her money well, when she sent me to the old Italian to learn his trade. Lotions for the complexion, and a discriminating use of poisonous drugs. I discriminated, and Theresa profited; and now she is his wife, and has left me here alone with the dead woman. Theresa, Theresa, come back and save me from the dead woman!'

Madam Hawtrey stood by, horror-stricken. 'Fetch the vicar,' said she, under her breath, to a servant.

'The village doctor is coming,' said some one near. 'How she raves! Is it delirium?'

'It is no delirium,' said Bessy's mother. 'Would to Heaven it were!'

Theresa had a happy day with her husband at Brighthelmstone before he set off on his return to London. She watched him riding away, his servant following with his portmanteau. Often and often did Duke look back at the figure of his wife, waving her handkerchief, till a turn of the road hid her from his sight. He had to pass through a little village not ten miles from his home, and there a servant, with his letters and further luggage, was to await him. There he found a mysterious, imperative note, requiring his immediate presence at Crowley Castle. Something in the awe-stricken face of the servant from the castle, led Duke to question him. But all he could say was, that Victorine lay dying, and that Madam Hawtrey had said that after that letter the master was sure to return, and so would need no luggage. Something lurked behind, evidently. Duke rode home at speed. The vicar was looking out for him. 'My dear boy,' said he, relapsing into the old relations of tutor and pupil, 'prepare yourself.'

'What for?' said Duke, abruptly: for the being told to prepare himself, without being told for what, irritated him in his present mood. 'Victorine is dead?'

'No! She says she will not die until she has seen you, and got you to forgive her, if Madam Hawtrey will not. But first read this: it is a terrible confession, made by her before me, a magistrate, believing herself to be on the point of death!'

Duke read the paper—containing little more in point of detail than I have already given—the horrible words taken down in the short-hand in which the vicar used to write his mild prosy sermons: his pupil knew the character of old. Duke read it twice. Then he said: 'She is raving, poor creature!' But for all that, his heart's blood ran cold, and he would fain not have faced the woman, but would rather have remained in doubt to his dying day.

He went up the stairs three steps at a time, and then turned and faced the vicar, with a look like the stern calmness of death. 'I wish to see her alone.' He turned out all the watching women, and then he went to the bedside where Victorine sat, half propped up with pillows, watching all his doings and his looks, with her hollow awful eyes. 'Now, Victorine, I will read this paper aloud to you. Perhaps your mind has been wandering; but you understand me now?' A feeble murmur of assent met his listening ear. 'If any statement in this paper be not true, make me a sign. Hold up your hand—for God's sake hold up your hand. And if you can do it with truth in this, your hour of dying, Lord have mercy upon you; but if you cannot hold up your hand, then Lord have mercy upon me!'

He read the paper slowly; clause by clause he read the paper. No sign; no uplifted hand. At the end she spoke, and he bent his head to listen. 'The Countess—Theresa you know—she who has left me to die alone—she'—then mortal strength failed, and Duke was left alone in the chamber of death.

He stayed in the chamber many minutes, quite still. Then he left the room, and said to the first domestic he could find, 'The woman is dead. See that she is attended to.' But he went to the vicar, and had a long long talk with him. He sent a confidential servant for little Mary—on some pretext, hardly careful, or plausible enough; but his mood was desperate, and he seemed to forget almost everything but Bessy, his first wife, his innocent girlish bride.

Theresa could ill spare her little darling, and was perplexed by the summons; but an explanation of it was to come in a day or two. It came.

'Victorine is dead; I need say no more. She could not carry her awful secret into the next world, but told all. I can think of nothing but my poor Bessy, delivered over to the cruelty of such a woman. And you, Theresa, I leave you to your conscience, for you have slept in my bosom. Henceforward I am a stranger to you. By the time you receive this, I, and my child, and that poor murdered girl's mother, will have left England. What will be our next step I know not. My agent will do for you what you need.'

Theresa sprang up and rang her bell with mad haste. 'Get me a horse!' she cried, 'and bid William be ready to ride with me for his life—for my life—along the coast, to Dover!'

They rode and they galloped through the night, scarcely staying to bait* their horses. But when they came to Dover, they looked out to sea upon the white sails that bore Duke and his child away. Theresa was too late, and it broke her heart. She lies buried in Dover churchyard. After long years Duke returned to England; but his place in parliament knew him no more,* and his daughter's husband sold Crowley Castle to a stranger.

EXPLANATORY NOTES

THE MOORLAND COTTAGE

3 *lyke-gate*: (archaic) 'the roofed gateway to a churchyard under which the corpse is set down at a funeral, to await the clergyman's arrival'. The *OED* cites the spellings 'lich-gate' and 'lych-gate', but not the variant Gaskell has used here.

ling: the northern English equivalent of Scottish heather.

German forest-tales: Peter Skrine has suggested two possible sources for this allusion. He writes, 'Is it a reference to *The Fair-Haired Eckbert*, that extraordinary fairytale by the German Romantic writer Ludwig Tieck (1774–1853) which Carlyle had translated and which had coined the haunting word "Waldeinsamkeit" (wood solitude) for a kind of loneliness felt only in the depths of a forest?' Or perhaps the tales are an allusion to 'the *Schwarzwälder Dorfgeschichten* or *Village Tales from the Black Forest* by Berthold Auerbach (1812–82), the German bestsellers of the 1840s?' Skrine quotes from the review of the first English translation of these tales in the *British Quarterly Review* in 1847: ' "The pleasure which they are calculated to afford is very much of the same kind as that which is derived from a quiet saunter in green fields, with pleasant summer breezes blowing freshly around one." Freshness of this sort is precisely the quality Charlotte Brontë admired in *The Moorland Cottage*.' See Peter Skrine, 'Mrs Gaskell and Germany', *Gaskell Society Journal*, 7 (1993), 42–3.

4 *crape*: a light, transparent fabric, mechanically crimped; in black, it was used extensively for mourning dresses, and for funereal trimmings.

6 *brae*: Scottish and northern dialect term for a steep slope, hillside, or bank of a river valley.

8 *shot*: small pellets of lead used in firearms, particularly sporting guns.

négligé: (French) careless.

9 *beau-pot*: a vase for cut flowers; altered form of the original 'bough-pot'.

10 *founder's line . . . presentation*: a reference to Edward's projected future as a clergyman. The term 'presentation' refers to the right, often held by private individuals, of awarding a clergyman a benefice or living, that is, the position of parson of a parish church.

12 *bombazine*: a twilled or corded dress-material; in black, it was often used for mourning garments.

pièce de résistance: (French) literally, the main course of a meal; the phrase is used in English to signify the chief item or principal feature.

13 *Margaret*: Gaskell refers to her heroine as Margaret only three times in the story, here and on pp. 93 and 96. There seems to be no reason for these changes and the use of 'Margaret' rather than the more informal, familiar 'Maggie' is curiously abrupt and distant.

14 *stone-coped*: describing a decorative covering or cladding of stone around window openings.

15 *yeomen*: small freehold farmers whose exact social position is often difficult to define, but who are often regarded as being below the rank of gentleman.

19 *Sleeping Beauty*: a reference to the well-known fairy tale, the long history of which is traced in Iona and Peter Opie's *The Classic Fairy Tales* (London, 1974). Gaskell uses the allusion in order to highlight aspects of Maggie Browne's character, domestic situation, and emotional development. She uses the same device to similar effect in relation to Molly Gibson in *Wives and Daughters* (ch. 2).

21 *the man in the Arabian Nights . . . hard, barren rock*: a reference to the story of Ali Baba who sees by chance a band of robbers entering a cave where they have hidden their stolen treasure. The robbers use a magic password, 'Open Sesame!', to cause the rock covering the mouth of the cave to open. Elizabeth Gaskell, like most of her contemporaries, was very familiar with the tales from the *Arabian Nights*, the English reading public having been exposed to a multitude of translations, imitations, and variations of Antoine Galland's *Mille et une nuits* (1704–17) for over a century before Edward Lane's immensely popular translation of the *Nights* in 1839–41. For an examination of the place of *The Thousand and One Nights* in English culture see Peter L. Caracciolo, *The* Arabian Nights *in English Literature* (New York, 1988).

27 *'ministers of Him, to do His pleasure'*: Psalms 103: 21.

those lines of George Herbert's, '. . . or grave.': 'Perirrhanterium' (from 'The Church-porch', the frame of 'The Temple'), ll. 89–90. In his edition of *The English Poems of George Herbert* (London, 1974), C. A. Patrides gives these lines as 'for all may have, | If they dare try, a glorious life, or grave'. Gaskell's misquotation may be deliberate or the result of imperfectly remembered lines or an emendation in the edition of Herbert's poems she may have used.

Joan of Arc: (1412–31), Saint Joan of Arc, the Maid of Orleans, French military heroine of the Hundred Years' War against the English, and religious martyr, burned at the stake for witchcraft and heresy.

28 *Virgil*: (70–19 BC), Publius Vergilius Maro, Roman poet whose works were studied widely in boys' schools and in the universities.

'Arma, virumque cano, Troiae qui primus ab oris': the opening line of Virgil's epic poem, the *Aeneid*, 'I sing of arms and the man who first from the shores of Troy . . .'

'Infir . . . noneis.': a schoolboy joke, with English rearranged to look (vaguely) like dog Latin, i.e. 'In fir deal is, in oak none is; in mud eel is, in clay none is.' Deal is the timber obtained from the fir tree.

'Apud . . . restis.': again, this is English rearranged, more convincingly in this case, to look like Latin, i.e.

> A pudding is all my desire,
> My mistress I never require,
> A lover I find it a jest is,
> His misery never at rest is.

29 *Don Quixote, . . . Sancho Panza*: the hero of Cervantes' satirical romance of the same name (1605, 1615), Don Quixote is a poor gentleman obsessed by tales of chivalry. Wearing rusty armour and riding an old horse, he wanders in search of chivalric deeds to perform accompanied by his squire, Sancho Panza, a simple but shrewd peasant.

private schools: Frank attends Eton, one of the great public schools which were exclusive to the aristocracy and wealthy classes. He is disparaging towards the more numerous private schools which were run for profit and varied greatly in quality of tuition and in the background of the boys who attended.

31 *taking orders . . . an attorney*: taking orders or entering the church necessitated completion of a university degree. To become an attorney, a term commonly used synonymously for solicitor for much of the nineteenth century, one was articled or apprenticed to a firm of solicitors and learnt 'on the job'.

36 *rubber*: in games such as whist and bridge, a set of three games in which a clear winner can be decided.

39 *lines of Wordsworth . . . 'Shall pass into her face.'*: William Wordsworth (1770–1850), 'Three Years She Grew in Sun and Shower', ll. 26–30.

40 *delf . . . China*: the former, also known as delft or delph, named after the town in Holland from which it originated, is lesser quality glazed earthenware. The latter is high-quality, semi-transparent earthen-

ware, named porcelain by the Portuguese who introduced it from China into Europe in the sixteenth century.

47 *the Princess Victoria*: may be a reference to Queen Victoria herself (1819–1901) before she became queen in 1837 and married Prince Albert of Saxe-Coburg-Gotha in 1840. *The Moorland Cottage* was published in 1850 (when Victoria and Albert's eldest child, also Princess Victoria (1840–1901), was only 10 years old) but the action of the story seems to occur some years before this date.

48 *potted charr*: or char, a small fish, like a trout, found in mountain lakes, and often prepared by being preserved in pots. Mrs Beeton refers to the char as 'the most delicious of fish, being esteemed by some superior to the salmon' (*Beeton's Book of Household Management* (1859–61; 1st edn. facsimile, London, 1968), 124).

a 'fool, rush in where angels fear to tread,': Alexander Pope, 'An Essay on Criticism', l. 625.

50 *gêne*: (French) constraint, discomfort.

53 *the 'melodies of the everlasting chime'*: cf. Elizabeth Gaskell, *Ruth*, ch. 5:

> There are in this loud stunning tide
> Of human care and crime,
> With whom the melodies abide
> Of th' everlasting chime.
> Who carry music in their heart
> Through dusky lane and crowded mart,
> Plying their task with busier feet,
> Because their secret souls a holy strain repeat.

I have been unable to trace this quotation and can only agree with Alan Shelston's comment in his edition of *Ruth* (World's Classics edn.; Oxford, 1985) that the lines may 'have been taken from one of the many common-place books or annuals that were popular in the period' (462).

'Whose faith is fixt . . . "I cannot understand: I love." ': Alfred Tennyson, *In Memoriam* (1850), 97, ll. 33–36.

54 *an old German engraving . . . 'Pleasure digging a Grave'*: books of engravings—of landscapes, of famous people, or, as here, illustrating moral themes—were commonly provided for amusement and improvement in middle- and upper-class drawing-rooms of the period. In *Wives and Daughters*, for example, Molly Gibson is provided with Edmund Lodge's *Portraits of Illustrious Personages of Great Britain. Engraved from Authentic Pictures* (1821–34), with which to amuse herself in Lady Cumnor's drawing-room (ch. 2).

55 *the Temple*: Middle Temple and Inner Temple were two of London's four Inns of Court (the other two being Gray's Inn and Lincoln's Inn). These are ancient colleges of law, at which a university graduate undertakes study of the law as the pupil of an established barrister.

61 *the widow . . . her mite*: Mark 12: 42–4.

62 *Evenings at Home . . . the 'Transmigrations of Indra'*: *Evenings at Home; or, the Juvenile Budget Opened. Consisting of a Variety of Miscellaneous Pieces, for the Instruction and Amusement of Young Persons,* was written by Dr John Aikin (1747–1822) and his sister Mrs Anna Laetitia Barbauld (1743–1824) in six volumes and first published in London between 1792 and 1796. The story 'The Transmigrations of Indur', the title of which Gaskell misquotes slightly, is found in volume two, and concerns the adventures of a man who is enabled, by magic, to take on the form of a succession of animals and to experience their mode of life.

   ' "*What's done . . . what's resisted,*" ': Robert Burns (1759–1796), 'An Address to Unco Guid'.

63 *Quixotic*: a reference to Don Quixote (see note to p. 29).

69 *struck off the Rolls*: to be banned from practising and to have one's name removed from the official register of those qualified to act as solicitors or attorneys.

74 *as hard as a nether mill-stone*: 'His heart is as strong as a stone, and as hard as the nether milstone', *Geneva Bible* (1560), Job 41: 14 (*OED*). The nether millstone was the lower, fixed, very hard stone upon which the upper stone moved in order to produce the action needed for grinding grain.

   keep to windward of the law: Shakespeare, *Twelfth Night*, III. iv. 183, 'Still you keep o' the windy side of the law', i.e. the safe side, out of reach of the law.

   make assurance doubly sure: Shakespeare, *Macbeth*, IV. i. 83.

75 *hulks*: old, dismasted ships anchored in the Thames river and off Portsmouth, and used to house the overflow of prisoners from England's already crowded gaols. They were used from 1778 until 1857.

78 *Ariel imprisoned in the thick branches*: an airy spirit in Shakespeare's *The Tempest*, rescued by the magician Prospero from the curse of the 'damn'd witch Sycorax'. Ariel refused to serve Sycorax so she imprisoned him in 'a cloven pine' where he remained 'a dozen years' uttering groans that 'Did make wolves howl, and penetrate the breasts | Of ever-angry bears' (I, ii).

80 *packet*: packet-boat, a vessel following a regular schedule between two ports, carrying mail, goods, and passengers.

shippen: (dialect) or shippon, a cow-shed.

Botany Bay: site on the east coast of Australia at which Captain James Cook landed in 1770. Although the British colony and penal settlement was subsequently established at Port Jackson, 'Botany Bay' remained in common parlance as the term for transportation to New South Wales.

85 *El Dorado*: (Spanish) the gilded. 'Originally the name given to the supposed king of the fabulous city of Manoa believed to be on the Amazon. The king was said to be covered with oil and then periodically powdered with gold-dust so that he was permanently, and literally, gilded. Expeditions from Spain and England (two of which were led by Sir Walter Ralegh) tried to discover this territory. El Dorado and Manoa were used by the explorers as interchangeable names for the "golden city". Metaphorically it is applied to any place which offers opportunities of getting rich quickly or acquiring wealth easily' (*Brewer's Dictionary of Phrase and Fable* (14th edn.; London, 1989), 377).

87 *Pizarro*: Francisco Pizarro (*c*.1475–1541), Spanish explorer who conquered the Inca empire and founded the city of Lima.

89 *Esau's craving for a blessing*: Genesis 25: 20–34; 27: 1–41; 32: 3–20; and 33: 1–16. Esau, the older twin of Jacob, was destined to be supplanted by his younger brother. Their mother, Rebekah, connived with Jacob to deceive their father, Isaac, into bestowing his blessing on Jacob instead of Esau as he had promised. The parallel with Maggie's situation lies in Rebekah's favouritism of Jacob over Esau which resembles Mrs Browne's preference for Edward over Maggie, and Jacob's guile and cunning which aligns him with Edward. Maggie, like Esau, is open and spontaneous, and, also like Esau, she forgives her brother for his sins against her.

steerage-passengers . . . cabin places: on board ship steerage passengers travelled at the cheapest rate in crowded, unpleasant conditions whereas passengers who paid more for a berth in a cabin enjoyed more space and privacy.

91 *"God's will be done!"*: The Lord's Prayer, *Book of Common Prayer*; also Matthew 6: 9–13; and Luke 11: 2–4.

95 *Llandudno . . . the little Orme's head*: on the north coast of Wales, west of Liverpool, along the route the *Anna-Maria* would have taken across the Irish Sea.

96 *Abergele*: also on the north coast of Wales, approximately ten miles east of Llandudno.

    Conway: anglicized spelling of Conwy, situated approximately three miles south of Llandudno.

97 *"in that new world which is the old"*: Alfred Lord Tennyson, 'The Day-Dream' (1830; 1842):

> And on her lover's arm she leant,
> And round her waist she felt it fold,
> And far across the hills they went
> In that new world which is the old.

    The quotation is particularly apt as the central section of the poem, 'The Sleeping Beauty', recounts the fairy tale of that name. Maggie had, earlier in the story, described her moorland cottage as 'like the place the Sleeping Beauty lived in' (see note to p. 19), and Frank has played the prince to Maggie's princess, rescuing her and restoring her to life.

    slop-shop: the ship's store which supplies cheap, ready-made clothing and other supplies, generally of inferior quality.

99 *car*: a horse-drawn vehicle.

100 *'stand and wait'*: John Milton (1608–1674), Sonnet XVI 'On His Blindness': 'They also serve who only stand and wait'.

THE SEXTON'S HERO

101 *Morecambe Bay*: on the north-west coast of England, between Lancashire and present-day Cumbria (which comprises the counties known in Gaskell's day as Cumberland and Westmoreland). In his history of the Lancashire landscape Roy Millward comments on the low-tide roads across the Bay. 'The most spectacular of these treacherous routes connected Hest Bank and Kents Bank, a distance of seven miles across the north-eastern recess of Morecambe Bay. . . . A picturesque relic of the route remains in a row of nine yew trees at Slackwood farm on the little limestone hills that come close to the sands at Silverdale. Travellers were warned not to leave the shore at Hest Bank until these trees appeared in line. But the pages of the parish register at Cartmel are the grimmest memorial to this road; they contain 145 entries of death by drowning on the sands.' (*Lancashire: An Illustrated Essay on the History of the Landscape* (London, 1955), 104–5).

102 *Martinmas*: the feast of St Martin, Bishop of Tours (fourth century), falls on 11 November.

Lindal . . . Grange: Lindale, and Grange-over-Sands, on the northern side of Morecambe Bay and on the western side of the sands which lie at the junction of the Bay and the mouth of the river Kent.

103 *osiers . . . coopers*: coopering, the art of making wooden barrels in which to store and transport a wide range of goods, would have been much in demand in the busy trading port of Liverpool. Barrels intended to hold liquid are made of oak and bound with iron hoops but those which do not have to hold liquid are made of much lighter wood and bound with hoops usually made of hazel or sometimes willow (osiers) which are twisted and nailed. See John Seymour, *The Forgotten Arts* (London, 1984), 27, 94.

104 *"quaker? . . . Jonathan Broad-brim"*: derisive names for members of the Society of Friends, founded in England by George Fox (1624–91). Fox recorded in his *Journal* that the Friends became known as Quakers because 'I bid them Tremble at the Word of the Lord.' The name may also be derived from a general term of abuse directed at religious radicals who shook and trembled at their meetings as the result of extreme emotion. (See *Brewer's Dictionary of Phrase and Fable*, 899). 'Jonathan Broad-brim' is derived from the Quakers' broad-brimmed hats. Eric Partridge notes Henry Fielding's use of the term in *The Spectator* in *A Dictionary of Slang and Unconventional English*, 2 vols. (5th edn.; London, 1961).

105 *threeped*: or threaped (dialect), 'to assert positively, especially to persist in or maintain a false accusation or assertion; to insist on'. See Joseph Wright (ed.), *English Dialect Dictionary* (London, 1961).

like the French radicals: the sexton's statement that his story refers to events of forty-five years ago places the action at the turn of the century, in the midst of the French Revolutionary and Napoleonic wars. He uses, appropriately, a country proverb to express his sense of a reversal of the natural social order, be it a humble clerk questioning the vicar's word or the common people deposing and executing a king and demanding the right to govern themselves.

106 *Kellet*: Over Kellet and Nether Kellet are a few miles inland from the eastern shore of Morecambe Bay.

the French coming and taking it away: Letty's fears for her baby reflect the invasion hysteria current in England during the period and are echoed in several of Gaskell's other works including *Sylvia's Lovers* and *Cranford*, in which Miss Matty recalls, ' "I know I used to wake up in the night many a time, and think I heard the tramp of the French entering Cranford" ' (*Cranford*, ch. 5).

shandry: in north-west dialect, a light cart on springs. The *OED* cites Gaskell's use of the term in this story.

King George: George III (1738–1820), who ruled from 1760 until 1820.

beener: the context suggests a dialect term meaning slower or wearier; however, I have been unable to find any other example of such a usage.

the fresh: the fresh water part of a tidal river, above the salt water.

Bolton side: Bolton le Sands, on the eastern side of the Bay and, as the sexton says, over 6 miles south-east across the Bay from Lindale.

107 *quick*: loose, easily yielding to pressure.

108 *a pillion*: a saddle, usually a woman's, or an attachment to an ordinary saddle to allow a second person (often a woman) to be carried.

109 *Flukeborough. . . . Arnside Knot*: Gilbert Dawson's body and the remains of the shandry and mare appear to have been carried in opposite directions by the tides of Morecambe Bay. Flukeborough (or Flookburgh) is on a piece of land which projects into the northern area of the Bay while Arnside Knot is a wooded hillside on the eastern side of the mouth of the Kent River.

CHRISTMAS STORMS AND SUNSHINE

111 *Johnson*: a puzzling reference which may possibly be an allusion to Dr Samuel Johnson (1709–84), critic, man of letters and staunch Tory. However, Gaskell's placement of the events of the story 'some dozen years ago', as well as other internal references, suggest that the tale is set in the 1830s, well after Johnson's death.

'Pro Bono Publico': (Latin) for the public good or benefit.

112 *having matched Greek with Greek . . . tug of war*: from 'When Greek joined Greeks, then was the tug of war' in Nathaniel Lee's play *The Rival Queens* (1677). The line refers to the determined resistance of the Greek cities in war against the Macedonian kings Philip and Alexander the Great, and implies that the struggle between two forces of equal strength and determination will be great.

113 *law for brute animals*: the first legislation against cruelty to animals, prohibiting the mistreatment of cattle and horses, was introduced by an Irish landowner, Richard Martin, and passed in 1822. When the proposed law was debated in Parliament, 'there were such howls of laughter that *The Times* reporter could hear little of what was

said. . . . Another member said Martin would be legislating for dogs next, which caused a further roar of mirth, and a cry "And cats!" sent the House into convulsions' (Peter Singer, *Animal Liberation* (2nd edn.; London, 1990), 204). It was not until 1849 that the Act was extended to cover all animals.

Radicals . . . Reform Bill: the Reform Bill of 1832 aimed to realign the boroughs and counties which sent elected representatives to Parliament in order to reflect the massive shifts in population which had taken place in the eighteenth and early nineteenth centuries. It also extended the franchise to more of the middle class. It was promoted and passed by the Whigs, only the most extreme of whom were known as Radicals.

115 *pyracanthus*: also known as Christ's Thorn, an evergreen, thorny shrub with white flowers and scarlet berries. Its popular name and its appearance suggest that, like the holly Gaskell also mentions here, it is a plant particularly appropriate to Christmas.

116 *croup*: an infection of the large airways (larynx and windpipe) in children, characterized by a distinctive cough and difficult, noisy breathing.

screw it up . . . slack on: a method of damping down the fire when not in use in order to save fuel. Slack consists of small pieces of waste coal; screwing up the fire probably refers to a fire in an open kitchen range, which could be adjusted by winding in or out one or two movable sides, known as cheeks. See Caroline Davidson, *A Woman's Work is Never Done: A History of Housework in the British Isles 1650–1950* (London, 1982), 57–9.

117 *'As Joseph was a walking . . . ' &c.*: 'Joseph and the Angel', part II of the three-part, traditional English 'Cherry Tree Carol'. 'The three sections evoke the journey to Bethlehem, the moment of the Nativity (Joseph's angelic visitation occurs while he is searching for a midwife), and the sojourn in Bethlehem' (*The Shorter New Oxford Book of Carols*, ed. Hugh Keyte and Andrew Parrott (Oxford, 1993), 211). The ballad, which probably originated in medieval times, and was reproduced in broadsides, is found in several early-nineteenth-century antiquarian works including William Hone's *Ancient Mysteries Described* (London, 1823).

118 *mustard plaisters*: plaister is an obsolete or dialect form of plaster, another term for which is poultice. The plaster or poultice was spread on the skin, usually the chest or throat, causing a mild surface irritation in order to relieve a deeper inflammatory process. Mrs Beeton's recipe for 'Mustard Poultice' calls for equal parts of dry

mustard and linseed-meal mixed in warm vinegar (see *Beeton's Book of Household Management*, 1063).

119 *Pharmacopoeia*: an official publication listing drugs, together with instructions for their preparation, identification and use.

121 *that old angelic song . . . Bethlehem Heights*: a reference to the hymn by Nahum Tate (1625–1715) and Nicholas Brady (1659–1726) 'While Shepherds Watched Their Flocks by Night', which paraphrases Luke 2: 8–15. Gaskell's message here is based on Luke 2: 14, 'Glory to God in the highest, and on earth peace, good will toward men'.

THE WELL OF PEN-MORFA

123 *Trê-Madoc, . . . Caernarvon*: Tremadoc or Tremadog and the larger neighbouring town of Porthmadog lie on the southern side of the entrance to the Lleyn Peninsula (referred to by Gaskell as the promontory of Llyn and properly spelt in Welsh Llŷn), on the north-west coast of Wales. Caernarvon or Caernarfon (Welsh) lies on the northern side of the entrance to the peninsula. 'Mr Maddocks, Shelley's friend' is cited in *The Oxford Companion to the Literature of Wales*, ed. Meic Stephens (Oxford, 1986) as William Alexander Madocks (1773–1828), industrialist and philanthropist, who built the town of Tremadog, named after its founder. In 1798 Madocks purchased an estate adjoining Penmorfa marsh and began reclaiming land from the sea. From 1808 to 1811 he built the Cob, an embankment which still stands today across the estuary of the Glaslyn river known as Traeth Mawr. I am indebted to Dr Helen Fulton, Director of the Centre for Celtic Studies, University of Sydney, for this information and for her generous assistance in compiling the explanatory notes to this story.

Welsh Wales: Dr Fulton notes that this phrase is used today, and no doubt in Gaskell's time also, to mean 'Welsh-speaking areas of Wales'. The Llŷn peninsula (and north-west Wales in general) is one of the bastions of Welsh Wales and still has a high proportion of Welsh speakers.

124 *names, . . . unwilling witnesses*: the family names described here by Gaskell seem to follow the patronymic system which was in use in Wales until the passing of the Act of Union in 1536, and the anglicization of the country, particularly its administration, which followed. The reference to baffling the barristers at Caernarvon assizes points to the clear 'us and them' attitude of the (Welsh-speaking) Welsh towards the English, who dominated law and government until the mid-twentieth century, an attitude which is still perceptible today, though less obviously. See *The Oxford Companion to the*

Literature of Wales, 567, for an account of the ways in which Welsh names were anglicized and a system of permanent surnames was adopted from the sixteenth century onward.

126 *Nest . . . Agnes*: the original Nest was the daughter of a twelfth-century Welsh king, renowned for her beauty and referred to by medieval Welsh poets as a symbol of beauty. *The Oxford Companion to the Literature of Wales* notes that she 'was known as "The Helen of Wales" on account of her abduction by Owain ap Cadwgan in 1109' although she 'may well have been Owain's willing accomplice. She had many lovers, including Henry I, and is reputed to have borne at least seventeen children' (428). The career of her namesake reflects ironically on Gaskell's Nest Gwynn and heightens the tragedy of her story.

triads . . . district: Dr Fulton notes that there are two kinds of triads. First, a formal generic kind in which legendary, legal, and medical information was catalogued in groups of three as a way of remembering it. A lot of these kinds of triads survive in manuscript collections, mainly of the fourteenth and fifteenth centuries. The second type of triad, which is the type obviously referred to here by Gaskell, is simply a literary device, used in medieval Welsh prose tales, and no doubt ultimately derived from oral tradition, as a means of description. The triple structure emphasizes or exaggerates some aspect of the object's appearance, such as a woman's exceptional beauty. Gaskell's example uses the same simile, 'as beautiful as', whereas the typical Welsh structure is to use three different similes. For example, 'Her hair was as black as jet, her skin as white as the snow, and the two red spots in her cheeks [were] like the blood in the snow', from the Welsh romance 'Peredur son of Evrawg', *c*.1250, trans. Jeffrey Gantz, *The Mabinogion* (Penguin edn.; Harmondsworth, 1976), 233. This collection of medieval tales known as *The Mabinogion* was translated into English by Lady Charlotte Guest and first published in 1846 as part of the 'Celtic revival' in England. So when Gaskell refers to the 'triads' she is certainly drawing on a well-established feature of the Welsh oral tradition and such a reference in her story would no doubt help to give it a touch of authenticity. On the other hand, her 'triad' is not quite like the genuine article in terms of its structure and the use of someone's name as part of the triad, and she has probably invented it to lend to her story that kind of 'Celtic magic' which English writers often looked for in Wales. For additional information on triads see *The Oxford Companion to the Literature of Wales*, 598–9.

the fairy-gifted child . . . gifts: the story 'Diamonds and Toads' was included in Charles Perrault's (1628–1703) *Histoires ou Contes du temps passé* (1697) as 'Les Fées' and was first translated into English as 'The Fairy' in Robert Samber's *Histories, or Tales of Past Times, By M. Perrault* (1729). In this story a beautiful and virtuous girl is drawing water at a well when she is approached by a fairy disguised as a poor old woman. The girl willingly gives the old woman a drink from her pitcher and is rewarded with the blessing that at every word she speaks a flower or jewel will come out of her mouth. In Gaskell's tale Nest Gwynn also draws water at a well and seems to be a 'fairy-gifted child', but she is also 'cursed'. See Opie, *The Classic Fairy Tales*, for a history of this tale.

127 *Moel Gwynn . . . 'The End of Time'*: Moel Gwynn is a hill, 'Moel' meaning 'bare, bald' and therefore 'bare hill (top)' and Gwyn(n) meaning 'white, pale, fair'. Criccaeth or Criccieth lies on the southern coast of the Llŷn Peninsula, approximately 5 miles west of Tremadog. J. G. Sharps noted in 1960 that 'on the Portmadoc–Criccieth Road one may find the "End of Time" farm—in Welsh *Penamser*' (*Mrs Gaskell's Observation and Invention* (Fontwell, Sussex, 1970), 99). Mrs Loan Leach, secretary of the Gaskell Society, located the name 'Penamser' on the gateway of a farm near Porthmadog in 1987 ('Summer Outing to North Wales', *The Gaskell Society Newsletter*, 4 (August 1987), 21).

coursing-match: the hunting of hares using greyhounds.

128 *Dol Mawr*: (Welsh) the great meadow.

freshet: (obsolete) a small stream of water.

131 *'to take her for better, for worse'*: Form of Solemnization of Marriage, *Book of Common Prayer*.

132 *Tynwntyrybwlch*: this phrase starts with 'house' (ty) and ends with 'pass' (bwlch), but is difficult to translate. It may mean something like 'the house at the edge of the pass', as Welsh farmhouses were often named using a descriptive phrase to do with the landscape. Gaskell may have spelt the name incorrectly or it may be her own invention.

'the Saviour . . . death to life': Luke 7: 11–16.

136 *John Wesley*: (1703–91), Anglican clergyman who found that his evangelicalism was not popular with the established Church. He travelled widely to preach his message of salvation through faith and, together with his brother Charles, established the Methodist movement. He recruited laymen such as Gaskell's character David Hughes who, as she describes, 'became one of the earnest, self-denying, much-abused band of itinerant preachers who went forth . . . to spread abroad a more earnest and practical spirit of religion'. Gaskell's sympathy with the Evangelical movement is obvious here

and may have something to do with her Unitarian faith and the fact that the Methodists were, for a long time, outcasts like the Unitarians.

Caernarvon slate-vessel: Caernarvonshire was the heart of the Welsh slate industry in the nineteenth century. In the absence of railways (which did not run in north Wales until 1848) the slate was sent by steam ship to Liverpool, the main industrial centre serving the north Wales region. In the early to mid-nineteenth century this was the largest shipping fleet in Wales. Gaskell's uncle and cousin, both called Samuel Holland, were involved in developing the slate quarries of the area.

he 'suffered long, and was kind': 1 Corinthians 13: 4.

137 *'the awful agony in the Garden'*: Mark 14: 32–50, in which Jesus in the Garden of Gethsemane prays to God to spare him the forthcoming trial of the crucifixion.

'He prayed . . . his face like sweat': Mark 15: 34—'And at the ninth hour Jesus cried with a loud voice, saying, Eloi, Eloi, lama sabachthani? which is, being interpreted, My God, my God, why hast thou forsaken me?'

streeked . . . head and feet: 'streek' is the northern English form of 'stretch' and means to lay out the body. Trefor M. Owen's, *Welsh Folk Customs* (1959; Llandysul, 1987) mentions that a pewter plate, with salt on it, was placed on the breast of the dead person, partly as a preservative, and partly to guard against evil (the devil was thought to hate salt). Lighted candles were placed at the head and feet of the body during the vigil or wake held on the night preceding the funeral (173–5).

'He giveth and He taketh away': Job 1: 21.

142 *waned*: all editions of the story I have sighted give 'waxed' here but, in the context of Nest's ebbing life, 'waned' makes more sense.

'they reckon not . . . dwell;':

> 'I have a son, a third sweet son; his age I cannot tell,
> For they reckon not by years and months where he is gone
>   to dwell.
> To us, for fourteen anxious months, his infant smiles
>   were given,
> And then he bade farewell to Earth, and went to live
>   in Heaven';

from 'The Three Sons', by John Moultrie (1799–1874), first published in his *Poems* (1837). Gaskell's quotation is not accurate but this is typical of her work in which she often misquotes slightly, probably because she is quoting from memory. The poem would have struck a chord with her in the writing of this story because her infant son died of scarlet fever in Wales in 1845.

matins: strictly, the ecclesiastical term for the order of public morning prayer, but often applied figuratively to the morning song of birds.

THE HEART OF JOHN MIDDLETON

145 *Sawley . . . water-power*: Gaskell sets her story in the bleak uplands near Pendle Hill on the border between Yorkshire and Lancashire, and she draws on the history of the area which saw the beginning of the cotton industry in Lancashire in the second half of the eighteenth century. Sawley can be identified with the town of Sawley, formerly known as Salley after the Cistercian abbey which stood there, or possibly with Whalley, further downstream and also site of ruins of a Cistercian abbey. The Bribble, named later in the story, is the River Ribble, which runs south from the Yorkshire dales into Lancashire and then south-west to the coast at Preston. The extensive cotton manufacturing interests of Robert Peel in East Lancashire began in the 1760s with the calico-printing firm of Haworth, Yates & Peel. Peel was the grandfather of Sir Robert Peel (1788–1850), second baronet and British prime minister. John Middleton works in one of the many cotton mills in the area.

146 *Ishmael . . . every man's against me*: Genesis 16: 12. Ishmael was the son born to Abraham and Hagar the Egyptian, his wife Sarah's maid. Sarah later bore Abraham a son, Isaac, and Hagar and Ishmael were cast out into the desert. The Jews trace their ancestry to Isaac and Abraham, and the Arabs to Ishmael.

blow-ball: the seeding head of a dandelion.

149 '*threaped*': see note to p. 105.

150 *the great gourd-tree of the prophet Jonah*: which God caused to grow in the desert outside the city of Nineveh to shade Jonah. However, as John Middleton points out, his hatred casts a blighting shade, unlike the 'merciful shade' of Jonah's gourd-tree. The simile is also inappropriate because Jonah's gourd-tree grew in a day and withered the next whereas John Middleton's hatred lasts for years and years. However, it is appropriate that Gaskell's hero draws on the imagery of the Old Testament both here and at various points in his narrative, for the stories of God's anger and vengeance strike a response in his heart far

more readily than the message of love and forgiveness contained in the New Testament.

151 *the Seven Champions*: *The Famous Historie of the Seven Champions*, by Richard Johnson (1573–1659?), printed about 1597, contains the legends of St George of England, St Denis of France, St James of Spain, St Anthony of Italy, St Andrew of Scotland, St Patrick of Ireland and St David of Wales.

the Pilgrim's Progress: an allegorical tale of Christian trial, endurance and salvation, by John Bunyan (1628–88), first published in 1678 (Part I) and 1684 (Part II).

Byron's Narrative: an account of the shipwreck of the *Wager* off the coast of Chile in 1741. The *Wager* was part of a fleet led by George, Baron Anson on his famous voyage round the world in 1740–4. The *Narrative* was written by John Byron (1723–86), midshipman, published in 1768, and used by his grandson, Lord Byron, as the basis for part of his poem 'Don Juan' (1819–24).

Milton's Paradise Lost: by John Milton (1608–74), first printed in 1667. This epic poem takes as its subject the Fall of Man through sin.

154 *Gehenna*: the 'Valley of Hinnom' outside Jerusalem which was a site of idolatrous worship, including sacrifices and the passing of children through fire (II Kings 23: 10). It was later used for the burning of city refuse and the bodies of dead animals and criminals. With such a sinister history, it is not surprising that by the first century BC its name had become a synonym of hell.

beehive chair: or lip-work chair, was made from coiled straw rope, either used on its own, or built around an elm stick chair. Its rounded canopy shows why it is regarded as the forerunner of the hall porter's chair. The name 'beehive' derives from the fact that the same techniques and materials were used to make beehives. Richard Bebb's *Welsh Country Furniture*, Shire Album series (Princes Risborough, Buckinghamshire, 1994), contains a photograph of such a chair (13), and the lipwork technique is described in J. Geraint Jenkins, *Traditional Country Craftsmen* (London, 1978), 151–3.

Peter: John Middleton's preference for Peter over the other disciples probably stems from the fact that Peter was the only one to use physical action to resist the arrest of Jesus in the Garden of Gethsemane (John 18: 10).

the mighty act of God's vengeance, in the old Testament: a reference to the Flood, Genesis 6: 5–9: 17.

155 *the cotton-crop had failed*: the Lancashire cotton manufacturing

industry relied on imports of raw cotton and was thus dependent on the success of the crop in its source countries. In the late eighteenth century India and Egypt were the major sources of supply but by 1820 this role had been taken over by the southern, slave-holding states of America.

My right hand had not forgot its cunning: Psalms 137: 5.

156 *"varmint"*: (dialect) vermin or, more generally, animals for hunting; the word also carries the connotation of clever or cunning.

list: (archaic) this word has several different meanings, two of which are applicable in this context—to desire, choose, or to listen to.

the hem of His garment: Matthew 9: 20–22 and 14: 36.

the publican and sinner: Matthew 9: 9–13.

Pharaoh . . . the King Agag: Old Testament enemies of the Jewish people. The book of Exodus tells the story of the Jews whose lives were 'made . . . bitter with hard bondage' (1: 14) in slavery to the Egyptians. Agag was an Amalekite king 'hewed . . . in pieces' by Samuel in revenge for crimes against the Jews (I Samuel 15: 33).

157 *broadcloth . . . fustian*: broadcloth is a fine fabric, its name originally referring to its double width but also denoting good quality, whereas fustian is a thick, coarse cloth.

158 *Padiham. . . . work*: Elizabeth Gaskell stayed at Padiham in June 1850 and again in August 1855 as the guest of Sir James and Lady Kay-Shuttleworth at Gawthorpe Hall. The inference is that John Middleton found factory work at Padiham, similar to his previous employment at Sawley. However, Gaskell may have made an error of local history because 'Until the 1840's the landowners prevented the building of factories, and Padiham was a village of handloom weavers' cottages' (Millward, *Lancashire: An Illustrated Essay*, 60).

the Fell: north-country term for high ground or a moorland ridge.

'Keep a stone . . . when the time comes.': Gaskell wrote of this north-country proverb, 'I remember Miss Brontë once telling me that it was a saying round about Haworth' (*The Life of Charlotte Brontë* (1857), ed. Alan Shelston (Penguin edn.; Harmondsworth, 1975), 61). Gaskell first met Charlotte Brontë at the Kay-Shuttleworths' Lake District home, Brierley Close, in August 1850, only four months before 'The Heart of John Middleton' was published. Interestingly, the same proverb is also found in Brontë's *Shirley* (1849; ch. 7), set in Yorkshire.

161 *houseplace*: the name given, in many parts of England, to the common living-room and kitchen in a farmhouse or cottage.

the Prince of the Air: St. Paul refers to the Devil as 'the prince of the power of the air' in Ephesians 2: 2.

lordly dish: Judges 5: 25.

162 *Jael and Sisera*: whose story is told in the Song of Deborah (Judges 5). Jael, a woman of a nomadic tribe, killed the Canaanite king Sisera after his defeat by the Israelites. He sought refuge in her tent and, after she had brought out food and drink as a sign of hospitality, she killed him with a hammer and nail.

163 ' *"There is a God . . . many mansions." '*: John 14: 2.

165 *it is better to be sinned against than to sin*: *King Lear*, III. ii. 59–60—'I am a man | More sinned against than sinning'.

MORTON HALL

167 *the Repeal of the Corn Laws*: the Corn Laws of the late eighteenth century and the first half of the nineteenth century were a series of regulations governing the import and export of grain. The legislation protected the local producers and so was supported by Tory landed interests. As followers of an old aristocratic family such as the Mortons, the Sidebotham sisters who narrate the story are, of course, staunch Tories. In 1838 the Manchester Anti-Corn Law League was formed, an alliance of Radicals and industrialists. The manufacturers wanted to pay lower wages and believed that this would be possible only if the price of bread dropped, that is, if grain could be freely imported. However, it was not until February 1846, after a failed harvest in 1845 and the first blights on the Irish potato crop, that the then prime minister, Sir Robert Peel, introduced measures to repeal the Corn Laws and abolish the duty on imported corn over three years.

Lord Monteagle . . . the Gunpowder Plot: Roman Catholic conspirators, the most famous of whom is Guy Fawkes, plotted to blow up Parliament and, in the process, to kill King James I, his queen, and his oldest son, on 5 November 1605. One of the conspirators, Francis Tresham, warned his Catholic brother-in-law, Lord Monteagle, not to attend Parliament on the day in question, and through Monteagle the plot was exposed. The Plot heightened suspicion of Catholics and expression of such suspicion ranged from restrictions imposed by legislation (not lifted until the Catholic Emancipation Act of 1829) to such common superstitions as those expressed by the Sidebotham sisters.

the Jesuits: members of the Society of Jesus, a religious order of the Catholic church founded in 1534 by Ignatius Loyola. The name acquired sinister connotations due to the power and secrecy of the order.

the Female Jesuit: a Gothic novel by Mrs Jemima Luke (1813–1906), first published in 1851 under the full title, *The Female Jesuit; or, the Spy in the Family*, and followed in 1852 by *A Sequel to the Female Jesuit; Containing Her Previous History and Recent Discovery*.

168 *Drumble*: Gaskell's name for Manchester, which she also uses in *Cranford*.

Liverpool Street: Gaskell's precise placement of Morton Hall and the Sidebothams' farm has prompted readers to try to identify their originals in the vicinity of Manchester. However J. A. V. Chapple has discovered, in the Brotherton Collection, Leeds University Library, a notebook belonging to Jane Adeane of Llanfawr, who knew Elizabeth Gaskell's friend Caroline Davenport, later Lady Hatherton. Chapple quotes from an extract of a letter copied into the notebook. The letter was from Gaskell to Lady Hatherton, and dated 27 December 1853 ('Morton Hall' had just come out in *Household Words* in November):

To recur to your note which I received at Knutsford, my Morton Hall was *Morton*, not Moreton, but indeed till receiving the half message from Miss Louisa Stanley I had utterly forgot that there was a Moreton in Cheshire, never having seen it, and not knowing its exact situation to this day. And about the 'poor starving people' the whole story originated in two little graphic sentences from the old Servant (aged 93) at Mr Brontë's at Haworth; I asked her why a certain field was called the Balcony Field (put a strong & long accent on cony) and she told me that when she was a girl 'while the Farmers were still about the country & before they had begun to plague the land with their Mills &c' there had been a grand House with Balconies in that field, that she remembered seeing Miss — (I forget the name) get into the Carriage with her hair all taken up over a cushion, and in a blue sattin [sic] open gown, but Oh! she came to sore want, for her Nephew gambled away the property and then she lent him money, and at last he & she had nowhere to hide their heads but an old tumbledown Cottage (shewn to me) where folk do say she was clemmed to death, and many a one in Haworth remembered him going to Squire (Name forgotten again) to offer a bit of old plate for sale to bury his Aunt rather than that the Parish should do it [.] The 'Blue sattin gown' and the 'clemming to death' were a striking contrast, were they not? (J. A. V. Chapple, 'Elizabeth Gaskell's *Morton Hall* and *The Poor Clare*', *Brontë Society Transactions*, 20 (1990), 47–9).

Gaskell had been a guest at Haworth in September 1853, and the tale told to her by Tabitha Aykroyd certainly contains the germ of the story Gaskell published as 'Morton Hall'.

the Alderney: a dairy cow.

169 *the Restoration. . . . old Oliver died*: the years of the reign of Charles II (1660–85) were known as the Restoration period. After the Civil War (which lasted for most of the period 1642–48) and the execution of the Stuart king, Charles I in 1649, Charles II was proclaimed king by the Scots in defiance of the English Republic but was defeated by Oliver Cromwell and forced to flee to the Continent. Many Royalists, such as Gaskell's John Morton, followed him, and many more had their estates confiscated or sold, often to the benefit of Cromwell's supporters, Roundheads such as Richard Carr. The Puritan Commonwealth could not be sustained for long after the death of Cromwell in September 1658 and Charles II was recalled and proclaimed king in May 1660.

General Monk: or Monck, George, first Duke of Albemarle, (1608–70), was instrumental in the restoration of the Stuart monarchy. He had fought for Charles I against the Parliamentarians, for the Parliamentarians against the Irish, and with Cromwell against the Scottish Royalists. After Cromwell's death he recognized the dangerous instability of the country and, as commander of a formidable military force, was able to create a situation favourable to the re-establishment of a stable, legitimate monarchy.

the Stuarts: one of the royal houses of Britain. The Stuart monarchs ruled from 1603–49 (James I and Charles I), 1660–88 (Charles II and James II), and 1689–1714 (William and Mary of Orange, Anne I).

calves' head for dinner every thirtieth of January: a dish eaten in ridicule of Charles I on the anniversary of his execution. However, Alice Carr would appear to be somewhat ahead of her time for *Brewer's Dictionary of Phrase and Fable* states that the Calves' Head Club was 'apparently first mentioned in a tract . . . of 1703 by Benjamin Bridgwater, stating that it first met in 1693' (184).

the first twenty-ninth of May: Oak-apple Day or Royal Oak Day, celebrates a triple anniversary—the birthday of Charles II, the day he entered London at the Restoration, and his escape from Cromwell's forces, after his defeat at Worcester in 1651, by hiding in the 'Royal Oak'. Thus sprigs of oak with gilded oak-apples were worn.

170 *the Duke of Albemarle*: one of the titles conferred upon General Monk (see note above) who was raised to the peerage by Charles II on 7 July 1660.

the Queen of Sheba . . . Jerusalem: according to the biblical account, Solomon did not court the Queen of Sheba to visit him but she, having 'heard of the fame of Solomon concerning the name of the Lord, . . . came to prove him with hard questions'. However, the traditional use of the phrase 'Queen of Sheba' to describe a proud woman who gives herself airs may derive from the fact that 'she came to Jerusalem with a very great train' (I Kings 10: 1–2).

good red gold: (archaic) 'red' is a conventional epithet of 'gold'.

the Virginian plantations: Virginia, one of the thirteen original American colonies, was dubbed the Old Dominion because, despite the imposition of Puritan control between 1652 and 1660, it remained loyal to Charles II during the Commonwealth. Thus, many Royalists, cavaliers such as Sir John Morton, fled there after the execution of Charles I and the exile of his son, and became involved with the tobacco plantations which were the basis of the colony's economy.

171 *Old Noll*: a disparaging reference to Oliver Cromwell.

172 *conventicles*: secret or illegal meetings, particularly religious meetings.

173 *post-horses*: horses kept at an inn, available for hire by travellers.

174 *cade lambs*: tenderly nurtured young animals, rejected by the mother and brought up by hand.

Worcester: site of Charles II's last defeat on English soil, by Oliver Cromwell's forces, in 1651.

176 *pillion*: see note to p. 108.

tire-women: (archaic) lady's maids.

mere: a lake or pond.

lists: (archaic) desires, wishes, chooses.

177 *the battle of the Boyne*: fought between James II and William III in July 1690 by the River Boyne in Ireland. James, a Catholic, who had been forced to abdicate in 1688, attempted to regain the throne from the new Protestant king, William III of Orange, who had married James's daughter Mary. William was victorious and the Battle of the Boyne is still celebrated today by Protestants in Northern Ireland.

huxters: obsolete form of hucksters, small shopkeepers or pedlars. As in this instance, the term has a derogatory implication suggesting a mean and petty grasping after profits.

charnel-house: a burial-house or vault.

178 *entail*: settlement of an estate or property so that the possessor's power as absolute owner is limited, usually by preventing the sale of part of the land or assets so that it is preserved intact for succeeding generations, and by settling it on specific people so that it cannot be willed away or heirs disinherited.

179 *Prince William of Gloucester, nephew to good old George the Third*: (1776–1834), son of William Henry, first Duke of Gloucester and brother of

George III. In 1816, contrary to the hopes of the Sidebotham sisters, he married his cousin Mary, fourth daughter of George III.

maréchale powder: (French) scented hair powder.

180 *making cheeses*: twirling around then sinking down, as in a low curtsey, so that a full skirt or petticoat stands out all around in the shape of a cheese.

185 *houseplace*: see note to p. 161.

190 *Northumberland. . . . an Irishwoman*: Philip Yarrow has noted that Mrs Turner's 'Donagh' represents 'quite a good attempt at a phonetic transcription of the Northumbrian pronunciation of Turner' on Gaskell's part. See 'Mrs Gaskell and Newcastle upon Tyne', *Gaskell Society Journal*, 5 (1991), 68. I am indebted to Philip Yarrow, Emeritus Professor of French at the University of Newcastle upon Tyne, for his expert and generous assistance in the preparation of the explanatory notes to this story, and to 'My French Master' and 'Crowley Castle'.

191 *the rule of three*: a method of finding an unknown number when three other numbers are known which exist in a specific relation to the fourth. The first and second numbers stand in the same relation to each other as the third does to the fourth, ie. 2 is to 4 as 3 is to x, x being 6; Miss Burrell is to a baron as Miss Annabella is to a ?

192 *an honourable*: an official or courtesy title, in this context referring to the title given to the younger sons of earls, and to the children of peers below the rank of marquess.

The Female Chesterfield; or, Letters from a Lady of Quality to her Niece: Miss Sophronia's work is obviously based on the Earl of Chesterfield's (1694–1773) letters to his illegitimate son, published by his son's widow in 1774. Not originally intended for publication, they dealt with questions of etiquette and became the model for many hand-books of manners and social duties.

193 *Pomfret cakes*: liquorice lozenges for ticklish throats, made at Ponte-fract since the sixteenth century.

194 *spinnet*: a small keyboard instrument similar to the harpsichord.

Santo Sebastiano; or, the Young Protector: (1806), a Gothic novel in the style of Ann Radcliffe, by Catherine Cuthbertson.

God save the King: has been attributed to John Bull (?1563–1628), the king's organist at the Chapel Royal and later organist at Antwerp Cathedral. The anthem did not come into popular use until the 1740s.

198 *consumption*: or tuberculosis, a chronic infectious disease, primarily of

the lungs, characterized by fever, wasting, chest pain and coughing. It was extremely prevalent in the nineteenth century, accounting for nearly 25 per cent of all deaths in England around 1850.

199 *gout*: a metabolic disorder characterized by recurrent attacks of acute arthritis, usually of the great toe. There is some epidemiological basis for the commonly held belief that gout was a disease of the aristocracy.

200 *fear God and honour the king*: 1 Peter 2: 17.

202 *the old Northumberland burr*: Philip Yarrow notes that, like the French and the Germans, Northumbrians use the uvular 'r'.

MY FRENCH MASTER

205 *his commission, and his half-pay*: officers in the army and navy purchased their commissions and these were, therefore, commodities of value which could be sold. To go on 'half-pay' was to remain in the service but withdraw from active duty.

Goldsmith's History of England, Rollins's Ancient History, Lindley Murray's Grammar: Oliver Goldsmith (?1730–74) published a *History of England in a series of letters from a nobleman to his son* in 1764. The French historian Charles Rollin (1661–1741) was the author of the uncritical *Histoire ancienne* (1730–8) which was translated into English in 1738–40 and thereafter went through many editions in the eighteenth and early nineteenth centuries. Lindley Murray (1745–1826), an American-born Quaker, published an English Grammar in 1795, a Reader in 1799 and a Spelling Book in 1804. Jenny Uglow writes that here Gaskell 'is deliberately listing books which all her contemporaries would recognize and smile at'. See Uglow's *Elizabeth Gaskell: A Habit of Stories* (London, 1993), 28 for a discussion of the place of these texts in girls' education in Gaskell's day.

206 *an emigrant*: the 'Emigration' of French nobles to England and the German states on the Rhine began with the fall of the Bastille on 14 July 1789 and the yielding of Louis XVI to the demands of a crowd which marched to Versailles in October of the same year. This migration accelerated in 1792 when the monarchy was abolished and France became a republic. Many, like Monsieur de Chalabre, were forced to flee during the Reign of Terror (1793–4). The Law of Suspected Persons, for example, passed in September 1793, allowed the imprisonment and execution of many noblemen and others sus-

pected of royalist sympathies. In 1797 it was estimated that there were perhaps 300,000 *émigrés*, whose property was confiscated. It has been suggested that Monsieur de Chalabre was based on Elizabeth Gaskell's recollections of another *émigré*, the Knutsford dancing master, Monsieur Rogier. However, Rogier's recorded eccentricities do not tally with Monsieur de Chalabre's quiet dignity. See Joan Leach, 'The French Master', *Gaskell Society Newsletter*, 12 (August 1991), 12–16, and Henry Green, *Knutsford: Its Traditions and History* (1859; Manchester, 1969), 134–6.

lion: a celebrity, the chief attraction of a place. The phrase derives from the custom of showing visitors the lions formerly kept at the menagerie in the Tower of London. Gaskell herself was lionized when she visited London after the success of her first novel *Mary Barton* (1848). Jane Carlyle described her as 'a natural unassuming woman whom they have been doing their best to spoil by making a lioness of her' (quoted in Uglow, *Elizabeth Gaskell: A Habit of Stories*, 225).

the fatal 21st of January 1793: when King Louis XVI of France was guillotined in Paris.

208 *a queue*: a pig-tail.

209 *a sous-lieutenant*: (French) a second-lieutenant.

Michaelmas: (29 September) the feast of St Michael and All Angels.

210 *Martia*: a suitably obscure nickname, given the way in which it is used by the narrator's mother. It is probably derived from Mars, the Roman god of war, thus suggesting 'martial'; tallness would be a useful attribute of soldiers.

'the Iris being blown down': the iris was formerly often called Fleur-de-lis or Flower-de-luce. Therefore the narrator's parents are making a covert reference to the execution of the French monarch via the fleur-de-lis on the French royal coat of arms.

211 *'The wicked, cruel boys had broken off the White Lily's head!'*: the lily is also a reference to the Bourbon dynasty as the heraldic fleur-de-lis is a representation of this flower. The lily also symbolizes purity, innocence and fairness and is thus, from a Royalist's point of view, an appropriate way of referring to Marie-Antoinette, Louis XVI's queen, who was guillotined in October 1793.

212 *crape*: see note to p. 4.

preux chevalier: (French) gallant knight; an archaism in literary use, denoting chivalry, gallantry, and bravery.

a lock . . . right for us: Monsieur de Chalabre emulates his sovereign, for Louis XVI was a locksmith in his spare time.

silk-winders: silk-reels.

213 *paste-board*: a pastry-board.

the peace of 1814: after over two decades of more-or-less continuous conflict, Paris was taken by the Allied armies fighting against France (Russia, Prussia, Austria, and Britain) and Napoleon abdicated on 6 April, retiring to the island of Elba. The Allies dictated that the resultant power vacuum be filled by the restoration of the Bourbon dynasty.

the Gazette: *The London Gazette*, first published (as *The Oxford Gazette*) in 1665, and the first real newspaper in England. It is still published, twice weekly, and contains legal and government notices.

The Bourbons: one of the principal ruling houses of Europe. Bourbons ruled not only in France (1589–1792, 1814–48), but also in Naples and Sicily (1735–1861), and in Spain (1700–1868, 1870–3, 1874–1931, 1975–).

214 *Grillon's Hotel*: 7, Albemarle Street, opened in 1803 by Alexander Grillon (see *The London Encyclopaedia*, ed. B. Weinreb and C. Hibbert (London, 1983), 192).

'devoirs': (French) respects, duty.

Gardes du Corps: (French) literally, bodyguards; a troop of cavalry, composed of noblemen under the *ancien régime* and of soldiers with the rank of officer under the restoration, with the task of guarding the person of the king. They were established in 1445, did not survive the Revolution, but were re-established under Louis XVIII.

the London mail: the coach used to convey letters and parcels as well as passengers between provincial centres and London.

215 *orangerie*: a garden or orchard where orange trees were grown in tubs. The orangerie at the royal palace of Versailles, principal residence of Louis XVI and Marie-Antoinette, was much imitated.

Miss Fanny: the narrator's sister has previously been named as Mary. This is one example of Gaskell's notorious carelessness with the names of minor characters, perhaps a consequence of the fact that she often wrote in haste and submitted work for publication without revision.

beautiful wreath: orange blossom, symbolizing fruitfulness and innocence, is the traditional bridal flower. *Brewer's Dictionary of Phrase and Fable* notes that the custom was introduced from France to England in about 1820.

Count de Provence . . . Louis the Eighteenth: King Louis XVI's brother, who reigned as Louis XVIII after the restoration of the Bourbons (the son of Louis XVI, who was recognized by the Royalists as Louis XVII, having died in prison in June 1795). During the Republican and Napoleonic years the Comte de Provence had sided with the Allies against France. He assumed Divine Right and resisted the constraints of the Constitutional Monarchy imposed on him. He was not a popular ruler, and died in 1824.

Duc de Duras: (1771–1838) Royalist who belonged to the Gardes du Corps until its dissolution during the Revolution. He emigrated in 1791 and returned to France in 1807 but did not resume any public office until the reign of Louis XVIII.

the Tuileries: a royal palace in Paris, built for Catherine de' Medici in 1564 and destroyed in 1871.

my sword . . . ploughshare: Isaiah 2: 4.

Rome was not built in a day: (proverbial) worthwhile achievements take time and patience.

216 *franked*: conveyed free of charge.

the Cent Suisses, the Gardes du Porte, the Mousquetaires: like the Gardes du Corps, all elite, mainly ceremonial regiments. The Cent Suisses or Swiss Guard were highly regarded mercenary soldiers who served throughout Europe. The Gardes de la Porte (Gaskell's 'du' is incorrect) guarded the doors inside the palace when the king was present. The Mousquetaires were two regiments of musketeers, formed by Henry IV in the early 1600s, and composed of noblemen belonging to the maison du roi (the king's household). They survived the Revolution but were suppressed in 1815.

217 *M. du Fay, Fils*: (French) Monsieur du Fay, Junior; a conventional form of address.

return from Elba . . . battle of Waterloo: Napoleon escaped from Elba in early 1815, received an enthusiastic welcome from the majority of the French population and the army, and entered the Tuileries in Paris on 20 March. His brief return to power, known as the Hundred Days, ended with his defeat at the Battle of Waterloo on 18 June. Paris fell on 3 July. Napoleon surrendered on 9 July and was sent to the island of St Helena where he died in 1821.

immortelles: everlasting flowers which keep their colour after drying.

218 *Duc de Feltre*: Henri Clarke (1765–1818), of Irish origin, was suspended from his position in the army as chief of general staff during the Reign of Terror. He was incarcerated but escaped to Alsace. He served Napoleon in various military and diplomatic posts and was given the title Duc de Feltre by him in 1809. However, his

loyalty to Napoleon wavered, he was quick to offer his services to
Louis XVIII in 1814, and from March to July 1815 was the king's
minister of war, charged with defeating the returned Napoleon.

219 *the 'de' was dropped*: 'de' in French names is an indication of nobility or
high social standing.

220 *Jupiter-ship*: Jupiter, or Jove, reigns supreme over the gods of Roman
mythology, just as, according to the narrator, husbands reign supreme, or like to think they do, in their little households.

221 *marraine*: (French) godmother.

Valetta: or Valletta, port city and capital of Malta. Built in 1565, it
was invaded by the French in 1798 and seized by the British in 1800.
After 1814 Valletta was an extremely important naval and military
base for Britain in the Mediterranean.

esprit: (French) wit.

catechism: a prescribed text for teaching elements of the Christian
religion, consisting of questions and answers; thus, more generally, a
method of teaching or learning that uses the question and answer
form.

222 *Sister of Charity*: Gaskell may be referring to the Daughters of
Charity, founded in Paris in 1633–4 by Vincent de Paul and Louise
de Marillac, a Roman Catholic order of non-cloistered women who
are engaged in active social work, particularly teaching and nursing.
However, she is probably using the term 'Sisters of Charity' generic-
ally; her letters show that she participated in the debate about
sisterhoods in the 1850s (see, for example, *Letters*, 116–18, and her
comments about Florence Nightingale, 320–1).

Three years ago I was in Paris: 'My French Master' was published in
December 1853, seven months after Elizabeth Gaskell's first visit to
Paris.

An English friend . . . French in manners and ways: a reference to Elizabeth Gaskell's friend Madame Mohl, born Mary Clarke in West-
minster in 1793, who lived most of her life in France and did indeed
marry a German professor, Julius Mohl. Gaskell was a frequent visitor
to the Mohls' Paris home, and kept up a lively correspondence with
Mary.

salon: (French) literally, a drawing-room, but carrying a special meaning in the Parisian context of a gathering of people carefully chosen
by an experienced hostess for the purpose of lively, witty, and entertaining conversation. Mary Mohl modelled herself on the *salonnière*
Madame Récamier (1777–1849), who entertained important liter-

ary and political figures during the Empire and Restoration, and she saw the creation of a salon as a career. 'Suitable guests were carefully brought together, likely topics "researched", debate skilfully stimulated, those at the start of their careers introduced to established figures, the famous of one country put in touch with the famous of another' (Margaret Lesser, *Clarkey: A Portrait in Letters of Mary Clarke Mohl* (Oxford, 1984), 101). Elizabeth Gaskell revelled in the atmosphere of Mary Mohl's salon and this influence may be traced in Gaskell's essay 'Company Manners' (*Household Words*, 9 (20 May 1854), 323–31).

224 *his daughter . . . in Ary Scheffer's sacred pictures*: the artist was a close friend of Mary Mohl's and it was through that connection that Elizabeth Gaskell and her daughter Meta dined at the Scheffers' in February 1855—'such a good dinner!' Gaskell wrote (*Letters*, 333)— and visited his studio. Ary Scheffer (1795–1858) enjoyed popularity and success during his lifetime. The subjects of his paintings are generally religious or Romantic, inspired by Goethe, Byron, and Schiller, among others. I have been unable to identify the 'portrait of his daughter which arrests every eye' but the context suggests that he used her as a model in a number of paintings.

THE MANCHESTER MARRIAGE

227 *Bond Street*: a fashionable shopping street in London's West End.

228 *the true Saxon accent*: Mr Openshaw's regional pride is expressed here through his use of language. Similarly, Elizabeth Gaskell's use of dialect is a significant feature of her writing, brought most prominently before her reading public in her first novel, *Mary Barton*. She included in that novel glosses to unfamiliar words which stress the way in which Lancashire dialect keeps alive its links with an Anglo-Saxon heritage.

229 *'breaking up'*: rapidly becoming infirm. It is an appropriate term for a retired sea-captain to use as it can also apply to a ship 'breaking up' in heavy seas or on rocks.

230 *the Cape*: the Cape of Good Hope, at the southern tip of the African continent.

Underwriters: in this context, those who insure a ship and/or its cargo.

231 *Ruth*: whose story is told in the Old Testament book of the same name, was a young widow who left her homeland in order to stay with her mother-in-law Naomi, whose husband and sons were dead.

232 *the famous Yankee motto—'England flogs creation, and Manchester flogs*

England.': if 'flog' is taken to mean 'excel' or 'beat', then the motto suggests that 'The English are the best in the world, and the Mancunians are the best of the English'. However one would not expect this to be a *Yankee* motto. Alternatively, it may be an observation on Britain's expanding empire (encompassing all creation), and the British drive to find and exploit cheap sources of raw materials for industries such as Manchester cotton manufacturing in the eighteenth and nineteenth centuries. When this story was published the northern American states (Yankees) were shortly to go to war against the south over the issue of slavery, upon which the southern cotton-growers depended; hence perhaps a pun on the flogging of slaves.

235 *thy wedded husband . . . honour me*: Form of Solemnization of Marriage, Book of Common Prayer.

236 *nesh*: (dialect) soft, weakly, tender.

237 *Richmond*: a town on the Thames, favourite summer resort of Londoners, now absorbed into the city's suburban sprawl.

245 *"any, good Lord, any"*: I have been unable to trace the source of this quotation.

253 *that poor father whom she had never seen*: of course Ailsie *did* see her father, in the pivotal incident of the story, although she did not recognize him as such.

CROWLEY CASTLE

255 *Merton*: may be based on Eastbourne where Gaskell holidayed in September and October 1862. Eastbourne is close to Brighton and Dover, both of which are mentioned in the story, and J. G. Sharps has suggested that either Pevensey Castle or Herstmonceux Castle may have provided the model for Crowley Castle (see *Mrs Gaskell's Observation and Invention*, 449–51).

portcullis: a means of defence of a fortress or castle; this strong, heavy grating fitted into grooves on the sides and floor of a gateway and was moved up and down by chains.

256 *bonne*: (French) maid.

257 *grenadier*: originally, a soldier whose duty in combat was to throw grenades. When grenades went out of use in the eighteenth century (they were reintroduced in World War I), the name was applied to a company of the finest, tallest men in the regiment.

260 *the meet*: the gathering of men, horses, and hounds for the purpose

of fox-hunting, traditional recreation of the aristocracy and landed gentry.

261 *bear-leader*: a travelling tutor.

county member . . . borough member: each of the English counties was represented in the House of Commons, as were boroughs, municipal districts located within a county. A voter belonged either to a borough or to a county. The opportunities for political corruption afforded by the boroughs were the main target of the 1832 Reform Bill. In a 'rotten' borough the population was too small to warrant representation and in a 'pocket' borough the votes were controlled by one individual, often the local squire.

262 *favouring the Stuarts*: the Stuart line of succession was disrupted in 1688 with the exile of the Catholic James II and the accession of the Protestant William and Mary of Orange to the throne. They were succeeded by Mary's sister Anne, and then by the Hanoverian kings, the third of whom was George III, in whose reign the events of the story take place. However, the Stuart claim to the throne remained in the form of Charles Edward, Bonny Prince Charlie, the Young Pretender, grandson of James II, and was realized in the Jacobite invasion he led in 1745. Jacobite alarms persisted into the 1750s, late enough to implicate Sir Mark Crowley in Gaskell's story.

King George the Third: see note to p. 106.

All Saints' Day: or All Hallows' Day (1 November), a festival of the Christian church held to honour the saints and martyrs.

filliping: a flicking movement of a finger against the thumb.

263 *the Duc de Richelieu*: (1696–1788) Marshal of France and third Duc de Richelieu, grand-nephew of Cardinal Richelieu, was one of the most notorious libertines of the age of Louis XV, and still an arbiter of fashion in his eighties.

bonton: (French) high fashion.

the Grand Opéra . . . the Français: the French national opera and the Théâtre Français or Comédie Français, the national theatre company.

264 *petits soupers*: (French) small, intimate, suppers.

maréchale: see note to p. 179.

'mouches': (French) patches; artificial beauty-spots made of black silk or court-plaster (silk coated with isinglass), used to hide blemishes or enhance the complexion.

265 *whose right hand had forgotten its cunning*: see note to p. 155.

Adonis: in classical mythology, a beautiful youth beloved by the goddess Venus or Aphrodite. As in this example the term is often used ironically to suggest a corrupt or dissolute character disguised by a handsome exterior.

268 *repent at leisure*: William Congreve (1670–1729), *The Old Bachelor* (1693), v. viii and ix—'Thus grief still treads upon the heels of pleasure: | Marry'd in haste, we may repent at leisure.'

269 *love . . . door*: proverbial.

270 *Some one waited fourteen years*: Jacob served fourteen years for Rachel, Genesis 29: 16–30.

271 *a poor prodigal*: a reference to the parable of the Prodigal Son, Luke 15: 11–32.

272 *Japan-ware*: wood, leather, tin or papier mâché objects decorated with black japan varnish in imitation of traditional Japanese laquerwork. The process known as japanning was popular in eighteenth-century Europe.

273 *monseigneur*: (French) form of address reserved for royalty, nobility, or those holding high office in the church.

widow's weeds: mourning clothes.

274 *pabulum*: (Latin) food, nourishment.

de facto: (Latin) in fact, in reality, as opposed to *de jure*, by right, according to law.

277 *spend it*: the manuscript version of the story ends at this point (see Note on the Text).

278 *nigh unto death*: Philippians 2: 27.

281 *the Marais*: a district of Paris, fashionable with the nobility in the seventeenth century, but thereafter deteriorating, with workshops springing up in the courtyards of the grand houses.

284 *Brighthelmstone*: the original name of Brighton, on the south coast of England, a poor fishing village until the middle of the eighteenth century when it began to be recommended to the wealthy for the beneficial effects of its sea bathing. It grew even more rapidly in importance as a fashionable resort when George IV, then Prince of Wales, first took up residence there in the 1780s and subsequently built the Royal Pavilion.

285 *an ague-fit*: a fit of shaking or shivering accompanying an acute fever.

287 *bait*: to rest horses on a journey, stopping to give them food and water.

his place in parliament knew him no more: Job 7: 10.

THE WORLD'S CLASSICS

A Select List

HANS ANDERSEN: Fairy Tales
Translated by L. W. Kingsland
Introduction by Naomi Lewis
Illustrated by Vilhelm Pedersen and Lorenz Frølich

JANE AUSTEN: Emma
Edited by James Kinsley and David Lodge

Mansfield Park
Edited by James Kinsley and John Lucas

J. M. BARRIE: Peter Pan in Kensington Gardens & Peter and Wendy
Edited by Peter Hollindale

WILLIAM BECKFORD: Vathek
Edited by Roger Lonsdale

CHARLOTTE BRONTË: Jane Eyre
Edited by Margaret Smith

THOMAS CARLYLE: The French Revolution
Edited by K. J. Fielding and David Sorensen

LEWIS CARROLL: Alice's Adventures in Wonderland
and Through the Looking Glass
Edited by Roger Lancelyn Green
Illustrated by John Tenniel

MIGUEL DE CERVANTES: Don Quixote
Translated by Charles Jarvis
Edited by E. C. Riley

GEOFFREY CHAUCER: The Canterbury Tales
Translated by David Wright

ANTON CHEKHOV: The Russian Master and Other Stories
Translated by Ronald Hingley

JOSEPH CONRAD: Victory
Edited by John Batchelor
Introduction by Tony Tanner

DANTE ALIGHIERI: The Divine Comedy
Translated by C. H. Sisson
Edited by David Higgins

VIRGIL: The Aeneid
Translated by C. Day Lewis
Edited by Jasper Griffin

HORACE WALPOLE : The Castle of Otranto
Edited by W. S. Lewis

IZAAK WALTON and CHARLES COTTON:
The Compleat Angler
Edited by John Buxton
Introduction by John Buchan

OSCAR WILDE: Complete Shorter Fiction
Edited by Isobel Murray

The Picture of Dorian Gray
Edited by Isobel Murray

VIRGINIA WOOLF: Orlando
Edited by Rachel Bowlby

ÉMILE ZOLA:
The Attack on the Mill and other stories
Translated by Douglas Parmée